Colonial Justice
and the Jews
of Venetian Crete

THE MIDDLE AGES SERIES

Ruth Mazo Karras, Series Editor
Edward Peters, Founding Editor

A complete list of books in the series is available from the publisher.

Colonial Justice
and the Jews
of Venetian Crete

Rena N. Lauer

UNIVERSITY OF PENNSYLVANIA PRESS

PHILADELPHIA

This book was published with the generous
assistance of a Book Subvention Award from the
Medieval Academy of America.

Published by
University of Pennsylvania Press
Philadelphia, Pennsylvania 19104-4112
www.upenn.edu/pennpress

Printed in the United States of America on acid-free paper
1 3 5 7 9 10 8 6 4 2

Library of Congress Cataloging-in-Publication Data
ISBN 978-0-8122-5088-6

In gratitude to my parents,
Phyllis and Chaim Lauer

Contents

A Note on Usage

Names and Orthography

Orthographic flexibility (or inconsistency, one might say) rules the Latin records used in this study. Even within one document, a single person's name may be identified using different spellings, for example: Kali, Cali, Calli, and Kalli. In addition, some of these individuals also have Hebrew names apparent in the Jewish sources. These names are usually related to, but different than, their Latinate names and must also be rendered consistently for this study. In recording names in the text, therefore, I have standardized the spelling either by using the common English spelling or by choosing a single orthography that reflects the most common usage (for example, Cali). I have rendered Isaac, Judah, and Joseph following standard English usage. The Hellenized-Latinate version of Elijah used so commonly in these sources has many spellings: Liachus, Ligiachus, Lingiachus, Lighiachus, and so forth. I have chosen the Italianate Liacho, which reflects how the name might have been pronounced. While some men named Elijah in Hebrew were called Liacho in the vernacular, many others were called Elia. This distinction remains consistent in the ducal records, and I have retained it according to that information.

When Hebrew is transliterated, the ח has been rendered h and the כ has been rendered kh.

Dating

Venice began its year on 1 March. The Jewish calendar follows a modified lunar calendar with a new year beginning in the autumn at the start of the month of Tishrei. For ease of understanding, I have changed all Venetian and Jewish dates to the familiar Julian calendar (solar, Christian, beginning the year with 1 January) unless otherwise specified. Thus, for example, a ducal record marked 4 February 1439 will be rendered 4 February 1440 in this study, since the 1439 dating is according to the Venetian calendar, which did not begin the new year until 1 March.

Coinage and Currency

In Crete during this period, the money of account was the hyperperon (a unit borrowed from the Byzantine coinage system), calculated in terms of the Venetian grosso. One hyperperon (in Venetian, a *perpero*) equaled twelve Venetian grossi. Twelve grossi also equaled about twenty-six soldi.[1] Notarial and ducal records almost always mention prices and fines in Cretan hyperpera, with smaller fractions of hyperpera calculated in grossi. Cretan hyperpera should not be confused with the hyperpera of Constantinople, nor should this money of account be confused with an actual coin. There was no mint in Crete during this period.[2] *Taqqanot Qandiya* mentions ducats (in this period, the gold ducat coin equaled about 2 Cretan hyperpera)[3] and florins, in addition to grossi, suggesting the range of coins and moneys of account used in transactions.[4] It also mentions *dinarim*, a general currency designation in Hebrew that probably refers to hyperpera.[5]

Abbreviations and Archival Citations

TQ = Elias Artom and Umberto Cassuto, *Taqqanot Qandiya u'Zikhronoteha (Statuta Iudaeorum Candiae eorumque Memorabilia)*. Jerusalem: Mekize Nirdamim, 1943.

Material from the Archivio di Stato in Venice (ASV) is rendered according to archive (ASV), series (usually Notai di Candia or Duca di Candia), *busta* (envelope-box) number, register number (that is to say, folder within the *busta*), and folio number. I then follow with the date of the entry in parentheses. For example: ASV Duca di Candia, b. 26, r. 8, fol. 7v (1 October 1437).

Colonial Justice
and the Jews
of Venetian Crete

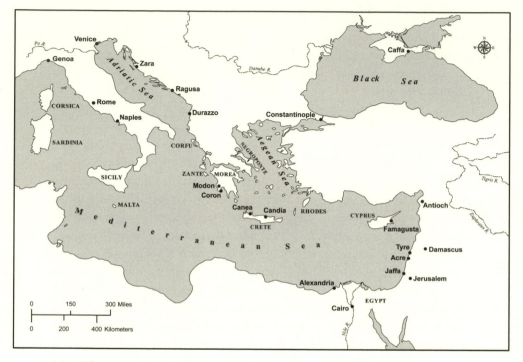

Map 1. The eastern Mediterranean in the late Middle Ages.

Introduction

Networks of Jewish Life in Venetian Crete

Soon after Passover in 1363, scandal consumed the Jewish community of Candia, the capital of Venetian Crete. A Sicilian Jew who had been living in Candia had spread a rumor that the Jewish women of the island were promiscuous. Having slept with Jewish prostitutes in the Jewish Quarter, he libeled all the Jewish women of Candia "and did not differentiate between the respectable and the easy women, between the married and the penetrated women, or between widows and prostitutes."[1] So recorded the community leaders who gathered to compose a Hebrew ordinance, or *taqqanah*, in an attempt to stop the Sicilian's slander from affecting the community's reputation. Their explicit goal was to protect the honor of God, the Torah, and those who keep God's commandments, and, finally, "the general honor of our praiseworthy community."[2] To solve their problem, they demanded that the Sicilian leave town. They did not care where he went: "He should go from here to wherever the wind carries him," just as long as he put a good distance between himself and their town.[3]

Thinking pragmatically about their problem, the Candiote Jewish officials added a provision to the *taqqanah*. If the culprit refused to leave or if he ever reappeared in town, they ordered the elected head of the community, the *condestabulo*, to turn him over to the Venetian government ("may their glory be raised") to be punished for adultery and slander. The authors further clarified that the *condestabulo* should do so without fearing that he would be committing a sin. This last legal datum is striking. "Informing"—that is to say, denouncing Jewish misdeeds to a non-Jewish authority—provoked great anxiety among rabbinic authorities during Late Antiquity and the Middle Ages. So grave was the misdeed of informing that, according to rabbinic law, the informer at times even merited capital punishment.[4] In this *taqqanah*, however, the Candiote Jewish leadership not only established that the *condestabulo* could not be considered an informer but even went so far as to decree that, should the *condestabulo* not turn over the libelous Sicilian to the Venetian government, the leader himself would be publicly shamed before the Jewish community for eschewing his sworn duty. Relying on the colonial island's justice system was not just an option; it was a mandate.

The case of the slandering Sicilian is not unique in the history of Jewish Candia. In a number of other circumstances when the reputation of the community as a whole was on the line, the *taqqanot* of Candia demanded that the leadership hand over Jews to the Venetian government for trial and punishment. Should a Jew be found buying and selling stolen goods on the black market, for example, the *condestabulo* was ordered to turn over "that man or that woman" to the secular authorities, since his actions undermined confidence in Jewish economic practices. In this case too, the ordinance threatened the *condestabulo* with public shaming were he to shirk his duty, whether "out of flattery or [personal] relationship or love or pursuit of bribes."[5]

What makes the case of the slandering Sicilian unique is that we know its outcome. Collected among *Taqqanot Qandiya* is a list, ostensibly authored by its sixteenth-century editor, Elia Capsali—community leader, rabbi, and historian—recounting a number of the community's *condestabuli* and their great accomplishments. The list records that a *condestabulo* named Malkiel (Melchiele) Casani "made a *terminazion* [agreement] regarding those who slander the virgin girls of Israel, that they would be punished and flogged around the city and will stay in jail. And it was done, and one Sicilian was punished, and they flogged him and incarcerated him, and this was done with the agreement of most of the distinguished men and masters of Torah in our community."[6] Not only was the Sicilian turned over to the authorities, but the *condestabulo* also worked with the Venetian government to come to an agreement over his punishment—an agreement known as a *terminazion*, as our text records, transliterating a legislative term directly from the Venetian dialect into Hebrew letters.

The world depicted in this Hebrew source seems unexpected in the context of *taqqanot*, a religiolegal genre common to the medieval and early modern periods. *Taqqanot* were rules relevant to the here and now of their production, binding only on the local community that produced them and aimed at a local Jewish readership (or listenership, as they were read aloud in the synagogue as well as recorded for posterity).[7] Moreover, *taqqanot* are often understood by scholars as texts intended to act as a potent symbol of the semiautonomy that the medieval and early modern Jewish community was said to enjoy, a corporate authority granted by a sovereign government for the sake of Jewish self-rule.[8] *Taqqanot* were indeed rules passed by the community, for the community, exemplifying the independence of the community. By putting out a set of *taqqanot*, the community leaders announced their own jurisdiction over religious life and practice in their town.

Yet this sense of self-sequester, idealized autonomy, communal unity, and rabbinic jurisdiction is not manifest in the texts from Venetian Candia. Though certainly focused on the language of Torah and rabbinic sensibilities, the Candiote community's leadership appears deeply involved with the sovereign government of Crete, not only turning over perceived criminals to be dealt with by secular channels but working side by side with the state to levy punishments. Though the authors of the *Taqqanot* wrote in Hebrew and generally spoke Greek, they also incorporated Venetian terms for state structures (such as *terminazion* and *condestabulo*) into their official Hebrew texts. We even read of Jewish leaders formalizing an internal financial penalty against potential wrongdoers through a Latin state notary.[9]

Taqqanot Qandiya does more than reflect relations between Jews and the state. The statutes also portray a community integrated into the broader town and thoroughly enmeshed in a wide range of economic exchanges with their non-Jewish neighbors. In the ordinances discussed so far, contact is portrayed negatively, as dangerous and illegal interactions on the black market and potentially in the sex trade. But other entries refer to Jewish-Christian contacts through patronage of artisan crafts and the hiring of apprentices. Nor were Jews immune from the moral complexity of Candiote society, as references to adultery and prostitution—here and elsewhere—suggest.[10] Moreover, the entry of a Sicilian into Candiote Jewish society hints at some of the ways that the Jews of Candia were connected to the wider Mediterranean world.

By convention of the genre, *taqqanot* tend to emphasize the values of segregation, piety, and localism. At the same time, these Hebrew sources demonstrate that, during the late Middle Ages, the Jews of Candia inhabited a social reality that was linguistically, politically, and institutionally woven into the social tapestry of the majority Christian town in which they lived, and tightly tied into the Mediterranean networks in which Crete functioned as a major hub. From the elite leaders who ran the governing board to its rank-and-file members, the Jews of Candia were thoroughly enveloped in the structures of Cretan colonial society and its governmental institutions.

In fact, it is through the lens of one of these institutions—the Venetian colonial justice system on Crete, and particularly the extensive surviving court records from the island's supreme judiciary—that we are able to discern with

real clarity, beyond the echoes of *Taqqanot Qandiya*, the contours and entangle-
ments of the Jewish community of Venetian Candia. Because the Jews of Candia were subjects of the Venetian empire, their lives were also intertwined with
the institutions of the colonial society. But the conventional view of colonial
institutions as tools for subjugation and control cannot fully describe how they
functioned in the lives of Venice's colonial subjects. In Crete, Jewish subjects
harnessed some colonial institutions and maneuvered through them for their
own benefit and interests. Most importantly, regular litigation by Jews against
other Jews in these Venetian courts became a primary outlet for the airing of
intracommunal and interpersonal disputes. Knowledge of Crete's colonial justice system, and the malleability of the system itself, allowed this secular court
to become a key venue for Jews—male and female alike—both to articulate
personal identity and to work the system for their own, individual benefit.

This book tells the story of Jewish individuals and families on Crete as
they engaged with their various social and legal networks, within and beyond
the Jewish community. It focuses primarily on the century between the Black
Death (1348) and the fall of Constantinople to the Ottoman Turks (1453).
These events, which reshaped the contours of the Jewish community on Candia as they shaped Cretan society more broadly, bookend a period of relative
peace. This allows us to witness Jews making daily choices without external
threats of war or famine. To be precise, peace reigned from the end of the
St. Tito revolt in 1363–64, though I have decided to begin my investigation
a bit earlier so as to track more closely with the dating of the sources I use.[11]
With the fall of Constantinople came an influx of Greek refugees into Crete,
and a drastic uptick in Greek anxiety, which manifested in the form of a rebellion, the so-called Siphi Vlastos conspiracy of 1453–54, and others in its wake.
At least in the short term, this event changed Venetian policies toward Greek
subjects and Orthodoxy in Crete, ending the century of relative quiet.[12] Comprehensive analysis, however, also requires some consideration of Jewish life in
the beginning of Venetian rule in the early thirteenth century and its state of
affairs in the sixteenth century.

Two overarching claims about Jewish life in Candia during this period are
made in this study. The first is that the Jews of Candia encountered and engaged
with Latin and Greek Christians not simply out of necessity or as a result of
the vicissitudes of daily life, although these certainly played a role. Rather, Jews
chose to participate in meaningful encounters through professional channels
and legal engagement with Venice's secular judiciary. This behavior was fostered, even if inadvertently, by Crete's colonial government, which saw in the

island's Jews a relatively safe ally and buffer against the less conciliatory Greek Orthodox population. Venice's strategy of colonial appeasement in Crete thus gave local Jews social leeway and legal opportunity that were often unavailable to Jews elsewhere at the time.

The second argument addresses the implications of such engaged interaction: that sustained encounter did not happen only at the fringes of Jewish society and that it left a decided and visible mark on the internal community. Engagement with Christians and with Venetian institutions—above all, the colonial justice system, and particularly in contexts of intra-Jewish litigation—influenced, shaped, and changed the Jewish community of Candia, allowing it to function as a traditional Jewish community without many of the anxieties and reservations of other medieval Jewish communities.

These two arguments are inextricably connected. That is to say, the internal relations of the community as negotiated in the colonial courtroom must be viewed in conjunction with the networks of which these Jews were a part. This interdependence explains why the Jews of Crete chose to behave in a fashion decidedly at odds with traditional understandings of rabbinic ideals, which dictated that all intra-Jewish disputes must be addressed within the confines of the Jewish community. In particular, the *beit din*, or Jewish court, was supposed to decide matters of Jewish concern. But Candiote Jews often chose to reject this directive, in part because of their relationships with people and governing entities outside the bounds of the local Jewish community. These relations were not simply pragmatic and temporary. They shaped the nature and the experience of the individual Jews who made up the community. The decisions made by these Jews then affected the nature of the Jewish community writ large.

Sources of Jewish History on Crete

The Jews who made up the *kehillah kedoshah*—the "holy community," as the Jewish corporate structure called itself—of Venetian Candia (modern Iraklion) during the late Middle Ages were mostly Greek speakers hailing originally from the Byzantine sphere. The community's story has been only infrequently and incompletely told.[13] Moreover, the story of Crete's Jewish individuals remains untold, and this book tells that tale by bringing to life Cretan Jews by looking at their interaction with Venetian colonial justice. The portrait of Jewish life drawn here looks quite different than those typically recounted about the

Middle Ages. Though Jewish sources have traditionally portrayed Jews as isolated, self-segregating groups, living almost accidentally within a given sovereign society, medieval communities were often engaged in the wider societies
that encompassed them. The Jews of Venetian Candia actively enmeshed themselves in the concentric social spheres of the colonial capital and beyond. They
were very involved in the life of the city, both in its capacity as a site of a great
deal of formal business and more casually as a hub of other sorts of quotidian
interaction. Jews regularly interacted with the Latin-rite (Catholic) Venetians
and Greek-rite (Orthodox) native Cretans who lived alongside them.

The fact that this book focuses on the Venetian colonial judiciary as a
central institution in the lives of Crete's Jews stems in significant part from
the exceptionally large collection of ducal court records that survived the
Ottoman takeover of Crete in 1669.[14] These court records are housed today in
Venice's Archivio di Stato, collected as part of the Duca di Candia series. This
study relies on both the records of sentences meted out (Sentenze Civili) and
long-form records of cases (Memoriali).[15] Jews appear in a considerable number of these records, acting as litigants, defendants, witnesses, and in other
capacities, including agents, executors of wills, and medical patients. Beyond
the legal context, references to Jews as neighbors, relatives, orphans, or guard-
ians offer even more information about the Jewish community. Though the
judicial records are a rich source, this study is the first to thoroughly address
their Jewish-related content.

This book's emphasis on the justice system, however, does not stem solely
from the wealth of evidence but also from the real importance of courts in
medieval Mediterranean life. Litigation was a far more common activity in
the late Middle Ages than it is today, and many more people were likely to be
swept up in late medieval court proceedings than in modern cases. Litigation
thus offers us access to a broader cross section of Candiote Jewish society than
is initially apparent. Moreover, emphasis on litigation also engages with the
Venetian state's own concern with "justice" as a primary ideological principle
through which it ruled in both colonial and metropolitan settings. The world
of litigation, legal recourse, and other modes of "justice" formed an essential
building block in the development of the Venetian empire and its political
philosophy. By asking how Jews fit into this picture of justice and judicial life,
then, this study contributes not only to debates over Jewish life but also to
considerations of the broader Venetian Mediterranean and medieval empires.

Ducal court records are not the only source available for an investigation of
the Jews of Venetian Crete. There are other surviving Latin materials marshaled

in this study. Notarial acts form one of these source bases. The Venetian bureaucratic engine was one of the most prolific record keepers of the premodern
world. Crete's thriving markets seem to have been constantly abuzz. Perhaps
because any business deal could end up as a legal battle, residents of Candia
patronized the city's many notaries, men who had the technical skills and legal
know-how to draw up binding contracts that would hold up in court. Though
Greek and Hebrew notaries were active in Candia as well, Venice's official notaries wrote in Latin, and it is almost solely these Latin registers from the capital
that survive in the archival series called Notai di Candia.[16]

Business was brisk for these men: for the fourteenth century, the registers of forty-seven notaries survive; in the fifteenth century, forty-one notaries'
materials have endured through war, water, book-boring worms, and time.[17]
The systematic exploration of the vast notarial records from the period under
study lies outside the scope of this project, but much notarial data from uned-
ited and edited registers have been incorporated, as well as references to notarial
acts discussed by other scholars. In addition, material from the town crier's
rolls has been examined.[18] Even a cursory glance at these sources shows how
deeply embedded in the economic and social life of the city Candiote Jews had
become by the mid-fourteenth century; their mark can be found everywhere.

And of course, there is *Taqqanot Qandiya*, the set of Hebrew sources
discussed above. In this collection, communal ordinances composed and
approved by the leadership of the Jewish community in Candia are gathered.
Alongside these ordinances that give the source collection its name are other
types of communal documents, including a few responsa (halachic decisions
written in response to specific questions) and some historical lists, such as the
important accomplishments of some of the *condestabuli*.[19] The collection orig-
inates from the first half of the sixteenth century, when the historian and rabbi
Elia Capsali gathered and copied the ordinances and the other materials in
the format that exists today. To be sure, *Taqqanot Qandiya* does not allow the
historian to hear the voice of all sections of Candiote Jewry; it is the product of
a male, elite, and rabbinically oriented subclass of the *kehillah*. Nevertheless,
because of the local nature of the ordinances, responsa, and other included
texts, as well as Capsali's own attention to the historical import of his home
community and its concentric spheres (he also wrote Hebrew histories of both
the Venetian empire and the Ottoman Empire), *Taqqanot Qandiya* does provide fascinating insight into not only the religiolegal life of the community
but also its day-to-day workings, its institutions, its tensions, and its relationship with Candia's non-Jewish majority.

An undated manuscript copy of Capsali's compilation discovered among the collection of David Salomon Sassoon, the famed Anglo-Iraqi collector of Jewish and Samaritan books, remains the only manuscript of *Taqqanot Qandiya* in existence. It now resides in Jerusalem, part of the manuscript collection at the National Library of Israel.[20] Its early pages are unfortunately in illegible condition, and an early attempt at conservation with what looks like contact paper has obscured some other pages. An edition from the mid-twentieth century, however, preserves material no longer visible in the manuscript. Umberto Cassuto and Elias Artom, scholars of Italian Jewry and classical Jewish texts, worked from this codex to create an edition with critical apparatus in Hebrew, and this published version remains the only such edition.[21] The editors intended their edition, published in 1943, to be the first volume of a two-part study of the Jews of Candia based on these ordinances, but exigencies of war and finances precluded the completion of this project.[22]

As a self-consciously prescriptive source, *Taqqanot Qandiya* offers a lopsided view of the Jews of Candia, emphasizing piety, community, and religious concerns, albeit sometimes honored in the breach. Rabbinic texts have long been the major sources marshaled by scholars studying the history of Jews. When doing social history using rabbinic voices, however, it is difficult not to trip over their decidedly prescriptive nature. An alternate approach that looks only at Jewish life through non-Jewish sources also has severe limits, stemming from the outsider's perspective they necessarily offer. This study surmounts that obstacle by bringing these kinds of sources into conversation with one another and by analyzing them in tandem. It marshals both primary sources produced by Jews and primary sources about Jews produced mainly by Christians in order to offer not only more angles of view but also a higher-resolution—and therefore clearer and more nuanced—image of the community in question, much as anthropologists do when developing their ethnographies of contemporary social groups.[23]

The resulting details of Jewish daily life, family concerns, economic activities, living conditions, and religious communal life are quite diverse. In some ways, what emerges looks like a typical portrait of medieval communal Jews: elites taking up local Jewish office to help liaise between the community and the sovereign; rabbis concerned with maintaining dietary standards and cleanliness in the Jewish Quarter; and wealthy and poor alike anxious to make good marriage matches for their children. But in other ways, this consilience of sources also offers a far less typically visible social landscape. Here we are privy to Jewish individuals concerned with their own interests, as well as those of the community—often contradictory though simultaneous aims. Some Jews were dedicated to religious practice and community leadership at the same time that they were comfortable going outside the community for resolutions to social and religious problems, for extended economic alliances, and even for sexual intimacy. Some happily watched the public courtroom spectacles in the town center, and some strolled around the harbor—even on Sabbath during the time of prayer services, despite the customary expectation that Jews should be in synagogue then.[24] Candiote Jews were probably not the only Jews in Europe doing these things; rather, the exceptional sources, and the juxtaposing of both secular and Jewish sources, permit us uncommon entry into the daily lives and concerns of the Jews of a medieval community.[25]

Jewish Life in Christian Society

Focusing on Candia's well-documented Jews, therefore, suggests new ways to think about medieval Jewry across the Mediterranean and beyond, particularly by pointing to the importance of historical contingency in Jewish-Christian relations and by identifying a complex *convivencia* outside the bounds of Iberia. As scholars have moved beyond the old models of reading medieval Jewish history through a lachrymose lens, one influential approach has been to reinterpret violence against Jews through a multifaceted prism of local social, political, and religious realities—and not as the inevitable product of prevalent rhetorical tropes.[26]

Yet explaining the contingency of anti-Jewish violence can only function as one part of this corrective. The other side of this coin remains essential as well: to recognize that violence was only one mode of interaction between medieval Jews and their Christian neighbors—one that characterized the minority of such contacts in many places across the medieval world. In Crete, as in locales throughout Christendom, quotidian interactions between Jews and Christians look rather different than the list of traumatic encounters emphasized by lachrymose narratives. Political alliances, professional reliance, sexual attraction, and even religious curiosity led Jews and Christians—Greek Orthodox and Latin-rite alike—to encounter each other on terms not defined by animosity and conflict. On a day-to-day basis, Cretan society exhibited a pragmatic acceptance of religious difference.

Scholarship on medieval Jews used to subscribe to the consensus opinion that Jewish life under Christian rule was generally harsh, malicious, and ultimately destined for destruction.[27] But more recent scholarship has recognized that any universalizing conclusions about "Jewish life under Christian rule" are untenable.[28] Christendom was a diverse and complicated place; local considerations—whether tense relations between the king and his Christian subjects, or policies of economic pragmatism—often played as important a role in informing attitudes and actions toward (or against) Jews as did uniform ideological prejudice. Indeed, internal Christian tension sometimes directly benefited Jews. Conflict between Venice and the pope (particularly over issues of authority and jurisdiction in its colonial sphere) helped protect Candiote Jews from papal and papally appointed Dominican Inquisition tribunals, which were not allowed to hold sway on the island except in rare cases.[29]

Regular, low-conflict interaction between Jews and Christians in Christendom tends to be identified as part of a phenomenon unique to the medieval Iberian Peninsula, the product of its exceptional cultural complexity in which pragmatic needs and proximity impelled Jews, Christians, and Muslims to accommodate one another. But other regions ought to be observed through a similar filter, and the Venetian territories provide an excellent natural laboratory in which to explore cross-cultural contacts that look like their own version of *convivencia*.[30] As in Iberia, Candia's reality of three different religiocultural groups—Greek, Latin, and Jewish—seems to have prevented the sort of binary tension (us versus them) that tends to set the stage for violent conflict aimed at Jews. Perhaps the tripartite social reality diffused the force of hatred of the Other by multiplying the targets defined as such. It seems likely that animosity aimed at the Jews in Candia was buffered by the reality of ongoing tensions between Greeks and Latins.

One of the most productive new methods for breaking through old approaches to, and artificial bifurcations about, medieval Jews is to explore the ways Jews utilized sovereign courtrooms as a venue of dispute between Jews. Scholars of Iberia and Provence have noted that Jews, male and female, chose to air their grievances against their fellow Jews not at the *beit din*, the Jewish court, but before secular, Christian sovereigns—despite rabbinic prohibitions.[31] The significant implications of this behavior are still being worked out, in this study as in others. Elka Klein's work on Catalonia has made an important step in recognizing that the reality of Jews in court, particularly women, ought to change our understanding of the daily functioning of Jewish society; as in other realms of medieval Jewish life, Jewish attitudes toward the court system were clearly not in line with rabbinic exhortations.[32] Uriel Simonsohn's work on Jews and Christians litigating in Islamic courtrooms in the early medieval Middle East and North Africa has demonstrated that this phenomenon extends beyond Christendom.[33]

Jews who litigated in sovereign judiciaries had diverse motives, and it is increasingly clear that these courts—in Crete, as in the Islamic world—offered certain benefits that made it more appealing to bring civil suits before judges of a different religion than to bring similar suits before the Jewish court: enforcement powers, a balance of professionalism and useful subjectivity, arbitrational neutrality, and even sometimes cultural familiarity. By looking at the kinds of cases Candiote Jews chose to bring against their coreligionists (from property disputes to marriage fights, from salary disagreements to synagogue crises) and the arguments made by Jews in the course of their suits (often marshaling Jewish, religious discourse deciphered and reframed for non-Jewish consumption), modern readers may imagine themselves present in the courtroom, hearing how individuals thought of the intersection of Jewish law and Jewish life, religious and secular interests, and how they crafted their own narratives for an outsider audience.

Through the pen of the courtroom notary, these Jews cease to be caricatures of rabbinic discourse. Indeed, intentional anonymity often renders Jews mentioned in responsa as nebulous "Reubens" and "Simeons," the medieval equivalents of the modern "John Doe." Seen through Venetian legal sources, Crete's Jews are revealed as three-dimensional individuals with competing values and complex social associations. Nevertheless, the image that develops from these sources is not one in which Jewish individualism exists wholly separately from Jewish communal membership. Rather, a major facet of Jewish choice related to the ways in which a Jew situated him- or herself in the community structure. In other words, for some Jews, the courtroom became a place in which they could express their own views on Jewish law and custom—not outside the frame of Judaism but with an eye toward their own agency within the religion. This helps explain why even the leaders of Candia's Jewish community saw in the secular courtroom an effective venue for resolving Jewish communal disputes and did not see that strategy as a repudiation of their communal responsibilities. In fact, at times, Jewish elites came to the Venetian courtroom to force their coreligionists to uphold the tenets to which their religious community was supposed to adhere. Likewise, Jewish women trapped in unhappy marriages did not use the secular court system to undermine Jewish marriage but to find workarounds that enabled them to stay faithful to Jewish law (oftentimes pushing for their own definitions of Jewish law) while also freeing themselves from marital misery and economic subservience.

As this discussion of unhappy wives suggests, a critical benefit of sin-
gling out personal choice, and particularly the ways that individuals used the
secular judiciary, resides in what it reveals about Jewish women. Medieval
rabbinic texts tend to assign Jewish women discrete, polarized identities as
either "good" or "bad." Responsa categorize women according to male, rabbinic concerns and offer moral judgments on them, based on whether the rabbinic sources approved of their behavior.[34] Recent scholarship on premodern
Jewish women has illustrated that once they are considered outside the frame
of rabbinical texts, women appear in the public sphere engaging in a variety
of public and professional activities, not only with other women but also with
men unrelated to them, Jewish and Christian alike.[35] This study takes seriously
the notion of Jewish women as agents of their own lives, both figuratively—as
deciders in their own lives—and literally, as self-representing figures in secular
courts, as well as economic actors functioning outside the purview of their
fathers and husbands.[36] The Jewish women of Candia certainly often married
according to their parents' wishes and lived within the communal confines
of the *kehillah*. Within these contexts, however, women in professional and
public capacities made decisions for themselves without constant requests for
permission of fathers or husbands; and they publicly asserted their own understanding of their identities as females and Jews. The secular judiciary, and
its common use by Jews, provided for Jewish women a venue for expressing
individual agency, as it did for Jewish men.

To be sure, the history of Jewish-Christian relations must not be seen
through rose-colored glasses. Cretan Jewish life during the century from the
Black Death to the conquest of Constantinople was marked by some dark
moments, including a massacre of Jews in the fortress town of Castronovo by
rebels during the St. Tito revolt in 1364.[37] Residential confinement in the Judaica, a precursor to the ghetto though never with gates or locks, emerged in stages
over the course of the fourteenth and fifteenth centuries. Anti-Jewish rhetoric
appears in many official sources. A claim of Jews crucifying a lamb around Easter time led to the arrest of nine elite Jews, and the death of two, in the early
1450s, a case addressed in Chapter 3. This study aims not to disregard crisis but
to contextualize it and to underscore the space between moments of trauma.[38]

Taken as a whole, the history of Jewish life on Venetian Crete represents a
successful experiment, in comparison with the broad, mounting anti-Judaism
that characterized much of western Europe in this period. It contrasts even
with Venice itself. Jews settled without barrier in Venetian Crete, but, except
for fifteen years in the late fourteenth century, they were prohibited from

living as a community in the Venetian metropole. In that short intervening period, Venice needed moneylenders for its war effort, and thus Jews were allowed to settle. Once the loan crisis was over, and as anti-Jewish enmity rose, Jews were forced to leave in 1395.[39] In the early sixteenth century, when Jews once again sought refuge from war in Venice, the government discovered it needed them as a source of revenue and as pawnbrokers. Unable to live with or without them, in 1516 Venice compromised by forcing the Jews into the neighborhood known as the Ghetto, originally a place for casting cannon (in Venetian dialect, *ghettare*) but soon an epithet that became a synonym for merciless segregation.[40]

Crete was different. For Jews from Germany, Iberia, France, and elsewhere, Crete was known as a haven and became a stable locus of immigration throughout this period. Jews from across western Europe and the Levant trusted that Venetian justice would serve them and their families. As a result, they not only moved to Crete but also involved themselves in the civil systems (including the judiciary) of the island. In many states across medieval Christendom, including in Crete, Christians doubtlessly mistrusted religious difference and regarded it as diabolical, the target of morally and religiously justifiable violence. As such, the ability of medieval Jews to benefit from a justice system that limited the effects of this ideology of intolerance is worthy of emphasis.

Individuals and Community

The reality of meaningful interaction between Jews and Christians does not mean that either side thought of itself as losing its essential identifying markers, particularly religious identity. But religion was not the exclusive marker of identity.[41] Undoubtedly both social reality and colonial law stratified Jews, Greeks, and Latins on Crete according to religious identities. Yet evidence from Crete demonstrates the importance of other axes of identity.[42] Some key markers existed outside the frame of religion: language group, professional affiliation, gender, and socioeconomic status. Some constituted subcategories within the frame of religion: identification with Ashkenazi (northern European), Sephardi (Iberian), and Romaniote (Byzantine) ideas and origins. These other markers were important identifiers both for Jews who possessed them and for the Christians and Jews with whom they interacted.

Crete's Jews also acted in the service of their personal identities. In the colonial courtroom, Candiote Jews made choices based on a sense of their own ability to decipher religiolegal concepts without consulting supposed "experts," argued for their rights as Jews and persons, and even prized their own concerns over the needs of the community. This reality of individuals shaping their identities, making choices, and exerting agency over their own decision-making processes breaks down another untenable generalization about the Jews of medieval Christendom: that premodern Jews were tradition bound and community oriented above all other values.[43] The evidence for the Jews of Candia suggests a different picture: an evolving relationship with Christian sovereigns and Venetian colonial law provided for individual Jews a space in which they articulated choices not squarely in line with the dictates of the community, even as they stayed tied to the corporate system of the *kehillah* and remained dedicated to Jewish law and custom.

The individuality of Candiote Jews becomes more meaningful when considering the broad heterogeneity of the community. On one hand, this complexity stemmed from the ethnic origins of community members. Candiote Jewry was made up of Romaniote (Byzantine) Jews of Greek origin but also newer immigrants from Iberia, Germany, and elsewhere whose arrival (especially in the decades after the advent of the Black Death and the 1391 massacres in Iberia) sparked new challenges and tensions related to Jewish law, social mores, and communal association. This study examines the difficulties inherent in a heterogeneously constructed minority community, something often considered only for communities changed by the Spanish expulsion.[44] In addition, the Candiote community was made up of individuals and families from vastly different socioeconomic backgrounds, including merchants and tanners, doctors and servants, grocers and masons, cobblers and scribes, teachers and tailors. Though poorer individuals are less visible in the sources, echoes in *Taqqanot Qandiya* hint that they too engaged in behavior of which the (generally wealthy) leaders did not approve, from choosing affordable food with questionable *kashrut* to engaging in prostitution.

The individualism and heterogeneity of the Jewish community of Candia call for a reappraisal of the perception of the medieval Jewish community organ as a unified, semiautonomous structure that used its limited corporate powers to build a defensive bulwark between the community and the outside world.[45] When evidence suggests otherwise, scholars tend to interpret that reality in quasi-religious terms. As Elka Klein noted, "Jewish autonomy tends to be studied in the context of halakhic theory and the degree to which practice fell short of it."[46] But this supposed boundary between permitted and forbidden behaviors was not nearly so fixed in Candia's *kehillah*. Not only did regular Jews choose to bypass the *kehillah* in making major decisions, but the leaders of the community drew the sovereign government into communal decisions that were legally within the *kehillah*'s purview according to Venice's own rules. The Venetian government considered the Jews as a singular *universitas*, but the Jews did not necessarily always see things the same way.[47]

By focusing on the importance of individuals and their choices, this study intervenes in a scholarly conversation that extends beyond Jews. If we are all intellectual heirs of James Harvey Robinson, E. H. Carr, and their revolutionary rejections of Great Man History, simultaneously we ought not throw out the proverbial baby with the bathwater, resigning ourselves to quantitative conclusions and tales in the aggregate.[48] For the individual tales of humans living ordinary lives with perhaps extraordinary or at least unexpected moments, the microhistorical approach to history reminds us that the daily habits of regular humans are the building blocks of the premodern world we historians are trying to reconstruct.

Venice, Crete, and the World of the Late Medieval Eastern Mediterranean

While this study homes in on the Jewish community of Candia, its implications extend beyond the study of medieval Jews and contribute to scholarly understandings of the broader world in which these Jews lived—that is, the social, political, and cultural spheres of the Venetian eastern Mediterranean in the aftermath of the Fourth Crusade. A tale of Jews in the Venetian empire contributes to our understanding of the Venetian project from a fresh perspective. It is to this context that I now turn with some background to the Venetian colonial project on Crete.

The Fourth Crusade redrew the political map of the eastern Mediterranean, marking a substantive rupture in the history of the lands of the Romania (as the formerly Byzantine eastern Mediterranean was known). In October 1202, a Latin Crusader army set out by ship from Venice. This mostly French force intended to capture Muslim Alexandria, but through Venetian intervention (the army was deeply in debt to the Venetian state for its ships) first detoured to Christian Zara (modern Zadar, Croatia), reestablishing Venetian rule in that Dalmatian city by military force and then eventually aiming its weapons at the Byzantine Empire itself. In April 1204, the Crusaders sacked Constantinople, overthrew the emperor, and installed a Latin princeling on the throne.

In retrospect, the Latin Empire of Constantinople, as this coup's resulting government was known, was an economic and political disaster for those
who ruled it, and in 1261 a Byzantine contingent from Nicaea restored an
Orthodox emperor to the throne. Nevertheless, the implications of the Fourth
Crusade were vast. Most important was the infamous Partitio Romaniae, the
treaty in which the Crusader leaders divided the former Byzantine territory
among themselves, and the subsequent land trades made in its aftermath.
After Constantinople returned to Byzantine hands, the new political realities
in the Romania would in many cases remain for centuries.[49]

No state benefited more from, or was more changed by, the Fourth Crusade than Venice. By 1100, Venice had begun to extend its naval power beyond
the Adriatic. The goal was commercial expansion, and in the next century, the
Republic harnessed the economic potential of the Crusader States for its own
goals. Venice secured trading concessions from the Latin rulers of the Levant
in return for occasional military assistance, particularly gaining mastery of
the Levantine coast in the 1120s.[50] In the century before the Fourth Crusade,
Venetian traders expanded their foothold across the wider eastern Mediterranean, building on inroads constructed before the Crusades. Evidence, including a letter found in the Cairo Genizah, indicates that Venetian merchants
were active on Byzantine Crete—buying and transporting Cretan foodstuffs
to Constantinople and Alexandria—already by the mid-eleventh century, but
around 1126, Venice obtained free trade privileges on Crete from the Byzantine
emperor John II Komnenos and thus increased its economic power on the
island and along its adjacent shipping lines.[51]

The Fourth Crusade thus offered Venice a chance to directly control
many of the ports it had long used as purchase points and way stations in its
Levantine trade networks. Venice could cut out the middleman, that is, other
sovereigns' laws, taxes, and diplomatic mores. It is in this commercial light
that we can understand the locations Venice acquired through the Partitio
Romaniae and in subsequent private trades, including Negroponte (modern
Evvia), connecting the Aegean Sea to the Greek mainland; the ports of Coron
and Modon at the southern tip of the Morea (as the Peloponnese was known);
and the Ionian island of Corfu, overlooking the southern entrance to the Adriatic (abandoned and then reconquered in 1401).

Among all these new territories, known collectively as the Stato da mar,
Crete quickly emerged as the flagship colony. Venice evidently intended only
a minimal occupation of Crete, perhaps just focusing on the port cities, but
securing the ports entailed capturing and controlling the island as a whole.[52]

The island's strategic location, directly between Venetian waters and the Levant, would render it almost as important as Constantinople itself (which Venice chose to influence but not to rule directly).[53] In 1264, Doge Ranieri Zeno wrote to Pope Urban IV that Crete, because of its position, was the linchpin in the Republic's maritime empire. The doge emphasized Crete's potential role in defending Latin political interests.[54] But the island's economic advantages were equally, if not more, fundamental. Crete's strategic location for protection was but one of its benefits, alongside its strategic location for trade and the island's natural fecundity.

Recognition of Crete's central role was not immediate. In the aftermath of the purchase of Crete from the Crusader Boniface of Monferrat, Venice saw the island's obvious economic potential but had not decided on a method of rule. Genoese pirates (or so Venice construed them) easily took most of the island in 1206. The spirit of rivalry awoke the Venetians; they quickly dispatched forces to chase off their sworn nemeses. When Venice finally defeated the Genoese in 1211, it imported settlers, at first predominantly military men, in the following decades.[55]

Unlike most other holdings in the Stato da mar where feudal barons were allowed to retain control, Venice saw that in order to develop Crete into a central hub of sea power, it needed to retain direct control. To be sure, Cretan land was given in exchange for military service; most of the Greek-speaking rural population lived under feudatories.[56] But feudal power was highly limited by the island's governor, the duke of Crete, who would become the most important colonial representative in the Stato da mar.[57] Venice sent its best and brightest to rule its prized possession: a full 25 percent of the men who served in Crete's top two positions, duke and captain, were also elected to the prestigious Avogaria di Comun, the primary metropolitan court hearing criminal prosecutions from subject territories.[58] Others, including Crete's first duke, Jacopo (Giacomo) Tiepolo (r. 1218–20), rose to the position of Doge of Venice. Venice and Crete, just eighteen days' sail by ship in brisk summer breezes, remained in sustained contact, and both the metropole and its favored colony were ruled at the top by many of the same patrician administrators.[59]

In its colony of Crete, Venice aimed to replicate itself, a virtual Venice "Beyond-the-Sea."[60] To a large extent, Crete modeled itself on the lagoon city in developing its roles as "import-export capital" and ship-building center.[61] At first, Venice even divided the island into six districts (sestieri), reproducing the very urban structure of the metropole. The inefficiency of this system when applied to Crete, however, led to redistricting by the early fourteenth century.[62] As the center of the Mediterranean naval empire, only Crete was outfitted with an arsenal—as in the metropole—in which to build and repair galleys that could be easily dispatched across the region.[63]

Unlike the city of Venice, Crete provided fertile land that produced staples for export, including grain, wine, fruit, olive oil, and products from the island's sheep, including cheese, hides, and wool. Venice's lack of hinterland in this period made basic foodstuffs essential not only for reasons of profit but for feeding the metropole and the Republic's army.[64] But more economically important in the long run, the capital city of Candia was a trade node for goods produced far to the east. The port also served as a hub for Venice's slave trade from the thirteenth century.[65] Until the Fourth Crusade, Crete played a secondary role in Venice's commerce, as most convoys took the route hugging the Peloponnese toward the Levant. But it would become a key point in the Venetian maritime networks after 1204.[66] Its star would rise even higher after the fall of the Crusader States in 1291, when Candia became the chief way station for Venetian vessels, and would hold this honor through much of the fifteenth century.[67]

A New Social World

While the economic advantages of Crete ensured its status as first colony of the Stato da mar, other considerations made ruling and inhabiting Venetian Crete more complicated. New social realities after 1204 were as important as the redrawn eastern Mediterranean map. Venice had sent Latin-rite settlers from the lagoon to the island, but Crete was no vacuum. Indeed, the maritime holdings were more diverse than Venice's mainland, or *terraferma*, territories, both in terms of the multiplicity of languages and religions of the inhabitants and in terms of the complexity of religious interactions especially between Latin and Greek Christians.[68]

In comparison to the island's native Greek inhabitants, Venetians would never make up more than a small fraction of the population. Greek speakers, loyal to the idea of Byzantium and dedicated to the Orthodox Church, chafed against their Venetian-speaking, Latin colonial overlords who contributed to the demise of the empire. But more than political resentments, the Greeks and Latins—alongside other minority groups, particularly Jews but also Armenians and others—had to learn each other's cultural sensibilities, holiday calendars, religious attitudes, and social habits.

For Venice, this called for new approaches to rule. It had to figure out how to be a successful colonial sovereign. Such heterogeneity was not only new for Venice and its government apparatus; the introduction of Venice, its agents and allies, into these colonies actually changed the nature of the dominions too. While the traditional narrative tells of a highly segregated, socially stratified colonial society in which Latins and Greeks did not mix, recent scholarship has shown the untenable nature of such claims.[69] Crete's Latin and Greek Orthodox populations became entangled through an emotional and biological web of marriage and childbearing that makes it difficult to separate the "Greek" and "Latin" strands. The entrée of Latins, particularly the nascent Veneto-Cretan nobility, onto the island began a wave of demographic and cultural shifting that is still not fully understood.[70] That Crete served as a locus of interaction between people of different cultures, religions, and ethnicities must inform our understanding of the island and indeed the whole eastern Mediterranean in this period.

The focus on Crete's Jews in this study allows for a reevaluation of this major social shift. The historiography of Venetian Crete—and indeed the eastern Mediterranean more broadly in its post-1204 context—has tended to characterize the societal reality and its concomitant tensions as a sharp bifurcation, a world of Latin versus Greek that influenced conflicts over politics, language, religion, and social affiliation.[71] Scholars have long noticed that the sources produce an enormous amount of information about Jews but have chosen not to frame that group as a central part of the narrative.[72] But, in the daily social life of Candia, Jews were a prominent subgroup. Jews and Latins each made up roughly the same percentage of Candia's demographic—about a thousand people in each community—in comparison to a much larger Greek Orthodox population. In Crete's social theater, Jews were neither numerically small nor minor in terms of available evidence about them. Expanding the colonial history of Venice so as to embrace the Jews helps delineate the contours of Candiote society more accurately and accounts for a significant amount of evidence that has not heretofore been considered.

This approach also offers a new layer to the ongoing debate over the colonizer/colonized divide, an enduring dichotomy in postcolonial studies that oversimplifies the realities of colonial society.[73] Sally McKee broke down the artificial Latin/Greek division in *Uncommon Dominion* by showing that the social and religious lives of Greeks and Latins intersected and that strict colonial divisions intended to create a formally segregated hierarchy were kept in the breach. Consideration of this Jewish dimension illustrates that other players existed—and that they do not fit neatly within a dichotomous colonial model. Rather, the Jews of Candia were in some ways aligned with the colonized populations: legally they were subjects without citizenship rights, and linguistically they spoke the same Greek as their majority subject neighbors. Yet in other ways they were nested somewhere between the Greek subjects and the Latin colonizers, serving the colonial cause through professional and economic channels, and allying with the Venetian government at important moments (in particular, during anti-Venetian rebellions).[74] Thus the position of Jews in Candia's society offers an alternative view of colonial reality that, instead of comprising two groups existing at opposite poles, consisted of groups that occupied various and variable points on a spectrum in relation to their subject status and colonialism.[75]

Indeed, the choice to emphasize the colonially inflected position of this Jewish population and the colonial nature of the justice they consumed is meant to situate this study within the apparent "Jewish Imperial Turn" that some scholars of modern colonial societies have recently identified.[76] The complexity of Jewish interaction with, and place within, colonial empires has emerged as an urgent scholarly focus among historians of modern Jews. As premodernists become increasingly comfortable, and even adamant about, using the language of colonialism and the scholarly tools of postcolonial theory, there is no reason to limit the lines of inquiry about colonial Jews to the modern period.[77] Moreover, in discerning the uniqueness of Candia—considering why Jewish behavior, local government, and social reality interacted as they did—I argue that a colonial model best explains the evidence. Colonial justice in Candia, and the society it reflects, may not be wholly other than medieval Iberia or northern Italy, but it is dissimilar enough to help explain why Candiote Jews fared differently than their Spanish or northern Italian counterparts. In short, colonial justice is good to think with, despite any limits we may find in applying such a model.

The social and political realities that obtained on colonial Crete, a setting that necessitated real flexibility of governance to accommodate the varying parties, made the island both squarely part of Christendom, a familiar and well-trodden transfer point for galleys and their crews, and something vaguely other, on the edges of "regular" civilization. That this was a common view becomes clear from a story in Boccaccio's *Decameron* in a story from the Fourth Day of his narrative, in which three sisters from Marseille elope to Crete with their lovers, only to find misery and death instead of love and freedom. For wealthy daughters of strict Marseille merchant society, Crete was a haven where they could live openly with their lovers without social repercussion but still reside safely within a familiar social world, going to banquets and meeting other well-bred young people.[78] This fictionalized depiction of Crete as a hub of civilization hovering on the frontier of Christendom indeed maps onto the wider narrative of Venetian Crete. A frontier-like flexibility appears repeatedly in writings on Candia, benefiting Jews and others. Like the frontier societies of medieval Iberia, and indeed like the colonial societies of the early modern period, social complexity and distance from the center of power enabled social mores to adapt and empowered individuals to move beyond their assumed statuses.

But Crete was also a place where justice could be redefined and where rules could be bent, for better or worse.[79] Boccaccio himself identified justice as a focus of Cretan governmental policy and believed that the island was a place where arrests and trials were common. He also portrayed the duke himself as an individual located at the center of the wheels of justice: empowered to define what constituted justice according to his whims, employing less than moral tactics under the guise of a sort of accommodationist justice (forcing sex on one sister to save another). Indeed, this tension also appears in many of the depictions of Venetian Crete that emerge from the sources. Justice, portrayed as unbending in the political discourse, met up with a different reality on the ground, where it appeared rather malleable. The claim of "justice" was manipulated for individual interest or as a rationale for undermining specific laws in favor of a perceived greater good.

For Boccaccio's three sisters of Marseille and their lovers, Venice's malleable "justice" led to their demise—in the narrative logic of the tale, a fair penalty for "the vice of anger."[80] This legal flexibility, however, as we will see, did not always punish those outside the colonial administration but offered particular advantages to other inhabitants of the island—including individual Jews and the Jewish community as a whole. Instead of imposing a uniform law on all subjects, the colonial system of rule in Crete reflected and acknowledged the social diversity of the island, particularly in the division of courts of first instance between Latin and Greek speakers (or between Venetian citizens and Venetian subjects, onto which these language groups mapped) and in its accommodation of local precedents and customary law into its judicial decision making.

Not only was the notion of Venetian justice well known to contemporaries, as the *Decameron* highlights, but it has also become a central discussion in modern scholarly circles, particularly focusing on notions of justice among the patrician elite in the city of Venice itself. Venice's emphasis on the tropes of justice and equality, its approach to crime and punishment, and the place of law in its civil life have become a major focus in Venetian historiography, particularly from the fourteenth century.[81] These studies tend to focus on criminal law and thus give a particular view of what constituted justice—a justice reflected through incarceration and punishment, in which violence plays a central role. But the rhetorical language of justice and equality also played a significant role in the civil courtrooms of Venice, where justice represented "a resource that could be used by the populace in pursuit of their own strategies."[82] And it played a particularly important role as a colonial tool through which to appease and placate Venetian subjects.

Though some Candiote Jews encountered Venice's criminal justice system on the island, most Jewish involvement with colonial justice came through the civil court. Thus the particular ways in which justice was interpreted by the judiciary when Jews were involved—including by respecting and incorporating Jewish law into adjudication and providing equal access to the civil courtroom for subjects, Jewish and Orthodox alike—shed new light on the meaning of these concepts so central to Venetian state ideology.

* * *

This study is not intended to be a synthetic account Crete's medieval Jews. Rather, each chapter offers a new lens onto Jewish life and its relation to the island and the island's colonial legal system. Chapter 1 introduces the Jews of Candia, their communal structure, and the evolution of the community from the thirteenth century. Chapter 2 looks to quotidian Jewish-Christian relations, considering the role of economics and space in fostering meaningful interactions between these groups. Moving beyond individually driven interactions between Jews and Christians, Chapter 3 considers the role of the state in controlling and fostering Jewish engagement with Christians; influencing and controlling Christian attitudes toward Jews and toward typical anti-Jewish tropes; and in limiting the impact of anti-Jewish claims through the reliance on the Venetian judiciary. Chapter 4 begins a series of three chapters focusing predominantly on Jewish use of colonial justice to dispute against their coreligionists. This chapter asks why the Jews of Crete chose to litigate against each other in secular courts and surveys the general variety of cases that Jews brought against each other. Chapter 5 looks at cases of marital strife in which a spouse (usually the wife) sought redress before the ducal court. Chapter 6 returns to the elite leadership and the ways in which it marshaled

Venetian justice, in the process inviting Venetian intervention into the workings of everyday Jewish self-rule.

* * *

In some respects, the Jews of Venetian Crete lived out elements of Boccaccio's colonial fantasy. They lived in a Mediterranean society that afforded them enough distance from the power center to enjoy a freedom uncommon for medieval Jews. At the same time, Candia was also central enough to access the economic, social, and intellectual currents of the Middle Sea and beyond. This is a tale of the consequences of such a tension, between the center and the periphery, not only in space but in culture and religion. It is also a study of the implications of other familiar tensions: the community and the individual; social pragmatism and religious ideology; political expedience and judicial rigor. But most of all, it is a tale of lives—of individuals, families, and communities—intersecting with each other and with the state in a highly mobile world.

Chapter 1

The Jewish Community of Candia

Late one Friday afternoon in 1546, Elia Capsali—rabbi, historian, and leader of the Jewish community of Candia—walked home from the ducal palace. He had been visiting with his "beloved" friend Carlo Capello, the current duke of Crete.[1] As he exited the ducal palace Capsali found himself on the city's central piazza. It was still commonly known as the Plateia (Greek for "the town square") in 1546, even though Venice had officially renamed it St. Mark's Square centuries before, soon after it settled its military colonists in the town in the early thirteenth century.

The Plateia was the buzzing nerve center of Candia, and as Capsali entered the square, he saw the municipal and business centers of the city, including the main marketplace, currency exchange, merchants' loggia, and the Latin church of Saint Mark. As he entered the open square, Capsali must have inescapably drawn in the scents of food sellers' stalls and the acrid tang from smiths' workshops. Merchants loudly hawked all sorts of wares, from bread to horseshoes, from their rented benches. He might have heard the sudden hushed attention to public announcements made by the public crier in the central arcade, or *lobium*. At one time or another, he surely saw a criminal doing time in the *berlina*, the pillory set up in the square.[2] Though the duke was not sitting in judgment at that moment, since indeed he had been visiting with Capsali, the Plateia was even the spot where the ducal court heard its cases "in the open air" of the square.[3] The Plateia was a theater of life in Candia.

To the horror of religious leaders like Capsali, even Candiote Jews loved to watch the spectacle of the market and court proceedings—especially on Saturday mornings, when they should have been at Sabbath prayers.[4] Though Capsali's personal visit to the duke, the highest colonial official and governor of the island, was certainly not typical, for at least three centuries before Capsali's

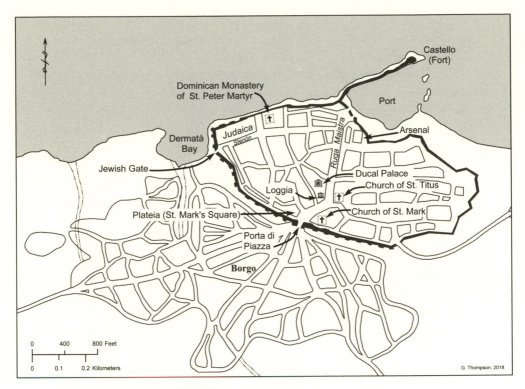

Map 2. Venetian Candia c. 1350–1450.

time, every Candiote Jew spent time in the Plateia, probably followed by a walk back to the Jewish Quarter. Such was Capsali's plan on that day.

The Candia in which Elia Capsali lived thrived as a cosmopolitan colonial capital. During his lifetime, the city's cultural life bustled even more than it had a century earlier. Byzantine refugees fleeing Constantinople in the aftermath of the Ottoman conquest of 1453 created a hub for literature, art, and classical philosophy in this Veneto-Greek milieu.[5] Nevertheless, even in the darker century after the Black Death, Candia served as a key node for travel, trade, and settlement, and had done so since surprisingly soon after Venice settled its first military colonists on the island in 1211. In fact, during the century or so after the Black Death, Crete hit her stride as a trade hub. With the Genoese controlling the hub city of Famagusta (on Cyprus) from 1374 to 1464, Candia became the key stopover point on the Venice-Levantine commercial route.[6] The first half of the fifteenth century witnessed the peak in Candia's role as a major emporium.[7] It was not simply that Candia was a hub for trade in other places' goods; the city and its hinterland produced highly desired items for export, including wine, cheese, wool, and tanned hides, among other lucrative merchandise.[8]

However bustling, Candia was nevertheless a small city, comprising 192 acres—only three-tenths of a square mile.[9] Today, a stroll from the Venetian piazza (now popularly known as Lion's Square), up the old main street known then as the Ruga Maistra (or Magistra), and right up to the harbor—a journey through the entire length of the walled city south to north—takes little more than five minutes. At least in the late sixteenth century, it was densely populated, with a 1583 census estimating the population inside the walls (not including the *borgo*) at 15,976. Only a relatively small percentage of these residents—fewer than a thousand people—belonged to Venice's noble class. Most of the city's inhabitants—over 80 percent—were middle-class Greeks, non-noble Italians, and Armenians. The city's suburb, the *borgo*, housed more of this community, especially Greeks but also Venetian elites who preferred some distance from the center of power and others who were priced out of central city living.[10] Jews made up another small but substantial population within the city's walls: about 950 souls, according to that census.[11] To be sure, we must add to this mix those who were not counted: people such as slaves and temporary visitors, including merchants and pilgrims.[12] Nevertheless, Candia remained a small town, physically and demographically. In comparison, even during the plague-ridden centuries after 1348, Venice managed to rebuild its population to above 100,000 souls; a census from 1500 puts the number at about 120,000.[13]

Unfortunately, no similar contemporary demographic assessment has survived for the century following the Black Death. Sally McKee has estimated Candia's demographics according to status and profession. She argues that "feudatories," the Venetian elites given land directly from the state, "and their families very likely never reached, much less surpassed, the figure of two thousand individuals" in the late Middle Ages. She also suggests that the "Candiote working population" (capaciously understood) hovered between at least five and eight thousand people.[14]

Yet any overarching total remains highly speculative. This fact—and a suspicion of numbers proposed by contemporary visitors—has led scholars to debate Candia's Jewish population numbers in the late Middle Ages.[15] But the census data for the late sixteenth century seem to me quite consistent with the earlier period. Counting the Jews mentioned in court documents, notarial records, and Hebrew sources from 1350 to 1454 suggests a similar population of at least 1,000 Jewish souls in the city—and probably more—in this century.[16]

These thousand or so Jews took part in the vibrant commercial life of the city, producing goods and offering services for Candia, for export, and for the internal Jewish community as well.[17] Some Cretan Jews busily made their livings in professions habitually associated with medieval Jews—moneylenders, merchants, and physicians. They were also notaries, religious scribes, and teachers, positions of high social standing.[18] Often these individuals involved themselves in more than one of these arenas, such as those who were both physicians and creditors. Despite the ubiquity of these high-status, "white-collar" jobs in the sources, many members—perhaps a majority—of the Jewish community in Candia worked in manual labor. Jewish laborers and skilled craftsmen hired themselves out and maintained their own workshops; these include tailors, artisans (*faber*), goldsmiths (*aurifex*), cobblers (*cerdo*), tanners, cork makers, butchers, healers, and dyers (*tintor*). Kosher food manufacture, including the production of kosher wine, dairy products, and meat, as well as overseeing their production for religious purposes, also employed a number of residents. Some Jews were domestic servants (*famulus/famula*), most likely serving in Jewish households.[19] Undoubtedly many unskilled laborers also existed among the community.

Though men predominantly filled these professional roles, Jewish women certainly also contributed to their own and their families' economic coffers across the spectrum: as creditors and merchants, health practitioners, domestics, and textile workers, actively and publicly taking part in the life of the city, as they also filled the at-home roles more commonly prescribed to them: wives and mothers.[20]

The Development of Candia's *Kehillah*

As he left the Plateia on that Friday afternoon in 1546, perhaps Elia Capsali glanced up at the clock on the bell tower to check how long he had before Sabbath began.[21] Though the clock was relatively new, the square—its organization and central role in the life of the city—remained much as Elia's ancestors saw it during more than three centuries that the Capsalis, once Byzantine Jews, had lived under Venetian rule. As a man keenly attentive to his family's and community's history—Capsali considered himself a historian and keeper of the community's memory—it could not have been lost on him that his situation was exceptional for a Jew of his time: his access to the halls of Venetian power, freedom in this colonial society, and, indeed, the place of the community he led.[22] In his book on Ottoman history, he himself would write of the trauma of other Jews that he had personally witnessed when some of Iberia's expelled Jews—poor, ragged, and hopeless—washed up on Crete's shores after the traumatic expulsion of 1492.[23]

In contrast to the insecurity of contemporary Sephardim, his community was confidently situated to help these homeless Jews. Despite burdensome taxation, the Jews of Candia were generally financially and politically secure; both the exigencies of Venetian imperial settlement and active negotiation by the island's Jews had created a safe space in which Jewish life could flourish.

And so it had, for centuries, both before and during Venetian rule. Jews did not come to Crete only as a result of the Venetian conquest. The Alexandrian Jewish philosopher Philo notes a significant Jewish community on Crete in the first century CE; Josephus Flavius married a woman from this Cretan Jewish community a few decades after Philo wrote.[24] Both reference to Jews in a tale recounted by the church historian Socrates Scholasticus and independent epigraphic evidence indicate that a Jewish community was settled on Crete in the fifth century.[25] To be sure, we do not know if Jews remained on Crete continuously, and Jewish settlement in this period seems to have been focused in Gortyna, the Roman administrative center on the southern coast of the island.[26]

Yet evidence certainly places Jews in Chandax (later called Candia) in the ninth and tenth centuries.[27] By the time Venice sent its first round of military colonists to hold the island in 1211, a Jewish community had struck deep roots in Candia, inhabiting its own neighborhood in the northwest corner of the city. This was the same district to which Capsali walked home after meeting the duke on that Friday in 1546.[28] This Jewish Quarter became known alternatively in Latin, Venetian, and Greek—the most commonly used languages of this multilingual colonial society—as the Judaica, Zudecca, and Obraki. In Hebrew, the quarter and its people were synonymous: both were known as the *kahal* or *kehillah*, simply "the community."

In fact, Elia's own ancestors were among those who lived in that thirteenth-century *kahal*. In 1228, Parnas Capsali signed his name to the first set of Jewish communal ordinances, *taqqanot*, which were meant to organize and unify Jewish life across the Jewish communities on the island.[29] Scholars assert that, since the community had long predated the Venetian colonial project, the Jewish communal structure was probably a holdover from Byzantine days.[30] Yet the authors of the rules of 1228, according to an introduction by its signatories, believed themselves to be innovators: this was the first unified attempt at bringing together representatives "from all four Hebrew [*ivrim*] communities" to agree to a set of rules aimed at all the Jews across the island.[31] Only seventeen years after Venice had established its rule there, a group of elites had amassed enough strength and trust within the community to gather the Jews, "young and old," in the Great Synagogue of Elijah the Prophet and to impose on them a set of ordinances prepared in advance.[32]

In his very signature, Parnas Capsali identified himself as part of this older, elite lineage. Not only did he record the name of his father, Solomon, but he traced for posterity one more generation: his grandfather Joseph Capsali, whom he proudly titled "the Rabbi."[33] Over the next three centuries, Capsali men remained at the forefront of communal leadership of Candia's *kehillah kedoshah*, the "holy community," as the corporate institution styled itself. While Parnas signed the first set of *taqqanot*, it was Elia Capsali—ever conscious of posterity and history—who collected these ordinances, along with letters and historical reflections, into a single text, the *Taqqanot Qandiya*, which survives in one lone manuscript until today.[34]

Communal Institutions

Between Parnas's life in the early 1200s and when Elia reached adulthood around 1500, members of the Capsali family and other elite clans developed a comprehensive corporate organization, similar to many Jewish *kehillah* (community) institutions in the Mediterranean and beyond.[35] As in other premodern Jewish communities, elected lay officials in Candia fulfilled the mandate of the corporate institution, whose chief goal was to enable, protect, and enforce local Jewish ritual life. These leaders, headed by an elected *condestabulo*, ensured that Candiote Jews had access to kosher food, including ritually slaughtered meat, and properly inspected dairy and wine. They organized and fostered liturgical life, with its ritual objects, Torah scrolls, synagogue spaces, and prayer leaders. They also convened a Jewish court, a *beit din*, although scant information about it survives.[36]

The *kehillah* was recognized as a corporate legal body—a *universitas*—by the Venetian government. As such, the *kehillah* owned real estate from which it derived income to provide housing for the poor and fund other community needs.[37] The leadership's other primary task was to serve as liaison between the Jewish community and the Venetian colonial government on matters that affected the community as a whole. Its most daunting task was to collect the Jewish tax, which was levied not per capita but on the community as a whole.[38]

Although some corporate institutions in the medieval world were empowered to deal with Jewish criminal activity, Venetian courts exercised control over all criminal cases.[39] The *kehillah* was allowed to mandate certain rules and ordinances for its members, an authority that other kinds of corporations, such as guilds and confraternities, also possessed. Thus any Jewish law and custom not contrary to Venetian law could be legislated for the community by the *kehillah*'s leadership. It is into this context of corporate self-rule that the Hebrew ordinances of *Taqqanot Qandiya* fit.

Like the Capsali family's enduring role as leaders, in some fundamental ways the community they led would maintain continuity during the generations between Parnas and Elia. The community's liturgical rite, the majority of its population, and its synagogues would remain "Romaniote"—that is, they identified with the ancestral ways of the Jews of Byzantine origin. Candiote Jews were generally native Greek speakers, and even as the community became more heterogeneous, it continued to follow Romaniote customs, rituals, and liturgy that—unlike Ashkenazi (Franco-German) or Sephardi (Spanish) liturgies—incorporated vernacular Greek into some parts of the service.[40]

In other ways, however, the Candiote Jewish community experienced significant changes between 1228 and the turn of the sixteenth century, not least because Crete's Jewish population was in constant flux. In particular, outbreaks of plague in the mid-fourteenth century decimated the community, a result of both death and families fleeing the island. In 1389, three representatives of the Jewish community, supported by testimony of three Venetian noblemen who had served on Crete, convinced the Venetian Senate that the collective tax, which had been recently increased, was an impossible burden for a community so weakened in number.[41] An influx of Jews from Iberia, Venice, and elsewhere, however, mitigated this loss soon after. Elia Capsali could have pointed to himself as an outcome of these demographic changes. Despite his well-known local patronymic, his mother came from the Delmedigo clan, an Ashkenazi family that arrived on the island in the late fourteenth century by way of Venetian Negroponte and quickly worked its way into the cadre of local elite Jews.

Given this population boost, Jewish economic fortunes on Crete changed for the better. As the nineteenth-century scholar of Venice Hippolyte Noiret noted, the expulsion of Jews (mainly of German and Italian extraction) from Venice was announced in late August 1394. A year later, the Venetian Senate voted to raise Crete's Jewish tax, citing not only the general wealth of the Jews but also the immigration of new rich Jews to the island.[42] The levied tax rose to 3,000 hyperpera, a 50 percent increase over the amount *kehillah* representatives had negotiated in 1389. If the tax rate correlated roughly to population, the Jewish community in the aggregate apparently remained economically successful over the course of the next century.[43]

To be sure, after 1492 and into the sixteenth century, faced with the challenge of poor Iberian Jews arriving en masse, and the need to ransom kidnapped Jews from Candia, Coron, and Patras, the Jewish community became so strapped for cash that it sold the silver finials from a Torah scroll; Elia Capsali even sold his personal library to an agent of Ulrich Fugger, the famed German businessman and bibliophile.[44] But at least until 1492, the influx of Jews from western lands offered Candia's *kehillah* some financial relief and demographic strength.

The leadership reacted to the challenges posed from the outside, such as raised taxes, through advocacy and negotiation with the colonial government—by working within the bounds of colonial justice and politics. The successful 1389 embassy to Venice is but one example of the direct approach Jewish leaders took in aiding their community; the support of the Venetian noblemen at that time suggests the value of maintaining close ties with the local administration. Capsali's visit to his "beloved friend" the duke should be read as part of this strategy, too.

Communal Reforms: 1363

When the challenges faced by the community arose from the internal realities of the *kehillah*, a different sort of strategy had to be employed. After the demographic crisis of the Black Death, the leadership convened a synod, perhaps recognizing in the moment an opportunity for unity and conformity that, they believed, would best serve the community. This synod of 1363 and its resulting *taqqanot* illustrate a community in need of a new leadership structure and new rules for relating both to each other and to the Christian communities with which they lived, worked, and even at times socialized.[45]

Their reforming ordinances of 1363 addressed problems with the structure of the system in place. From the century and a half beforehand, we have only the first set of *taqqanot* from 1228, the ones signed by Parnas Capsali and others, and a revision of the same. The 1228 set are written in rhyme; the revised set are written in prose and reordered, though the same ten ordinances remain. The prose revisions are undated and are ascribed to an otherwise unknown Rabbi Tzedakah. The initial ten ordinances address aspects of Jewish life, such as interactions with Gentiles, ritual purity, and synagogue attendance.

Regarding communal structure, the early ordinances identify communal leaders only as "appointed officials" (*ha-memunim ha-reshumim*) and assert that they have sole authority to impose excommunication.[46] An organizational structure that included these *memunim* (sg. *mamun*) seems to have lasted until 1363.[47] Deterioration in the surviving manuscript of *Taqqanot Qandiya* makes much of these first ordinances unreadable, and so it is unclear whether the community's "president," the *condestabulo*, existed yet in the early thirteenth century. One of the signatories is referred to as the *manhig*, "leader," but the designation is imprecise. A century later, however, the office of *condestabulo* was well established. In the revision of the first ten ordinances by Rabbi Tzedakah, likely from the first half of the fourteenth century, the right to call a ban is no longer the purview of unspecified officials but only allowed with prior approval from "the *condestabulo* who will be [in that position] at that time."[48] The Hebrew text transliterated the Venetian term without a translation, suggesting it had become standard by this point. From 1363 on, this official's name would often be listed in the introduction or signatory sections of ordinances; the first man identified in March of that year is "our leader, our president [*nesiyeinu*]" David the son of Judah, "the *condestabulo*."[49]

In 1363, however, this synod spelled out a more formalized leadership hierarchy. Each time the community elected a *condestabulo* (apparently annually), he was directed to choose seven men, "important men from the good men of the community" (*hashuvim mi-tuvei ha-kahal*), and have them swear on the Torah Scroll to uphold the rules of the community.[50] By choosing seven "good men," the leadership enacted a familiar medieval custom with origins in the Talmud.[51] In a *taqqanah* dated a month later, though apparently part of the same synodal texts, the legislators referred to additional leadership roles, positions more unique to the Cretan context: the *condestabulo* was given a panel of aides called *hashvanim* (councillors), the number of whom is not specified.[52]

The seeming precision of these new ordinances does not always bear out in the sources. In 1369, an ordinance is signed by the *condestabulo* and eight *memunim*, using the old term and an unexpected number—neither the seven "good men" mentioned above nor any councillors.[53] But by 1407, the *condestabulo*'s privy council was indeed comprised of three men known as *hashvanim*, and this remained the standard arrangement for the next few centuries.[54] The *condestabulo*'s councillors were chosen internally within the community, although by the mid-fifteenth century Venice also recognized them as officials of the Jewish community: ducal court records refer to the *condestabulo* and his three *camerarii* (chamberlains or advisors).[55] The community leaders continued to tweak the structure of the institution over time; in 1489, they decided that a single scribe, officially appointed by the current *condestabulo*, should be the only one to write official communal documents, since documents coming out of the *kehillah* seem to have been intentionally or accidentally misrepresenting the aims and words of the leadership.[56]

Many of the ordinances published by the reforming synod of 1363 repeat injunctions from earlier times, concerning mandatory gatherings, limitations on excommunication, maintaining the ritual bath, and the need for men to come pray in the synagogue. Despite their antique content, their repetition indicates the perceived importance of this synod and underlined the synod's goal of reunifying the community under common rules. In contrast to these repeated statutes, other ordinances were decidedly new and suggest novel social challenges faced by the community. Three ordinances seek to control the production, import, and purchase of kosher foodstuffs. Three others attempt to stem desecration of the Sabbath. Two ordinances sought to curb cheating in business deals with Christians.

These new ordinances suggest a community large enough to produce and regulate kosher food but also a community diverse enough to have members for whom Sabbath was evidently a lower priority. They also point to increased commercial relations with Christian neighbors—and, apparently, a concomitant rise in an attitude among some Jews that ethics need not apply in business transactions with individuals outside the *kehillah*. Although these are not unusual complaints to find in texts written by medieval Jewish communities, these new ordinances suggest an evolving focus and new challenges for the Candiote leadership.

Two new ordinances from 1363 point to a novel difficulty: Jewish prostitutes, Jewish pimps, and whorehouses in the Jewish Quarter of Candia. At least in part, this sprang from poverty, since the statute records that some of the prostitutes attempted to secure housing in the Jewish community's poorhouse.[57] The authors of the *taqqanah*, however, were not concerned with the sources of the problem. Rather, they sought only to root out the practice: first, by forbidding landlords to rent apartments to known prostitutes, and second, by publicly shaming those involved—including the clientele.

In the very next ordinance, the authors expressed dismay over the implications of prostitution in terms of the reputation of Candia's Jewish women. Knowledge of Jewish prostitution in the city had apparently spread far and wide, particularly because of Jewish visitors who patronized the prostitutes and then told others of their existence.[58]

Faced with crisis and disorder—unruly excommunication, unethical business practices, shirking the Sabbath, Jewish whorehouses—the leadership responded by erecting legal frameworks it hoped could reunify, solidify, and reorient the community under its leadership. Although the ordinances themselves were not revolutionary, the very act of calling a synod to pass new statutes aimed at the community as a whole, and the emphasis on the structure of the Jewish leadership, speaks to the belief among the elite that Jewish life needed to be reformed and that the community needed to be reminded of its unity. The new *taqqanot* achieved a measure of success, in as much as they were meant to form the basis for communal self-rule. The structure set out in the ordinances of 1363 remained mostly in effect; they were frequently reissued in the following centuries. No consistent reform project would ever replace it. Instead, individual ordinances were penned at key moments of perceived social and religious need.

Jewish Life and the Jewish Quarter

After taking leave of the duke, Elia Capsali began his stroll home from southern end of the city. The Plateia sat inside the main land gate, an enormous vaulted archway known as the Porta di Piazza, which led south from the town proper to its extensive suburbs, the *borgo*.[59] But the *borgo* primarily housed the Greek Orthodox population of Candia, and Capsali headed in the other direction. Walking to the northwest corner of the walled city where the Jewish Quarter was located, Capsali had to head north from the Plateia, up the Ruga Maistra, the major north-south thoroughfare that tracked through the center of the town, from the southern land gate to the northern gate at the harbor. Along the Ruga he saw Jewish stalls set up among the homes and stores that lined the street.[60] He also likely saw garbage neatly piled up next to each home and stall: since the 1360s, residents and shopkeepers on the boulevard were required to sweep up on Friday mornings in preparation for a communal trash cart, which would collect it on Saturday morning while Capsali would be in synagogue.[61]

At some point before the road hit the port, Capsali turned west and entered into the labyrinth of neighborhoods that made up much of the walled city. Before reaching the Judaica, navigating the narrow alleys, he passed by Jews rushing to bake their savory pies, a dish known even in the Hebrew text as a *torta*, in bakehouses shared with their Christian neighbors. Even though this had gone on for centuries, Capsali regarded it with such pious dismay that soon after, he built kosher ovens on his own property, at his own expense.[62]

Capsali entered the Judaica through the southeastern gate, erected in the 1390s and decorated with the Lion of St. Mark and Venetian coats of arms.[63] He strode down that neighborhood's main street, nicknamed Stenón (Greek for "narrow").[64] The tall buildings that marked this quarter as different from other neighborhoods—buildings of three or four stories, as opposed to the usual single-story homes occupied by most non-Jewish Candiote residents—would have shaded him on this late summer afternoon.[65]

By Capsali's day, the Judaica was a city within the city—enclosed by walls, some of which were also the exterior walls of Jewish homes. The south and east sides were shut up with walls in the fourteenth and fifteenth centuries. On its west and north sides, the Judaica abutted the water, where the seawall overlooked Dermata (Tanners') Bay, west of the city's main port. Lines of Jewish mansions faced the northern waterfront.

Did the noxious odors from Dermata Bay tanneries, constant threats from the sea, and narrow crowded streets make Capsali's neighborhood undesirable, as some have claimed? Perhaps not.[66] Lorenzo da Mula, a Christian visitor to Candia in 1571, wrote that the Jewish Quarter (or at least its parts closest to the water) was the "most beautiful part of the city."[67] Likewise, the keen-eyed visitor Meshullam of Volterra, in Candia in 1481, noticed other negative parts of Jewish life in the city but did not disparage the Jewish Quarter itself. Of course, perhaps these visitors saw what they wanted to see or saw what their guides showed them.

On the way home, Elia may have walked past the Jewish slaughterhouse or through the web of streets known as the "Cobbler's Area."[68] The quarter's synagogues, its mikvah (ritual bath), and its public well were not far from his route. Although the mikvah and the public well kept the same place over the course of the three centuries between the first *taqqanot* and Elia's own tenure as *condestabulo*, the number and locations of the synagogues did not stay constant. The oldest synagogue that had been in use in 1228, the one named for the Prophet Elijah, seems to have closed down at some point after 1369. But another major synagogue appeared around 1400, when the Delmedigo family founded the Allemaniko ("German") synagogue.[69] An unidentified synagogue, created in the 1260s, closed down in 1421 as the result of a Jewish convert to Christianity—and descendant of one of the founders of the synagogue—successfully suing in the ducal court for control of the land.[70] The *taqqanot* indicate that in 1369 and 1406 there were three synagogues worth mentioning; in 1424 a number of synagogues existed, but there were two major ones (*hashtayim hagdolot*).[71] But a *taqqanah* likely from the 1530s lists four, with its representatives: the Great Synagogue, represented by Samuel Cohen Ashkenazi; the Synagogue of the Priests, represented by Moses Del-medigo; the Synagogue of the Ashkenazim, represented by Aba Delmedigo; and the High Synagogue, represented by Solomon Cohen Balbo.[72] Already by 1369 and still in 1518, the Seviliatiko Synagogue, ostensibly the commonly used name for the Great Synagogue, was a major focus, where communal synods at least sometimes took place.[73]

The synagogue was a meeting house as well as a house of prayer. In the early part of the fifteenth century, the Synagogue of the Priests filled the role of a communal center, a place where community leaders "sat time and time again" to debate their responses to communal problems, such as the ongoing crisis in which Jewish-owned stores remained open for business too close to the start of Sabbath, and also sold goods during the intermediary days of holidays (*hol hamo'ed*).[74] In the later years of the fifteenth century, the leadership met at the Great Synagogue (Beit Knesset HaGadol) to discuss religious crises such as the laxity in separation between fiancés and their betrothed before the wedding.[75]

Jewish Migration and Settlement in Candia

The Jewish community of Crete grew and evolved during the Venetian period because of a steady flow of Jewish immigration. Nevertheless, many of the Jewish families in Candia were not newcomers. Naming patterns suggest that many Candiote Jews in this century were of Byzantine origin or at least had been in the Greek milieu for a long time.[76] Some families had lived on Crete before the Venetian conquest. A member of Casani family, Anatoli the son of David, for instance, wrote liturgical poetry on Crete in the twelfth century.[77] His family remained among the Jewish elite during Venetian rule. Other migrants arrived on Crete from within the contemporary and former Byzantine Empire and from Venetian colonies such as Coron and Negroponte.

Others came from farther afield, some with little in their pockets. In 1428, a Majorcan Jew agreed to serve a Candiote physician on his travels to Venice in return for food, lodging, and a salary of three hyperpera per month.[78] Others arrived with far greater resources. And just as their socioeconomic status varied, their origins did as well. Surnames suggest a wide variety of places of origin: Turco (from Ottoman lands or Asia Minor), de Damasco (Damascus), Ciciliano (Sicily), Tzarfati (northern France), and even one Jew oddly named

Saracenus. Many other non-Byzantine Jews came to Crete from Iberia and German lands.[79]

Venetian rule on Crete coincided with periods of upheaval in many other parts of Christendom, marked by plague, riot, and massacre, especially in Iberia and Germany. This turmoil provoked a Jewish exodus from the traditional centers of settlement in western Europe. Northern France expelled its Jews in 1182 and 1306 (only to allow the Jews to return in 1189 and 1315) and again in 1395. England definitively drove its Jews out in 1290. German Jews suffered the Rindfleisch and Armleder massacres in 1298 and 1336, respectively, and the Black Death provoked a sharpened set of anti-Jewish legislation, financial disabilities, and mob hostility across Europe that began in 1348 but continued in various incarnations for another century.[80] The massacres and burnings of the so-called Pestpogrom in the immediate aftermath of the plague gave way to devastating economic persecution around 1390, when the Luxembourger king Wenceslas IV canceled Jewish debt.[81]

Likewise, Jews began to flee Iberia in this same period. Before 1348, anti-Jewish violence certainly took place, as David Nirenberg has illustrated.[82] With the advent of the plague, however, Catalonia and Navarre became "the center of violence and killings" of Jews, and the Inquisition "accompanied the crescendo of violence," seeking out German and French converts to Christianity who had returned to their Judaism upon moving to Iberia.[83] The many Jews who sought refuge in Castile, however, were not to have peace in the following decades, as vitriolic anti-Jewish preaching led to mob riots and massacres across Iberia in the summer of 1391. Beginning in Seville, the riots spread to Valencia and Catalonia, and from there across the peninsula; many Jews were killed and others were forced to convert en masse.[84] In the first half of the fifteenth century, popular preachers such as Vincent Ferrer continued to rouse the masses to attack Jewish quarters and force Jews to convert under fear of death and pressed the governments of Iberia to pass ever-harsher anti-Jewish legislation.[85] Long before the expulsion of 1492, many of those who were able to fled Iberia, as did Jews from the German lands.

Though northern Italy was generally a locus of Jewish immigration, at various times Jews found the peninsula unwelcoming, particularly when mendicant preachers riled up town leaders and residents.[86] The Franciscan friar Bernardino di Siena (d. 1444) stoked hostility against Jews (even if temporarily) in bustling commercial towns such as Florence, Padua, and Siena.[87] Some Italian cities, such as Genoa and Milan, simply forbade Jewish settlement altogether; others expelled Jews in the late fifteenth century.[88] Venice

finally allowed Jewish moneylenders to settle in the city and its adjacent mainland (*terraferma*) in the decades after the Black Death, most explicitly from
1382. But Venice soon turned out its Jews, at the end of the century.[89] In
1394, for economic reasons—there was no longer an urgent need for moneylenders lending credit in the city—the government decided that it would not
renew the charter granted to the Jews when it expired in 1397.[90] From that
time, individual Jewish moneylenders were allowed into the city for no longer
than fifteen days. Jewish merchants and doctors were allowed in sporadically
according to other sets of rules. All Jews had to wear a yellow circle on their
clothing. Enormous fines were levied on practicing their religion in the open
during their short stays in Venice, for example by holding prayer services.[91]
Families left for more welcoming towns, and Venice ceased to be a tempting
destination for those seeking to relocate from regions further west.

As western Europe turned more hostile to Jews, Crete came to be regarded
as a haven, where Jews escaping expulsion (or worse) could start over. The
Venetian government evidently had no problem with immigration to Crete.
Likewise, there was no attempt by the Jewish community to control the influx,
as some Ashkenazi communities in previous centuries had done.[92]

The fourteenth and fifteenth centuries have often been seen as a period
of increasing economic disabilities for Cretan Jews, part of the crisis spreading across Christendom. Undoubtedly this period witnessed residential,
financial, and professional limitations for the community in Candia. Beginning in 1325, Jews in all Venetian colonies were required to live in Jewish
quarters only. Residential rules tightened in 1391, when the Signoria ordered
that some of the homes considered part of the Judaica, but across the street
from Christian homes considered not part of that district, had to be walled
off. This culminated in a final enclosure of the Judaica in 1450 at the request
of the adjacent Dominican monastery of St. Peter Martyr.[93] Meanwhile, in
1423, Venice prohibited Jews in all of its domains from holding real estate
outside Jewish quarters.[94]

Jewish trade was also limited in this period. Generally, Jews were allowed
to use shipping lines to Venetian colonies in the Levant, but they usually could
not secure rights to ship goods to the metropole.[95] Moreover, for about two
decades beginning in 1429, Venice prohibited its vessels from transporting
Jews or their goods to any Mamluk-held territory, thereby extending a papal
ban against Christian ships conveying Jews and Jewish-owned goods to the
Holy Land.[96] Jewish economic outlets in Venice's colonies were increasingly

restricted, which probably led more Jewish capital to be directed toward moneylending.[97]

In addition, during the 1430s and 1440s, when Venice needed funds for its war efforts, Cretan Jews found themselves taxed heavily and forced to make war loans. In 1389 the community's ambassadors successfully convinced the Senate to lower the Jewish tax to 2,000 hyperpera. But by the 1430s, the community was forced to pay 4,000 hyperpera in taxes, 12,000 ducats to help pay Venice's war debt, and another 3,000 measures of wheat.[98] Furthermore, Crete's Jews were legally compelled to wear the yellow badge beginning around the turn of the fifteenth century. This regulation, though, apparently did not meet with great success. [99]

Nonetheless, despite policies aimed at limiting Jewish residency, cutting Jewish market share in overseas trade, and burdensome tax increases and other obligatory payments, these impediments seem relatively minor in comparison to the Jewish experience in other parts of Europe. In particular, the residential limitations appear not to have provoked much anguish, especially since they were sometimes honored in the breach. Segregation thus did not mean isolation or alienation, nor did it discourage new Jewish settlement in Candia. Moreover, it is likely that the Jewish tax rose not simply as a result of Christian mistreatment but also, at least in part, as a result of surging Jewish settlement.[100]

Perhaps more importantly, the Jews of the Stato da mar lived in Venice's colonies without a specific legal charter or *condotta*, which Jews in many other parts of Europe and even in the *terraferma* holdings needed for legal settlement. Residence, thus, was not provisional but seemed more secure in its permanence.[101] The lack of *condotte* also meant exceptional economic freedom, in contrast to Jews who had to abide by specific charters in Italy and elsewhere. Although the prohibition on landownership and the shipment restrictions had the effect of limiting trade (especially in luxury items and spices), Crete still offered Jews a wide variety of professional opportunities. Likewise, although Jews were never given citizenship, their status as legal residents and formal subjects of Venice provided Candia's Jewish merchants certain advantages, such as legal protections when abroad, use of Venetian warehouses, and even, at times, access to state-sponsored shipping.[102]

Crete thus became a choice destination not only because its government allowed entry to refugee Jews but also because it offered significant attractions to businessmen seeking to expand their trading networks. Crete's position at a crossroads between the Italian peninsula and the Levant made the island, and particularly the town of Candia—arguably the most important way station in the Mediterranean, at least until the rise of Famagusta on Cyprus toward 1500—an attractive and lucrative destination for Jews.[103]

Paths Toward Integration

Although the majority of Jews, and indeed the most powerful Jews, in Crete throughout the Venetian period identified as Romaniote—following the Byzantine-Jewish liturgical and ritual rites—the immigration described above brought a heterogeneous mix of predominantly Ashkenazim (German Jews) and Sephardim (Spanish Jews) to the island. Their integration into Candiote society can sometimes be tracked through their interaction with the *kehillah*'s leadership, their business contracts, and their dealings with Venice's colonial court.

Most of the Sephardi Jews named in Latin and Hebrew sources on Crete appear after the massacres of 1391, and it seems likely that most arrived fleeing those terrible events. Some Sephardim, however, came earlier. A Catalan Jew, resident of Candia, contracted to sell honey in Candia as early as 1339, working alongside his business associates, Jews from Sicily and North Africa.[104] The widow Archondisa, in her will from 1358, recorded her late husband as Elia *catellanus*, although her name suggests that her own origins lay in the Greek-speaking world, a marriage pattern common for Sephardi men and Romaniote women.[105] Another Elia Catellan, son of Solomon, already lived in Candia in 1386 when he made his will.[106]

Of the Sephardim who settled in Candia before the *annus horribilis* of 1391, the Astruc (or Astrug) family's tale appears in sharpest relief, nicely suggesting the possibilities available to Iberian Jewish immigrants. Members of the Astruc family, most likely from Catalonia, settled in Candia in the mid-fourteenth century and quickly amassed wealth and prestige.[107] They used strategic marriages and business partnerships to secure their new positions as elite members of Candia's Jewish community. By 1359, Solomon Astrug (as the name is spelled in the Latin sources) had married and was in the midst of divorcing a well-connected Romaniote wife, Elea, daughter of a wealthy Greek Jewish businessman, Liacho Mavristiri, and soon married into another Greek Jewish family.[108]

Solomon Astrug built up a successful moneylending business and bought lucrative real estate.[109] He also made useful contacts in the colonial government. During the early 1390s, when the ducal court limited Jewish residence outside the Jewish Quarter, the court exempted Solomon Astrug—the only

Jew identified by name—from selling his residential buildings outside the neighborhood. He had no problem paying a high fee for this favor.[110] With their father's wealth to back them, Solomon's seven children flourished in Crete and for generations this lineage helped lead the Jewish community.[111] One descendant named Solomon even served as the *condestabulo* in 1446.[112] Other Iberian families in the next century would follow Astrug-like paths toward social integration and political leverage. Of course, money paved the way, and only a relatively small number of Sephardi Jews achieved the communal triumph of the Astrugs.[113]

While most Iberian Jewish immigrants appear to have come to Crete in the aftermath of the traumatic events of 1391, the contours of German Jewish migration to the island are less clear-cut. As in the case of Sephardi newcomers, there were certainly some German Jews in Crete before the Black Death. One Elia Allemanus contracted to buy wine there in 1271, only sixty years after Venice had colonized the island.[114] Migration from the German lands was in full swing by 1378.[115] In that year, a German Jew named Ysacharus (probably Issachar), ill and expecting death, recorded his testament. He was not an official resident of Candia but rather was currently living there with his wife, Hebela; a son remained temporarily in Ashkenaz. Ysacharus had arrived too recently to have learned a language in common with the Latin notary hired to compose his will, so he asked two Jewish landsmen to translate for him. These two men, each identified as German (*theotonicus*) and as official residents (*habitator*) of Candia, were able to navigate in local languages. Undoubtedly grateful for their assistance, Ysacharus labeled these men as being among "the better" German Jews living in Candia, indicating that more compatriots lived in the city.[116]

German Jews came to Crete by way of a number of different routes. Some came via Venice and north Italy. Maria, the widow of Heschia Theotonicus, lived both in Candia and in Venice in the 1390s, although her daughter and son-in-law, Samuel Theotonicus, were members of Crete's Jewish community.[117] Local Jewish leaders wanted Maria to pay Jewish taxes in Crete, though Maria held property, paid taxes, and was currently resident (so it was argued) in Venice itself in April 1391. Even during this short period in which Jews were allowed to settle legally in Venice, some Ashkenazi Jews—including Maria's son-in-law Samuel—preferred to put down roots in Crete, although Maria's husband seems to have remained in Venice until his death. Jews from German lands began to migrate to Venice's mainland holdings in the thirteenth century. The example of the widow Maria and her family suggests that some turned from the mainland to the even broader possibilities available in Crete.[118]

While some Ashkenazim chose to leave Venice even when they were temporarily allowed to live there, more German Jews who had been living and working in Venice immigrated to Crete after August 1394, when Venice refused to renew the Jewish charter. This quasi-expulsion brought "an influx of wealthy Jews" to Crete, likely including many Ashkenazi Jews.[119] The route of some of these Jews from Germany to Venice sometimes took them via Spain. In the later decades of the fifteenth century, Moses Cohen Ashkenazi migrated to Crete, where he quickly became embroiled in a famed debate over Kabbalistic notions of reincarnation with the local-born Cretan rabbi Michael Balbo.[120] In fact, Moses Ashkenazi spent time in Iberia, then traveled to Venice with his father, and from there moved to Candia.[121]

Other Ashkenazi Jews came through Venice's other colonies before settling in Crete, as did the Delmedigo family.[122] The actual connection between Germany and this family, the most famous example of a family of Ashkenazi origin in Crete, is lost to history. Latin legal material, however, indicates that the brothers Judah and Shemarya Delmedigo came to Candia by 1359 after significant residence in Negroponte.[123] They must have spent enough time in the Italian sphere to have adopted the last name Delmedigo, meaning "of the doctor."

Both Moses Cohen Ashkenazi and the Delmedigos thought of themselves as Ashkenazi and were considered as such by their coreligionists in Candia. Abba Delmedigo the Elder, for example, supposedly founded a synagogue in Candia called the Allemaniko ("German") around 1400.[124] In his Kabbalistic-philosophical fight with Moses Cohen Ashkenazi over competing ideas of reincarnation, the Romaniote Michael Balbo emphasized the alien character of his opponent's ideas by highlighting his foreign birthplace.[125] But their affiliations and practices did not always align with our assumptions of Ashkenazi behavior; if we can rely on the Delmedigo family's seventeenth-century prayer book, the family (at least by then) prayed according to the Romaniote rite.[126] This apparently was not a novelty: in the sixteenth century, members of the Delmedigo family acted as communal representatives for both the "Synagogue of the Ashkenazim" (the Allemaniko) and the "Synagogue of the Priests" (also known as the Chochanitiko), one of the old Romaniote synagogues.[127]

Just as the Delmedigos came to lead Cretan Jewry, other Jews of German origin also joined the elite ranks of the Cretan kehillah, including Lazaro Theotonicus (Eliezer Ashkenazi Katz), who in 1411 acted as condestabulo and spearheaded a project to build a new sewer to protect water quality.[128] In a taqqanah, Elia Capsali identified a rabbi and scholar named Yitzhak (Isaac) Ashkenazi as his revered teacher.[129]

Some German Jews had gained status in the community before the fifteenth century. In 1369, Malkiel Cohen Ashkenazi signed an ordinance of *Taqqanot Qandiya*, an act that indicated he had achieved a certain status within the community.[130] Malkiel, however, was a respected member not only of the Jewish community's elite but also of the wider town's elite. Melchiele Theotonicus, as he is called in the Latin sources, was a doctor in independent practice who was also employed by the Venetian judiciary to treat injuries and testify about them in court. The German Jewish surgeon identified as Magister Iaco appeared before a Latin notary to translate for the dying Ysacharus as he dictated his will in 1378.[131] Ashkenazi immigrants to Crete thus included respected physicians who were part of the colonial system and its institutions already in the 1360s and 1370s.

A small number of Iberian Jews also joined the leadership roster in Crete. In addition to the Astrug family, only two identified Iberian Jews appear in leadership positions. Isaac Catellan, son of Elia son of Solomon, acted as *hashvan* in 1444; his father had been in Candia by 1386 and thus was not of the post-1391 migration.[132] Emmanuel Sephardi, a doctor, signed a *taqqanah* in 1439.[133]

Connections Beyond Candia

As Candia's immigrants settled the city, they often remained tied into broader networks on the island, in the Venetian sphere, and in the broader Mediterranean world. In his youth, Elia Capsali had been sent to study in the Ashkenazi yeshiva in Padua and then lived in Venice. In studying abroad in an Ashkenazi setting, he emulated his father, Elqanah, who also studied in Padua, and his uncle Moses Capsali, who had apparently even attended yeshiva in Ashkenaz itself. By 1450, Rabbi Moses Capsali had moved to Constantinople, where he served as chief rabbi of the city under the Ottomans.[134]

The port city of Candia was, then, a place of transience and travel. Unsurprisingly, Jews from all over the island were in regular contact. Significant Jewish communities lived in Rethymno and Canea (modern Khania), although Candia boasted a larger population. Ducal court records and notarial registers from Candia also mention Jews based in other fortified towns and, to a smaller extent, villages of the hinterland, including Castronovo, Castro Belvedere,[135] and Castro Bonifacio.[136] The last of these fortress towns even housed a kosher slaughterhouse (*becaria iudeorum*) in 1439, when a predatory castellan tried to exploit it for profit.[137] In 1419, some Jews clearly lived in the village of Casale de Evgenichi; a local Jewish man and woman were murdered there (an event about which we know very little).[138]

In the fourteenth century in Castronovo, the Jewish community fell victim to Greek rebels during the great St. Tito revolt of 1363–64. Regarded by the rebels as agents of Venice, the Jews were massacred in the summer of 1364.[139] Jews did not abandon Castronovo, however; the surgeon Joseph Carfocopo was living in Castronovo in 1369, only a handful of years after the massacre, while another Jewish surgeon, Moses Gradnelli (or Gadinelli), resided there sixty years later.[140] Two Jewish families, the Chersonitis and the Stamatis, lived there in 1370.[141] Two other Jews from the town appear in the ducal records in May 1373, after one seriously wounded the other.[142] A decade later, enough Jews lived in Castronovo for a judicial sentence regarding payment for water use to simply refer to them collectively, "the Jews residing in Castronovo."[143] Although the Jewish population was expelled from Castronovo and Bonifacio at some point in the fifteenth century, once again this was not permanent, and evidence of Jewish settlement in both those locales reappears in the following century.[144]

Many Jews had interests in more than one town on the island, including some who owned property in more than one location.[145] Branches of the same family often lived in different cities, especially in both Candia and Rethymno. Members of the Capsali family lived in Rethymno;[146] and in the 1420s, Magister Monache, a doctor and resident of Candia, had his son settle in Rethymno, at least in part so that they could take up two ends of the cloth trade that linked the two towns.[147] Sometimes marriage connected families across the island. Herini, the widow of Sambatheus Chasuri, lived in Candia when she dictated her will in March 1348, but her two brothers, named as executors of her will, resided in Canea.[148] Likewise, Liacho, a Jewish cobbler, called Candia home, though earlier his father, Lazarus, had lived in the district of Milopotamo, west of Candia.[149]

Most of the evidence of Jewish settlement from areas outside Candia exists because these Jews journeyed there from their hometowns, often to petition the ducal court. While in Candia, these Jews relied on the institutions of the Judaica for food, shelter, and other needs, such as prayer services. *Taqqanot Qandiya* attests to connections between the elites of Candia and other cities. Jewish leaders from Rethymno appear as signatories on various ordinances, and one from Rethymno was adopted whole cloth in Candia.[150] As such, it is not surprising that the Jews of these cities worked together to promote common communal interests. When fighting a steep tax increase levied on the island's Jews during the 1440s, the *universitas* of Candiote Jews joined with representatives of the *universitas iudeorum* of Rethymno to appeal before the ducal court.[151]

Shared Venetian sovereignty also facilitated regular and easy connections between Jews living in Crete and those in other parts of the Stato da mar, particularly Negroponte.[152] Jews moved back and forth between Crete and Negroponte; marriages between Jews from the two islands were not uncommon.[153] Even the prominent Delmedigo family evidently moved to Candia after a stint in Negroponte.[154] Beyond the Venetian sphere, marriage, trade, and resettlement took place between Cretan Jews and those nearby on Rhodes, controlled by the Hospitallers from 1309 until the mid-fifteenth century.[155] Jewish traders from Rome, Barcelona, and Majorca came to Crete, sometimes to partner with their Cretan Jewish counterparts. Jewish traders set off from Candia to sell their wares in Sardinia, Tunis, Alexandria, and Constantinople.[156] The great Venetian wine trade to Alexandria enabled Jews like Elia Capsali of Rethymno (a relative of the Candiote leader) to reap profit exporting both kosher and conventional Malvasia di Candia (Malmsey), a rich varietal derived from Greek grapes.[157] In Constantinople before 1453—and indeed after as well—Candiote Jewish traders exchanging Cretan wine and cheese for leather hides often stayed in the Venetian quarter, where they met Catalan and Genoese Jewish merchants.[158] Finally, Cretan Jews had a profound connection to Jerusalem, a place where Candiote men and women went on pilgrimage but also sometimes to stay, to die, and to be buried.[159] The holy city loomed large in their imaginations. Some sent money "to the great Jewish men who are in Jerusalem," as one 1348 testator put it. Some named their children after it—such as Çigio, the daughter of Chaluda Balbo, whose name is most likely the feminized form Tziona—Zion.[160]

Anxiety, Acceptance, and Other Jews

Jewish community leaders welcomed newcomers, whether refugees or businessmen, from east and west, absorbing them into the *kehillah kedoshah*. These newcomers brought practical skills and knowledge, and (at least, ideally) contributed to the Jewish tax once they had set up in business. Naturally they arrived in Candia with their own experience of Jewish rite and tradition, as well as their own approaches to Jewish law. On one hand, the Jewish hierarchy demanded adherence to local Jewish custom from newcomers, a theme that sounds throughout *Taqqanot Qandiya*. At the same time, newcomers worked their way into the Jewish leadership hierarchy and into the tight cohort of Jewish elite families who had traded power among themselves for generations.

But some Jews caused the Jewish leadership a sense of anxiety. Only three times in *Taqqanot Qandiya* are wrongdoers identified by name, and in each case, they are outsiders. "A Sephardi Jew, and his name is Abraham Tofer [i.e., the tailor]," provoked a 1439 ordinance demanding all marriages take place before ten witnesses.[161] The ordinance not only stresses improper marital behavior but highlights the individual and, even more so, his Spanish origin. Likewise, when a rumor spread that Candiote women were promiscuous, the *taqqanah* targeted a specific man, "the Sicilian, Shalom."[162] In 1531, when another Jew libeled the reputation of Candiote Jewish women, the *taqqanah* identified him as "Judah Kirkus . . . who came to live in our land" from Egypt.[163] It was outsiders—Jews, but outsiders and newcomers nonetheless—who were presumed to threaten the reputation and sanctity of the Candiote community.

To be sure, blaming reprehensible behavior on newcomers was not confined to these specific instances. Elia Capsali, among others, engaged in this practice. Writing in the 1530s about a practice he despised—selling certain honors on the holiday of Simhat Torah instead of awarding them to learned and pious men—he blamed the behavior on "new people who have recently come, whom your ancestors could not have imagined" (an expression he borrowed from Deuteronomy 32:17). Later he complained of "immigrants [*gerim*] from a far land" who thought they could purchase themselves good reputations.[164]

Remarkably, the most egregious Jews, from the perspective of *Taqqanot Qandiya*, were outsiders but still residents of Crete—in particular, the Jews of the fortress town of Castronovo. Jews from this nearby community sparked long-lasting anxiety among the pious leadership. Two statutes from 1363 offer a clear set of complaints against them. Castronovo's Jews sold supposedly kosher meat that could not actually be trusted; their dairy products were equally suspect.[165] Such behavior touching on both religion and the economy was deemed "evil," and the rabbis feared that Castronovo's Jews would act "in secret" to trick Candiote Jews into eating impure foods.[166] Only if their cheeses were officially certified could Jews from Castronovo sell to their coreligionists in the city. The spatial rhetoric that divides "us vs. them" is striking: the Castronovans and their ilk are "outside of our community" (*mi-hutzah le-kehilateinu*), in contrast to Candiote Jews, who are "men of our place" (*anshei mekomeinu*).

To be sure, rabbinic attitudes likely did not align with those of the common flock. Not all Jews saw their coreligionists in Castronovo as beyond the pale; some were eager to buy their unapproved foodstuffs—a fact that sparked the *taqqanah* in the first place. Likewise, some Candiote Jews were pleased to marry their children to Jews from Castronovo, as Solomon Torchidi did in 1451 when he betrothed his son to an affluent girl from Castronovo.[167] In general, though, for the authors of the *taqqanot*, these Jews were regarded as problematic and had to be carefully watched.

The key issue was control: the Candiote rabbis wanted to take charge of ensuring the *kashrut* of the Judaica's food, while Castronovo's Jews—and likely its own leaders—judged themselves perfectly capable of producing fare without the imposition of the capital's rabbis. This tension over control came up again in 1567, when the Candiote leadership reacted with horror that the local religious leadership in Castronovo excommunicated a member of the community. In a letter recorded among the *taqqanot*, the Candiote leadership reminded the Jews of Castronovo that only Candia's rabbis had that right—bestowed on them by Venice itself, they claimed—and that their behavior, if continued, would provoke a wholesale excommunication of Castronovo's Jews by the Candiote *kehillah*.[168]

A well-known mid-fifteenth-century letter from the chief rabbi of Constantinople, Candiote Moses Capsali, further attests to tensions between the town and country Jews, as well as to the problems of newcomers bringing their own traditions. A writ of divorce was given by a husband to a wife in a place identified in Hebrew as "Kastell" or "Kasteel," likely referring to one of the fortress towns (*castelli*)—perhaps even Castronovo itself.[169] Yet Capsali does not ultimately blame Cretans. Rather, he writes: "And all this has happened to you because of new people who have recently come, whom your ancestors could not have imagined, until they have overcome you with sins, to lead you in the customs of their lands, which your fathers and your fathers never knew. And who would say that the customs of the rest of the communities [*kehillot*] were better than the customs of the holy community of Candia and the rest of the holy communities on the island?"[170] He also remarks on the widespread nature of the newcomer problem. In his current home of Constantinople, "a few of the wise men [*hakhamim*] from other lands came, and they were wise in their own eyes" for they tried to persuade the local Romaniote community to follow their alien ways. Capsali boasts that he and others proudly "stood in the breach against them." Local customs, he repeatedly stresses, are the sole legitimate customs.[171]

Nevertheless, while Moses Capsali could speak generally of interlopers promoting their innovations, he too was powerfully influenced by outsiders: when the innovations came via Ashkenaz, they were desirable.[172] Answering another query from the Candiote rabbis, Moses Capsali wrote about choosing a *hazzan* (literally, "cantor") for each synagogue.[173] On Crete as elsewhere a *hazzan* functioned as the chief executive officer for that synagogue during his

tenure—a powerful, high-status, and lucrative job. Vexed by Venetian government intervention in the choosing of Candia's *hazzanim*, Capsali expounded
the proper method.[174] Instead of suggesting that they go back to the old ways,
though, Capsali told the Jews of Candia to follow another example: that of the
Jews of Ashkenaz. Their practices are better, wrote Capsali, and in the course
of his responsum he referenced the Ashkenazi liturgy and even quoted a story
from Cologne, borrowed from the Ashkenazi rabbi Eliezer ben Joel HaLevi
of Bonn. In idealizing Ashkenaz, Capsali reinterpreted Candiote practice, an
increasingly prevalent trend as Candiote Jewish elites sent their sons to study
at the Ashkenazi yeshiva in Venetian Padua. Ashkenazi ways inflected Crete's
broad, community-wide halachic practices, including kosher slaughtering of
animals, and also affected a certain segment of Candia's Jewish philosophical
perspectives.[175]

Crete's Jews, however, absorbed cultural influences from beyond Ashkenaz. Sixteen Hebrew manuscripts of text collections copied for patrons and
reflecting their own interests have survived from fourteenth- and fifteenth-
century Crete.[176] These manuscripts suggest an elite interested in a wide variety
of topics, including biblical commentary, mysticism, homilies, and Jewish law
(halacha), as well as Euclidean geometry, Hebrew grammar, Spanish poetry,
Aristotelian philosophy, and medicine. These elite texts, particularly the explicitly religious works, highlight the impact of Iberian and Provençal scholars and
scholarly trends on Crete's Jews.[177] In addition, responsa evidence indicates that
already in 1300, some Candiote Jews sought religious rulings from Solomon
ibn Adret of Barcelona; links between Crete and Barcelona's rabbis continued throughout the century.[178] No matter what anxiety individual Sephardi
Jews, such as Abraham the tailor, brought to Candia, Sephardi ideas—mystical,
medical, or otherwise—held sway among the island's Jewish leaders.

This mixture of Jewish cultural traditions, as well as the ongoing connection between Jews in Candia and those farther afield, is attested in a will composed on behalf of Joseph Missini, a wealthy community leader who died in
Candia around 1411.[179] The Missini surname suggests that the family was not
local to Crete (likely from Messinia, the region encompassing the southwest
extension of the Peloponnese/Morea). But the family appears to have been on
Crete for at least a generation (perhaps more) before Joseph was born and was
deeply ensconced in its Jewish community and its Romaniote traditions.[180]
The Jewish community in Candia played a large role in Joseph's life. He served
a successful term as *condestabulo*.[181] He had even represented Cretan Jewry
before the government in Venice, when he and others successfully convinced

the senate to lower Crete's Jewish tax in 1389.[182] Beyond this performance, Joseph himself appealed to Romaniote practices at times in his life.[183]

When Joseph dictated his will to a Latin notary in August 1411, he provided large bequests both for his extended family and for the Candiote Jewish community at large, including through the funding of the salary of a scholar of Jewish text and law to whom would be bequeathed Missini's own library. He also left money to educate Jewish boys and to furnish dowries for impoverished Jewish girls.[184] He was clearly concerned with the local benefit his considerable wealth could bestow.

Joseph's generosity extended beyond Candia, however. He also bequeathed charity for the Jewish poor in Rethymno. Moreover, he stipulated that a third of his significant investment profits was to be given to German and French rabbis living in Jerusalem.[185] For Joseph, as for many of his Candiote coreligionists, Jerusalem was not an abstract or distant land of hope but a final destination on a well-known sea voyage. Joseph's dedication to Jews both at home and abroad, and to both Romaniote and Ashkenazi Jews, points to a Cretan Jewish community deeply tied into broader Jewish networks in the Mediterranean and beyond. Such connections to the Ashkenazi world began at home. Missini had brokered a marriage between his daughter, Crussana, and Israel Theotonicus.[186] As a fixture of the Judaica's elite, he likely sympathized with Ashkenazi intellectual and halachic ideas at the same time that he married his daughter to a German immigrant. Nevertheless, when pressed to comply with the Ashkenazi ban on bigamy, Missini refused to assent and remained married to a second wife, according to Romaniote tradition.[187] For Missini this was a normal negotiation of legitimate value options, not a contradiction.

* * *

Almost a century and a half after Joseph Missini led the Candiote community, on the Friday in 1546 when Elia Capsali walked home from the ducal palace, it was now Capsali who was in charge—and had been for a number of decades already, since his first stint as *condestabulo* around 1515. On that afternoon, Elia Capsali entered his sizable yard and passed into his family's residence compound, where he prepared for the incoming Sabbath. His prosperous family probably owned their own home; most inhabitants of the Judaica rented from rich Jews or from Venetian Christian feudatories.[188] But thoughts of business and property could be left for another day. As the sun began to set late on Friday, he gathered with his family for the Day of Rest, prayed the evening service, and, like his ancestors before him and his fellow community members around the neighborhood, enjoyed Sabbath dinner.

Yet the calm communality of this Sabbath-inspired domestic scene veils Elia's own reality of integration into the wider, non-Jewish society of Crete and beyond. Capsali, like the earlier authors of *Taqqanot Qandiya*, did not live in isolation. Jewish internal heterogeneity in Candia met a parallel reality of an interdependent wider society across the colonial city. The reality of daily encounters between the city's Jews and their Latin and Greek coresidents—interactions that were sometimes positive, sometimes not—had been part of Cretan life since before Venetian rule, and they only mounted during the colonial era. Capsali's ancestor Parnas, among the first signatories of the *taqqanot*, recognized the reality and necessity of daily commercial exchange, as he and his cohort voted to pass an ordinance against cheating in Jewish-Christian trade. Joseph Missini dealt with Christians at the highest level of government when he traveled on embassy to Venice, but when he returned to Crete, he encountered his Greek Christian neighbors, from whom he had bought his own home. As each man turned inward to lead his community, he simultaneously turned outward, forging enduring associations—commercial, legal, domestic—with Christians on the island they all shared.

Chapter 2

Jewish-Christian Relations, Inside and Outside the Jewish Quarter

Although Christians appear throughout *Taqqanot Qandiya*, one of the very few times in which the Hebrew text collection mentions Greeks specifically can be found among the reforming ordinances of 1363, in a statute that seeks to ensure that wine production complies with the laws of *kashrut*. Jews did not own the vineyards or presses used in making kosher wine. Instead, they sometimes purchased grapes and rented presses to produce wine for the community and for export elsewhere. But, at least until April 1363, the Jews who supervised wine-pressing in the villages near Candia often did not fulfill the requirements for keeping the drink suitable for Jewish consumption. Rather, claims the *taqqanah* written that month, they allowed the grapes to run through the pressing system without the proper cleansing process. Moreover, they let non-Jews load grapes into the press, and they did not carefully observe. Some Jews dispatched to oversee wine production did not enter the premises at all, claims the *taqqanah*, but simply took Gentile-made wine must and claimed it as kosher.

Blame is assigned all around by the *taqqanah*'s authors. On the one hand, the fault lies with the Jews themselves, labeled teenage ignoramuses, such boors that they "do not know how to pray." But the ordinance also offers a more sympathetic reading. The main reason that the Jewish men acted negligently resulted from "their fear of the Greeks, who say to the Jews '*Go away, impure one, they called to them, go away and do not touch.*'"[1] According to the *taqqanah*, sometimes these verbal attacks on Jews as polluters turned violent, and Jews were banned from even entering into the building in which the wine presses sat. Those sent to guard wine production shirked their duties to the Jewish community in order to avoid being physically assaulted.[2]

This *taqqanah* certainly evinces tense and brutal relations between Jews and Christians on Crete and, in particular, between Jews and Greeks. Certainly such violence can be corroborated. Elia Capsali recorded that, probably in the 1530s, a Jew from Canea who had been sent to guard the *kashrut* of wine had been killed.[3] Moreover, the claim that Greeks held the Jewish touch to be polluting was not just a product of Jewish imaginations, despite the use of a biblical verse to paraphrase the verbal attack. Throughout the Byzantine world, Greeks feared Jewish contagion transmitted to food and drink through touch.[4] On Crete in particular, a late fourteenth-century Byzantine monk and preacher stoked this contagion anxiety. In addition to concerns over grapes and wine specifically, Crete's Greeks also did not want Jews manhandling any fresh produce in the marketplace. In the mid-fifteenth century, Venetian authorities on Crete "bowed to Christian, mainly to Greek popular pressure," legislating when Jews could shop for produce—that is, only when they could be appropriately surveilled.[5] Meshullam of Volterra, an Italian Jewish visitor in Candia in 1481, noticed that the social custom banning Jews from touching produce was in full force during his time in the city, even if the law no longer applied.[6]

In fact, this anxiety was part of a larger fear of Jewish contagion that evolved among Christians in both eastern and western traditions during the Middle Ages. Unease about Jews touching grapes and wine during winemaking was expressed in the Latin west in the early thirteenth century by Pope Innocent III.[7] As in the Byzantine sphere, the fear was not limited to wine, as Kenneth Stow has noted: "Laws passed by lay councils in southern France and Perugia in Italy in the fourteenth and fifteenth centuries prohibited Jews from touching all food in the marketplace and required them to purchase food they did touch."[8] So the Christian fear of Jewish contagion was not solely a product of the Greek world.

Jews likewise utilized a rhetoric of contamination when referring to Christians in the *Taqqanot*. When Christian artisan apprentices are allowed into Jewish homes, the authors of a *taqqanah* from 1518 write, "*We are all become as one that is unclean*, woe to us."[9] By 1363, Gentiles are even conceived of as a force that, when allowed to interact with Jews, debases their very quality: "The Jews have established and accepted upon themselves, upon themselves and upon their descendants, so that they do not fall into [God's] wrath, to separate Israel from all the nations, *so that the most fine gold will not change, and how has it become dim*."[10] As Benjamin Arbel has noted, the ordinances on wine—as other *taqqanot* as well—"reflect a marked interest of the Jewish establishment in preserving segregation between Jews and Christians, an interest shared with the Christian establishment, though for different reasons."[11]

Yet these texts themselves also express a more nuanced everyday reality alongside the ideological screen. In the world described in the *taqqanot*, Jews and Christians relied upon each other economically. Cross-confessional apprenticeships and employment of artisans across religious lines form the backdrop to the ordinances above. In reality, these behaviors were limited, not entirely forbidden. Even when wine produced was not deemed kosher, the authors of the *taqqanah* authorized the Jewish owners to sell it to a Gentile, not to dump it. Furthermore, it is clear that, at least in the 1360s, when the first ordinance regarding wine production was enunciated, fear of violent Greek winepress workers was not considered significant enough to warrant finding other ways to secure Jewish wine. The authors of the *taqqanah* from 1363 placed the final onus on Jewish men, exhorting them to do their jobs properly.

There were real tensions between Jews and Christians in Candia. Jews did fall prey to attacks, disenfranchisement, and social prejudice. Concerned with this reality, *Taqqanot Qandiya* seems to promote self-segregation and locates the Jewish Quarter as the safe space for Jews to remain separate. It also assumes economic trust was hard to come by.

But the texture of Jewish-Christian interaction is necessarily more variegated. Pairing *Taqqanot Qandiya* with evidence from legal and notarial sources, it is clear that meaningful Jewish-Christian interaction in Candia was quite common and often without violence or tensions. The reality of everyday life for most Jews was not segregation but interaction—both positive and negative—with the city's Christian residents. Much of this interaction took place because of economic dealings, which were often built on relationships of varying amounts of trust. Trade and production partnerships, loans in money and kind, and the composition of contracts to solemnize these deals brought Christians and Jews, male and female alike, into regular contact across the city of Candia. Moreover, physical separation was never achieved (or, it seems, wholly desired) by focusing Jewish life in the Judaica. Jewish engagement with Christians took place all over the town, including inside the Jewish Quarter and even inside Jewish homes.

Economic Encounters and the Development of Trust

Let us return to Jewish wine, this time to a story told during a Latin inquest found in the ducal court records.[12] In 1424, near a Greek nunnery outside the walls of the *borgo*, a party of five Jews and one Greek Christian were on the road. They had set off together from the Judaica and were traveling to the Christian's home to collect wine Jews had bought from him. We know nothing about the wine's production or its *kashrut*[13]—only that it had been bought by Joseph Sacerdoto, who along with four other Jews was now traveling alongside the Greek seller.

Just as they left the city, highwaymen attacked. Assaulted, his clothing ripped, fearing for his life, Joseph Sacerdoto struggled off his she-ass and stumbled to the gates of the Monastery of Christ, the Greek convent. Witnessing these events, the nuns chose to save the Jew and close the gates with him safely inside.[14] When it was safe to leave, another Christian, a stranger, offered to escort the Jews back to town; the Jews trusted him (*ita confisi isti de ipso*) and safely followed him back to the road.[15] The Greek Christian wine seller, George Turcopulo, had also been attacked by the highwaymen and set off to catch them, in defense of the Jews and their possessions.[16] In this harrowing moment, a business relationship had transformed into something else. Turcopulo testified alongside the Jews in the ducal court inquest as they worked to bring the highwaymen to justice and recover their belongings.

None of this behavior on the part of the Christians was given. To be sure, the highwaymen's behavior perhaps surprises us least. Beyond attacking the party, they used an epithet known as an insult often leveled against Jews. Attempting to unsettle their targets, they shouted at Joseph and the Jews with him calling them "dogs."[17] But the behavior of those whose kindness was instinctive and, later, considered seems more unexpected. The Greek nuns, liable to be most influenced by claims of monks such as the one who preached against Jewish contagion through touch, let Jews into their hallowed ground without hesitation. Other Christians stepped up, and the Jews trusted them with their safety. More generally, the event itself was precipitated by another act of trust—that is to say, the agreement of Jews and a Greek Christian to engage in business dealings, an act that aimed to bring the mixed group from the Jewish space of the Judaica to the Greek man's home.

This is not a lone case of Jews and Christians trusting one another. There are a host of such instances, and they are best seen not in moments of crisis but rather in the kinds of considered economic relationships intentionally built by Jews, Latins, and Greeks in Crete. The island's notarial records provide evidence of regular business deals between Jews and Christians from the thirteenth century on. Among the sorts of transactions that took place across the religious divide were: loans given and repaid; goods including cloth, hides, precious metals, wood, spices, furniture, and foodstuffs bought and sold; houses and apartments rented and sold; confirmation of investments of capital and their repayments; contracts for short-term hires and apprenticeships; and hiring of doctors and healers for medical treatment.

Some Jews trusted Latins. When the late thirteenth-century Jew Elia, known as Sapiens, needed to have substantial cash, plus gold, silver, books, and other costly items delivered to his son Samaria, living in Negroponte, he entrusted the valuables to his agents: two Latin noblemen.[18] Some Greeks trusted Jews with their property. The Jew Leone Thiadus acted as an estate steward (*yconomos*) for the elite Greek Andrea Kalergi and was named as such in a proclamation from 1325.[19] This is not the only time the Kalergi family relied on Jews to deal with their real estate and other affairs. The Candiote Jewish businessman Liacho Mavristiri acted as procurator for the Kalergi family in the 1350s.[20] A decade earlier Mavristiri had proven his loyalty by helping the Greek archon Alexios Kalergi (illegally) purchase a feudal holding supposedly reserved for Latin nobles; Mavristiri made significant profit, Kalergi got his *cavalleria*, and the trust between the two was sealed.[21] As this suggests, Jews and Christians—Greek and Latin both—relied on each other in professional capacities to deal with their possessions with fidelity and honesty, even if the deal itself smacked of the illicit.

Not only trusted to work as each other's employees or agents, Jews and Christians at times became partners in a range of professional capacities and business ventures. Such cooperation took place across the socioeconomic strata of Candia. A Candiote Jew and a Christian co-owned a small ship in the 1350s. A Latin and a Jew paired as legal advisors to a Jewish woman in the next decade. Two masons, one Jew and one Christian, contracted to work together to repair a Jewish physician's cistern in 1420.[22]

Sometimes the equal nature of the partnership was specified in the very terms of the surviving act. Sambatheus, son of the late Vlimidi, a Candiote Jew, in 1303 made a partnership agreement known as a *societas* with the Christian Victor Paulo to buy, store, and sell wine at profit. Paulo was responsible for investing a hundred hyperpera to buy the must; Sambatheus had to convey and store it, giving an extra key to the warehouse to Paulo. All profits were meant to be divided equally.[23] In other cases, the language of partnership is less clear-cut, but the content of an act reflects a form of partnership. When Jewish Michael Carvuni gave an interest-free loan of ten hyperpera to the Christian Petrus Clarenvianus a decade after the Black Death, it actually was an investment in a joint partnership. Carvuni supplied the money, Petrus produced "Jewish wine" to sell in Candia's Judaica, and they split any profit beyond the original investment.[24] This is but one example reflecting the ubiquity of Jewish-Christian deals for the production of wine. Whether the wine was considered kosher by Jewish standards is not addressed; it could be that Jews helped produce it, and Sambatheus's role as conveyer and warehouser of the wine could potentially align with kosher rules. But in any case, at least at this level of commercial relations, this looks quite different than the world of violence described in *Taqqanot Qandiya*.

The reciprocal nature of these economic relationships reveals itself in interesting ways. When Jeremiah Nomico, a Jew, bought a hundred hides from the Candiote Christian butcher Raynerius in 1271, the latter was willing to give Nomico a monopoly on this commodity, contractually promising not to sell this type of hide to anyone else.[25] When the Jew David Rodhothi was hired to stretch hides by the Christian Leonardo Dragumano of the village of Selopulo for payment of six measures of wheat flour, David simultaneously gave Leonardo an interest-free loan.[26] Although the layers of relations and agreements that undergirded this reciprocity remain opaque, such mutual reliance betrays a different sort of relationship than either transaction might suggest alone. While David would be Leonardo's creditor, he was also his hired help, perhaps balancing the power dynamic that either act might produce individually. Christians and Jews also depended on each other to provide other sorts of confirmations and support: a Jew named Moses was called as a witness for the defense in a case against the Christian Nicolas Serigo, who was accused of cheating a business partner out of the profits from their salted fish scheme.[27]

David Jacoby was certainly correct in his assertion that "joint business ventures between Jews and Christians were common at various levels of society" in Crete.[28] As Ricardo Court has noted, "The joint venture . . . was itself a bulwark of trust."[29] The long-term goal of common profit encouraged both sides to work together earnestly and energetically. This notion of "trust" has recently come under the lens of a number of scholars considering the meaning of cross-confessional business relationships. While conventional wisdom has long held that premodern businessmen preferred to employ relatives, whose commonalities and kinship ties would ensure successful cooperation, a number of scholars have pointed out the problems with such assumptions. As Court has noted, kinship was "not the best basis for a business relationship" even in the premodern period because of the messy problems of disentangling oneself from the relative in case of problems; firing a relative is rarely good for family harmony.[30] Likewise, the Sephardi Jews of Francesca Trivellato's *The*

Familiarity of Strangers sometimes chose Sephardi non-relatives over relatives who lived in northern Europe; they also sometimes preferred to trade with Christians and Hindus, building relationships over time and across vast swaths of the planet, despite religious, ethnic, and cultural differences.[31] They made this work through a "creative combination" of strategies, including "group discipline, contractual obligations, customary norms, political protection, and discursive conventions."[32]

Candiote Jews used these same strategies to build lasting relationships with their non-Jewish business partners. Successful joint ventures, even when strictly limited to the realm of the professional, called for trust, a level of mutual confidence that fostered a sense of connection. Such trust can be both reflective of the circumstances that empowered the professional venture to be built in the first place—the sociocultural environment of colonial Candia—and generative of a furthered trusting relationship that moved beyond the professional under certain conditions.[33]

Complicating the Creditor-Debtor Relationship

Many Jewish men and women in Candia acted as moneylenders and pawnbrokers, whether on a small or large scale. Although regular business dealings often cultivated goodwill between Jews and Christians, a common notion holds that the limit of Jewish-Christian economic trust stood fixed at the boundary between business and moneylending—that famed locus of enmity between Jews and Christians in Latin Christendom.[34] This tension can certainly be found in medieval Crete, when Christian debtors occasionally if vociferously sought freedom from supposedly unfair debt they owed to Jewish creditors.

Nevertheless, loan contracts from the notarial registers reveal that even moneylending relationships could be more complex than a simple opposition between a Jewish lender and his Christian debtor. The loans often hide partnership considerations that go beyond what appears on the surface. As in the case above in which a Jew's loan to a Christian actually hid a deal to produce Jewish wine for the Candiote market, many transactions that appear to be loans are actually investments in larger ventures. Sometimes so-called loans are a convenient if unbalanced investment in futures, such as when a Jewish lender advanced a loan in the form of an amount of wheat (or wine), with the proviso that the borrower will repay the loan in new wheat at the beginning of the next harvest season. This may illuminate the practice, surprisingly common among Candiote Jewish creditors, of giving Christians interest-free, unsecured

loans in the form of both goods and cash.[35] Instead of typical loan acts, these
are best understood as a proxy mechanism of joint venture or futures sale. Most
significantly, this type of transaction must have involved a significant amount
of trust between parties.

Economic trust was not only incumbent on Jewish lenders. Rosters of
negligent Candiote debtors do not list only Christians who owed money to
Jews. Instead, we see a far more complex situation in which Jewish men and
women acted both as creditors and as debtors to Christians. While listed debtors apparently did not deserve the trust that had been placed on them (since
they had defaulted), some Jews were trusted enough to have received interest-
free loans from Christians, as did the Jew Elia from the Christian Leonardo de
Bonhomo in the thirteenth century.[36]

The existence of cross-confessional trust is readily apparent when Jews
and Christians were not on opposite sides of the broker's table. In Candia's
culture of moneylending, Jews and Christians sometimes acted as each other's
loan guarantors, such as when the Jewish Joste (Joseph) Adamero acted as
guarantor (*plecius*) for the Greek cobbler Alexius Stavrachi, who received an
interest-free loan of six and a half hyperpera from the Jewish moneylender
David Angura.[37] Over the course of at least eighteen years, the Jewish businesswoman Cherana, daughter of Abraham (Cherana tu Avracha), borrowed
money with, guaranteed loans for, and had as guarantors two Greek sisters,
Hergina Pantaleo and Petrucia Steno, both widows of elite men.[38] The three
women even found themselves mounting a defense together (albeit unsuccess-
fully) in the Curia Prosoporum, the court of first instance for Greeks and Jews,
when they were sued by a creditor.[39] This enduring partnership suggests that
these women were in business together, ventures most likely based on deep-
seated trust developed over time.

Jewish moneylending, as William Chester Jordan has explained it, became
the focus of great enmity in the Middle Ages because it created an "unnatural
aspect of dependency," an upending of what Christians saw to be the proper
hierarchical balance between them and Jews.[40] Jewish loans to Christian debtors undoubtedly sparked anger and hatred. Yet not all moneylending produced these results. Evidence for wider use of loans as proxies for other sorts
of transactions, especially when these "loans" involved significant amounts of
money or goods, presses for a reconsideration of the broader category of moneylending. Likewise, as in the case of Cherana tu Avracha and her Christian
partners, if one side of the creditor/debtor divide contained members from

multiple religious communities, any lender/borrower discord springing from the loan cannot be seen simply as a product of religious tension.[41]

These kinds of partnerships in Candia's lending marketplace offer a prime example of the ways in which allegiance to religion-based segregative dichotomies found in the official documentation conceals the complexity of interactions fostered by Venice's credit economy. Moreover, as opposed to other Christian governments facing the challenge of intrareligious economic interaction, the Venetian government in Crete allowed for, or at least assumed, the possibility of economic trust across confessional lines, at least regarding loanmaking. By the mid-thirteenth century, the Crusader kingdom of Jerusalem expressly forbade the use of guarantors who were not of the same religious community as the borrower; no such limits existed in Crete.[42] While Latin sources, inflected with ecclesiastical ideology about usury and filthy lucre, portray a strict bifurcation between Jewish creditors and Christian lenders, the reality—both in terms of the choices made by lenders and borrowers and in terms of the legal messages signaled more subtly by the government—was far more complicated and sometimes even far from contentious.

Mistrust and Tension in Jewish-Christian Business Relations

To be sure, examples of trusting professional relationships do not undermine the reality that numerous professional relationships were not nearly so felicitous—and that this sort of economic tension provoked anxiety among the leaders of the Jewish community. In the first centuries of Venetian rule on Crete, the authors of *Taqqanot Qandiya* feared that Candiote Jews were cheating Christians in business, ostensibly because they were Gentiles. In the first set of *taqqanot* from 1228, the third ordinance forbids swindling Christian business partners, whether through actual theft or through what is known as *geneivat da'at*, "theft of knowledge"—that is, tricking them, likely about the value of an object or transaction.[43] The authors highlight the effect of such behavior: it ruins the reputations of Jews, causing a *hilul hashem*, literally "desecration of God's name." In the revisions of the same ordinances rewritten by Rabbi Tzedakah from sometime the next century, this ordinance remains, although it simply reads: "No one is allowed to lie to the *goyim* or to trick them [*lignov da'atam*], whether in what Jews buy from them, or in what Jews sell to them." Once again the audience is reminded that such behavior ruins the Jewish reputation among Gentiles.[44]

But by the year of reforms in 1363, the problem of dishonest merchants had evidently become more worrisome. Fraudulent business dealings are the target of two ordinances. One outlaws the use of dishonest weights and measures to make more profit. The decree, however, makes no specific reference to Christians and indeed points to the victims of dishonest merchants as mostly Jews. Punishment for this behavior is a complete excommunication.[45]

A second *taqqanah* directly addresses the cross-confessional crisis and its seriousness. Although this *taqqanah* is labeled "Fence not to buy anything from the male slaves and female slaves of the Gentiles," it is actually a decree forbidding Jews from buying goods from or selling goods to anyone, though especially from/to unfree or free servants of non-Jews—or "even from a Jew"— for less than they are worth.[46] The *taqqanah* lists the sorts of goods at issue: silver, gold, bronze, iron, ore, tin, clothing, leather goods, pearls, precious gems (particularly garnet, sapphire, and diamond), silk, linen, wool, "or anything worth three grossi or more." Strikingly, the implications of such cheating were deemed so grave that the *taqqanah* ordered the *condestabulo* to hand the guilty party over to the Venetian government. If the *condestabulo* refused, the council of seven "good men" was obligated to publicly rebuke him for his negligence. The staunch prohibitions against *mesirah* or *malshinut*, informing on a Jew to the secular authorities, were thus suspended.[47]

The anxiety of the authors of the *taqqanot* should not necessarily be seen as evidence of rampant cheating of Christians by Jews but rather as a sense of the truly grim ill effects they believed even minimal cheating would have on the reputation (and perhaps safety) of the Jews of Candia. Moreover, even though the Jewish leadership feared that Jews were cheating Christians and coreligionists alike, it was still not only Jews who were suspect. In 1304, Zagha, son of the late Solomon, a Jew, bought a *millaria* (one thousand pounds) of "good Cretan cheese" from Bartholomeus Karavelo, a Candiote Christian. Their contract suggests that Zagha did not trust his supplier: "and I [Bartholomeus]," reads the act, "have to weigh and give you this [cheese] for you with your scales." Zagha apparently suspected Karavelo not only of skimping on his hefty *millaria* but of weighing the cheese with deliberately skewed instruments.[48]

This sort of proviso was meant to avoid litigation, but it was not always successful. A business agreement made in 1398 by the Latin nobleman Ser Amocatus Geno and the wealthy Jew Protho Spathael exploded into litigation that worked itself all the way to the ducal court over a handful of years. Although a lower court found in favor of Spathael, the highest court found for the Latin Geno and stripped the Jewish litigant of all profits from their undertaking. The ducal court decided that Spathael's role in the business arrangement was "against all justice, equity, and good practices" (*contra omnem justiciam, equitatem, et bonas mores*), language that had probably been put forth by Geno's camp.[49] Importantly, the essential disagreement appears to have had little to do with the different religions of the two men. No matter the religious affiliation of the men on each side of the deal, if both could live up to "justice, equity, and good practices"—the basic building blocks of trust—cross-confessional business could be effective and continue for years to come.

Much of the mistrust that occurred in business between Jews and Christians did not necessarily arise out of religious tensions but rather resulted from the common suspicion and standard difficulty that occur—now as then—between those who seek profit together or those who are competing for the same piece of the market pie.[50] Disappointment over broken trust only arose from situations based upon a certain degree of trust in the first place, a fact that illustrates that Jewish-Christian business partnerships were viewed as normal more than as suspect. In England, the crown established a Jewish Exchequer to deal with Jewish business. The Venetian state, in contrast, did not accentuate the difference between Jewish and Christian business. Christians engaging in business with Jews likewise did not overemphasize the religious affiliations of their business partners but rather their ability to deliver on the contract.[51] Business disputes between Jews and Christians in Crete do not reflect a social pathology set in motion by religious divides. Instead, as legal anthropologists have stressed, "disputes, far from being pathological," can often be read as "normal and inevitable" interactions between any individuals working to "secure their objectives."[52] However unfortunate or uncomfortable, dispute is a normal part of business relationships for all parties regardless of religious affiliation. Jewish leaders, nonetheless, saw animosity and misdeed as a potential threat to the stability of the community, and they thus forbade such behavior by summoning up its strongest weapons: excommunication (for fraud between Jews) and handing over the culprit to the Venetian colonial government (for egregious fraud against Christians in particular).

The Notary and the Wise Jew

Every sale, loan, or hire needed a contract written up based on the recording of a well-known litany of reliable formulae meant to ensure a deal would be upheld in a court of law. The most pragmatic relationship between two people, one might argue, is between a businessman and the man who writes up his contracts: a cursory, if regular, transaction. Candia's Latin notaries were agents of the Venetian state, a status that ensured that all transactions recorded in their registers had legal validity. The Latin notary, then, provided the seal of government; he was an ostensibly impartial instrument guaranteeing contractual legitimacy.

Nevertheless, regular contact between Jewish businessmen and the notaries they frequented could also initiate relationships beyond the technical confines of contract writing. Notarial registers illustrate just how often individual businessmen sought out notaries and that many Jewish businessmen patronized particular notaries. In just three months during 1388, for example, the Jewish moneylender Abraham Angura employed the notary Nicolo Tonisto thirteen times.[53] This same notary was a favorite of businessman Solomon Astrug, who hired Tonisto for twenty-three transactions during this same period.[54] Apparently Tonisto was known as a notary trusted by the Jewish community; other Jewish businessmen also appear over and over again in his records for these months.

Tonisto was but one Christian notary with a dedicated Jewish following: two decades earlier, Solomon Astrug had faithfully patronized the Latin notary Egidio Valoso. Valoso was also a favorite of Judah Balbo, a prolific moneylender who employed Valoso for forty separate contracts between April and August 1370.[55] Judah Balbo's son, Lazaro, however, patronized another Latin notary, Giovanni Catacalo: Lazaro appears in Catacalo's register engaging in fourteen separate transactions over just three days in May 1389.[56]

A court case from 1420 illustrates the tricky implications of Jewish loyalty for this last notary, Giovanni Catacalo, whose surviving registers show him to have been a favored notary for Jews—patronized not only by Balbo but also by many Jewish businessmen and businesswomen of Candia.[57] Likely in the context of his notarial work, Catacalo developed a relationship with a Jewish client that went beyond the pragmatic. Catacalo would soon turn to this Jew for more personal reasons. The official story, as told by Catacalo, was that the notary had bought himself a Bible (ostensibly the Hebrew Bible or "Old Testament") in Greek but had trouble with some of the difficult language.[58] Through his work, he knew a Jewish man who was both a businessman and a scholar—one we already met when he was engaged in business litigation with a Latin nobleman—by the name of Protho Spathael. The latter, active in business in the first decades of the fifteenth century, had also served as *condestabulo*, according to *Taqqanot Qandiya*.[59] Spathael was known to

Catacalo as an intelligent and wise man (*hominem intelligentem et sapientem*) and thus turned to him for guidance regarding the meaning of the text and its vocabulary, which Spathael provided at his own house over a couple of weeks.

This behavior was considered beyond the pale. Denounced as a heretic, accused of doubting the truth of Christianity and of Judaizing—defined here as participating in Jewish ceremonies—Catacalo was quickly imprisoned, tried, and found guilty. The case against Giovanni Catacalo is revealing for a number of reasons. It is the only time the Inquisition was permitted to intervene in Candia's own judiciary.[60] Indeed, the investigation was run by Dominicans sent by the Roman curia, and the language of heresy and Judaizing and the explicit claim of Jewish contagion (*contagia Judaicè*) is decidedly atypical in Candia's legal records until this point. Equally unusual for Candia, the tribunal interrogated (and probably tortured) Catacalo for three days, after which he confessed to having lost faith in the very foundations of Catholic dogma, including the messianic and divine nature of Christ, the intercessory power of Mary, the prophecies of Isaiah as foreshadows of Christ, and the spiritual potency of saints and icons.[61] After his confession, he "begged for mercy from our God for his sin, that he recognized that he had acted wickedly."[62] It seems likely that Catacalo was indeed on the brink of doing that thing not done: converting to Judaism. But after his treatment at the hands of the state and its ecclesiastical associates, he seems to have decided such a radical jump was not worth his life.

It is clear from Catacalo's punishment that the Inquisition believed that he came into contact with his heretical ideas by virtue of his work as a notary. Following two years of jail and other acts of public humiliation, Catacalo was allowed to return to his old profession. But he did so with one caveat: he was forbidden to notarize for Jews ever again. Moreover, his son Gabriele Catacalo, who had followed his father into the notariate, was also banned from ever working with Jews. It is apparent that the Inquisitorial court recognized that the ostensibly cut-and-dried matter of notarial work actually could and did promote a deeper relationship between client and notary.

At the same time, the relative ease of Catacalo's punishment is striking. So too is the lack of larger legislative or social implications, for it points to the contrast between Roman Inquisitorial fears (rarely allowed sway in Crete) and the broader approach of the local Venetian bureaucracy. Following Catacalo's ordeal, the ducal administration did not make any sweeping legislation against Jewish use of other notaries, nor did they hunt down other "Judaizing" notaries. Jewish businessmen continued to patronize favorite Latin notaries.

In the early 1450s, the Latin notary Michele Calergi often served Jewish clients, including the Delmedigo family.[63] The colonial government appears to have accepted this reality. For the most part, Jewish contact with notaries was supported. Pragmatically, it expedited the active trade and moneylending on which Venice and its subjects relied. A certain amount of sustained contact could be tolerated—as long as the Christian involved shunned the temptation of confessional perfidy. And, in truth, most likely there were few notaries in Candiote Christian society as inquisitive and spiritually intrepid as the unfortunate Catacalo.

The Space of Jewish-Christian Encounter

These economic transactions and the relationships they forged took place throughout the city of Candia and its environs. The countryside was the setting for the winepress fiasco, while the highway robbery of the wine merchants took place in the *borgo*, beyond the walls of the town. Everyday moneylending, buying and selling of goods, and writing up of contracts likely took place in many locations—workshops and warehouses, pawnshops and open-air stalls, and inside homes. Notarial contracts from Candia do not share nearly as much data as those from other Mediterranean cities; they do not identify where they were signed. But Jewish-Christian encounters were not constrained in location. When the Inquisition questioned Catacalo, they did not seem to mind that he had been in a Jewish home; rather, it was the sheer length of time he had been inside the wise Jew's home—fifteen days—that provoked suspicion. Moreover, Jews and Christians shared much of the spatial infrastructure of daily life, even sharing communal ovens until the mid-sixteenth century, when Elia Capsali built a bakehouse on his own property. But even after that moment, we do not know if all Jews shifted their baking to the specifically kosher ovens.[64]

To be sure, the story of Jewish residential life in Candia in the fourteenth and fifteenth centuries is one of increasing restrictions. The Jewish Quarter as a singular, defined space became increasingly reified and limited over that period, a trend paralleled in many other locations across Christendom.[65] Until the fourteenth century, Jews lived both in the area that became known as the Judaica and in a particular area of the suburban *borgo*.[66] Even the very boundaries, the streets that constituted the Judaica, were fluid for a century. By 1334, however, when for the first time Jews were ordered to own and rent homes only inside the Judaica, the boundary lines had become clearly defined.

A further order compelling Jews to live exclusively within these streets was also passed in 1350, perhaps part of the pan-European response to the Black Death.[67] In the early 1390s, the ducal administration ordered that some homes along the southern boundary of the Judaica, directly across the street from Christian homes, had to be walled off.[68] The east side of the Judaica was similarly bricked up in 1450, following complaints by the nearby Dominican monastery of St. Peter Martyr.[69] By the mid-1450s, then, the Judaica was no longer simply a neighborhood where Jews chose to settle together but a walled-in, discrete quarter whose inhabitants no longer lived there solely by choice.

Yet the narrative involves more than increasing segregation or a residential division of Jews and Christians caused by a Venetian change in policy. Segregation was not imposed solely by the Christian state but instead co-opted as an ideal by the leadership of the Jewish community itself. Moreover, despite this ideal found in both Jewish and Christian discourses, the reality for Jews and Christians was that that encounter took place both inside and outside of the Jewish Quarter, even as that space became increasingly identified as "Jewish."

Co-opting the Narrative: Jewish Delineation of Jewish Space

Despite Venice's accruing policies limiting Jewish residence, the Jewish community leadership did not chafe very much against the strictures. To the contrary, we see that the physical neighborhood of the Jewish Quarter had long been a comfortably limited area for the community's leaders—at least since the mid-fourteenth century, when Rabbi Tzedakah revised the rhyming ordinances of 1228 into a more legalistic prose version. Rabbi Tzedakah's text mandates that, for the sake of maintaining the sanctity of Sabbath and prayers, no Jew may leave the *kahal* (read: Jewish Quarter) until morning services are over.[70] Here, the Jewish leadership co-opted the spatial limitations that had ostensibly been imposed on the community and reinterpreted them as helping construct a protective neighborhood. A typical example of the intermeshing of imposed segregation and self-segregation, it tells us much about the way the Jewish elite, at least, had long thought of their micro-city.[71]

There can be no doubt that the leadership of the ethnoreligious communities of Candia emphasized and idealized segregation. As David Jacoby has written, "Both Jewish and Venetian ordinances envisaged the corrosive effects of social contacts and promiscuity between Jews and Christians and the benefits of the Jewish segregation."[72] While Venetian legislation certainly aimed to separate Jewish and Christian residence, Jewish segregation was, at least in part, self-segregation. Per Jacoby, Jews kept to themselves "by choice. Their lifestyle, customs, culture, social cohesion and residential segregation emphasized their identity as a distinct ethnic and religious group."[73] For Capsali and his ilk, then, the closed-in walls of the *kahal* felt comfortably familiar and protective. Moreover, instead of considering the Judaica a limiting factor, a close reading of *Taqqanot Qandiya* suggests that its authors saw the increasingly defined and confined space of the Judaica as a benefit to the leadership itself. It enabled them to simultaneously define the boundaries of their power, assert control over their communities, and perhaps even boost morale by assuring their flocks that they did indeed have a place to be among themselves.

The authors of *Taqqanot Qandiya* certainly saw and depicted the Jewish Quarter of Candia as an insider space. As in the example above, they regularly use the term *kahal* (or similar, *kehillah*), community, not only in reference to the people but as a name for the physical Jewish Quarter. The semantic field often seems to conflate the two, people and place. The leadership decries Jewish prostitutes dwelling in residences located "in our community [*be-kehillateinu*]."[74] Even more explicitly, in the ordinances forbidding Jews from leaving the confines of the Judaica during Sabbath and holiday prayer services mentioned above, we read: "From today forward, no one among the people of our community [*me-anshei kehillateinu*] will be permitted to leave the community [*kahal*; read: Jewish Quarter] on Sabbaths, the New Months, or holidays, without a compelling reason, until the exit from the morning synagogue service."[75] A revision of this ordinance passed by the reforming synod of 1363 makes the conflation more specific and more concrete: "From this day forward no Jew among the people of our community [*me-anshei kehillateinu*] will be permitted to leave from the street of the community [*rehov hakahal*] during the morning services during the time that the synagogue is open for prayer."[76] For the Jewish leadership, the space of the Jewish Quarter was one and the same with the confines of the Jewish community.

But the conflated language of the *kahal* as a human and spatial designation not only functioned as a vocabulary of inclusion, marking everyone inside as a member of the community. It could also help draw the barriers of exclusion and difference. In a list of all the *taqqanot* passed in 1363, the Sabbath ordinance is identified with this extended title: "That no Jew may exit from the community [*min hakahal*] into the alley of the Gentiles [*le-mevo'i hagoyim*] on Sabbaths and holidays at the time that the congregation [*tzibbur*] is praying, and all Jews are obligated to come to the synagogue to be as a single association [*agudah*] in their prayers."[77] The Jewish space of the *kahal* sharply and definitively contrasts with Christian space in this schema. One must exit, making a formal transition, from one to the other. Although it is unclear whether this alley refers to a specific street or a general category of streets, the choice of contrasting words is suggestive: the language of the *kahal* evokes openness, while the alley calls to mind narrow confinement.

The contrast between Jewish space and the Christian space beyond the walls appears most explicit when the authors of an ordinance mention the vesper bells "which are rung by the friars [lit. the brothers], the priests who are on the border of the *kahal*."[78] The Dominican monastery of St. Peter Martyr—and its human embodiments of Christianity's conversion ethic—stood to the east of the Judaica. It formed not only a physical boundary between the Jewish Quarter and the Christian world outside but also a conceptual boundary indicating where the *kahal* (qua persons and place) ended.

Even as the Jewish leadership saw the Judaica as a definitively Jewish space, they also recognized that they were not alone inside. The boundaries were not impermeable, nor did they need to be. Even the Dominican monastery, which starkly delineated the border of the Judaica, was not purely external to the Jewish space. The vesper bells could be easily heard within. In fact, the *taqqanah* that mentions these bells demanded that Jews utilize the sound of their ringing as a sign to cease working, once and for all, as Sabbath began.[79] The Christian sound invading Jewish space could be repurposed for a squarely Jewish aim. The seeming encroachment of Christian things into Jewish space should thus be read as multivalent, not to be simply and single-mindedly repelled but rather to be controlled—or better, in the spirit of Jewish exegesis, to be reinterpreted. Even a monastery—probably intentionally built in this location so as to abut the Judaica, perfect for turning Jewish souls to Jesus— could be co-opted by the Jewish establishment for its own goals.

Jews and Christians Inside the Judaica

The reuse of the vesper bells hints that Candia's Jewish leadership was well aware that the idealized self-segregation—the private, insider Jewish world they imagined existed in their Judaica—was not fully consonant with reality. First and foremost, this monastery and church had stood side by side, cheek by jowl, with the Jewish homes for over two centuries before a wall was erected.[80] Its waterfront compound lay so close to the Judaica's easternmost street that the friars could see into Jewish homes through windows and balconies that overlooked the monastery. It was this visual proximity to the Jews that threatened the friars' souls, or so they said in the complaint that sparked the 1450 walling in of the Judaica's street.[81]

It must be noted that 1450 is quite a late date to fully enclose a Jewish quarter. In contrast, the Venetian Senate ordered the Jewish Quarter of Venetian Negroponte to be separated from the rest of the city by a wall already in 1304 "for reasons of security."[82] Such a difference in policy highlights that each Venetian colony must be investigated separately, as legislation, contingencies, and enforcement of law regarding Jewish settlement and interactions with Christians did not necessarily apply uniformly to the whole Stato da mar. Here, it must suggest to us that the Cretan colonial government in this period did not obsess over the mixing of Jews and Christians in residential space as other colonial governments seem to have done.

Perhaps the government could not effectively enforce segregation; the need to repeat the orders in 1334 and 1350 may indicate this. But even the laws of the 1390s, which for the first time ordered the walling off of the southern boundary of the Judaica, incorporate a flexible understanding of the implications of the wall. The decrees explicitly permitted specific Jewish homeowners whose real estate fell outside of the technical confines of the Jewish Quarter to continue living in their homes and to rent apartments to other Jews.[83] We must imagine that cash had changed hands, from the listed Jewish homeowners to some colonial officials. But this phenomenon of looking the other way in not unique to Crete. That is to say, Venice in general does not seem to have been terribly strict in enforcing the Jewish residence policy in any of its colonial holdings. Even in the case of Negroponte, a senatorial decree intimates that neither the residential requirements nor the wall truly limited Jewish mobility, leading to further orders in 1402 to block off all but three entrances to the Jewish Quarter.[84] David Jacoby has noted that even after Jews were forbidden from owning real estate outside Jewish quarters across the Venetian overseas territories in 1423, Venice looked the other way as Jews continued to buy, sell, and rent outside the Judaica even in parts of Crete over the course of the next centuries.[85] In 1577, alongside his more famous grievance over Jewish prostitutes in the city, *provveditore generale* Giacomo Foscarini complained that he still found Jews living outside Candia's Judaica, albeit in the vicinity.[86] As in other cases, it seems that the law was upheld mostly in the breach.

But the concept of "Jewish space" in Candia is complicated not only by the fact that some Jews lived outside the quarter. Rather, the Judaica itself was a locus of mixing, a space where Christians could and did enter, for a whole array of reasons. Structurally, even the closing of the walls over the course of the fourteenth and fifteenth centuries could not—and was never intended to—enforce this kind of complete separation. Venice did not prevent nonresident Christians from entering the Judaica. The arched gate built in 1390 to demarcate the southeast limit and provide a formal entrance into the Jewish Quarter was neither closed nor locked.[87] Thus we find Christians who lived in other parts of the city and from the countryside present in the Judaica's streets and squares, and even inside Jewish homes and on Jewish property.

That it was absolutely normal for Christians to enter the Jewish Quarter, rather than an exceptional experience, is perhaps best expressed in a court verdict from 1449.[88] The judiciary specifically banned three Christian men (whose crimes unfortunately were not recorded) from entering the Jewish Quarter for any reason, on pain of both incarceration and monetary fine.[89] Should one of them enter the Jewish Quarter, the monetary fine would be divided between the denouncer and the commune. Only if another inhabitant of the city were to denounce the men would this restraining order have any teeth. It would be very easy for one of these men to walk right in. Obviously it was quite common for Christians to enter the Judaica as they pleased.

Although we do not know precisely why these particular three men wanted to enter the Judaica (a vendetta against a former Jew and a Christian lawyer seems to be the background plot), we can certainly witness other Christians in the midst of their engagements in the Jewish Quarter. Just as Jews often used the rest of the city for economic transactions, much of the Christian activity in Jewish space that is visible to us was economic. The many Christian landlords who rented to Jews, for example, must have entered the Judaica to deal with their property and tenants. In another kind of exchange, the Jewish prostitutes seem to have serviced their clients (including Christians) inside the Judaica's whorehouses and poorhouses.[90] Christian masons contracted to build walls for Jewish homes inside the Judaica.[91] Christians provided other goods and services for Jews in the Judaica's streets and public squares—such as a Christian seller of dairy products (probably from a surrounding village) whose goods were deemed insufficiently kosher for Rabbi Meir Ashkenazi, who ordered the man's milk to be dumped.[92]

Despite the negative valence of a malicious and fraudulent Christian food seller assumed by this tale of the dumped milk, proudly recorded by leaders asserting their right to control foodstuffs within the walls of their domain, Jews actually brought Christians into their very homes inside the Judaica for economic and professional purposes—even at the behest of the very same leaders.[93] Indeed, such evidence comes directly from *Taqqanot Qandiya* itself.

An ordinance from 1363 instructed that, although it was preferable for Jewish tailors to sew clothing for members of the community, should a Jew need to hire a Christian tailor, he was permitted to do so—on the Jew's turf. The Jew "should bring him [the Christian tailor] into the Jewish home, and he should sew for him on Jewish property" in order to assure that the tailor would not transgress the biblical prohibition against mixing wool and linen in one garment, a combination known as *sha'atnez*.[94]

Although in this ordinance the Jewish leadership sought to limit the entrance of Christian artisans into Jewish homes, a later *taqqanah* indicates the flock did not limit Christian access as the rabbis had dictated. In 1518, the Jewish leadership wrote that some Jewish artisans, specifically tailors and cobblers, were regularly bringing Christian apprentices into their homes.[95] Unsurprisingly, the Jewish leadership reacted to this practice with horror. Not only does such behavior make the Jews "impure," they wrote, but such interaction inside the home defied Venetian law. Though the reasons to forbid Christians in Jewish homes were "too many too count," the authors nonetheless chose to recount a few: "The teenage boys of Israel will follow along after them in their deeds and in their habits, and they will mix in with the *goyim* and they will learn their deeds." Moreover, they wrote, the Jewish masters should be forbidden to bring in apprentices "because of their wives and their daughters."[96]

The authors of this ordinance, particularly the current leader Rabbi Elia Capsali, worked hard to make this seem like an atypical and perhaps new activity. Nevertheless, the threat warranted its own community-wide decree. In fact, it is likely that a significant number of young Christian men would come to the homes and workshops of Jewish artisans every day, perhaps even staying overnight and being fed and clothed by the Jewish master, like apprentices in Christian settings. This behavior was not new; a notarial contract from 1338 shows a Jewish weaver hiring two Latin assistants for an entire year to help him finish woolen cloth.[97] These apprentices were obviously not walled off from the artisans' Jewish families but instead interacted with both the male and female family members in a way deemed seriously worrisome by the Jewish authorities, but apparently less concerning to the Jews who hired them.

While the *taqqanot* hint at these regular Christian visitors, they hide another reality that becomes clear when we look to the records from the ducal chancellery. There were not just occasional Christians staying over in houses in the Judaica. Other Christians—wealthy, elite Christian families—lived full-time in the Jewish Quarter, in homes they owned. In the aftermath of the anticolonial rebellion known as the St. Tito revolt (1363–64), as Venice's administration sought to reassert its control, it confiscated homes of rebels; a 1365 proclamation notes that many of these homes were not only *in civitate candide* but also *in iudaica*.[98] Lest we think that all of these Christian-owned homes were rented to Jews—as many Christian-owned residential buildings were—other evidence illustrates that some Christians lived there.[99] Sometime in the mid-fourteenth century, the Jewish businessman Liacho Mavristiri bought a home in the Judaica from Hemanuel Jalina, a successful Greek Orthodox businessman and tavern owner.[100] The Jalinas, however, were not selling their home to move out of the Judaica but rather owned a second home next door to the Mavristiris' property where they actually lived. By 1393, the Mavristiris had sold their home to another wealthy Jew, Joseph Missini, but the Jalinas still lived on their property next door.[101]

The Judaica housed not only Greek Christians but also prominent Latins. In a family fight over ownership of a house in the Jewish Quarter in 1358, the court record denotes the relative position of the residence by specifying all the neighboring homes.[102] On the east side, the house faced the street (*ruga comunis*). On the west and north stood homes with Jewish residents. On the southern side, however, the disputed house abutted the residence of Ser Johannes Gradenigo, a member of an elite Venetian family that had owned real estate in the Jewish Quarter since around 1300.[103]

The Judaica's close quarters suggest daily interaction between Jews and their Christian neighbors on the street, and perhaps inside homes. To be sure, the decision to live next to Jews did not mean that Christian neighbors necessarily felt warm to them. When told that the new Jewish owners who had bought the Mavristiris' home, the Missinis, should be able to share the water cistern that lay underneath the property of both neighbors, a member of the Greek Jalina family stated what he saw as a truism: "It is neither just [*iustum*] nor fair [*equum*] for Jews and Christians to mix at one cistern."[104] We hear echoes here of the anxiety of pollution through touch expressed by medieval Greeks and Latins alike in the beginning of this chapter. This staunch refusal by the Jalinas to share a water source with the Jewish Missini family sparked litigation that passed through all of the lower courts until it was heard by the duke himself.

Importantly, from a legal perspective, Cretan colonial justice cared little for the ethnoreligious fear of sharing water and looked to issues of property rights to make its judgment in the case of the shared cistern. The Greek family was indeed ordered to accommodate the Jewish family with whom they shared the cistern, although the judges did authorize a division in the cistern so that each side would have separate access to the water. A Solomonic solution of sorts, a judgment meant to appease both sides. Social attitudes, then, were not always translated into legal limitations, even as the Venetian government sought to keep all its subjects mollified.

A Coda: Surveillance, Suspect Jews, and the Theory of the Jewish Quarter

This reality of Jews and Christians rubbing shoulders inside the Judaica was not lost on the authors of *Taqqanot Qandiya*. The ordinances regarding Jewish artisans may point to a divide between the rank-and-file Jews, who seem to have related more casually to sharing Jewish space with Candia's Christians, and the religious leaders, who appear in these sources more anxious about such interaction. But even for the community leaders, the inevitability of such interaction led them to sometimes take a different tack on how to protect their flock from the Christian threat. For example, the ordinance from 1363 that instructed Jews to bring Christian tailors into their homes was approved only because it enabled surveillance. The Jewish home could be controlled by the Jew, and thus the Christian's behavior—that is, the choices of cloths the tailor used—could be watched and controlled. In the 1518 ordinance on Christian apprentices, the leadership appeared concerned about a lack of surveillance once again; the long-term relationship of the master and apprentice had led to a situation in which the Christian was no longer guarded while in the Jewish house and instead influenced the thoughts and behaviors of the weak and susceptible members (read: women and children) of the Jewish household. The Christian milk seller whose dairy products had to be spilled, likewise, did not break the rules of the *kahal* by being inside the Judaica but instead had not subjected his goods to the rigorous guarding demanded to ensure a kosher product.

Thus, from the perspective of Candia's Jewish leaders, within the confines of the Jewish Quarter a surveilled Christian was an unthreatening Christian. Like the vesper bells ringing atop the Dominican monastery at the eastern border of the Judaica that could become reinterpreted as a sign marking the entrance of the Sabbath, individual Christians could be co-opted; they could be socially neutered through surveillance, thus made unthreatening, and rendered useful.[105]

Even Elia Capsali himself could agree. Upon opening a kosher-only bakehouse on his own property, he "discovered" that no Jewish bakers lived in Candia and thus hired a Christian baker to come work on his property each day.

Capsali taught this Christian the laws of *kashrut* and not to bake on Sabbath. But even after learning the rules, this baker was rarely left alone. As Capsali told his reading audience, he built the two ovens right between his front door and his synagogue, so that "I enter them and certify them [*u-makhshiram*] at all times [*be-khol et v'et*]." [106]

An important addendum to our understanding of the Jewish leadership's approach to the Judaica as a space of surveillance lies in the groups intended to be excluded by the Candiote definition of the *kahal*. Without a doubt, the *taqqanot* illustrate that the *kahal*'s Jewishness contrasted with Christian atmosphere outside: it was a place where Sabbath happened, while outside the rest of the city went about their regular business; it limited the power of the friars whose Dominican monastery loudly perched on the very border of the Judaica. But the *kahal*'s guarded space also enabled the leadership to keep out other Jews. As we saw in Chapter 1, the rhetorical language of "us and them" implied by the term *kahal* was at times marshaled not only against Christians but also against Jews found equally threatening. A particular target of such anxiety were the Jews of Castronovo, producers of questionably kosher meat and dairy products, against whom were written two Candiote *taqqanot* in 1363.[107] Only if their cheeses were approved through a method of investigation, interrogation, and certification—that is to say, sustained surveillance—could Jews from Castronovo legally sell to their coreligionists inside the city.

In short, the Jewish rhetoric of a bifurcation of space—the complicated "us and them" that goes beyond ethnic affiliation—should be read as a way in which the Jewish religious leadership sought to divide their community (qua "holy community") from anyone, Christian or otherwise, who could threaten the order and organization, piety and religious strictures, and well-established social hierarchy these elite families had carved out for themselves within the small set of rabbit-warren alleys of Candia.

* * *

In idealizing segregation, Venice and the Jewish leadership could agree with one another. As Elia Capsali wrote in 1518, the colonial government's prohibition forbidding Jews from hiring regular apprentices from among the Christian population was decreed "out of their wisdom" and "for many reasons," with which he seems to have fully agreed.[108] The goal and rhetoric of separation, however, do not mask the reality that Jews and Christians regularly encountered one another, not just in the Plateia or in other parts of the city but inside the very Jewish Quarter. After all, engaged encounter—much of it by choice—was a fact of daily life in medieval Candia. Common cross-confessional business connections went beyond the medieval stereotype of Jewish moneylender and his Christian debtor, although Jews did often lend money to their Christian neighbors. But business in Candia did not always place Jews and Christians on opposite sides of a deal. Instead, Jews and Christians worked together in a wide variety of professional and economic capacities, and these ventures illustrate the ways in which trust could and did obtain between Candiote businessmen across the religious divide. Notarial evidence as well as material from other Latin sources reveal Jews and Christians collaborating in a variety of ways, including as employees, partnering for short-term work, and developing joint investment ventures. The Jewish Quarter was not a space apart but one deeply tied into the wider city and its inhabitants, nor was it a neighborhood in which the Jews matched the leadership's picture. Thus Candia's Jewish Quarter was not an impermeable space; nor would it even be the "urban condom" of the Venetian ghetto, to use Richard Sennett's graphic expression.[109] Prostitutes, Christians, impious Jews, and the sounds of the nearby Christian monastery intruded on the elite's idealized space.

Moreover, Venetian segregating legislation was decidedly ambivalent; this was not an age of the ghetto, though certainly this period witnessed increasingly ghettoizing trends (though what this means ought to be parsed carefully, as the sixteenth-century Venetian Ghetto is in no way the ghetto of the Holocaust). Even from the perspective of Candia's Jewish leadership, the rabbis themselves had a pragmatic approach to the Jewish nature of the Judaica—an approach that focused on surveillance of those who entered the quarter.

The elite leadership of Jewish Candia left for posterity a self-conscious portrait of its community: an image of a neat and controlled organizational structure, a unified and safe Jewish Quarter, and a community of mostly pious members. In moments of crisis, the leadership marshaled custom and law to reconnect the people of the community. Increasing residential segregation laws imposed from outside and the reality of Jewish-Christian interactions both inside and outside the Jewish Quarter necessitated a response. Community leaders were able to marshal the image of Jewish Quarter not as a locus of imposed segregation, as it appears in much of the historiographic discussions of medieval Jewish life, but as an insider space where the Jewish community could expect protection from outsiders, an emotional community of like-minded Jews, and a home base. Even intrusions could be reinterpreted and controlled through the language of communal ordinances. Understanding the reality of the Jewish Quarter, that it would never be a closed space truly reserved for the good members of holy community, the rabbinic elite developed an alternate approach to maintaining authority in their own space.

Yet, as Capsali's comment about the agreement of sovereign and subject community suggests, the leadership of the Jewish community remained well aware that its ultimate local authority was secondary to that of the Venetian state—an authority to which they were highly sensitive. Indeed, the colonial government in Venice played an important role of both facilitating and limiting the accepted modes of cross-confessional interaction on Crete, and it is to this state intervention that we now turn.

Chapter 3

Colonial Justice and
Jewish-Christian Encounter

If in the 1520s Elia Capsali insisted that both the Jewish leadership and the Venetian government aimed to keep Jews and Christians separated from one another, this was not the lived experience of Judah de Damasco in the early decades of the fifteenth century. A lay leader of the *kehillah* who had signed a *taqqanah* in 1399 as "Judah son of Joseph, the doctor," Judah was indeed a surgeon from a family of doctors. In his medical capacity, he treated patients privately and in a more public capacity served the Venetian colonial government as a judicial wound evaluator and expert witness. This was a common pairing for the Jewish doctors of Crete.

It was also in his medical capacity that Judah met Maria (nicknamed Marula) Sithiacudena, a Greek Orthodox resident of the *borgo* whose husband and family Judah treated. It remains unclear whether the sexual relationship began before or after her husband died, but they enjoyed that sort of ongoing relationship throughout her widowhood—at least until she was found dead on her bed in July 1419. A rope tied tight around her waist and a dead fetus in her womb provided the only clues to her demise. The five doctors sent in to examine Maria's body could not provide a conclusive cause of death, though they suggested that—perhaps—the tightly bound rope may have killed the woman. Some witnesses noted that she had been quite sick for over a week. The gossip mill, however, blamed Judah for poisoning his mistress in an attempt to abort the unwanted child.[1]

Following a series of decidedly inconclusive and contradictory interviews with twenty-one Greek neighbors and friends of the dead woman, most of whom proved reluctant in their testimony to admit to having any knowledge of the circumstances, the ducal court reached a verdict: Judah was guilty of murder. As punishment, he was to be hanged to death outside of Maria's home after his right hand had been cut off. His corpse was meant to be left hanging in situ for some time, a graphic message intended for other potential criminals.

But Judah was not in custody, and the court could only demand that he turn himself in to receive justice. Unconvinced that justice was what had transpired, however, Judah escaped the island and traveled to Venice—into the jaws of the beast, one might say—to demand his case be retried before a higher appeals court. Indeed, the case was retried, and Judah was eventually acquitted of all charges. Satisfied with the result, and confident of his freedom, Judah returned to Crete. A decade after the fateful day of Maria's death, Judah could be found back in Candia working as a medical expert for the very government that had once tried to have him executed.[2]

On the surface, this bizarre, poorly evidenced criminal case against this doctor, a Jew in a position of power, might suggest hostility toward the Jews of Venetian Crete, or at least toward those who could be thought to have risen above their proper status or station. Such a case would be expected to reveal the sentiment of anti-Judaism that is said to characterize much of medieval Jewish-Christian relations. Some official source materials from Candia certainly made use of anti-Jewish tropes connected to Jewish greed and contagion, among other images, as this chapter will explore.

A close reading of the case against Judah de Damasco, however, provides an unexpected dearth of such evidence. Not a single witness explicitly mentioned Judah's Judaism. No one referred to the religiously forbidden nature of the relationship in the testimony. The relationship was no secret. The affair had been allowed to progress by her friends and family; there is no suggestion in the records that anyone had complained publicly about the cross-confessional sex before being called as witnesses at Judah's trial.

In the entire case file, we find only one vague epithet perhaps referencing Judah's Jewishness: one Greek friend-cum-witness claimed that Maria herself, in a sick and angry state, had called Judah a dog, *canis Jocudas*.[3] In some contexts, the epithet carried a set of meanings linked to notions of filth, contagion, and segregation—a trope marshaled, among other uses, to rationalize why Christians should not let Jews into their private spaces or, more urgently, have sexual contact with Jews. A fourteenth-century French judge, for example, argued that Christian sex with Jews constituted "bestiality" because it was akin to copulating with a dog.[4] We must find it ironic, then, that this insult is put in the mouth of Maria, the very woman who chose (and it was indeed her choice) to bring a Jew into her home, to allow her family to be touched by him in his capacity as a doctor, and then to engage in an extended sexual relationship with him.

The previous chapter demonstrated Jews and Christians engaged in normalized, if sometimes trying, relationships, at least in the economic sphere. Clearly other sorts of relationships were also in play; scholars have long noted the reality of Jewish-Christian sexual interaction, despite staunch prohibitions from Church and state. Yet as the case of Judah de Damasco demonstrates, we need to dig deeper into Jewish-Christian relations to understand their structural features. That is to say, as this chapter argues, Jewish-Christian interactions were the product not simply of individuals making choices but of individuals acting in the context of a Venetian colonial society influenced and shaped by the Venetian and Cretan colonial governments' policies and attitudes. Maria's and Judah's behaviors—the choice for a Jewish doctor to treat Christian patients, the couple's well-known sexual relationship, Judah's choice to flee to Venice, and his confidence in the power of the Venetian judicial system—cannot be fully understood without being framed inside Venice's colonial policies on Jews and on Jewish-Christian relations. This murder trial and its outcome, then, offer a window onto Venice's impact upon Jews and Jewish-Christian relations.

The position of Jewish doctors, for one, arose from the very public support given to them by the colonial government. Jewish doctors, in fact, were exempt from a variety of taxes; they were given explicit rights to treat Christian patients; and they were given titles ("Magister") and sometimes official offices, recognized or bestowed by the ducal chancellery. Many Jewish elites in Candia were doctors who served the Venetian judiciary as wound evaluators and medical expert witnesses. They were therefore not just Jews but agents of the colonial state, a reality that facilitated the kinds of Jewish-Christian relations we witness in the ongoing affair between Magister Judah and the late widow Maria Sithiacudena.

Second, the doctors' role as agent of state took place in the context of the judicial needs of the colonial government, and it is this judicial world that both controlled and limited Jewish rights and Jewish-Christian relations in Candia. That is to say, not only was the relationship between Judah and the Greek Maria enabled by his official status as judicial employee, but we must consider Judah in his capacity as a defendant and the light it sheds on the colonial justice system as an agent of control in this society. The notion of a Jew killing a Christian (whether truthful or not) did not lead to rioting, chaos, and bloodshed; rather, the iron fist of Venetian "justice" controlled the outcome.

Although the particulars of Judah's case are unique—it is the only extant record of a murder trial in which a Jew was accused of killing a Christian—in other important ways, it reflects broader trends and realities that defined Jewish relations with the state and sheds light on the ways in which the state mediated and fostered relations between Jews and Christians. Venetian policies, and particularly its approach to providing "justice," part and parcel of its colonial appeasement project, fostered an environment in which anti-Jewish rhetoric was controlled and defused, though certainly not absent. This enabled a political and social reality of Jewish-Christian relations that looks quite different in Crete than in many other parts of medieval Christendom.

Venice's Jewish Doctors

Although scholars have often identified meaningful premodern Jewish-Christian relationships as taking place among those living on the very peripheries of their respective societies, Judah de Damasco was a man squarely in the center—not only in the center of Jewish society but also in the center of wider Candiote society.[5] A master surgeon trusted by the Venetian government to treat and evaluate non-Jewish patients, Judah appears in the sources as a professional wound expert employed by Candia's court system in many entries of the legal record beginning in 1401. In doing so, he joined his father and brother, who were already in the same profession and working for the ducal judiciary.[6] It seems that Judah met Maria in the context of his work as a physician, since he was known to frequent her house when caring for her husband, Johannes, during his eight-month, ultimately terminal illness; he also came to treat their three children whenever they were ill.[7] After Johannes's death, Judah continued to come around regularly—he was constantly in the home (the term used is *conversabatur*, perhaps suggesting he was even living there), as witnesses note over and over again.

It was his professional credentials that gave his visits a credible veneer of social legitimacy. Jewish doctors were not a minority of those hired by the Venetian government to act as wound evaluators. They also played a very active role in caring for patients—Greek, Latin, and Jewish alike—in Candia and its outskirts: in fact, Jewish doctors treated Christians across the socioeconomic spectrum, from slaves and poor Greeks to Latin nobles.[8] Jewish doctors seem to have played similar roles in other Cretan towns such as Canea.[9] The doctors who appear regularly in the ducal records lived and worked inside the town of Candia, in the predominantly Greek suburb south of town known as the *borgo*, and in a number of outlying fortress towns and villages, including Castronovo, Belvedere, and Castro Bonifacio.

Substantial data from the ducal records allow for a statistical evaluation of the doctors associated with the administrative region of Candia just outlined—and permit the conclusion that Jews did not just make up a significant portion of doctors in Crete; they made up a majority, at least of those utilized by the state. From the first mention of doctors in the ducal record in 1366 until 1420 (the year after Judah's trial), we find thirty-seven Jewish doctors caring for and evaluating patients in Candia and its environs. In contrast, for the same period, twenty Christian doctors appear. This ratio of slightly less than 2:1 Jews to Christians, however, is somewhat misleading, since in an average year, Jewish doctors outnumber Christian doctors by a higher proportion. By way of example, in 1416 thirteen Jewish doctors and five Christian doctors appear in the sources; in 1417, ten Jewish doctors and three Christian doctors are represented; in 1418, eleven Jewish doctors and three Christians appear; in 1419, the year of Judah's trial, nine Jewish doctors and four Christian doctors appear in the sources. In addition, and by way of explaining the discrepancy, while the same individual Jewish doctors appear in the records year after year, many Christian doctors—some of whom do not appear to be residents of Crete but rather spent a limited time on the island—only appear intermittently, for one or a few years.

In fact, the flight of Christian doctors was indeed a crisis that provoked anxiety among Crete's government, which, at least in the later fourteenth century, regularly sent ambassadors to Venice in an attempt to convince Venetian doctors to take up two-year salaried positions on the island. Relatively low wages and the sense of Crete as a colonial backwater (as Sally McKee has argued) kept metropolitan doctors away or prevented them from staying for long.[10] This unwillingness to settle in Crete on the part of Venetian Christian doctors became local Jewish doctors' gain, as the colonial government turned to their Jewish subjects.

Despite the particulars of the Christian doctor shortage on Crete, the ubiquity of Jewish doctors concurs with current scholarly thinking, particularly that of Joseph Shatzmiller, who claims that, "next to moneylending, medicine seems to have been the most preponderant profession among Jews" in the Mediterranean after 1250.[11] What is striking here, however, is the nature of the relationship between Jewish doctors such as Judah de Damasco and the state apparatus. Jewish doctors rarely limited their work to private practice, though they did treat Cretans across the socioeconomic spectrum. Moreover, they were not only hired by the government to treat poor patients, a common function of the "municipal doctor" in the medieval Mediterranean.[12] Rather, the Venetian colonial judiciary employed them to offer expert opinions about whether a given patient (usually wounded severely by someone else, though not always in cases where charges might be brought) was out of danger of dying from their wounds (*extra periculum mortis*). Jews at times played similar evaluative roles in courts across the Mediterranean and beyond, but their prevalence strikes anyone reading the records from Crete: these short testimonies, almost always involving at least two Jewish doctors among the minimum three, are perhaps the most common type of entry in the archives of the Duca di Candia.[13] One imagines that dealing with these wounded patients in whom the ducal court was interested took up an immense amount of these doctors' schedules, between visiting and caring for patients and then reporting on the record before the notary.

To some extent, the Jewish ability to publicly and reputably practice medicine in the medieval Mediterranean always involved the state. Since for the most part Jews were not allowed to study medicine in the university, those seeking to learn the medical arts gained expertise through private study and apprenticeship, often from a father or father-in-law as part of a family dynasty of medical doctors.[14] Thus, when a Jew appears in the Latin record as *magister medicus*, whether at the grade of *physicus* (physician, also spelled *fisicus*, the higher-status doctor who was understood to have had a superior, well-rounded education) or *cirurgicus* (surgeon, often *ciroicus*, a lower-tier doctor who was "expected to deal with wounds and to perform a variety of surgical operations"),[15] this indicates that the government had evaluated and approved these qualifications.[16] In Candia, these Jewish doctors acted as part of the recognized *collegium medicorum*, with the same status as non-Jewish physicians and surgeons.[17] Some Jewish doctors held other formal titles that came with salaries. The records reveal Jewish doctors named to official salaried positions with Candiote feudatories in the fourteenth and fifteenth centuries, a tenure that had to be both confirmed by and discontinued with permission of the ducal court.[18] More fully tied into the state apparatus, the surgeon Magister Lazaro held the position of *deputatus medicus maleficiorum* (ostensibly the number two in the ministry in charge of criminal medical inquiries) until mid-April 1454 and was paid by the government (*ad salarium comunis*) for his work.[19] Though Lazaro was summarily removed from his position to be replaced by a Christian—it cannot be a coincidence that his removal took place during the period in which a group of Cretan Jews were accused of lamb crucifixion and sent to Venice for trial, discussed below—he was one of a number of Jewish doctors who held official positions, whether with the ducal curia or with the noble feudatories, behind which stood the authority and the salary of the government and its elites.[20]

The public role of the doctor made his work one in which he regularly found himself in the close working company of Christians. After Maria's body was discovered, for example, five doctors and a representative from the police force known as the "officials of the night" were sent to investigate. Four of the doctors were Jewish, and they obviously worked closely with a Latin doctor and a Latin lawman. Mixed Jewish/Christian teams appear extremely frequently in the ducal court record. A Jewish doctor was regularly trusted to act as the *fisicus* leading the team of three doctors sent to evaluate wounds, usually made up of a physician and two surgeons. In their official capacity, then, Jewish doctors working on behalf of the state were enabled by the state to share knowledge, build working relationships, and engage in scholarly and practical give-and-take with Latins on an equal—if not superior—footing.

When this relationship between the Jewish doctor and his Christian medical colleagues played out in the open, it likely influenced the perceptions of Christian potential patients. As Andrée Courtemanche has remarked, doctors' group outings to the sites of deaths and evaluations were decidedly public ventures that not only placed the health/death status of the patient in the public sphere but also "lent official status to the medical expert visiting the home" of the dead or wounded.[21] When a Jewish doctor was involved, this public display must have cemented his power and status in the eyes of the laymen who saw his association with other civic officials and Christians.

Perhaps it was this state-approved authority (along with the shortage of Venetian Christian doctors) that enabled wealthy Latin nobles to hire Jewish doctors without concern for the religious divide. For example, Ser Urssius Justinian hired Judah's brother, the surgeon Nathan de Damasco, to care for a dangerous illness of his shin and foot, which he treated for eight months until his patient was healed, a process that apparently spanned most of 1412. To be sure, in this case, litigation ensued: Ser Urssius thought his care worth only fifty hyperpera, and Nathan sued for his full contracted payment of one hundred hyperpera. Yet this was a common enough phenomenon among doctors and patients no matter their religion, and in this case, the ducal court agreed with Magister Nathan, commending his medical intervention undertaken "with great industry and effort."[22]

If Latin aristocrats comfortably employed Jewish doctors, even more so did this obtain for Greeks like Maria and her neighbors. It seems probable that, although many witnesses knew about Judah's all-too-regular visits to the widowed Maria, no one was willing to question the legitimacy of his behavior because of his position of power relative to these poor, low-status Greeks. He may have been a Jew, but he was a doctor, virtually an agent of the colonial state that had stripped these Greeks of status and heavily controlled their social and physical mobility.

While this power dynamic kept these Greeks silent, it may have also been this same hierarchy that made the sexual relationship attractive to Maria, who may have seen in Judah an opportunity to care for her now fatherless family. We do not see any gifts explicitly exchanged between the two, but a well-off man could use his money and connections in many ways. This kind of quiet support is hinted at in the colorful testimony of George Vlagho, who reports a conversation he had with a Greek friend, Costas, whom he ran into at the Church of St. Eleftherios.[23] An unhappy Costas told Vlagho (as the latter testified) that Judah had helped Maria sell her dead husband's sheep, shutting Costas out of his role as middleman for this deal. We are left to imagine that Judah's intercession netted Maria a higher final profit than what Costas would have given her after his own cut. According to Vlagho, Costas had blamed his loss of the deal on the sexual relationship between Maria and the doctor. This elliptical conversation presents only one thin sliver of the events that surrounded the relationship but suggests that Maria gained more than a sexual partner: she gained an economically savvy, well-connected man who was willing to assist her as she sought to rebuild a financial life without the primary earner in her household.

A consideration of the power dynamic produced between a male, officially sanctioned, educated Jewish doctor and a poor, socially disadvantaged, widowed Greek woman provides an important lens into the ways in which intimate, opposite-sex relationships formed between Jews and Christians in Venetian Candia. We cannot only consider gender and religion; we must consider precisely what "sort" of Christian woman the Jew interacted with: her status and her ethnicity, her financial and social needs, all of which helps situate this Christian woman in the pecking order of Candiote society. Likewise, a Jewish doctor with ties to the colonial apparatus and successful business connections must be understood to fill a different social position than the average Jew—that is, the one who induced anxiety in a Greek grocer when the Jew would touch the fruit he wanted to buy at market. The sorts of Jewish contagion in play in the previous chapter, it seems, could disappear when the Jew was not "just" a Jew but an agent of the colonial order whose potential benefits outweighed any fears.

The Cretan colonial government's choice to support Jewish doctors is all the more remarkable when we compare this policy to that of other states of the fourteenth- and fifteenth-century Mediterranean. As we have seen in many polities, Christian legislators, both Catholic and Orthodox, passed laws meant to prevent Jews from spreading "Jewish contagion"—often understood quite literally, as in laws forbidding Jews from touching produce or bread at the market. A Jewish doctor was potentially a particularly egregious source of such contagion. After all, what did a doctor do but come into close contact with his patient? Just as this period witnessed increasing legislation against Jewish sources of pollution, starting in the thirteenth century, both ecclesiastical and secular bodies in locales across western Christendom enacted laws expressly forbidding Jewish doctors from treating sick Christians, perhaps because they were concerned that the Jews would prevent the dying from receiving last rites, or perhaps because of this increasing anxiety over Jewish contagion.[24] In addition, in fourteenth-century Iberia and France, laws explicitly forbade Jewish doctors from treating Christian patients out of a fear that Jewish doctors would pretend to treat patients but actually intentionally murder them with their so-called remedies.[25] We do not hear such claims in Crete.

Nevertheless, we ought not overstate the unusual nature of this state hiring practice in its Italian context, at least in this period. As Ariel Toaff has demonstrated, until the mid-fifteenth century, when popular preachers turned their razor tongues against Jewish doctors, communes across Umbria regularly hired Jews—known to be less expensive than their Christian counterparts—to act as municipal doctors, though retained predominantly to care for the indigent.[26] Occasionally Jewish doctors were brought in to consult "in cases with complex legal implications."[27] Crete's particular shortage of Venetian Latin doctors apparently took an extant practice that seems to have been acceptable in parts of the Italian mainland and created a circumstance of greater and more widespread opportunity for Jewish doctors on the island. Increased visibility of Jewish doctors in state-recognized positions, it seems, begot a process of normalization and even social acceptance—a process that made Judah's relationship with Maria relatively unremarkable, until she and her fetus ended up suspiciously dead.

Jewish Subject Status and Its Advantages

By the time the ducal court of Candia pronounced judgment against Judah de Damasco in late summer 1419, he was gone from the island. Judah did not appear in the courtroom to hear that he was meant to have his right hand amputated, be hanged to death, and then have his corpse strung up in front of his dead lover's home. Judah had managed to find a way off of Crete without alerting the authorities; he became a fugitive.[28] He could have gone anywhere that shipping lines and his money allowed: out of Venetian dominions, to hide within another Jewish community. A man with professional training could have started over.

But he chose a different route. Instead of running away, Judah intentionally entered the mouth of the lion, running directly into the arms of the justice system that wanted him dead. But why? What rights did Judah have? He may have been a doctor on Crete, with local respect and authority. Nevertheless, he was a Jew, and a subject living in the colonies. How would he be seen by the Venetian metropolitan government when he appeared before an appeals court?

According to David Jacoby, Jews were most commonly treated as Venetian nationals. Sources typically refer to Jews as the "faithful" or *fideles* of Venice, a political affiliation whose irony stems from the fact that, according to typical medieval rhetoric in Crete as elsewhere, Jews were also the exact linguistic opposite: perfidious.[29] *Fideles* was a category often bestowed on foreigners who moved to Venice's dominion, and it came with a series of privileges particularly when overseas: diplomatic and legal protection, as well as the use of Venice's economic institutions and facilities.

Reinhold Mueller has stressed the unique nature of the "subject" (Latin: *subditus*) status of Jews in the Venetian dominions, both in the Stato da mar and the *terraferma*. Unlike in the contemporary kingdoms of Christendom, the Jews were not "servants of the king's chamber," a term that took on distinctly pejorative valences in the later Middle Ages. However, the language of *subditi*, like the language of *servi*, indicated in its context that Jews were under the protection of the given sovereign and, in the case of Venice, had a "direct bond" to the republican government.[30]

Despite the decidedly hierarchical valence of both terms, it was the legal valence of Jewish status as *subditi* and *fideles* of Venice that ensured that the protection promised to their Greek Orthodox neighbors was also upheld when it came to Jews themselves. As Eliyahu Ashtor has demonstrated, Venetian authorities took an active role in protecting Cretan Jewish subjects, particularly in the realm of commercial rights vis-à-vis non-Venetian actors. At least four times over the course of the thirteenth through fifteenth centuries, the Venetian government sought redress for their Jewish subjects: in the late 1270s, against the Byzantine government; in 1407, against Genoa; in 1411, against Sicily; and in the mid-fifteenth century, against the Byzantines again. In each case, Venice sought to protect Jewish trade rights and to ensure the safety of the Jews' trade goods, despite the fact that these Jews were "only" subjects and not citizens.[31]

This protection was not simply a matter of commerce; it could even override papal pretensions and will—suggesting the ways in which protecting Jews was a by-product of Venice's push to assert her own autonomy vis-à-vis the pope. When a papal Inquisitor attempted to persecute an important member of the Jewish community in Candia in 1314, the Cretan duke prevented inquisitorial involvement. Moreover, Venice then requested from legal jurists an opinion on the jurisdiction that should be granted to inquisitors vis-à-vis the Jews; the jurists confirmed Venice's view, that Jews were entitled to their ancestral customs.[32]

Protection, to be sure, never meant any sort of citizenship for these colonial Jews—neither as citizens of Venetian Candia nor as citizens of Venice.[33] Though a number of Cretan Jews sought citizenship or citizen-like privileges, the central government explicitly forbade Jews that right, since Venetian and city-specific citizenship generally necessitated a Christian legal reputation that Jews could simply never obtain.[34] The case of David Mavrogonato, who some scholars have claimed had been given citizenship on Crete, offers an important case in point. Mavrogonato, a Jewish merchant and translator for Greek priests, reported to the Venetian government a conspiracy to overthrow colonial rule he had overheard when working for the Greek community. A few years after the events, in 1463, Mavrogonato requested special privileges as a reward for his loyalty. The Venetian government granted him a tax break (including the right to not pay additional taxes demanded by the Jewish communal organization) and the right to be in public without the Jewish clothing badge. In 1466, he also received permission to live anywhere in the city of Candia, permission to wear clothing not strictly identifiable as "Jewish" wear, and the right to an annual stipend. He was even allowed to send his merchandise on Venetian ships. The rights Mavrogonato received highlight the diminished freedoms of the Jews of Crete in the second half of the fifteenth century. As Mavrogonato's case indicates, however, these limitations were not insurmountable, even without citizenship.

Yet while these privileges mimic those given to citizens, that mimicry is precisely the point: Mavrogonato was allowed to live like a citizen but was never given the actual title or status.[35] Even in the years after the Black Death, when Venice eagerly sought to attract settlers to its maritime lands with citizenship privileges, the stipulation excluded Jews: "Non intelligendo in hoc Iudeos."[36]

David Jacoby notes that the exclusion of certain groups in these types of policies was not limited to Jews. "Although not specifically mentioned in the legislation" passed in the post–Black Death year of 1352, offering citizenship to non-Jews who resided in Venice's main colonial cities for ten years, "Greek immigrants to the colonies were also barred from Venetian citizenship." However, Jacoby ascribes the Greek exclusion to "social and political considerations," and not stemming "from religious attitudes as in the case of the Jews."[37] Whether we accept Jacoby's distinction or not, perhaps these two cases are more similar than different: this policy, aimed at both Greeks and Jews, is part of a typical colonial approach toward maintaining a division between the colonized and the colonizer, not simply one aimed at a singular socioreligious group. As non-Latins, both Greeks and Jews had to be categorized in a way that legitimated and maintained their subjugation; religious status compelled Venice to see both groups as subjects and legitimated their maintenance as such. But being a subject had its advantages, and for Judah de Damasco—as other Jews and Greeks from the colonies—that meant trusting the possibilities found in being part of the Venetian system.

Colonial Justice

In large part, Judah's confidence must have stemmed from the fact that, at the same time the Venetian government limited both Jewish and Greek subject enfranchisement and political rights, it also offered subjects something that ultimately proved quite empowering: Crete's Jews, like its Greeks, had widespread rights to seek justice through the Venetian judiciary, whether in civil or criminal court settings.

Judah likely arrived in Venice before the official reports from Candia had reached the Senate; he had time on his side, stealing the march on the government that had sentenced him, making connections and finding allies in the metropole. Two years after his conviction, Judah appeared before the Avogaria di Comun, the state prosecutors' office that was empowered to initiate appeals of subordinate courts' decisions.[38] His case was sent to the highest appeals court, the Quarantia (the Council of Forty), in April/May 1421.[39] After two inconclusive votes, the Quarantia completely acquitted Judah on the third vote, overturning the ducal court's ruling. He could thus return to his family, his profession, and his life back on Crete.[40]

The Cretan administration recognized the acquittal in writing, entering a cancellation of the sentence into the court record on 9 August 1426, seven years after the initial court case. The town crier even announced the acquittal across the city.[41] By 1429, Judah was once again working as an expert wound evaluator for the very administration that had sought to mutilate and execute him.[42] Less than a decade after the sensational trial, Judah was once again living an ordinary life.

Perhaps Judah was lucky. His contentious acquittal meant he was freed only by the skin of his teeth. Despite this outcome, however, it is clear that Judah believed from the start that he had a good chance to rehabilitate his image and have the charges dropped if only he could have his case appealed. It seems that he did not believe he would have a fair shake if he stayed in Crete, since there was no higher court to which he could appeal, but this did not make him lose confidence in the Venetian judicial system as a whole. It simply spurred him to appeal higher up the ladder.

What was it about Venetian-style justice in particular that gave Judah the confidence to walk right into the halls of power to appeal his case, despite having fled as a wanted fugitive from Candia? An essential part of that answer lies in the Venetian patrician attitude to justice—that is to say, the idealization of the notion of justice by the government, alongside its somewhat amorphous and irregular implementation. Moreover, the sources attest that the idea of "justice" was known to be more important than the rigid enforcement of a specific set of laws and that it was meant to be applied to all those under Venetian rule, regardless of status, including colonial subjects on Crete—Jewish and Greek Orthodox alike. Jews long before Judah had accessed Venetian justice, both for their individual cases and as a community as a whole—as part of the *universitas iudeorum*.

This emphasis on "justice" for subjects stems from Venice's larger republican and imperial project. In establishing and ruling its colonial empire, Venice implemented a justice system in the Stato da mar that went far beyond the apprehension and punishment of criminals for the sake of maintaining social order. For Venice, "justice" and "equality" were bywords of an ideology that was understood by Venice's ruling class as the epitome of the republican, patrician ideal. As Monique O'Connell notes, throughout the colonial period, "the idea of justice was the centerpiece of Venetian self-promotion as a good republic."[43] From as early as 1205, upon taking office, the doge himself would swear an oath to render justice and treat all men equally.[44] He was obligated to personally "visit the law courts periodically and give ear to any complaints of denial of justice."[45] This act, and the primacy of republican justice as part of its pragmatic approach to empire, remained a fundamental (if propagandistic) ideal throughout the centuries of Venetian rule in the eastern Mediterranean.[46]

In part, Venetian emphasis on justice originated as a republican ideology that placed "equality" as the highest value. To be sure, sometimes this notion of equality referred to "the equality of rights, privileges, and status" only conferred upon the noble class of Venetians.[47] For the most part, patrician understanding of equality and justice did not overlap with our modern sense of the terms; rather, justice was a patriarchal good for the aristocracy to bestow upon lessers and a benefit that provoked obedience. Nevertheless, as Stanley Chojnacki has argued, patricians do not seem to have been above the law either theoretically or in practice. Likewise, equality also meant equal opportunity to be prosecuted for crimes committed.[48]

Just as the paternalistic nature of justice and equality did not exclude the nobles from having to live within the frame of law, the ideology also did not bar non-nobles from the benefits of law. In fact, a correlative meaning of equal justice applied broadly beyond the confines of the ruling class and became increasingly important in the age of Venetian dominion in the Stato da mar. This other sort of "equality" represented fairness for all before the law, including nonpatrician, noncitizen residents of Venice and even "inhabitants of the subject territories."[49]

This patrician notion was safely applied to those outside the closed aristocracy through jurisdictional equality, that is, the right to access law courts of the Republic no matter the class or status of the claimant. For subjects and citizens alike, the quality of the justice rendered was meant to be assured by a system of human checks and balances; no single judge could offer a sentence—individual power remained suspect—but instead a panel of judges conferred together.[50] Thus a justice system that promised equal access and impartial hearing to all of Venice's subjects, citizen or not, became an essential part of Venice's republican-imperial ideology and an essential tool in its propaganda campaign following the successful capture and settlement of colonies in the wake of the Fourth Crusade. This judicial equality was realized in two primary ways for the subjects of the Republic: through the implementation of an appeals-based system of due process and through the ability of all subjects to bring lawsuits before the Venetian court.

Judicial Appeals and the Jews

As we have seen, the status of belonging to the state judicial apparatus could improve the social position of Crete's Jews, in particular its medical doctors. But Venice's judiciary could provide other advantages to the Jews of Crete, and to the community as a whole, particularly through its guarantee that subjects could appeal its decisions. Venice claimed jurisdiction for all penal violations, and in doing so, it promised its own version of due process to all those suspected and convicted of crimes.[51] Part and parcel of this due process was the guaranteed ability to appeal a verdict, sometimes even after sentencing, as Judah de Damasco effectively did before the Venetian Senate. Subjects could also appeal noncriminal judgments, for example, appealing new tax burdens or other financial legislation. Gaetano Cozzi has identified this right to appeal as a "nodal point" of Venice's governing policy.[52] In fact, the right to appeal a verdict was considered so important that appeals judges known as the *sindici da mar* "were obliged to go circuit every two years . . . through the towns of Dalmatia, Greece, and the Levant" because the expense a colonial subject might suffer should he need to travel to an appeals court in Venice might be prohibitive.[53]

For Jews, the right to appeal criminal cases and new legislation benefited not only individual members of the community like Judah but the corporate community as well, for example in the case of a growing tax burden levied on the *universitas iudeorum* as a whole. On 25 February 1387, the Senate in Venice passed a resolution ordering the Jews of Crete to pay their communal tax at a rate of 2,500 hyperpera annually. This high assessment came with an explicit rationale: the island was full of very rich Jews.[54] Moreover, between 1387 and 1389 the Senate raised the annual tax fee again to an even more exorbitant rate of 3,500 hyperpera a year.[55] The perception of Jewish economic success, it seems, was here a detriment to the Jews, who experienced this taxation as a crushing burden. It was simply too much to let pass with gritted teeth and open wallets. In response, three prominent members of Candia's Jewish community including Joseph Missini were chosen to travel to Venice and represent the island's Jews before the Senate. Their appeal was heard on 25 May 1389.[56]

The main thrust of their argument was one of utility: we Jews are too useful to the state for it to be reasonable for you, Venice, to overtax us so heavily, claimed the representatives. The weight of the tax was not only causing Jews to suffer personal financial setbacks but also spurring some to abandon Crete—and leaving those who remained to shoulder an even larger portion of the burden. All in all, they argued, the tax rate provoked a spiral of poverty that would eventually undermine Venetian interests. And indeed, Venetian experts on Crete agreed with the Jews' determinations. Three noblemen, including a former duke and a former *provveditore* of Candia, testified that in fact the tax burden was ultimately detrimental to Venetian interest in maintaining a successful and wealthy Jewish community on Crete.[57] The Senate was convinced by the argument's logic and by the people who argued for it: the government lowered the tax rate to 2,000 hyperpera, a very significant 43 percent reduction.

This tax appeals case suggests that the Venetian perception of Jewish wealth and success created both benefits and detriments for the Cretan community. Though it was undoubtedly a burden that provoked exploitation from a Venice especially thirsty to fill its coffers, perhaps counterintuitively it sometimes provided the Jewish community with a defensive weapon in its arsenal of self-protection. In addition, of course, this case illustrates the ways in which the promise of access to Venetian institutions for the sake of appealing legislation was not simply lip service but could function effectively and to the benefit of the Jewish community as a whole.

The right to appeal could also enable Cretan Jews to leap over the hierarchy and access the very top of it. Appeals allowed Jews to fight across social class boundaries and against those who wielded direct power over them. An illustrative case stems from Rethymno, a Cretan city on the northwest coast with a substantial Jewish population. In 1356, a Rethymniote Jew named Samaria appealed to the Senate in Venice to overturn an impost of corvée labor, an *angaria*, instituted by a former rector of the town. Samaria argued that this demand for labor on top of steep taxation would render the Jews of that city villeins—virtually serfs—of Venice, and therefore unfree, which would be illegal. The Senate concurred and overturned the rector's Jewish *angaria* in this case.[58] Samaria's ability to directly access the halls of power enabled him to leapfrog above the immediate Venetian representative in Rethymno and instead appeal to a higher Venetian council—to the Senate itself.

For Samaria, his very freedom seemed to be at stake. Sometimes, however, this access was utilized for less than virtuous aims. Ottaviano Bonavita, a member of Candia's Jewish community (and, incidentally, the late Joseph Missini's son-in-law), was accused in 1433 of having successfully convinced three Cretan noblemen—all former councillors, that is, ducal advisors and judges, in Candia—to decide a case in his favor.[59] The three men, so the case file claims, were seduced by his smooth talk.[60] Somehow (perhaps a bribe was involved, though this is not articulated), Bonavita was able to induce the judges "to sell law and justice, offices and benefices of our dominion on the island of Crete."[61] Unfortunately no other details survive, and much of the story remains opaque. What is clear, however, is that Bonavita's direct access to the councillors and his ability to argue his case behind the scenes enabled him to get his way, though not without accusations of judicial misconduct. Perhaps Judah de Damasco made use of similar opportunities during the time he spent preparing to appeal his case in Venice; the strangely repeating votes may suggest something of the sort, thought we cannot know for sure. If so, Judah, unlike Ottaviano Bonavita, did not get caught. Access, then, had its many benefits, even if they were not necessarily all unequivocally ethical.

The Limits of Appeal

It must be said that the right to appeal was in no way a panacea for Venetian subjects, including Jews. On the simplest level, appeals against taxation were not always effective, for either individuals or communities. In 1439, a Jew from Rethymno found himself rebuffed in the ducal court, despite his claim that the wheat tax imposed on him was neither just nor reasonable (*non erat iustum nec rationabile*).[62] Two years earlier, a request by the Jews of Candia to revisit the Jewish tax was rejected outright by the ducal court.[63] An embassy from the three Jewish communities on the island of Negroponte, another Venetian colony, had its petition for lowering the Jewish taxes turned down in 1452. Nevertheless, in an act indicative of the seriousness with which Venice's governing bodies took each petition, two other simultaneous requests made by the Jewish representatives from Negroponte were approved: the first to lower shipping taxes for the island's Jews to the level of all other subjects and a second to defend Negropontan Jews against extortion by Venetian soldiers.[64]

There were also further limitations to the appeals process. While multiple appeals were allowed, a court could put a stop to the process. For example, Crete's ducal court sentenced the Jewish woman Elea Mavristiri to remain "in perpetuum silentium"—effectively forbidding any more litigation on this topic—after they determined she had brought too many (to their minds, unfounded) appeals to her case.[65] In addition, from a financial point of view, not only were court cases expensive, but embassies to Venice were even more costly, necessitating contributions from community members. In 1314, for example, a town crier read a public proclamation reminding everyone who had promised to contribute to the Jewish embassy to Venice to pay up by the following Sunday.[66] Suggestive of the importance of this communal financial support for enabling the mission, the proclamation came with an enforceable threat to ensure timely payment: a penalty of two grossi for each hyperpera pledged but not paid. According to David Jacoby, in addition to the expected costs of this 1314 trip, the Jewish community probably paid bribes to the duke and his councillors to facilitate the embassy, as indicated by a set of other expenses mentioned in this record.[67] Successful appeals could happen, but various less than pristine wheels at times needed to be greased.

Finally, while the Jews could continue to appeal, so could their adversaries. In a tragic case beginning in 1451, a nun (apparently a Latin-rite nun)—perhaps a converted Jew herself—accused prominent members of the Candiote Jewish community of crucifying a lamb on Holy Friday. She claimed that this was done each year, ostensibly as a way of mocking Christians' celebration of Easter, the holiday that highlights Jesus as the lamb of God. When the accusation was brought to the attention of the authorities, the Venetian doge ordered the Cretan duke to investigate the charge, and the duke in his turn assigned the affair to a fiercely anti-Jewish syndic (circuit judge and investigator) named Antonio Gradenigo. Gradenigo's investigation, supported by the state prosecutors, the Avogaria di Comun, led to the arrest of nine community leaders.[68] Imprisoned and tortured in Candia, two of the men died on the long voyage to Venice, where they and their compatriots were to be tried before the Grand Council (Maggior Consiglio). On 15 July, the case was tried and the remaining seven Jews were acquitted.

It was not over, however, since Gradenigo appealed the ruling, charging that the Jews had bribed members of the council. In the retrial, held in March 1453, six men were found guilty—and punished. However, in one final appeal by the Jews in June 1454, the six community leaders were retried and finally found innocent. While the appeals process finally ended with an overwhelming call for the freedom of these Jewish men, the many layers of appeals had led to the death of two, the torture of all, and almost two years of incarceration for the very leaders of Candia's Jewish community.

Venetian Colonial Justice versus Mob Justice

Even more than Judah de Damasco's personal trials and tribulations, this terrible communal trauma suggests just how manifestly Venice's emphasis on court justice led to different outcomes for the Candiote Jewish community and its members than in other parts of medieval Christendom. These sorts of specifically anti-Jewish accusations came late and rarely to Crete. When such events did happen, the accused Jews were not left entirely powerless to face massacres and summary executions but rather could at least wield the weapons of the courtroom, the appeals process, and the concept of "justice" to defend themselves. The results might not have uniformly fallen in the Jews' favor, the trauma was real, and the appeals process could hinder as well as help. But these tools were not illusory; they could and often did protect Jewish subjects of Venice from the explosive vicissitudes of minority life in a volatile social environment.

The strange lamb crucifixion libel places the difference between the Venetian approach on Crete and other locations across Christendom in high relief. Undoubtedly, the Jewish community found the death of two leaders and the repeated trial of a number of others traumatic. Jeremiah Nomico, a leader of the Jewish community, wrote in a colophon to a manuscript he commissioned that he had begun and completed the manuscript in prison in 1452 and hoped vengeance would be wrought for this injustice during his life.[69] But the scale and the majority's approach to this blood libel were quite different from those of other blood libels across Europe. Most basically, the response to these accusations involved a judicial process, and not rioting by the masses, such as the massacres of 150 Jews by mobs in London and York in 1190 following claims of blood libels around England. Moreover, the result for the Candiote case was an acquittal (twice)—far different than the public burning of over thirty Jews in Blois following a blood libel there in 1171, the execution of eighteen Jews following the accusation of the murder of Hugh of Lincoln in 1255, or—closer in time and place—the fifteen Jews burned to death for the supposed murder of Simon of Trent in 1475. In contrast, as well, child murder accusations across Germany did not merit judicial examination but relied on miracle accounts to condemn Jews, who were summarily and publicly executed.[70]

To be sure, the Jews of Candia were "only" accused of crucifying a lamb, not a child (though the Venetian records suggest that the accuser claimed the Jews chose a lamb because they could not find a child). But that is precisely part of the point: in Candia, no accusation of a ritual murder of a human being was ever leveled against the Jews, and when a similar accusation regarding a symbolically potent animal was made (quite late in the scheme of these accusations), the government apparatus took it on as a legal matter, refusing to let it spark public riots or a massacre. Venetian "justice" and the rule of law as it was understood and respected by the Venetian authorities offered Crete's Jews a benefit that, if not a panacea, certainly could protect the community as a whole—despite the undeniably horrific reality of torture and death for a few.

Moneylending Revisited

This is not the only example in which the judicial culture of Crete fostered circumstances in which anti-Jewish rhetoric was mitigated, channeled, or prevented from escalating into widespread violence or mob behavior dangerous to Jews. Two further examples will help us parse the place of state institutions in Jewish-Christian relations. The first brings us back to the Jewish role as moneylenders. We saw examples in the previous chapter that highlight the ways in which moneylending did not always fit into medieval stereotypes. But, to be sure, Jewish credit did at times spark real enmity from Christian debtors, particularly when the debtors were Veneto-Cretan aristocrats fallen on hard times. Most notably, over the course of a few decades in the first half of the fifteenth century (in 1415, 1428, and 1449), Latin debtors in Crete complained to the Venetian Senate about the "unfair" debts they owed to Jews. In the 1410s, in the aftermath of a "financial crisis which overwhelmed the nobility during the first two decades of the fifteenth century," debtors petitioned Venice about Jewish lending practices (and the fact that Jewish lenders had already sued in court to recover the debts), leading to a new policy whereby Jews were ordered to lower their interest rates, from 12 percent to 10 percent plus pawns.[71]

Nevertheless, Venice did not cancel the extant debt, as did a number of monarchs across Latin Christendom who saw the opportunity to make money for themselves and build loyalty among their subjects. In a famous example, in the early years of the reign of Philip Augustus of France, the French king not only had his guards raid Jewish homes and seize anything of value, demanding a ransom of 15,000 marks, but then he also canceled debt owed to the Jews, as long as debtors paid a fifth of what they owed—directly to the royal coffers. He then expelled Jews of the royal domain. Even in the Crown of Aragon during the reign of Alfonso III, a ruler who was so concerned to ensure that Jews were generally repaid by debtors that he also held trials over debt crises, Christian debtors in some areas had their Jewish debt canceled in 1286 and 1288. Later, debt cancellation would become a norm.[72] In contrast, the Venetian government heard statements from ambassadors for both sides, from the Jewish and Latin parties, in the summer of 1416. Then, the state ordered a commission of three noblemen to work out compromise settlements that would ensure the repayment of a significant portion of the debt owed by each of these 1,970 men, depending on the financial state of the debtor. Ironically, not even one Cretan nobleman could be found who did not hold any debt to a Jew, and since holding debt would bias them, these local aristocrats were banned from serving on this commission. Thus three Venetian patricians were sent from the metropole to deal with the debt crisis.[73]

A smaller-scale debt crisis took place in 1428, when thirty-six "poor, loyal" archers in the employ of the state (soldiers whose names and home villages suggest that they are Greek) "humbly" complained to the Senate that they could not repay their debts to the Jews (adding up to about 750 ducats). Venice canceled a quarter of the debt, but not all of it, and as in the previous case worked out a payment plan whereby the men would pay the Jews in annual installments over the course of a decade.[74]

Anti-Jewish rhetoric and "othering" played a role in the archers' arguments. The petitioners, echoed by the Senate in its statement, stressed their own loyalty repeatedly (*fideles*; *fidelitate*). The Jews, on the other hand, are characterized as seeking the worst kinds of filthy lucre—seeking unfair profit and engaging in extreme usury.[75] Once again, however, the government sought a compromise solution in place of complete "forgiveness" of the debt; ostensibly only a quarter of the moneys owed could be seen as unfair interest, worth forgiving out of sympathy for the poor archers. The rest should be returned, fair and square, to the Jewish creditors. In 1449, further complaints by defaulting debtors led to yet another commission, this time seeking to make concessions in the sale of pawns as a way to mitigate financial disaster.[76]

As in other parts of Christendom, the association of Jewishness with moneylending made Jewish creditors a particularly soft target for disgruntled defaulters. In the case of these crises, governments and unhappy debtors had a choice in how to respond. But in each instance, the Venetian government chose to take Jewish moneylenders, the debts owed to them, and their position in Candiote society seriously as one side of a disputing party. Venice's centralized power and emphasis on judicial control prevented a parallel to what had happened in England in the 1260s: knights deeply indebted to Jews, and in open rebellion against King Henry III for ignoring their complaints, not only broke into the Jewish Exchequer to steal and destroy debt records, and then ordered all debt owed to Jews canceled, but also killed many Jews in London and in other cities in the process.[77] Although King Henry would undo the cancellation upon recovering power, his successor, Edward I—in his attempt to appease his knights and other Christians—entirely prohibited Jewish moneylending and eventually expelled the Jews entirely in 1290.[78]

Venice's approach was quite different. The powerful Senate sought solutions that would immediately appease the Christian debtors while simultaneously protecting Jewish moneylenders' rights to continue to lend at reasonable interest, recover debt (even if not in full), and maintain their place in Candiote society. Instead of letting anti-Jewish sentiments become a vehicle for violence and vitriol, Venice turned to its judiciary. It treated Jewish creditors and Venetian debtors as two sides of a legal dispute, preferring (like many contemporary Italian courts) not to cave in to a zero-sum game but rather to provide an arbitrated compromise to appease both disputants. In other words, Jews were not external to this world of compromise, but as Venice worked hard to promote itself as the republic of justice and equity, it included Jews in Crete in its realization of this turn to justice. Venice certainly acted this way for its own reasons: self-promotion, pacification of a volatile region, and the need for Jewish credit to continue flowing. The result, however, was that Jews felt confident that the Venetian government in Crete could be relied upon to act with measured responses, whether Jews were the petitioners or the defendants.

Jewish Dogs, Jewish Officials

Venice's judicial appeasement strategy—and its limiting effect on anti-Judaism—is also visible in a senatorial decision from 1433 that puts on display the most graphic and fully articulated Cretan example of the rhetoric of Jewish contagion. In content, it appears decidedly disconnected from questions of contagion.[79] In May, two Veneto-Cretan noblemen serving as ducal councillors petitioned the Senate in Venice to forbid Jews from occupying two semiofficial roles. Over the course of the previous centuries of Venetian rule, Jews had indeed held lucrative tax-farming positions.[80] The positions of *messetarius* and the *sansarius*, which appear to have involved both a tax-farming element and a role as broker between the parties making deals in the marketplace, were two that Jews had been allowed to hold, and did.[81] But these two Cretan councillors decided that putting such power—to mediate the business contracts between two good Christians—in the hands of Jews was wrong in every way. Indeed, according to their petition, Candia's bishop annually admonished his flock that those who let Jewish brokers mediate should be excommunicated.[82] As enemies of the Cross, Jews should not be allowed to hold any benefices or honors. Such a prohibition, they claimed, was gospel truth, quite literally: "Moreover, because we are taught by the Gospel's warning that it is not good to take up the bread of the sons and give it to the Jewish dogs, of course, who by various methods hunt Christian blood to suck it up."[83]

The comparison of Jews to dogs derives from an interpretation of Matthew 15:26 that the councillors paraphrased exegetically in their petition.[84] In this verse, Jesus talks to a Canaanite woman who sought his help to save her demon-possessed daughter. Jesus at first refuses, because his mission is to help the people of Israel, not Canaanites. According to Matthew, Jesus says to her, "It is not right to take the children's bread and toss it to the dogs," meaning, it is not right to give the spiritual nourishment that Jesus provides to the people of Israel to those who do not deserve it. Those who do not deserve his help are equated with dogs. Christian exegesis of this verse—with Jews representing the dogs of Jesus' parable—underpinned segregationist attitudes and policies from the fourth century onward and was a primary image utilized to communicate fears of Jewish contagion across the medieval Christian world, as the dog, deemed a filthy animal, became associated with Jews.[85]

The petition from the Cretan councillors conflates a number of anti-Jewish images: the Jew as dog, of course, but also an implication that the dogs do not simply pollute but actively seek to hurt Christians and draw blood (like the claim of Jews as Christ-killers, which of course the host desecration is understood to emulate). The novelty here lies in the association of blood as a metaphor for money. The classic blood libel of Jews consuming Christian blood (a libel that, as we saw, is not recorded as having ever appeared on Crete) is reinterpreted as an analogy for Jews stealing Christian money by seeking profit. Through this play on images that were known to have been marshaled by fifteenth-century Italian churchmen, the blood libel and classic claims of usury come together to form a new meta-image of the bad Jew through the reference to the Jewish dog.[86] Over the course of the rest of the petition, the councillors further characterize Jews as enemies (*inimicos*) and treacherous (referring to the *infidelium iudeorum*, the treachery of the Jews), unworthy of playing any role in the loyal and Catholic Venetian order, even in semiofficial positions.

In responding to the petition in September 1433, the Venetian Senate overwhelmingly approved the ultimate request of these two Venetian men, banning Jews from holding the positions in question.[87] Instead of replicating the graphic vitriol of the local councillors, however, the metropolitan Senate simply affirmed that such a prohibition would be honorable and praiseworthy to God and the world, and useful to the Christians who would occupy the offices.[88] The Senate also articulated that God's law does indeed demand that "the perfidious Jews are deprived of all offices and benefices of the Christians" and that the new ban applied to the whole island of Crete.[89] And with that, the Senate in Venice turned to other business. The language of the blood libel, the image of the dog, and even references to usury were left out of its consideration.

For the government in the metropole, the moral rightness or political expediency of a cause—for indeed, we cannot know if the senators voted to approve the ban because they thought it right or convenient—had to be balanced with other considerations. In this case, it seems, in a move consistent with its general policy, the Senate did not want to produce or replicate language of incitement but rather language of relative appeasement. From its vantage point looking over all of Venice's holdings in the eastern Mediterranean, the peninsula, and its trading posts beyond, the Senate had much larger concerns than the worries over profiteering of two Cretan councillors. This middle position, supporting the petition but rejecting its particular language, offered a compromise aimed at maintaining the quiet across the colonies. The efficiency and quiet of the colonies were undoubtedly goals of much of the Senate's decisions, and though this particular instance took away a mode of profit-making for Jews, in the aggregate this pragmatic approach could benefit the colonial Jewish communities.[90]

Judah, Jewish Power, and the State

The councillors who composed the petition in 1433 may not have said so explicitly, but they appear to have been concerned about a broader culture in Candia in which Jews were not kept in their proper place (below Christians) by the governmental system but rather were able to further their goals (financial, certainly, but perhaps also social). This power was given to them by the colonial government itself through its permitting of Jews to hold certain semiofficial positions. In this assessment of the relationship between state-approved roles and Jewish social and financial mobility, the angry councillors were not quite wrong; they may have, however, located their ire in the wrong semiofficial position. That is to say, other professional circumstances fostered by the government played a much larger role in empowering Candia's Jews than collecting taxes on market goods. The position of Jews as doctors to Christians, both Latin and Greek, a role supported and encouraged by the policy of hiring Jews as medical experts in the island's sovereign courts and allowing Jews to treat these same groups, played a far more significant role in empowering Jews, upsetting the "proper" hierarchy between Jews and Christians and giving the Jews access (both broad and intimate) to the world of Christian society.

To be sure, real social taboos existed across Latin Christendom, in Candia as elsewhere. Indeed, we must be careful not to impose an anachronistic conception of tolerance on any discussion of premodern cross-confessional contact. In the words of Benjamin Arbel, "Segregation was (*avant la lettre*) and still is an ideological concept. . . . Integration, on the other hand, has become an ideological concept only recently and had no place, as such, in the framework of Jewish-Christian relations in early modern Europe. It can only be considered in retrospect as a praxis, or better as a consequence of social, cultural, and economic forces."[91] The rhetoric of separation, like the legal moves to isolate Jewish residential settlement we have seen in previous chapters, were part and parcel of an ideological policy in which ecclesiastical and state concerns met.

Nevertheless, Venice's other, competing values—particularly its strong desire to promote itself as the most just republic—led to circumstances in which its Jews, as subjects, benefited from its colonial project. The classic motifs of medieval life under Christian rule—claims of the Jew as usurious dog, murderous bearer of contagion, tricky stealer of Christian money—were present here, in varying degrees. But they were often nonstarters, limited by government protection, broader interests, and wider understandings of Jews' identities as agents of state. Venice made Jewish identity flexible in its implications, if never mutable in its existence (short of conversion).

Moreover, Venetian flexibility seems to have helped foster—or at least dovetailed with— Jewish social flexibility, as in the case of Judah de Damasco. We have seen that when Judah sailed back to Candia after being acquitted and vindicated by the highest court in Venice in 1426, he returned to a city willing to accept him again. His position as wound evaluator working for the colonial administration was returned to him, and he was certainly back at work in that role by September 1429.[92] He once again received a government salary for his work.[93]

Perhaps even more surprisingly, the Jewish community of Candia welcomed him back into his old social position. His now well-known behavior, his long-term sexual relationship with a Greek woman, did not change his standing among the Jews. He appears in the record over the course of the next

twenty-plus years energetically taking part in Jewish public life. In 1444, acting on behalf of the Jewish community, Judah brought an update on certain
Jews' tax statuses before the ducal court and reported on a new holder of a
communal position.[94] In 1451, he took the stand in his capacity as recent *cam-
erarius* of the Jews (i.e., *hashvan*) in order to defend the nonpayment claims
of the former *condestabulo* under whom he had served, Mioche Demedico
(Delmedigo), against the current *condestabulo*.[95] He was also named one of the
four executors of the estate upon the death of the community leader Sabatheus
Casani, alongside Casani's widow and two sons.[96] Apparently, then, his behavior did not strip him of his normative leadership position within the community, nor did it alienate him from his friends and confidantes. Neither of the
social circles in which Judah traveled saw his behavior as wholly beyond the
pale; he could still be trusted by fellow Jews and Christians alike.

The connection between the opportunities given to Jews by Venice and
the reaction and behavior of the Jewish community itself is here suggestive
only. Correlation does not prove causation. But it is not facile. Jews utilized
Venice's institutions at a great rate—particularly the other side of justice, the
right to litigate against others in the state's judiciaries. It is the Jewish encounter with Venice's colonial justice, and its implications for Jewish life in Candia,
that makes up our next subject of inquiry.

Chapter 4

Jewish Choice and the Secular Courtroom

It was a truth widely acknowledged, among both Jews and the Venetian government, that the Jews of late medieval Venetian Crete were highly litigious. It was equally self-evident that Jews expressed this litigiousness not simply in the Jewish court, or *beit din*, which existed in Candia, but also in the Venetian secular judiciary. In many ways, Venice welcomed this wide use of its judiciary. Access to the justice system played a primary role in Venice's self-definition as a benevolent colonial power, as we have seen. But Venice did not always like every part of how its justice system played out in the hands of its subjects. In 1321, the Cretan colonial government ordered the town crier to announce to the Jews that they could no longer turn their court dates into spectacles. To be more specific, any Jew who brought a case before any Cretan court had to limit his companions to the *condestabulo* and two or three people who were close enough to the claimant to be allowed to legally plead or submit petitions for him or her.[1] The ostensible prehistory to this, it seems, is a roomful of potential character witnesses, moral supporters, and voyeurs clogging up the wheels of justice—or at least giving a headache to the judges.

The Jewish leadership of Candia also criticized its flock's use of judiciaries. But their complaint originated from a different concern: the timing of suits. The rabbinic authors of *Taqqanot Qandiya* worried that Jews were so eager to sue their fellow Jews in Venice's court that they were even initiating these suits on Friday—Sabbath eve—and on the eves of holidays. This had created a situation in which the court case might continue past sundown, into the holiday, causing a serious religious transgression. This sentiment already weighed heavily on the authors of the poetic first set of Hebrew ordinances dated to late summer 1228—less than two decades after the Venetian conquest: "In order that everyone will be happy in his rest [or: on his Sabbath], he and his children and his wife, and all of his entourage who accompany him, and each one cannot mold what will be his own verdict, we have decreed that no one is allowed to bring a lawsuit against his fellow Jew, from noon forward, whether before the Gentile [court] or the Jewish [court]."[2] As in the colonial government's 1321 complaint, the fact of Jewish use of the court seems unproblematic, and unquestioned. That much is taken for granted, as was the spectacle of the event. Indeed, Venice's later prohibition against bringing along too many supporters echoes here, too: the reference to "all of his entourage who accompany him" intimates that it was generally accepted that a trip to court meant a horde of other people accompanying the litigant.[3] But this was not a specific concern in Jewish eyes. Rather, for the authors of the *taqqanot*, the problem arose because local Jews accessed justice without consideration of other factors, such as Sabbath. This ordinance, meant to be binding upon all Cretan Jews, suggestively places the use of the Venetian court before reference to the Jewish rabbinic court, or *beit din*, tacitly if unintentionally approving of the use of either option. Indeed, the reference to the Jewish court is likely superfluous, as rabbinical judges would not likely allow their cases to extend past an appropriate time. We might even suspect that this *taqqanah* only mentions the Jewish court for the sake of keeping up appearances.

Such blatant acceptance of Jewish recourse to the secular court does not map onto the rabbinic theoretical conception of Jews and justice. In fact, it may at first seem that the communal leadership of Candia was acting in opposition to the prevailing, canonical opinions of the great rabbis of the age that recourse to secular courts was forbidden. Over the course of the tenth through fifteenth centuries, influential rabbis developed systematic theories of how Jews should live and function communally under non-Jewish sovereigns. Retaining as much intracommunal control as a community could muster became a major element of many of these political philosophies.[4] Although this rabbinic political philosophy will concern us far more in Chapter 6, it is worth noting here that a major facet of maintaining intracommunal control was the assumption and protection of as much jurisdictional independence as a sovereign would allow—and in many places that meant the right to adjudicate intra-Jewish civil suits.[5] Jews, in short, were meant to sue each other only in the confines of the Jewish court, the *beit din*. The assumption that halacha forbids Jews from suing each other except in the most extreme situations remains even today.[6] In its medieval social context, rabbinic rulings against using state judiciaries aimed in part to protect Jews from cruel treatment at the hands of non-Jewish judges, as explained by Rabbi Meir of Rothenberg.[7]

The prohibition also targeted assimilation. Solomon ibn Adret, the influential Catalan rabbinic authority, believed that if Jews comfortably used secular judiciaries, they would soon adopt the broader non-Jewish culture.[8]

Writing the volume of his magisterial account of Jewish life that touched on Crete in 1980, Salo Baron noticed the regularity of Jewish litigation in Venetian Crete's state judiciaries, to the apparent neglect of the *beit din*. Deeming this an outlier among Jewish communities, he suggested that this behavior stemmed from Byzantine times and was prevalent throughout the Byzantine Empire's Jewish communities, in contradistinction to the behavior of Jews in other milieus.[9] But a slow aggregation of scholarship over the past half century indicates that Cretan Jewish decisions to litigate in secular courts cannot be seen as a product of the Byzantine milieu alone. Rather, while Ashkenazi Jews seem to have stayed out of the secular courtroom, Jews in the Christian Mediterranean—particularly in Iberia and Provence, and likely elsewhere—chose to air their grievances with one another not in a *beit din*, a Jewish court, but in the halls of justice administered by their current sovereign.[10] Moreover, this move to sue in secular courts cannot be seen as a result of sovereign force: many Jewish communities in Latin Christendom had fairly broad rights to internal justice, yet their members still often chose the secular route.[11] In fact, recent scholarship has demonstrated that this trend stretched beyond the Christian Mediterranean: Jews living under Muslim rule took advantage of Muslim courts to litigate with their fellow Jews.[12] Thus, like their coreligionists from the Atlantic coast to the far edges of the Black Sea, Crete's Jews adopted the habit seemingly without concern for the (supposedly sweeping) prohibitions outlined by Ibn Adret and his contemporaries.

For Crete's Jews, the secular courtroom, manned by Venetian judges, became a comfortable place to air grievances and seek resolution of disputes. To be sure, for some Jews, the courtroom served as another locus of encounter with Christians, a fact we have seen played out in previous chapters, whether in business disputes, as fights over shared cisterns, or even occasionally when new Christians sued their former Jewish community members and families. But this was not the main object of ire for the Catalan Solomon ibn Adret, the Ashkenazi rabbi Meir of Rothenberg, and others; it was the intra-Jewish litigation that they found most problematic. Yet these suits between Jews were the more widespread sort of ducal court litigation in which Jews appeared, and it is this sort of litigation that is mentioned nonchalantly in the *taqqanah* addressed above. As Jewish litigants made the decision to encounter Venetian justice in a public courtroom, they chose to do so as a medium of encountering their fellow Jews, an act of public spectacle that brought intracommunal disputes beyond the community's jurisdiction—and beyond the community's purported private space.

Crete's Jews initiated suits against their coreligionists, not just about business disputes but more often about family inheritance drama and other ostensibly private affairs. But how did this work? What were the contours and motivations of this intra-Jewish litigation—the how and why of this behavior? To answer these questions, we must first consider the facts on the ground: the nature of the Venetian court system, the Jews who used the secular court, and the kinds of lawsuits they brought before the secular judiciary. Next, it is important to consider why Crete's Jews chose to litigate in the secular courtroom—why they engaged in a sort of "forum shopping" among judiciaries. Rationales for using the secular court certainly shed light on the Venetian judiciary itself, but perhaps more trenchantly, they offer insight into the limitations and complications of the Jewish legal system itself, as well as the social and emotional motivations that drew individuals to take on the public, performative role of litigant.

Jews in the Halls of Venetian Justice

As the Hebrew ordinance of 1228 limiting Friday litigation makes clear, less than two decades after Venice had sent its first military settlers to colonize and administer Crete, the Jews of Venetian Candia were already regularly and unselfconsciously bringing suits against Jews (and non-Jews) in the relatively new Venetian courts.[13] As we saw in the previous chapter, the rush to utilize Venetian courts was promoted by Venice itself, as it built its self-image as a good patriarchal republic, ensuring justice and equality for its people—patrician, ordinary citizen, and subject alike. We have already explored the ways in which this amorphous promise of "justice" created the legal space for appeals against Venetian taxation and criminal law. Likewise, when it came to civil cases, all subjects, regardless of citizen status, could bring lawsuits before Venetian courts. As with the right to appeal, the right to sue for civil damages brought many Jews to the Venetian judiciary.

In order to understand this right to civil litigation, let us first consider the venues for such activities. Though Venice promised equal access to justice, this did not mean that all justice had to be meted out in a singular venue. Scholars have noted the jurisdictional complexity, and indeed the confusing overlap, of the Venetian legal system. Multiple midlevel appeals courts, for example, could hear civil petitions in Venice, including the *auditori di sentenze* and the Avogaria di Comun.[14] We see the same phenomenon in Crete. Indeed, in Candia, by 1340, no fewer than five bodies could be expected to deal with various kinds of justice. When Latins in Candia wanted sue each other, if the first-instance civil suit dealt with inheritance matters, they would litigate before the Giudici di proprio; suits regarding debts and commerce would be heard by the Giudici di petizion.[15] Justice was also the business of the Officers of the Night (Signori di Notte, a sort of police force and investigative judiciary) and the Officers of the Peace (another police court)—two other judicial offices that could be involved with facilitating the processes of civil as well as criminal justice. Many of these judiciaries were parallel to those in the metropole.[16] The same institutions as in Candia were found across the island's towns, including at Canea and Rethymno.[17]

As non-Latin subjects, however, Crete's Jewish and Greek Orthodox residents did not have access to the same court of first instance as their Latin, citizen neighbors. Instead, when their cases involved only Jews and/or Greeks, they went to a separate court of first instance, known as the Curia Prosoporum (also known as Giudici di prosopo). Although this may look like a case of second-class marginalization, and could indeed be read this way, Venice also maintained a second court for Grecophone inhabitants for practical reasons. First, it engaged with a slightly different set of laws: certain Byzantine and Jewish precedents were taken into consideration for the relevant communities, and the judges *di prosopo* had to be somewhat familiar with these.[18] Second, Jews and native Greeks both spoke the local Cretan-Greek dialect, and this court could focus on Greek speakers and their documents. To be sure, the three judges who made up the Curia Prosoporum were ostensibly Venetians, or at least citizen Latins, but the focus on Greek language must have affected the choice of judges, while "Greek notaries and scribes were indispensable for the operation of the Venetian administration" and especially in this court.[19]

Unfortunately, the records from the court do not survive. What we know of the Curia Prosoporum has come indirectly through other sources, referenced in passing during the appeals process and echoed in notarial registers. For example, a solution of debt from 1450 mentions that tensions over a loan had brought the two parties—the Jew Judah Balbo versus Greek Christian brothers Georgius and Philippus Avonale—to the Curia Prosoporum.[20] Likewise, in 1359, the Jewish woman Elea Mavristiri had sued and won against another Jew, Mordachai Plumari, before the *iudices prosopii*.[21] We know of this latter case because when Elea brought another suit a few months later, this time to the island's court of appeals, known as the ducal court, she produced the earlier court decision as proof of the legitimacy of her claims. In fact, it is these court records from the ducal court, the court of appeals for Crete's Jews, Greeks, and Latins alike, that have lasted through the centuries; we have already seen stories culled from these records throughout this book. These survive because they were transported to Venice in 1669, as part of the final treaty ending Venetian rule on the island following a two-decades-long siege by Ottoman forces. The ducal court records are an essential part of the Archive of the Duke of Candia (filed now as the series titled Duca di Candia). It is in these records that Jewish activity abounds.

Jew Versus Jew in Civil Court

The Jewish leadership accepted the reality of intra-Jewish litigation at the secular court, at least to a point. But what were the disputes that brought these Jews to the secular judiciary? The same ordinance that seeks to prevent suits brought too close to Sabbath and holidays offers some insight into the types of cases Jews brought—or at least those that were deemed legitimate to bring. It notes that suits revolve around "silk cloth, or about the business of buying and selling, or about the other issues of things and merchandise."[22] At least as portrayed in this context, business and financial dealings were the primary stressors driving Jews to sue their coreligionists in Venice's court.

To an extent, this poetic assertion matches the ducal court records from around 1350–1450. To be sure, we must remember that the records of the court of first instance do not survive, and therefore we do not know how many, or what sort of, cases were settled definitively in the Curia Prosoporum without appeal. Undoubtedly there were many. But when looking at the ducal court records from this century, around 160 individual lawsuits appear in which a Jew initiated a suit against another Jew; the exact number is difficult to count because it is sometimes hard to decide precisely when a given case is actually a continuation of a case heard earlier by the ducal court or if it ought to count as a new lawsuit. Nevertheless, it is clear that a good number of intra-Jewish cases that made it to the ducal court—around thirty-five—revolve around business arrangements gone sour, including fights over business-related debts and real estate disputes. And indeed, cloth sales and the import/export of other goods could spark such fights. In spring 1402, a Candiote Jew brought suit over "a certain quantity of pepper and some cloths and Jewish books" he was importing from Alexandria. He sent the merchandise with a Jew sailing to Candia while he himself remained in Egypt, but he was never able to recover the goods upon his own return to Crete.[23]

Aside from business discord, Jews also sometimes sued their coreligionists because of disputes provoked by their close living arrangements and the nature of some legally shared property features. A common water cistern, which could provoke anxiety between Jewish and Christian neighbors over Jewish "contagion" (as we saw in Chapter 2), could likewise cause enmity between two Jewish neighbors—as happened in 1430, when Samaria Delmedigo sued his neighbor Meir Astrug, claiming that Meir refused him access to their co-owned water source. Deciding that both men should have access to the water, the court ordered the men to pay jointly to have a locked door constructed so that each would be able to access the cistern with a key.[24]

Jewish neighbors likewise fought over each other's rights to renovate, especially if their properties shared a common wall. Just a month before the fight over the cistern, Nathan, son of the late Vitale, and the surgeon Stamati Gadinelli came to court, fighting about a wall that separated their properties. Nathan wanted to add timber to the top of their common wall, but Stamati did not approve of the plan, provoking the lawsuit.[25] Good fences make good neighbors, we might say, but only if both parties can agree about the nature of the fence. Even when neighbors did not co-own a fence or a cistern, other stresses and strains of tight, urban living provoked angry lawsuits, as Protho Spathael (the community leader we witnessed teaching Bible to the Greek notary) and his neighbor Liacho, son of the late Moses, discovered. In a sitcom-ready situation, Liacho's renovation project, a new balcony, broke Protho's wall—a home addition undertaken by Liacho only after Protho's own renovation, covering a path between their homes, blocked sunlight from entering Liacho's home.[26] The reality of community-based life—inside a crowded urban neighborhood in which Jews worked with and lived near their coreligionists—accounts for some of the intra-Jewish tension that led Jews to the secular judiciary.

But commerce and neighborly property were not the only—or the primary—kind of stressors that led to long-lasting litigation between Jews. Around half of the intra-Jewish lawsuits that made it to the ducal court involve Jews using the judiciary to air family disputes. In over twenty-five of the cases, Jews sued each other over marital crises, a topic to be taken up in the next chapter. Even more noticeably, in over fifty of the aforementioned 160-plus disputes, it was family strife caused by the death of a wealthy patriarch that drove Jews to sue their close relatives. These inheritance fights, unlike many of the disputes over neighborly discord, could drag on for years in the ducal court, hardly settled through one court appearance, or even through one set of litigation. New suits connected to the same inheritance dispute developed over time, with new family members taking sides and seeking their own pieces of the estate pie.

The illustrious Balbo family, particularly the family of Isaiah Balbo, who died in the first years of the fifteenth century, offers a clear example of the ways in which family enmity over possessions (and, undoubtedly, all of the emotional meanings of those possessions) played out over time, and in ever-evolving ways, in the ducal judiciary. Isaiah's survivors fought bitterly and repeatedly in the ducal court over his significant estate. Brother fought brother, as Isaiah's sons Judah and Shabbetai (Sambatheus) Balbo did in February 1409, utilizing Shabbetai's own marriage contract as evidence of what their father intended to hand over to each child.[27] Only a few months earlier, Judah and Shabbetai had been united in court—against Judah's own wife and father-in-law!—in an attempt to seize goods held by the defendants that the brothers claimed belonged to Isaiah's estate.[28]

Then Isaiah's son Judah also died. Obviously this further complicated the attempts to parcel out the estate. In 1411, Judah's daughter Tziona (Çigio), named the heir of her recently deceased father, came to court to fight her uncle Shabbetai, again calling on evidence from previously made marriage contracts to seek a portion of her father's part of Isaiah's estate.[29] On the very same day, the court heard Isaiah's widow, Chana, petition against Tziona in an attempt to secure her dowry from part of her dead husband's estate.[30] Settling the inheritance from a single death was complicated enough, but when a second death occurred within a few years of the first, and the first estate had not been settled, any hopes for a peaceful arrangement within the Balbo family must have disappeared.

The Balbo family represented the epitome of the Candiote Jewish religious elite—wealthy, active, and respected community leaders.[31] Their use of the Venetian judiciary to play out this long inheritance battle illustrates the well-accepted nature of such behavior, though clearly their wealth—having possessions to fight over—created the litigation-ready circumstance, a factor not present when the poorer members of Crete's Jewish community died. Nevertheless, they could have dealt with the estate dispute internally, through private arbitration, or through the assistance of Jewish legal experts. But the

Balbos chose the secular judicial route, and they were certainly not the only
elite family to do so. In 1427, 1430, and again in 1433, for example, the children
of the late Elia Astrug used the secular court to fight over dowry money left
in Elia's will.[32] Over the course of the second half of 1445, and into 1446, the
widow of Sabatheus Casani (a former *condestabulo*) and his sons bickered over
the dead man's estate, resulting in no fewer than ten entries in the register.[33]

Fights over inheritance make up a large number of the cases in which Jews
fought other Jews. They also make up a large number of the Jewish intrafamily
disputes. The Balbo case can be counted as four separate lawsuits; but they all
stem from one primary death. Through either lens, they certainly outweigh in
number the cases that appear in the records of the ducal court over business
deals gone bad. This may be a result of the reality of the nature of appellate
cases: while two businessmen might be eager to settle their financial dispute
and move on to the next deal, the emotional component to family fights may
have led to unceasing appeals processes, resulting in a hefty historical record
from the ducal court register.

Lest we take for granted Cretan Jews' use of the secular judiciary in cases of
inheritance, let us contrast such behavior with a medieval letter discovered in the
Cairo Genizah. In it, two orphan girls in Egypt, desperate for help in obtaining
their inheritance, turned to their Jewish congregation for assistance. They hint,
ominously, that if help did not come from the Jews, they would turn to the non-
Jewish courts for assistance: "We cry to God, may he be exalted, and to you, the
House of Israel—do not leave us empty handed. . . . You [who] excommunicate
on the Mount of Olives all who obtain their inheritance through the judgments
of the Gentiles."[34] In the Genizah community reflected in this letter, seeking
judicial interference over inheritance was not simply frowned upon but merited excommunication. In reminding their Jewish elite audience of the possibly
severe implications of their own non-action, the orphan sisters attempted to pull
at the community's heart-strings, compelling them to act. In sharp contrast, the
taqqanot from Candia never oppose the practice, and indeed, evidence suggests
that the leading families of Candia's *kehillah* comfortably accessed Venetian justice to help resolve inheritance disputes.

In considering the threat to litigate above, a final comment regarding
the types of Jews who chose to engage with the secular court is worth adding
here. If we think about the inheritance cases above, we find that it was often
female family members who took the initiative in these cases. This is not an
anomaly among these sources, nor is this unique to Crete. In litigating in the
secular court, whether over inheritance, marriage, business, or other disputed

moments, Candiote women acted in step with Jewish women around the Mediterranean.[35] Over the last two decades, scholars of the Middle Ages have unearthed evidence of a widespread pattern of female litigation, a phenomenon shown to obtain not only in the Mediterranean but also beyond, and across Christian and Muslim states.[36] Scholars of Jewish women, however, have been slower to take up this area of study, in part because the traditional rabbinic source base obscures this reality under a series of normative prohibitions of such behavior. Rabbinic prescriptive views mandating that women remain in the private sphere have often been taken as depictions of reality.[37] Were one only to read the rabbinic literature from the later Middle Ages, one would likely come to the conclusion that Jewish women not only generally stayed at home but particularly did not litigate in courts. Rabbi Solomon ibn Adret, for example, famously stated that, because of modesty, it was especially important that "women do not display themselves in Jewish courts [*batei din*], nor especially in non-Jewish courts [*archaot*]."[38]

Despite these idealized Hebrew portraits of medieval women that show them safely behind the curtains, recent scholarship on medieval Jewish women, particularly studies looking at the rich Latin archives from Iberia and southern France, has demonstrated that Jewish women did not remain silent partners. Indeed, they lived public lives, accessing public institutions and partaking in the surrounding economic and quotidian life of the majority culture.[39] Evidence from Latin judiciaries makes it apparent that rabbinic theory did not correlate to the reality on the ground. Jewish women regularly appeared as claimants, defendants, and even witnesses in the state courts, in Crete as elsewhere.

Forum Shopping: Choosing the Venetian Court

When Candiote Jews chose to bring suit before Venetian judges, they engaged in forum shopping. That is, they had a choice when deciding where to bring their lawsuits. This was true in Candia, as it was in Venice itself in later centuries, and in lands across the Mediterranean. They were not compelled to air disputes in the secular judiciary. There was a Jewish court to which Jews could, and did sometimes, resort. Though no records from this court survive, reference to the court can be found in the ordinance of 1228 discussed earlier. The prose edition of these same ordinances, dated to the first half of fourteenth century, confirms the continuing existence of the Jewish court a century after the first set of decrees, in a *taqqanah* to which we have already been introduced: "From here on out, no man among us is permitted, on pain of anathema, to make a complaint against his Jewish brother in any court [lit. house of justice], whether at the Gentiles' [court] or the Jews' [court], on Sabbath eve and holiday eve."[40] We learn a bit more about the sixteenth-century iteration of the rabbinic court, or at least its setting: in an ordinance from 1518, the authors note in passing that "the seats of justice" were located in the Great Synagogue, that is, the *beit din* met there.[41] It was still located there two decades later.[42] Beyond these off-handed references, however, we hear little about the workings of the rabbinic court.[43]

Ostensibly this *beit din* was a court in which judges understood not only the litigants' language but also their mind-set, their lifestyle, their religious practices, and, most important, the religious law that affected the ways in which Jews were supposed to deal with other Jews, whether in business or in family life. Nevertheless, although the Hebrew ordinances suggest that some Jews did seek out Jewish justice, the lack of internal evidence (i.e., from other Hebrew ordinances) and the placement of the "Gentile court" first in both versions of the aforementioned ordinance, alongside the lack of references to the Jewish court in the Latin records, all conspire to suggest that the secular court commonly won out when a Jew was deciding between the Venetian court or the *beit din*—or, at times, the two venues might have been accessed simultaneously.

What motivations could have compelled the Jews of Crete out of their (ostensible) social comfort zone to enter the Venetian domain?[44] The next section suggests some of these factors, both structural—the weakness of the Jewish judiciary, in contrast to the perceived efficiency, power, speed, and malleability of the Venetian court system—and socioemotional, including a sense of Venice's "neutrality" and the public nature of the secular court venue. These latter rationales are admittedly somewhat speculative. Yet they are drawn from a large body of recent scholarship on law and society deeply informed by legal anthropology, suggesting one more way in which Jewish choice was not wholly different than the decision-making mechanisms of non-Jewish litigants.

Institutional Weakness in the Beit Din

The *beit din* in Candia appears to have been a weak institution. The impotence and unimportance of the rabbinic court is suggested by the *taqqanah* addressed above. Even the authors of communal ordinances placed the Gentile court before their own. Perhaps the problem was an old one: rabbinic courts in pre-Venetian Crete may not have developed fully as a result of Byzantine policies that, though recognizing the corporate rights of Jewish communities, had first an ambivalent policy toward the *beit din* and later a negative one.[45] Justinianic Jewry-law "banned the Jewish judiciary," notes Amnon Linder, "but tacitly accepted Jewish jurisdiction in cases between Jews." At least in Constantinople, however, beginning "on some unspecified date" and until 1166 or so, "they established a special court for the Jews" under the aegis of the Byzantine magistrate responsible for the area comprising the Jewish Quarter. This effectively eliminated the possibility of a licit Jewish-run court. After the period of the specialized Byzantine court, Jews had to seek justice in the secular judicial system, though they were entitled to give an oath that did not run counter to Jewish belief.[46] It is possible that these restrictive Byzantine policies resulted in a weak and disorganized Jewish court that, though it existed in the first half of the thirteenth century, did not find a substantial footing during the first centuries of Venetian rule.

The notion of the Candiote *beit din*'s inherent weakness also finds support in the fact that the religious leadership often sought Venetian aid in the enforcement of their legislation, a subject taken up in Chapter 6. To be sure, the elite leadership could impose powerful social punishments, particularly excommunication and shaming. A typical example of this punishment scheme can be found in a Hebrew ordinance from among the rewritten decrees of Rabbi Tzedakah, dated to the first half of the fourteenth century. In this ordinance, titled "A decree that one may not encroach on his friend's territory and evict him from his home," the authors forbid a Jew seeking housing to offer a landlord an above-market rental price if a fellow Jew is already living in that apartment and if he has not sought prior permission from the current tenant.[47] Probably indicative of a severe housing shortage in the Jewish Quarter, the result of such offers had led lucky landlords to evict current tenants "within a day or two days" in order to rent at higher prices to new tenants.[48] This decree not only declares illegal the initial offering of a higher price point but also forbids anyone to live in a house where this has been done for a full year following the event.

The punishment is a declaration of anathema (*knas brakhah*, literally, "a penalty of a blessing," a euphemistic term for a curse), which is here described in detail. The community leaders must "gather the entire community together in one of the synagogues, and there his peer [the man who was evicted] should reveal to the community what he [the landlord] did, and he [the illegal renter] is called transgressor [lit. 'one who breaks through a fence'] within Israel, and there they must obligate every Jew to separate themselves from him. You shall not take part in his happy occasions, and do not come close to him in his time of mourning, and peace will be upon Israel."[49] The very public nature of this humiliation is spelled out: the intentional gathering of the whole community and bestowing on him an official status as a recognized lawbreaker or transgressor, known as one who "breaks through the fence."[50] This status is meant to act as a curse in itself, as it refers to a quotation from Ecclesiastes 10:8 in which one who "breaks through the fence, a serpent should bite him." He is publicly excommunicated, which means not only that he be exiled from religious venues but also that the community is meant to ostracize him at his life-cycle events: "happy occasions" refers to births and weddings, for example; "mourning" refers to burial and the week of *shivah*, when a mourner is regularly visited, fed, and cared for by fellow members of the community. He no longer deserves such treatment.

Although excommunication could be a powerful enforcement tool in a functioning community, it in no way offered a catchall solution. Social ostracism can only be as strong as a leadership's authority. If the flock chose to ignore the call for the ban, there was little that the *condestabulo* could do; indeed, this suggests that such ultimatums could actually be a sign of the weakness of its authors. Moreover, if members of the flock chose to take it upon themselves to excommunicate whomever they wanted, a problem addressed a number of times in *Taqqanot Qandiya*, the leadership's only recourse was a verbal reaffirmation that this power should be left to the *condestabulo* and a threat to publicly shame the individuals imposing the extralegal bans.[51] By 1527, even excommunication was deemed powerless without Venetian teeth. As is articulated explicitly in a *taqqanah* from that year, the *kehillah* announced that it sought governmental permission—in particular from the *gastaldo*, the town-crier—before it excommunicated Jews (discussed further in Chapter 6).[52]

Venetian Strengths

Where the Jews had recourse only to internal excommunication, Venice could use its bureaucrats, policing agents ("officers of the night"), prisons, and financial control to force a party to pay its fine or live up to its verdict. This is not to say that Venice was an Orwellian police state. Plenty of people fled their sentences, prompting angry *bandi* (town criers' proclamations) and threats of heavier fines for those harboring fugitives.[53] Men ordered to make payouts in civil court sometimes simply neglected to pass along the funds.[54] Nor was every case settled as soon as judgment was rendered, a feature of an open appeals system. But as compared to the Jewish community, Venice's enforcement was far more effective.

But there were other advantages to choosing Venetian justice. As Shatzmiller has suggested, there was always a certain pragmatic logic to choosing secular courts in general. In his estimation, Christian state courts expedited matters in a way that the Jewish court did not. Like other sovereigns' systems, Venice promised—and delivered—ready access to a regular court with levels of appeal. Indeed, the Venetian curia was a full-time institutional court, even going so far as running a circuit to the villages "when required."[55] Elisabeth Santschi has noted what she considered the relative speed with which the Cretan ducal court closed cases, for example, never taking more than two years from inquest to judgment during the criminal trials she explored; these cases were often concluded in a matter of days or weeks from the time of the initial complaint or crime.[56] In contrast, the *beit din* utilized judges who were the same men busy with many other aspects of communal leadership, not to mention their own businesses.[57] The ordinance against evicting a fellow Jew discussed above also hints at the inconsistency of access to the Jewish communal leadership. As they describe the proper way to punish one found guilty of causing such an illicit eviction, the signatories mandate that "the *condestabulo* or whichever of the appointed men [*memunim*] who is available on that day" should send out the call to gather the members of the *kahal*.[58] Despite their official positions, the community's very leaders were often unavailable, perhaps out of town on other business.

The regularity and consistency of the secular judiciary certainly provided an incentive for Jews across Christendom to choose to air their disputes in that venue. But Venetian justice was not wholly efficient or actually "professional." In fact, some of the greatest advantages that benefited Jews and other litigants in the Venetian judiciary were a product of its distinct legal flexibility, its judicial amateurism, and even its disorder. Venetian judges on Crete were given a great deal of judicial discretion in deciding cases. To be sure, Venice's own body of statutory law applied on Crete; indeed, its codification in the thirteenth century into the Statuta Venetorum was influenced by its guiding doge's own experience as the first duke of Crete.[59] But statutory law was only the beginning of any legal decision-making process. By the mid-thirteenth century, judges sent to serve a stint in the courts on Crete were explicitly instructed that, should they be unable to find a solution in Venetian statutory law, they should turn to precedent from similar cases (*de simile ad simile*), then to local custom or approved use (*consuetude*). If neither provided a solution, they should turn to their own best judgment (*bona conscientia*).[60] This recognition that statutory law was not enough stemmed from the Statuta itself. In its prologue, Doge Jacopo Tiepolo directed judges to use their best God-given reason, if statute, precedent, and customary law were insufficient.[61] Codified within the legal framework itself was the idea that the statutes would have but limited applicability in the long run.

Thus, the consideration of statutory law was one of a number of potentially valid approaches toward deciding legal matters, and a judge could quite easily rationalize putting statute aside for the sake of a wider sense of justice. As Edward Muir has put it, "Venetian law was more 'oracular' than guided by statute or precedent."[62] This "oracular" approach—in part an ideological rejection of the all-encompassing Roman law and its perceived papal and imperial ties—paved the way for Venice to deal flexibly with the legal circumstances they found in the colonies they annexed.[63] But such approaches were also highly malleable in the hands of smart litigants and their experienced procurators or advisors.

This malleability becomes all the more evident when we consider the nature of Venice's judges: they were almost all amateurs. Venetian judges (and governors, who acted as judges in appellate cases) were usually politicians little trained in legal minutiae, not professional jurists.[64] As James Shaw has noted, "The only requirement to become a judge was that candidates be of good patrician stock: there was no need for any formal training in law."[65] Noblemen were "amateur judges armed with a strong self-belief in their innate capacity for justice," and therefore needed neither education nor experience to guide them.[66] Patrician administrators and judges could and would use their own positions to further the position of kin, patrons, and clients.[67] A lack of expertise in the Statuta Venetorum, then, could be easily masked by recourse to local custom and one's own "best judgment." Indeed, it could be explained away as an example of judge's discretion, *arbitrium iudicis*, valued highly in the Venetian legal sphere. For Cretan Jews, the judge's own lack of expertise or professional dedication to "law" could offer significant benefit. The litigant could rely on forceful logical or emotional argumentation to sway a lay judge himself little versed in the technicalities of law and statute.

Initially, the system of amateur judges was built with the intent of preventing the accumulation of too much power among any one person or family within the nobility—a squarely intrapatrician problem. As a result, one of the key principles was that no judge could hold his post for too long.[68] A regular rotation of the bench meant that no single person or family could make the law a personal fiefdom. But this solution to an internal, elite problem also aided Jews and others who utilized the courts: regular turnover served to ensure that badly educated, bribable (or unbribable!), anti-Jewish, or otherwise poor-quality judges would not remain long in office.

Finally, Venice's appeals system benefited Crete's Jews because of its overlapping courts and long-lasting strings of litigation. If the speed of an individual suit incentivized litigants, as Santschi has suggested, the slowness of the overall litigative experience served in tension as a parallel incentive. As Edward Muir and Monique O'Connell have each emphasized, Venice's complicated jurisdiction could actually benefit non-elites, particularly low-status communities in the rural hinterlands of Venice and in the colonies. An appeals process facilitating a "semipermanent state of litigation" avoided a firm resolution against the rural populace and created space for these individuals and communities to negotiate with and maneuver against powerful oligarchs. The justice system became a locus in which they could exert their own agency despite low status—a "weapon of the weak," to use James Scott's expression.[69] A system that seemed primed to oppress them could instead be marshaled as a productive method of arbitration and negotiation.[70]

But we need not limit this discussion to those in the rural hinterland. Jews, in particular, were primed to marshal this system because of the multiple judicial outlets at their disposal. Particularly in civil suits, Jews could engage in forum shopping, choosing where to litigate in light of perceived best outcomes. Allowed to access the *beit din* should they choose, given their own court of first instance, and ultimately enabled to appeal ad infinitum (unless explicitly ordered otherwise, as very occasionally happened) before the duke, and even before the senate in the metropole, the unending series of litigative moments provided Jews with space to maneuver and negotiate—whether the fight was against the government itself, as in Muir's discussion, or against fellow Jews. Jewish individuals found in the very structure of the colonial apparatus—and indeed, in its complicated, overlapping, sometimes contradictory structures—methods through which to maximize their own utility.

The Benefit of Neutrality

A further factor attracting Jews to the Cretan colonial court had little to do with the particulars of the Venetian justice system itself but rather stemmed from a general consideration of the outsider nature of the secular court—that very same quality that made rabbinic authorities such as Ibn Adret uncomfortable. In a fairly small minority community where the socioeconomic elite play the roles of rabbis and judges, it would be difficult for someone going against the status quo to expect a fair hearing at the Jewish court. This problem is evident in other Jewish communities. In a sixteenth-century Italian case brought before a *beit din* in the northern Italian city of Ferrara, for example, a fight broke out "which turned largely on the question as to whether the case could be impartially tried in Ferrara" because of the power of one of the litigants. The banker Immanuel Norzi "wielded considerable influence" over the rabbis who would act as judges.[71] A significant concern was that if one side was a powerful elite, the rabbinic judges might be swayed. Yet even if in Candia neither side was as powerful as the banker Norzi, simple familiarity and widespread kinship ties among Jews in a fairly small, fairly endogamous community could breed just as much bias.

In contrast, a certain impartiality could be expected in secular court—not because the Venetian court system was inherently any more unbiased than that of the Jews but because the Venetian judges were not nearly as invested in the Jewish political and family wrangling that inevitably stood as the backdrop to many suits. Because he was an outside arbiter without insider biases, old enmities and favoritisms simply could not play a role when a Venetian judge decided a case between Jew and Jew. For members of the small community of patrician Venetians living in Candia, perhaps cliquish biases frustrated their own attempts at impartial justice in the ducal court, but as semi-outsiders, the Jews were almost paradoxically empowered by their liminal position.

It should be noted that Jewish recourse to Venice's courts reflects a strategy employed by many disputants involved in a variety of means of dispute resolution, particularly those seeking arbitrated settlements. Thomas Kuehn has articulated a similar point for Renaissance Italy, arguing that those seeking arbitration sometimes chose "distant, even unknown arbitrators (e.g., lawyers)" because they "might be more evidently neutral than closely related persons who, after all, had their own view of matters and their own interests."[72] But neutrality was not the only motivation when the chosen arbitrators belonged to the ruling majority class, as Lauren Benton argues in her discussion of the occasional Muslim use of Christian arbitrators (i.e., not in a court setting) to resolve disputes in post-Reconquest Aragon.[73] Although just as for Jews the use of a Christian authority ran counter to Muslim juristic opinion, for individuals Muslims, "the strategy made sense when litigants believed that judgments made by Christian elites would have greater legitimacy and possibility of enforcement."[74] Access to a "foreign" legal system, or at least to its judges and arbitrators, offered medieval Muslims and Jews alike a mechanism by which they could call upon not only a more neutral party but one who also had the status and authority of sovereign power behind him.

Social Emotions and Public Shame

In theory, the goal of justice necessitates the choosing of a neutral arbiter. For premodern (and likely modern) people, however, the goal in seeking arbitration and airing disputes was not necessarily impartial justice. Legal anthropologists, who explore the human, cultural, and often emotional elements of jurisprudence, argue that humans have long manipulated court systems to protect their own interests and to act out power struggles that, strictly speaking, have little to do with the contemporary notion of "justice." As some scholars have concluded, "Courts must have been of some use for the disputants; we should not assume that people went to court out of a disinterested love for the law."[75] Looking at those who "consumed" the justice offered by the courts of medieval Marseille, Daniel Lord Smail has asked why late medieval litigants would have chosen to replace their vendetta-oriented systems for pursuing conflict with a formal case pleaded before a royal official.[76] In answering this, he has emphasized the emotional benefits—imposing shame and humiliation on others, for example—afforded to those who chose to use Marseille's judiciary.

This suggests a final reason why Candiote Jews, like their Christian neighbors, brought disputes before the secular court system: it offered the opportunity to air grievances and to publicly impose shame and humiliation in a way that Jews perceived to be more satisfying and socially powerful than seeking Jewish justice. Smail has shown that the open courtroom in Marseille was quite literally open—it was centered in the city's markets, allowing anyone and everyone to hear the plaints brought before the judges.[77] Likewise in Candia, the ducal court was held outside in the Plateia, the central piazza of the city that housed all the major public buildings.[78]

The court's public nature, and its function as a site of well-attended entertainment, is made clear in a Hebrew ordinance from the first half of the fourteenth century. In a scathing critique of the Jews of Candia, the decree's authors detail the disinterest that many of the community's Jews had in attending Sabbath services. "We seek even ten men," the number necessary for a proper prayer quorum, "and we cannot find them in the synagogue to fulfill the law of prayer. They are causing the *Shekhinah*[79] to be angry at us because of their avoidance of being found in the house of God at the time of prayer."[80] Where, then, were these Jews if not in the synagogue? The authors answered this unambiguously: "Some head toward the vineyards and gardens and orchards, some head to the beaches to [watch] the *reed boats*,[81] and some head to the law courts, also in the markets and in the streets, without any purpose."[82] The law court, like the market or the beach, was a place to spend a relaxing or invigorating morning, where one could watch the latest case—or perhaps a serial drama, another round of appeal!—unfold just as easily as one could watch the boats enter Candia's harbor but with a more exciting plotline.

Thus, Venice's judiciary offered a very public venue for the pursuit of emotional satisfaction. Court proceedings were truly a public spectacle in which a claimant could openly impugn an opponent's reputation and present the most sympathetic account of his or her own self-narrative. The audience could hear and remember this version, no matter in whose favor the court officially decided, and then spread these stories and social judgments to friends and acquaintances. As a result, a defendant might technically win the case against him but lose social and maybe even financial credit—trust in his word and deed—among the wider community. The legal courtroom thus doubled as a court of public opinion, influencing social standing within the Jewish community (and likely beyond) in a way that only loosely correlated to the strict legal outcome. The ability to present a case not only to the judges but to an active audience of peers—Jewish and not—may have thus aided Jews in their decision making when they chose to try their cases in Venice's colonial court.

Jewish Legal Rationalizations

In making the decision to litigate in the colonial judiciary, the Jewish individuals of Venetian Crete—and their leaders—clearly did not believe themselves to be transgressing Jewish law. One loophole familiar from the halachic opinion of the Ashkenazi authority Rashi (d. 1105, Troyes) and the Catalan sage Nachmanides (d. 1270, Acre) permits a Jew to take his coreligionist to the secular court if the *beit din* cannot compel the defendant to appear before it. Maimonides (d. 1204, Fustat) codified into his law code a more lenient perspective: that as long as the *beit din* approved the behavior, and gave its permission, one could sue his coreligionist in the secular court.[83] The nonchalant language of *Taqqanot Qandiya* alongside the variety of Jewish defendants found in the ducal court in Candia suggests that this community had no notion that only recalcitrant defendants could be dragged to the secular judiciary. Perhaps they assumed a blanket acceptance of the practice by the *beit din*, in a sort of expansion of Maimonides' type of answer. But if this is true, it needs further consideration: how could the Candiote *beit din* rationalize such behavior whole cloth?

Perhaps the Jews of Venetian Crete, as the Jewish community in Venice itself in later centuries, had an atypically capacious understanding of the Talmudic maxim coined by the sage Samuel: "dinah de-malkhutah dinah," or "the law of the land is [valid] law."[84] This principle is understood by the rabbis to mean that, in specific cases (namely property and business law), Jews living as minority subjects must adhere to the legal structures of their secular rulers.[85] The rabbis limited the legitimacy of secular rulers' laws by juxtaposing this principle against another concept, *hamsanutah de-malkah*, or "the robbery of the king": if a law was deemed by the Jewish establishment to be arbitrary or unethical, or if a royal whim undermined the laws on the books, Jews could safely (at least in a religious context) ignore the mandate.[86] This principle of *dinah de-malkhutah dinah* was usually applied broadly to obligatory secular laws, such as taxation, sanitation, and real estate laws. As the famed fourteenth-century Catalonian rabbi Nissim Gerondi (the Ran) wrote, when it came to secular taxation, "the question needs no deliberation, for certainly concerning tax matter we follow the custom," that is, the local secular law, "even if it is unlawful [according to Jewish law] [*she-lo ka-din*]."[87]

That Jews in the Venetian milieu accepted a wider reading is known to us from a century later in the metropole. The rabbinic leadership of Venice in the sixteenth century was notoriously flexible in interpreting Jewish law according to the precept of *dinah de-malkhutah dinah*, stretching the authority of their Christian sovereign government beyond the usual bounds of the maxim. The Venetian rabbinical response to the phenomenon of Jews testating in the Venetian style, as explained by Howard Tzvi Adelman, provides a compelling example.[88] As in the Candiote case, Venetian testaments "departed from Jewish tradition both in that they were made before Christian notaries and also that they were based on the principle of granting a bequest rather than following traditional lines of succession."[89] Yet Venice-based rabbis overwhelmingly defended the practice, some citing it as an example of "the law of the land" and therefore binding—despite the fact that Jews were not obligated to testate in this way. Some rabbis even went so far as to claim that it had become in itself a Jewish custom by extremely common use and, as such, was subject to the complicated Talmudic concept that "custom takes precedence over law" (*minhag mevatel halakhah*).[90]

Utilizing the concept of *dinah de-malkhutah dinah* was in no way obvious in the case of testaments; as mentioned above, the precept usually applied only to obligatory secular laws, and the Venetian testament undermined traditional Jewish (male) succession lines. Yet the communal benefits of the secular testament were seen as so vast that the rabbis co-opted halachic language in order to legitimate it. This was not a uniform practice; in direct contrast to the Venetian case, when rabbis in the Ottoman Empire were asked to judge the merit of these wills (for example, in cases where a male member of the family was left out of a will and wanted to press for a portion of the inheritance based on Jewish inheritance law), they often threw them out, arguing that secular wills had absolutely no standing.[91]

But across the Mediterranean, internal legalistic language was used by the Venetian rabbis to validate the use of local, secular practices. The Talmudic idea dictating that "the law of the land is law" provided a loophole for the Venetian Jewish communal leadership. This principle enabled them to benefit from what they must have seen as convenient, and even superior, methods of transmitting significant wealth and goods from one generation to the next. In these cases, the use of the Venetian standard, in place of the equally available Jewish standard, must have seemed to confer better benefits, because of the reasons addressed above.

Moreover, Venetian flexible judicial procedure and its emphasis on "justice" over a singular law code (as reflected in the judge's oath and its reliance on local law and *bona conscientia*) or a singular language allowed Jews to enter the courtroom without anxiety that they would have to leave Jewish law behind. Generally, Jews understood that—to quote a *taqqanah* from 1527—"according to the power that we have from our sovereign, [we are] able to act according to our religion and our customs," even if, often, they still needed Venetian permission for certain behaviors (in this particular case in the *Taqqanot*, intra-Jewish excommunication).[92]

The Jewish right to maintain traditional Jewish customs extended specifically into the Candiote courtroom, where they knew they would not need to make blasphemous statements in oaths or break Jewish marriage laws by accepting Venetian judgments. When Joseph Ferer swore an oath to care for (i.e., act as legal *tutor* for) his orphaned granddaughters before the ducal court in 1415, he swore that he would care for the children according to Venetian statutory law. But the oath itself was done according to Jewish law—*secundum legem moysi*—with the understanding that only such a vow would be binding

on a Jew.[93] Beyond keeping oaths, Venice promised Jews that when they came
to its colonial courts, they would be able to have the judges adjudicate according to their own ancestral personal law—particularly marriage and divorce
law, a topic the next chapter takes up at length. Undoubtedly this sense that
Venetian judges did not aim to uproot Jewish law, but at times to support it,
made Cretan Jews more comfortable to enter the secular judiciary—and likely
gave them a sense of empowerment to shape the legal narrative by defining
Jewish law for the court.

Like other areas of Venetian judicial culture, this right to adjudication
according to Jewish law was at times a powerful weapon and, at times, highly
arbitrary. The reality of appeals could intersect awkwardly with extreme
judicial discretion in the lower courts. For example, in the mid-fourteenth
century, in Negroponte, another Venetian colonial center of Jewish life, a
family of Jewish serfs called the Galimidis believed that they could wield
the right for Jews to live according to Jewish law—here referred to as "the
law of Moses"—to gain freedom from their Jewish masters, the Kallomitis.[94]
Members of the serf family, owned since the 1260s (over seven decades), sued
for freedom in the court of the *bailo*, the Venetian colonial governor and
highest judge, knowing that he was empowered to make decisions according
to local and ethnic custom. Likely with the prodding of the Galimidis, the
bailo looked to Jewish law to adjudicate this dispute and decided according
to his understanding of biblical precedent (the law of the Hebrew slave in
Exodus 21:1–6) that a Jew had to free his Jewish slave after seven years. The
Galimidis were free. Unfortunately for the newly freed serf family, however,
the Kallomitis were not satisfied with this ruling and appealed it all the way
up to Venice's supreme court. There, the judges of the Quarantia decided that
biblical precedent was not what they had meant when they said that local
judges could decide based on local custom. In fact, they stated, this use of
biblical precedent was against God and justice, against the laws and customs
(*ordines et consuetudines*) of Negroponte, and was even against the commission of the *bailo*. The Quarantia thus overturned the Galimidi family's free
status, sending them back to their coreligionist masters.

In Crete, in contrast, the limits of adjudication according to Jewish law
were far clearer to both judge and litigants: only in cases regarding marriage
and divorce did Jewish law apply. But the nature of litigation here—the
knowledge of what Jewish law and Jewish custom could make for compelling
arguments, alongside the ability to consistently appeal, the public nature of

the courtroom making the "court of public opinion" a second social judge and jury, and the other facets of forum shopping explored above—further facilitated Jewish choice to litigate in the secular courtroom.

* * *

The Venetian justice system was undoubtedly complicated but could be molded to meet many of the needs of those who used it—noble, citizen, and subject alike. To be sure, bringing suit was not cheap, and thus one had to be solvent to take real advantage of the civil court. Yet the very structure of the system and the evolving notion of justice for subjects ensured that it was not only patricians who could gain from access to Venice's councils and courts. Subjects, too, gained significant control over their disputes by marshaling Venetian justice. This was surely, in part at least, an intentional by-product—a visible piece of propaganda on which the Republic could carry through and show its benevolence, securing loyalty and social quiet. This imperial pragmatism thus served colonizer and subject, facilitating a symbiotic relationship that could empower both even within the decidedly uneven power dynamic that defined the colonial environment.

That is to say, if justice was a propaganda piece, it successfully met its goal of attracting those at whom the campaign was aimed. Although the intentions of the Venetian patriciate in providing access to justice and flexible law were not nearly as pure as their ideological mouthpieces would have their readers believe, the subjects who utilized their judiciaries could nevertheless harness the power of the court for their own needs, benefits, and motivations. Such was the case with Jewish subjects across the dominions, including the Jewish community on Crete and in other colonies.[95] The Venetian colonial administration of Crete thought that the bestowal of justice promoted a pacified populace; but pacified did not mean passive. And if Crete's Jews were certainly pacified in one sense—willing to accommodate and facilitate the Venetian political project on the island—they can only be characterized as active facilitators of their own legal and social fate, both on a grand scale (e.g., sending embassies to Venice) and on an individual scale, through lawsuits against family, neighbor, and business partner alike. Jews used Venice's colonial court because they believed they could achieve their desired outcomes in the courtroom in ways they could not via the Jewish judiciary, with its particular rules and judges.

But in noting that Jews chose this path, it is essential to stress that they did not deem their behavior religiously transgressive, nor did their leaders, despite the many decades (if not centuries) of Jewish and scholarly conventional wisdom that has treated such behavior as outside acceptable bounds. We must revisit our assumptions about how rank-and-file, "typical" Jews did and did not act within the confines of their normative Jewish behavior. Perhaps the claims of medieval rabbis' aversion to the use of secular courts are overblown. To be sure, location matters. The prohibitions of Ashkenazi rabbis in German lands, such as those of Meir of Rothenberg, were far more adamant, and far more concerned with the unjust behavior of the courts themselves than with the resulting behavior of Jewish litigants. Perhaps Ashkenazi Jews did mostly stay within the Jewish court system as a result. In the Mediterranean world, however, even old evidence can produce a new narrative. As Elka Klein has illustrated, scholarly references to Ibn Adret's anti-court statements have overstated the man's own behavioral practices: not only does Ibn Adret's writings in other places seem to prohibit only certain types of Jewish use of secular courts, but Ibn Adret himself brought suit against another Jew in the royal court in Barcelona, in his capacity as guardian of an orphan![96] Certain kinds of cases, then, were less problematic than others, and even Ibn Adret understood that reality sometimes necessitated outside intervention.

The medieval Jews of Candia did not strictly limit their use of the Venetian courtroom to issues safely outside the purview of Jewish law. In fact, Jews found a way to directly bring Jewish law into the secular courtroom, particularly in the space of personal law of marriage and divorce, a form of "customary law" that obtained for Jews in the Venetian courtroom. But this was not the only frame in which Jewish legal and social ideas encountered and engaged with Venetian legal and social contexts, even when both claimant and defendant were Jews. In the following two chapters, then, we will explore the ways in which the rationalizations set out in this chapter took on a life of their own, both for Jews in unhappy marriages and for the very leaders of the *kehillah*, using the secular court as a venue to litigate over intracommunal fights.

Chapter 5

Marriage on Trial

Among the hundreds of Jewish litigants who appeared before the duke's judicial bench, Elea Mavristiri stands out for sheer tenacity. Over a quarter century in the later 1300s, she came before the ducal court twelve times. Like many of the Candiote Jews we met in the previous chapter, she used the court to fight both Jews and Christians, relatives and business contacts alike, litigating over breached contracts, refusal of owed payment, and unfulfilled work agreements. Others sued her, making similar allegations of moneys owed.[1] In some ways, Elea Mavristiri acted atypically among Candiote Jews. Twelve appearances at the ducal court—and ostensibly many more at the Curia Prosoporum, the court of first instance for Greeks and Jews—ranks among the highest number of any individual Jew, particularly since these appearances represent many different suits. In one instance, her constant appeals even led a frustrated judiciary to condemn her to "perpetual silence," ending that particular case.[2] She was clearly frustrated with her circumstances, too. Elea took a step at some point in her life that appears exceptionally unusual among the Jews of Candia: abandoned by her father, the unscrupulous businessman Liacho Mavristiri, and divorced by her prominent husband, Solomon Astrug, she sought community elsewhere, making the drastic decision to become a Christian known as Maria Cornario. But the litigation continued after Elea/Maria's baptism, and it was Solomon who often drove Elea/Maria to seek court intervention both as a Jew and as a Christian, and both while he was Elea's estranged husband and then later as Elea/Maria's ex-husband.

Although after the previous chapter we may not find it surprising that Elea, qua woman, came before the ducal court, we may still find it noteworthy that Elea used the secular judiciary to litigate over issues of marriage and divorce. Let us remember that we are immersing ourselves in a world without a concept of secular or civil marriage.[3] All marriage took place under religious auspices, and divorce was allowed for Jews but not for the Latin Venetians. Here was a locus in which Jews and Christians could not encounter one another; there was simply no mechanism for Jews and Christians to marry. They could have sex, as we have seen happened among doctors, widows, and prostitutes alike. But marriage was something different.

So was divorce. Rabbinic theory deemed it essential to keep divorce inside the community. Although the rabbis often affirmed the validity of secular legal instruments for Jews (such as business contracts), and marriage contracts often appear in Latin (as discussed below), Jewish law explicitly prohibited Jews from using a secular mechanism of divorce, such as writing up a divorce agreement—a contract that enacted a status change and did not just reflect one—before a Latin notary.[4] In addition, although a Jewish divorce must be initiated by the husband and the divorce writ (the *get*) given by a husband to his wife, by the Middle Ages, the *get* needed to be produced through, mediated by, and approved by the *beit din*. In some high and late medieval Jewish communities, in fact, divorcing couples needed the consent of multiple rabbinic authorities from multiple communities.[5] The *beit din* thus played a mandatory role in Jewish divorce. We might therefore expect that marriage and divorce litigation remained outside the purview of the secular court and stayed primarily under the jurisdiction of the *beit din*—especially if we consider that marriage litigation generally fell to ecclesiastical courts in Christian contexts, too.

Let us add one more stipulation: to be sure, one might assume that Elea's decision to convert renders her an unusual case. Perhaps hers were the actions of a pariah who did not care about rabbinic convention but simply took advantage of the fact that Venice generally assumed that men and women ought to have equal access to justice.[6] Perhaps she was simply an "immodest" woman, to mimic the language of Solomon ibn Adret, who deemed modesty a major reason for women to refrain from litigation.[7] Perhaps Elea was simply careless about airing her most private dirty laundry, already intent on leaving the Jewish community and caring only for the funds she could take with her in her new life.

All of these assumptions prove incorrect. Most basically, Elea Mavristiri's divorce was done through proper Jewish channels, as both she and her ex-husband attested, and it was not until years later that she chose baptism. But beyond Elea's own life story, the fact that she sought resolution at the secular court of Candia is not in any way unique among the town's Jewish women. Women were regular consumers of Venetian colonial justice. Even the colonial

administration recognized that a significant number of the Jews who brought
claims were women: the town crier's proclamation from 1321 that limited the
number of supporters a Jewish litigant could bring along to court explicitly
addressed both male and female claimants, *iudeus vel iudea*.[8]

Furthermore, although Jewish women were involved in suits of all types,
Jewish women most often initiated marriage- and divorce-related litigation.
In fact, among the over 160 intra-Jewish lawsuits visible in the ducal court
records, over twenty-five of these disputes revolve around marriage and
divorce. Most of these lawsuits (and indeed, every single one of the initial
petitions that sparked first rounds of litigation) came from female petitioners,
and as far as we can tell, when it came time to litigate, these Jewish women
generally presented their own cases.

Some of these female claimants were already divorced according to Jewish legal practices and hoped the secular court could force an ex-husband to
hand over funds owed to Jewish divorcees. But many were not divorcees. Many
women who came before the ducal court were unhappily married because their
husbands were negligent, abusive, absent, or mishandling their dowries and
dotal assets. Some were "imperfectly married," to coin a term: they claimed
their grooms refused to go through with a full marriage after a legally binding
(at least according to Jewish law) betrothal contract had been signed. They
were not totally married according to Jewish law but were not able to discard
their betrothal and marry other men without legal intervention. These women,
whether betrothed or fully married, did not seek resolution through a litigated
divorce—the secular court could not offer such a service. Some imperfectly
married women wanted the court to force the fiancé-husband or his family to
return dowry money. Others hoped that litigation would convince the absentee
man to actually marry his betrothed quasi-wife according to Jewish ritual.

Often, though, unhappily married Jewish women were looking for resolution through another mechanism more familiar to scholars of Catholic
marriage, or modern life: a legal separation. This formal category, also known
as "separation of bed and board," set the stage for a payout of alimony and a
living stipend.[9] It could be demanded and collected from a husband, his family, or another agent—an important caveat, since many a negligent husband
could not actually be brought to court, often because he was either running
from debtors or because he was happily (and bigamously) married to another
wife elsewhere in the Mediterranean. If the *beit din* could not get these women
a complete divorce, an "imperfect divorce" (as the separation of bed and board

is sometimes known) would have to do. The ducal court thus had power to order payouts, providing an alternative to divorces that these unhappy wives could not obtain or perhaps did not want.

Both Jewish law and the legal principles that underpinned the state legal codes of late medieval Christendom assumed that female modesty would keep women out of the courts. Both were mistaken, or at least oriented toward a prescriptive, and not descriptive, perspective.[10] But women, Jewish and Christian alike, were able to play on this assumption. As this chapter argues, female litigants (to be sure, ostensibly with the help of their legal teams) managed to wield these and other assumptions about women's roles and gender ideals as weapons in their fight to convince courts of the justice of their causes.

As this consilience of Jewish and secular Christian law suggests, bringing gendered family law into the secular courtroom involved a meeting of legal spheres. In fact, Venice facilitated this overlapping of legal jurisdictions in precisely this realm of law. When Jews brought cases that engaged with marriage or divorce practices, the Venetian Catholic colonial judges were mandated to adjudicate according to Jewish law. Thus when Elea Mavristiri or other Jewish women sued their husbands, the judges had to ascertain what Jewish law demanded (or what they believed Jewish law demanded) in each case.

But these judges were, of course, themselves Catholic and, although amateur judges with no specific legal training, they were generally educated in—and sensitive to—the Catholic and Roman-law-inflected legal and social milieus. Apparently aware of this, Jewish women—and men, too—accessed conceptions of marriage and divorce, gender roles, and social expectations more familiar from these non-Jewish contexts. This chapter, then, continues the discussion of the ways in which Jewish residents of Candia intentionally engaged with non-Jews and non-Jewish society by arguing that, in the courtroom, Jewish women and men not only brought Jewish law and Roman-law-inflected state law together when useful but also, in crafting arguments, utilized typical legal strategies and displayed their familiarity with Christian notions of marriage, divorce, and womanhood. Finally, this chapter peels back another layer of the complexity of Candiote Jewish society, as seen through marital challenges, their social causes, and gendered responses. Marriage, deemed by many the last bastion of nonacculturation among medieval Jews, was thus actually subject to, and part of, the common discourse shared by Jews and Christians alike; law, gender systems, and their points of overlap became primary vocabularies of this shared discourse.

Translating Jewish Law in the Secular Court

The Talmud articulates the mechanisms of Jewish marriage as a transaction: "A woman is acquired through three things," write the rabbinic authors of the second-century law code, the Mishnah, "through money, a contract, or intercourse."[11] Though one of the three options was an actual written contract, over time, all elements of the marriage process took on contractual significance. Even the betrothal agreement between two parties, before the actual marriage, carried legal weight, conferring a new status upon the woman as a "married woman," unable to engage in sexual intercourse with another man without committing adultery.[12]

As Michael Berger notes, "Talmudic marriage was essentially of a legal, not sacral, nature," a fact "most evident in the requirement of a marriage document."[13] This marriage document, the *ketubbah*, obligates a husband to provide his wife with food, clothing, and conjugal rights. The importance of the *ketubbah* particularly lies in its provisions for the wife should the marriage end in divorce or the death of the husband. In these cases, the *ketubbah* contracts the return of the wife's dowry, plus an additional amount of money from the husband's estate that was supposed to be set aside for this potential purpose at the beginning of the marriage. Essential to understanding the importance of such a payment is the fact that halacha directs all of the husband's inheritance to his children, and none to the wife; the *ketubbah* thus provides all of the support she would get from her husband's estate.[14] Rabbinic marriage, however, does protect the woman's right to maintain the title to property she brought into the relationship and to sell it if she so desires. In the eyes of the Talmudic authors, the *ketubbah*'s role was explicitly to protect women; the mechanisms of financial payment would ensure that a husband did not "regard it as easy to divorce her."[15]

This concern to limit easy divorce evolved because of biblical and rabbinic understandings of divorce, which dictated that only a husband could initiate and carry out a divorce. Deuteronomy 24:1 is explicit in the matter, and the rabbis found no way to mitigate the unidirectionality: "A man takes a wife and possesses her. She fails to please him because he finds something obnoxious about her, and he writes her a bill of divorcement, hands it to her, and sends her away from his house." The Mishnah suggests a wide variety of opinions regarding the situations in which a man is allowed to divorce his wife; while some rabbis demanded divorce in situations of sexual misconduct or physical repulsion, others enabled a man to divorce his current wife simply if he had found someone else whom he would prefer.[16] In contrast, the Talmud limited to very few cases the reasons for which a wife could ask the *beit din* to compel her husband to divorce her.[17] Therefore, within the rabbinic framework, the husband must grant the wife a divorce, in the form of a written divorce decree, the *get*; the wife remains legally quite passive in this process. Marriage is a contractual agreement based on joint consent; the rabbinic divorce procedure, though male initiated, is the only means by which the marriage contract could be canceled.

Because contract claims were a commonplace of civil litigation, the contractual nature of Jewish marriage provided Jewish women on Crete with a familiar language when they litigated over it in the secular courtroom. In 1370, Cali Chersoniti of Castronovo (the fortress town not too far from Candia) sued her almost-husband Peres Stamati, from the same town. A valid Jewish marriage had been contracted between the two of them according to Jewish rite (*secundum ritum iudeorum*), Cali contended. But then, before carrying through with the actual nuptials, the ostensible groom went and contracted marriage with another girl. "Girl" is the mot juste here, since the new bride was identified by Cali as a young girl—about seven years old. As a result, Peres refused to marry Cali. Her request in this case was to have the court force Peres to take Cali as a bride "secundum formam pactorum suorum"—that is, according to the terms of the betrothal contract they had signed.[18]

Peres's rebuttal relied equally on the contractual nature of the marriage. After noting that in fact he and Cali were not even able to speak for this contract, since indeed their respective fathers had made the marriage contract in the first place, he claimed that the fathers agreed to cancel the marriage contract and that he and Cali had indeed also agreed to call off their marriage. After examining the evidence, the court sided with Cali, noting that the contract never appeared to have been canceled.

Cali was empowered to sue the man who shamed her by contracting marriage with her and then marrying a child because she was able to frame the emotional (and financial) violation against her as a breach of contract. The importance of the contractual nature of marriage, and the potential for the contract to be interrogated in court, appears to have been recognized widely; though the court seems to have accepted Hebrew-language contracts in general, some Jews chose to write up marriage contracts in both Hebrew and Latin, as did a couple named Stamata and Joseph, who appeared before the ducal court in the early decades of the fifteenth century, no longer happily wed.[19] Many Jewish betrothal contracts—a legal agreement preceding marriage, in which two parties (usually the parents of the bride and groom) agree to a future marriage, outline the potential dowry and other gifts, and generally set a date by which the actual marriage must take place—appear in Crete's Latin notarial registers. In creating these Latin betrothal contracts, the Jews of Candia engaged in a practice familiar from Venice's notarial record and used, in variation, across the broader northern Italian context.[20]

But it was not these binding agreements, familiar to the Venetian judges, that the court used as a deciding factor in the case between Cali Chersoniti and Peres Stamati. After agreeing to Cali's contract-based argument, they next pointed out that Peres had continued with the betrothal long enough to take possession of Cali's dowry and to exchange further marriage gifts; the couple had gone so far as to exchange rings. The court explicitly understood that the exchanging of rings constituted marriage "according to the rite and custom of the Jews" (*secundum ritum et consuetudinem iudeorum*). As such, the marriage could not simply be dissolved by reference to an invalidated contract, as Peres had claimed.

Claiming Jewish Law's Jurisdiction

Notably, in the case of Cali and Peres, it was the court that refused to frame the question simply as a matter of contract law. To be sure, they did find for Cali, judging that the betrothal contract itself was still valid. But they recognized that marriage was constituted not only in the realm of the written word but also in a whole host of other ritualized behaviors. They noted that an exchange of goods in the form of dowry, other gifts, and in particular rings (which had come to represent the Mishnaic notion of acquiring a wife through money) had indeed taken place, and thus they could not relegate their judgment to a simple matter of contracts.

Both Cali, in highlighting the validity of the marriage contract as some-thing done "according to the Jewish rite," and the judges, in moving beyond the claim of a breach of contract, were calling on the legal principle set down in Venice's Cretan system that Jews should be able to live according to their own law in cases of marriage and divorce. Specifically, Venetian judges were instructed to allow Jews to uphold their ancient law (known as the "Law of Moses," *lex moisis*, or the "rite/s of the Jews," *ritus iudeorum*, among other variations) in cases related to marriage and divorce. As we will see, Cretan Jews certainly knew of this accommodation by the mid-fourteenth century. But a further formal precedent, used later by litigants, was set out by 1400 by Cretan duke Albanus Baduario, who made it explicit that "Jews are able to act according to their rites" for marriage and divorce.[21] Divorce, of course, was not allowed by the Latin Church, but Jews were entitled to legally engage in divorce if they followed the traditional Jewish processes. The key point here is that Jews were not mandated to follow their own laws only in their own court system, as they were under Jewry law in Germanic areas, but were entitled (and indeed, obligated) to have Jewish law's jurisdiction obtain when litigating before the Venetian judiciary.[22]

The knowledge that Venice's judges were sensitive to Jewish law and custom regarding marital crises produced a situation in which the claim of Jewish law's jurisdiction became a common defense. Such was the circumstance during the defense of a lawsuit brought by Elea Mavristiri in one of her early litigative moments, in November 1359.[23] She was in the midst of indirectly suing her father, Liacho Mavristiri. By that time he had moved to the island of Rhodes and was thus represented by a relative and procurator, the Jew Samuel.

The slightly convoluted backstory is as follows: Liacho, an unscrupulous but sometimes successful businessman (we met him earlier negotiating an illegal land sale for the Greek Kalergi family), had recently married a Jewish widow named Eudochia Plumari. The prospect of this marriage had apparently caused the family much aggravation. In fact, four years earlier, in 1355, Elea had convinced Eudochia's brother-in-law Mordachai Plumari to sign a Latin contract in which he had sworn never to give permission for a marriage between Liacho and Eudochia, his brother's widow. Should a marriage occur, he had promised to pay Liacho's daughter Elea an extremely large fine of 7,000 hyperpera. Somehow, however, Mordachai Plumari was cajoled by Liacho— even from his faraway perch on Rhodes—to ignore the contract he had made with Elea and to give permission for the nuptials. The marriage took place.

If Mordachai Plumari was at fault, how did this evolve into a case against Liacho's agent? Mordachai Plumari had not paid Elea the fine for allowing the marriage to go through, and Elea had successfully sued him for the money in the Curia Prosoporum, the colonial court of first instance for Jews and Greeks. She won her case in January 1359. By November, however, Mordachai had not paid his debt, and thus Elea appeared at the ducal court to press for her payment. But her tactic was different now. Her father, Liacho, was already in debt to his new brother-in-law Mordachai (likely it was Mordachai's money that made the marriage so appealing to Liacho). Therefore, instead of attempting to get the money out of Mordachai directly, Elea petitioned to have the court force her father (through his procurator) to pay her from the money he owed to Mordachai.

This labyrinthine case is not about marriage; it concerns first and foremost a breach of contract, and second, the unsuccessful collection of a fine already imposed by a Venetian court. Marriage is secondary, if not simply irrelevant, to this round of litigation. Liacho's procurator, however, attempted to utilize the court's attention to Jewish law in the case of marital rulings as a defense. He announced that the permission to marry Eudochia Plumari was valid, "according to the Law of Moses" (*secundum legem moisi*). He concluded with a statement that offers us the clearest Jewish articulation of this personal law principle found in these sources: "The law of Moses was divine, according to which [law] the Jews are ruled in their marriages, and the temporal ruler must govern the Jews [through it], namely by their laws and rites, and by the power of these personal privileges that the *universitas* of the Jews had."[24]

It is clear that the procurator-agent Samuel knew that this was not, strictly speaking, a lawsuit about marriage. That is why he followed this initial line of defense with a second rationalization, claiming that Liacho and Mordachai had no financial connection and that Elea had mischaracterized the original contract. As a result, he claimed, Liacho should not have to pay Elea for Mordachai's potential wrongdoings. Samuel's first argument, however, appealed to this realm of the Jewish law, which seems to have become a catchall defense whether or not the facts of the case precisely applied.

The court, importantly, was not convinced. Nor were they tripped up by Samuel's use of the "Jewish law" argument, just as they did not limit their judgment of Cali Chersoniti and Peres Stamati's marriage contract case to the contractual frame the claimants attempted to utilize. They found in favor of Elea, awarding her 1,000 hyperpera from Liacho's estate.[25]

Drawing the Boundaries of Jewish Law's Jurisdiction

Venice was one of a number of medieval polities to consider Jewish law and custom in its own jurisprudence, a fact that must have played a role in attracting Jews to its courtrooms. Scholars have pointed to a few other medieval polities that, at least to some degree, did the same. In the thirteenth and fourteenth centuries, Castile, Aragon, and Navarre also adjudicated according to Jewish law in family or marital matters, and the Jews who litigated in these secular courts expected halacha to obtain.[26] In this Iberian context, at times the courts were instructed by the crown to consult with the sages of the Jewish community in order to come to a resolution that would be considered religiously valid in the eyes of rabbinic experts.[27]

Though it seems that the Candiote court did not turn to local rabbinic experts—at least, we have no evidence for this practice in Crete—the judges were nevertheless serious about coming to conclusions that they believed squared with authentic Jewish law. In pronouncing judgment in a marriage suit brought by a Jewish woman in 1406, the duke and his councillors announced that in assessing the case, they had to consider Jewish law, and in particular, had to examine the provisions of the Jewish marriage gift, given according to Jewish law.[28] A later appeal of the same case once again reiterated and emphasized the court's responsibility to consider Jewish law if both parties remain alive.[29] The degree of autonomy granted to Jewish marriage law by the Venetian judiciary, however, was highly constrained, even within the boundary of cases understood by the ducal court as marriage-law cases. The stipulation in the case above—that consideration of Jewish law only applies when both parties are living—illustrates this limited scope. The judges stressed that should the wife die first and/or die intestate, the court should then adjudicate on the basis of Venetian law, ostensibly because the case would cease to be one that deals with marriage and instead would become an issue of inheritance—a lucrative area the colonial government retained for its own jurisdiction.[30]

This respect for Jewish marriage law even extended to instances when it directly clashed with canon law. In a 1409 ruling, the court noted that some Jewish practices "differ from the rites of the Christians" but that, despite this fact, the court could not impede the practice of Jewish law—a tenet of the precedent set in 1400 by Duke Baduario.[31] This certainly included the Jewish right to divorce but could even allow bigamy. But emphasizing that some Jewish customs could only be undertaken within the rabbinic structure, the court recognized its own limited jurisdiction over Jewish divorce, at times even admitting that it had no jurisdiction to make certain decisions.[32] It is to this complicated arena of divorce that we turn next.

Divorce, Jewish Law, and Secular Jurisdiction

The ducal court and Jews alike understood that Jewish law itself limited the court's jurisdiction. Jews could not be married or divorced by the secular judges but rather only could have marriages and divorces that had been solemnized under the auspices of the Jewish legal system upheld. Claims for legal separation—which will be addressed later in this chapter—were a safe zone; the court did not have to consider a status change under Jewish law but rather created a nonreligious, essentially financial status category. Likewise post-divorce cases, which simply involved the enforcement of already decided financial settlements. Cases in which divorce was involved, though, complicated the court's consideration of the *ritus iudeorum*. Most of the time, it seems, Jews respected this division of jurisdiction and did not bring cases before the court that explicitly petitioned for the court to get involved in forcing a divorce. But occasionally arguments about what validated Jewish divorce made it into the courtroom. An investigation of these cases not only suggests a delicate dance played by Jews and judges alike but also reflects a sharing of knowledge and attitudes—whether conscious or not—between Jews and Christians regarding certain facets of marriage law.

Between 1443 and 1445, Abba Delmedigo and his wife, Potha, fought over the terms of a separation and divorce.[33] Abba, an elite member and elected leader of the Jewish community, claimed that Potha had defects that were unknown to him at the time of marriage, a rationale he used in his attempt to convince the court to compel Potha to come before rabbis somewhere "in the west" so as to end the marriage without having to pay financial recompense.[34] At first glance, it seems that Abba's reference to Potha's defects stems from the common tactic of attacking a woman's reputation.[35] But this claim carries heavier baggage. Although this is not made explicit, it seems that Abba was presenting the rabbinic concept of a fraudulent marriage, *kiddushei ta'ut*, a well-known example of which occurs when a spouse enters into marriage without disclosing a serious physical defect (*mum*). From a rabbinic perspective, such nondisclosure is serious enough to invalidate the marriage, and if the wife carries the grave defect, the husband need not pay out her contracted *ketubbah* money upon divorcing her.[36] But only a *beit din* qua religious experts can approve a claim that a defect constitutes a fraudulent marriage.

The case files only hint at the ways in which the early stages of this fight had escalated. Abba, it seems, desperately tried to convince a Venetian court that Crete did not have local rabbis with the necessary expertise to ascertain whether Potha had the requisite severity of defect. Perhaps he had already been turned down by his fellow Jewish leaders; perhaps his involvement in the community leadership caused him to desire a more neutral party. Either way, by 1443, an appeal had traveled all the way up to the Quarantia, Venice's supreme court back in the metropole; it refused Abba's claim that no local rabbis had enough expertise to deal with his case.[37] Nevertheless, all of the Venetian courts involved in this case refused to address the actual question of divorce, comfortably assigning such decision to expert rabbinical jurists, whether near or far. In this case, the judiciary understood the obligations of upholding the *ritus iudeorum* as entirely taking such decisions out of its hands.

This case underscores that the choice to litigate in the secular court did not mean a complete rejection of the Jewish legal system. After years of fighting between Potha and Abba Delmedigo over the nature and implications of her "defect," the ducal court's judgment in November 1445 (ordering Abba to pay her 150 hyperpera annually) seems to have convinced one or both halves of the unhappy couple to resolve the problem once and for all. An entry tucked after the last case records that the couple had managed to agree to terms of a complete Jewish divorce.[38] It seems likely that this case had been playing out simultaneously in multiple venues—that just as Abba brought his plaint before the ducal court, he was also trying to work through the *beit din* and probably through other Jewish family and friend networks.

It is likely that women and men sometimes used secular court litigation as a means to another end, perhaps divorce or reconciliation. The public shaming and public burden may have compelled intransigent spouses to change their minds. This would not surprise scholars of premodern disputes, who have long pointed to simultaneous modes of dispute resolution as a norm and to courtroom litigation as a vehicle for forcing an alternate settlement.[39] Moreover, taking legal action simultaneously at both a religious and a secular court during marital crises would not be atypical, as Joanne Ferraro has shown for sixteenth-century Venice.[40] The lack of *beit din* records from Crete certainly limits our ability to see the full panorama, but we cannot discount the idea that for many Jews, following parallel avenues would be the normal approach.

* * *

Only one case in these records demonstrates an activist Venetian court willing to push a Jewish husband toward divorce. In 1447, Fumia, a daughter of the well-known Politi family, came before the ducal court to seek assistance with her marriage, which had been something of a nonstarter.[41] She had married Avraghuli (Abraham) Mosca sometime before, but the marriage had never been consummated, and Mosca had never lived with her. He, in fact, had left Crete altogether for most of their marriage, and when he did come back for short visits, he would not stay with her. He would not give her a *get*, a Jewish divorce, but he also would not invest himself in the marriage on Crete. The social and religious embarrassment caused by such abandonment must have, in part, driven Fumia to the court. Perhaps more important, however, was the question of money: Avraghuli was in control of her substantial dowry. In its judgment, the court came as close as it could to forcing a divorce: the judges demanded that, should the husband not take back his wife and live with her in a normative married sense, he must give her a writ of divorce, a *libellus repudii* according to Jewish legal ways.[42]

Yet even in this case, the duke fundamentally upheld the *ritus iudeorum*, whether intentionally or not. The court did not grant a divorce but acted as a *beit din* is authorized to. As noted earlier, religious law dictated that only the husband could initiate a divorce. In some very specific cases, however, the Talmud indicates that a rabbinical court was supposed to help a woman get a divorce, such as if the wife felt physical repulsion or if her husband refused to engage in sexual activity.[43] Fumia articulated that, in her case, her husband had not and would not engage in sexual intercourse with her. Theoretically, since she could not initiate a divorce process, the Jewish court was called upon to act "as [the wife's] agent in requiring divorce."[44] The theory contends that since the wife cannot act, the rabbinical court must become her protector and agent, acting on her behalf.[45] Whether they acted with intentional knowledge of this point of Jewish law, or not, the ducal court in practice pressed Mosca to act according to Talmudic precedent.

The court's reaction to Fumia's case, to be sure, must also be understood in the judges' Christian context as well. As Joanne Ferraro has illustrated, Venetian ecclesiastical courts that heard Christian marital litigation, and primarily heard claims initiated by women, had a bifurcated approach to dealing with these claims. Claimants who asserted that a marriage was coerced or unconsummated were supposed to petition for an annulment.[46] Indeed, "marriage not consummated, according to canon law, was not valid" since the time of Gratian's *Decretum* and thus was liable to dissolution.[47] Those who argued that husbands were guilty of cruelty or neglect (which we will see in the next section), on the other hand, were entitled to petition for "separation of bed and board" but without the legal dissolution of the marriage.[48] Jewish women typically appeared in court making the second claim, that a husband was abusive or neglectful, and thus they sought provisions that would enable them to live separately. In this unique case, in which sexual consummation functioned as the primary node upon which this case pivoted, the ducal court of Venice acted as the ecclesiastical court would have done and demanded that the marriage be dissolved. Yet, it recognized its limited jurisdiction; it was neither an ecclesiastical court nor did they hold jurisdiction to end Jewish marriages at all, so all they could do was demand that a divorce take place. In doing so, the court pushed its ruling only as far as it believed it could. Jewish and Christian law thus intersected here, helping the court frame its decision in a way that seemed suitable perhaps from both perspectives.

Litigant Power: Defining Jewish Law

Despite the judges' attention to Jewish law and its limits in the Venetian judiciary, the secular venue of such debates undoubtedly influenced the outcome of Jewish marriage cases. Because the Catholic judges were not, in fact, experts on Jewish life and law, the litigants themselves—both male and female—harbored great power to define halacha, in some cases creating precedents that would be applied to later cases. Two vivid lawsuits portray this particularly well, each featuring a Candiote Jew we have met before. The first features Elea Mavristiri again, suing her ex-husband. The second stars Joseph Missini, the community leader, Jewish representative to Venice, and wealthy philanthropist—and as we will see, a fairly proud bigamist.

First let us turn to Elea Mavristiri, who appeared before the duke in 1368 to fight her ex-husband, Solomon Astrug. The marriage had not been a happy one. A decade earlier, around the same time Elea was busy fighting her father's proxy, the ducal court had upheld a lower court's ruling that Solomon owed his wife a thousand hyperpera and ordered him to pay within the week.[49] Less than a year later, the ducal court was asked to intervene again and ordered Solomon to pay his wife separation alimony: forty hyperpera a year.[50]

By 1368 the divorce had been completed. Yet it was particularly painful for Elea, who insisted to the judges that she did not want the divorce but that her legal passivity in the face of the Jewish divorce process had left her without recourse.[51] Despite her inability to control the end of her marriage, Elea had accepted this reality; besides, her ex-husband had already remarried. Perhaps expressing her discontent with the events surrounding her divorce gave Elea some emotional redress. It was not solely for this reason, however, that she approached the court. Money was the medium of vengeance in civil court, and Elea had reason to seek a payout from Solomon.

Indeed, the case from 1368 deals with the money owed to Elea according to her *ketubbah*, funds that had not made it back into her hands despite the completion of the divorce. She asked the court to compel Solomon to pay that which was owed her "according to the rite of the Jews," listing: her dowry, worth 700 hyperpera, plus an additional 36 *exagia* of silver, 36 *exagia* of gold, and 200 silver coins. The additional significant sums—one *exagium* of precious metals weighed over four grams[52]—constituted the money that "is imparted to women according to the rite of the Jews, as is contained in a certain cadastral writ," which had been made on the order of the former duke of Crete, Marino Grimani, in December 1361.[53] Though it is unclear why this order was made in 1361 (perhaps this dated to the beginning of the divorce proceedings), it is important to note the implications of Elea's claim: that the rules for Jewish divorce penalties had been spelled out by the ducal court in its own records, thus tightly entwining the secular legal system with the supposedly autonomous (and actually flexible) Jewish rites of marriage and divorce.

Solomon defended himself by denigrating Elea; she was oppressive and troublesome to him (*sibi gravis et molesta*), and he could no longer tolerate her unending burden and attacks (*gravedens et impugnationes*) on him. Their marriage had been legitimate; the divorce, too, was legitimate according to the Law of Moses and rite of the Jews. That much he conceded. But, he claimed, the data were wrong. First and foremost, the dowry had only been 500 hyperpera. Most importantly for our understanding of the use of Jewish law claims, Solomon then argued that, as for the additional payments, he did not have to pay them because they were only usual Jewish custom (*ritu solito iudeorum*), not Jewish law (*legem iudaicam*). Note here the halachic argument being made: all parties agreed that the divorce was done correctly, according to Jewish law, but Solomon claimed that the ducal court in 1361 misunderstood the additional payments it claimed he owed—and misunderstood what constituted real Jewish law. It was his choice, he argued, whether or not to pay out the additional moneys because it was simply a matter of Jewish custom (ostensibly the Heb. *minhag*), a semibinding tradition that might look to an outsider as a part of Jewish law, but in reality it was not.[54] The Law of Moses and the rite of the Jews, he seemed to say, are about those things that are absolutely binding; Jewish custom, a flexible phenomenon, should not count.

Despite Solomon's attempt to parse the case's logic according to the law/custom divide, familiar to a rabbinic court, Elea had already set the tone of the debate—and established the precedent for the Catholic judges—years before, when she had convinced the court that the additional moneys were owed to her according to Jewish rite. The court did not consider the difference between custom and law in this case. Or, at least, in this case, local Jewish custom won out over a general Jewish law. Indeed, the ducal judges reaffirmed that, with a valid divorce, Elea had the right to her dowry, which—they confirmed through investigation of the contracts—was equal to 700 hyperpera. They also confirmed Elea's right to the additional moneys, mimicking the very language she had used: the extra silver and gold is the money that is "imparted to Jewish women according to the rite of the Jews."[55]

By disputing before the secular court, Elea not only was able to define the parameters of the case but also was able to establish the understanding of "correct" Jewish law that the court would perceive as authentic. Venice's amateur judges, no independent experts on Jewish law (or on any law, for that matter), had to rely on her convincing description of the facts of the case. Had she chosen to utilize Jewish channels, all decisions about how to read Jewish law would have been made by the rabbinical court judges themselves, since they were perceived as the authorities on such matters. The woman's own views of Jewish law could play no role there; but they could—and did—before the duke and his councillors.

The sad tale of Elea Mavristiri's divorce did not end here; documents from the ducal court show that Elea continued to sue her ex-husband for at least another seven years for money she claimed he owed her. She even hired a team made up of one Christian and one Jew to help her recover the funds (though she later successfully sued them, too, claiming she had been pressured into hiring them and that they had benefited her not one bit).[56] Yet it is this initial case that sheds bright light on the plight of Jewish women in Candia and the utility of accessing the Venetian court system. Because Jewish marriage was based on a contract, the clauses of the contract (the *ketubbah*) could be parsed in the secular court of law according to its own standards. But in essence the *ketubbah* was an instrument of Jewish law, and thus the realm of the contractual (Venetian jurisdiction) and the religious (meant to be dealt with under Jewish law's specifications) intersected in a place that gave Jewish women in Candia power unimaginable in a rabbinic court: the power to define Jewish law and its parameters. By turning to the secular court, Elea and women like her did not have to reject Jewish law and custom; yet the definitions of Jewish law were malleable in this context. Elea could shape the court's view of the Jewish legal approach toward giving over goods in the wake of a divorce, and her now ex-husband could offer a counternarrative of his own view of proper Jewish law. This case, however, also suggests the limits of this power; Elea's continued litigation indicates that Solomon continued to refuse to pay the money and that the ducal court was also unable (or unwilling) to enforce its judgment.

Bigamy and Arbitration: Shaping the Jewish Law Narrative and the Courtroom Experience

Another vibrant case demonstrates the extreme extent of litigants' power to shape Jewish law before the Catholic judges and indeed to use the court quite differently than one would use the *beit din*. In October 1401, using a Christian lawyer, Channa Missini brought a suit against her husband, Joseph Missini. Channa claimed Joseph had kicked her out of their home and had taken another wife, "against the customs of the Judaica of Candia."[57] Although she was supposed to have been given provisions, time passed, and no care was given to her.

Unlike the short, pro forma defendant responses often recorded in the registers, in this case Joseph Missini offered a far more extensive defense recorded by the court notary. "With all respect to his wife," Joseph said, he did not kick her out; she left of her own accord. As such, Joseph offered Channa a counterproposal. Should she want to come home, he would welcome her back and treat her honorably. But then, Joseph proceeded to present his wife with some other options. First, he offered to pay her provisions, precisely as she had requested. Alternatively, he explained, if she did not want to come home, he would be willing to pay for her food and clothing "honorably and appropriately" (*honorifice et decenter*)—and provide her with a different home. According to this new option, Missini would provide for her as a wife (not separation provisions) but give her a separate home away from Missini's new, second wife.

The judges reacted to Missini's proposal by turning to Channa and asking her if she was interested in her husband's counteroffer. She agreed, stating that she was willing to remain his wife, though in a separate home from the new wife, and receive the provisions suggested during Joseph's defense. As such, the court ordered Joseph to pay for the following provisions for her: food, clothing, and a home, totaling six years of annual payments worth 150 hyperpera annually, paid out as 50 hyperpera every four months. But this was not separation alimony. The agreement's validity hinged on a specific condition: that Channa allow her husband into the new home he would provide her at any time ("day and night"; *die noctuque*) and engage in conjugal relations, that is, the behavior of a man to his wife (*videlicet vir ad uxorem*).

This compromise solution appears particularly unusual in the context of Candiote Jewish marital lawsuits because the court did not rule according to the petition articulated by the unhappy wife. Instead of the easy (and far more typical) solution, finding for the female plaintiff while borrowing language from her petition, the judges involved themselves in brokering a new deal. As such, this court case looks far more like an act of arbitration than a strict legal hearing. Perhaps that is exactly how we should interpret these happenings. As Thomas Kuehn has explained, this was precisely one of the functional roles of the Renaissance courts of Italy, where lawsuits were not necessarily brought in straightforward hopes of a cut-and-dried judgment. Indeed, "many suits were initiated to culminate not in formal adjudication but in a compromise settlement. The lawsuit was not an end in itself but a form of leverage to force a settlement, at times with the encouragement of a judge."[58] Channa's case plays out as a microcosm of these overlapping systems of suit and arbitration, since both approaches to dispute appear in her case. The judges acted in the role of mediators, presenting to Channa the compromise solution, which she readily accepted.

But the mechanism by which this case evolved from a zero-sum game into an arbitrated compromise stems from the couple's ability to utilize claims of Jewish law about bigamy. In fact, it was the discourse regarding the *ritus iudeorum* that provided a language through which conciliation could be reached. Channa claimed that bigamy was "against the customs of the Judaica of Candia." She did not make a comprehensive claim that bigamy was against the *ritus iudeorum* or the *lex moisis* but only that it violated local Jewish custom—*consuetudinem iudaice candide*—an unusual and highly specific expression. We know from the fight between Elea Mavristiri and her ex-husband that this could be quite a persuasive tactic.

In presenting his defense, Joseph did not deny that he took a second wife. In contrast to Channa's claim of local Jewish custom, Joseph defended his actions in terms of broader Jewish law. It is commonplace, he argued, for Jews observing the Jewish rite around the world to keep two wives. He spelled out a number of cases in which this is so, including a provision for marrying the widow of one's brother (Levirate marriage) and marrying a second wife when the first cannot produce a male heir. In fact, it seems that Missini actually referred the judges to a specific Mishnaic passage, though the notary seems to have entirely misunderstood its point. The record repeats precise data that appear in Mishnah Yebamot 1:1, albeit confusing what is actually a list of forbidden spouses as a list of recommended spouses.[59] Joseph also asserted that in many parts of the world, according to the Law of Moses and the rite of the Jews, it is admirable and permissible to take a second wife, "especially when a Jew does not have a male child, and there is no hope of having a male child with whatever wife he has, in which situation the afore-mentioned Joseph is now."[60]

Joseph's religious rationale was not wrong. Rabbinic authorities from the Talmud onward had indeed argued precisely some of these points, suggesting a deep knowledge of rabbinic law on Joseph's part—unsurprising in light of what we know from Joseph's will and his communal activity, as we saw in Chapter 1.[61] Nevertheless, this was likely not the accepted custom in Crete, where much of the communal leadership adhered to the strict Ashkenazi ban on bigamy. Candia's elite Jewish families sent their sons to the Ashke-nazi yeshiva in Padua, and the halachic approach often mirrored the Ashke-nazi positions. This is not surprising, as most of northern Italy, including the Veneto, followed the ban on bigamy that had been put in place around the year 1000 CE by Rabbi Gershom ben Judah.[62] At his synod in Mainz, Ger-shom instituted a ban on bigamy and polygamy, as well as a ban on husbands divorcing their wives without the wives' consent.[63] The extent of the ban, how-ever, remained controversial. The Talmud had explicitly allowed bigamy (i.e., two wives) in a number of cases, including those in which the first wife was immoral, infertile, or insane, or had abandoned her husband. It also specified the possibility of bigamy in the case of levirate marriage, as Joseph Missini had correctly indicated. In Ashkenaz, however, Gershom's ban quickly superseded the Talmudic leniency, even in cases of infertility and levirate marriage. In Spain, on the other hand, and to some extent in Provence as well, some polyg-amy did take place, particularly in cases of infertility or levirate marriage.[64] Yet even here it was still considered a poor choice, and many *ketubbot* were written with specific added clauses forbidding the husband to take a second wife.[65]

This suggests a key reason for Channa's choice to litigate in the ducal court instead of before the local *beit din* and Joseph's choice to mount a rigorous, fact-based defense: the strictness of the Ashkenazi ban would likely have prevented a compromise. We can also speculate that Channa may have intended from the start to use the suit to create a space in which an arbitrated compromise could be reached—without having to accept the permanent loss of her husband. Had her case and its intentions been simple—if her husband was indeed acting bigamously against local Jewish law—the rabbinic court would have likely awarded her the *ketubbah* money; perhaps the *beit din* would have encouraged or compelled Joseph to divorce her or the second wife. But Channa may not have wanted a simple resolution in which she would accept provision money and lose her husband, nor leave her husband with only herself and no chance of a male heir. As such, Channa's choice to seek redress in the secular court may be read as an attempt at reconciliation. This could only be done by avoiding the *beit din*, which likely would have decided her case on the basis of legal considerations, not social factors. The Venetian court appears to have been better equipped to straddle the line between law and arbitration than the Jewish court. In addition, because it was less familiar with the politics of the Jewish law by which it was mandated to decide this case, the Venetian court proved a more malleable medium for Channa's intentions.

The goal was never, however, to avoid an answer framed in Jewish law. Indeed, Venice's accommodation ensured that both Channa and her husband could come to a resolution that was acceptable according to their own interpretations of Jewish law. But the interpretations were noticeably not mutually exclusive: Channa said that local Jewish custom forbade bigamy; Joseph claimed that, technically, Jewish law (writ large) allowed the practice. Neither was wrong; the Jewish law/custom divide would appear in argumentation again, though this time it became precisely what enabled the Venetian court, here sensitive to the distinctions between law, local statute, custom, and common sense, to look beyond a rigid interpretation of the law; they were presented with two, potentially equally legitimate, versions of Jewish law's perspective on bigamy. Each side carefully constructed a case in which each could appeal to Jewish law for different reasons, neither side offering a false tale.[66] And the ducal judiciary, ever careful to ensure that they were perceived as respecting their subjects' customary law, indeed took the bait.

Before rendering judgment, the panel of judges added into the record a reference to past precedent, eagerly affirming that Jews be allowed to act according to their rite.[67] Forced to decide whose version constituted legitimate Jewish law, the court allowed both to be possibilities, paving the way for a compromise between the two. In the end, Joseph's claim that the *lex moisis* allowed bigamy provided enough space for both husband and wife to be correct, thereby enabling reconciliation. It also set a precedent for the future. When a fellow Cretan Jew and fellow leader of the Jewish community named Lazaro Vetu came to court nearly eight years later to defend himself against his wife, he claimed he had kicked her out in order to take a second wife. Vetu would treat bigamy as his right. He defended his behavior only by maligning his wife's integrity. He had exiled her from the marriage home, he claimed, because she was a thief and had done other "entirely indecent" things our notary chose not to record for posterity.[68]

In the Missinis' lawsuit, a convincing accounting of the capaciousness of Jewish marriage law not only overruled the notion of local Jewish custom (where Solomon Astrug had failed) but also enabled the allowance of something explicitly forbidden in Venetian and canon law.[69] Indeed, in 1288, the Maggior Consiglio of Venice had outlawed bigamy not only for citizens but also for foreign residents in Venice. Punishment specified for a bigamous husband included a financial penalty or, if not paid within the specified time, a year in jail.[70] Though not specifically aimed at overseas dominions, this law emphasizes the seriousness with which bigamy could be taken.[71] The admission of the *ritus iudeorum* into the litigative logic, however, forced the ducal court not only to permit but to facilitate an action that was usually explicitly illegal. This legal flexibility enabled the ducal court to act beyond the bounds of its own law, and even outside the bounds of strictly legal considerations, and become an ad hoc body of arbitration.[72]

The Court as Theater: Gendered Pathos, Honor, and the Christian State

Knowing that the Venetian court accepted Jewish law, Jews certainly strategized the ways in which claims of Jewish law could make for more convincing arguments. But they were well aware that this was not the only way to build a compelling case. Certainly, careful legal logic and knowledge—whether about contracts or precedents—aligned with statutory knowledge to play an important role. But claims of legality and logic are not the only tools present in the courtroom. As theoreticians of law have begun to notice, the courtroom is a theater, a stage upon which all sorts of disputes are performed.[73] The space of a courtroom is often similar to a playhouse; the speech is formal and ritualized. Performative behaviors that implicate the audience—think of the audience rising as the costumed judge enters—also resemble theater. The audience to the dramatic performance, here including the judge, is meant to simultaneously believe that the act being performed conforms to reality, while also recognizing the contrived, theatrical, semiscripted nature of the courtroom drama.

Indeed, the courtroom is a nexus of law and culture, a theater where "justice" is performed amid competing social values and personal goals.[74] The litigants who come before the court frame a narrative performance for the goal of convincing the judiciary of the righteousness of their case.

But every performance needs a script. Claims of Jewish law provided one. But what other scripts did Candia's Jews use in crafting compelling performances? As Marie Kelleher has stressed, a primary courtroom script for Christian women can be found in the gender stereotypes of the later Middle Ages, particularly as articulated legally in the set of principles underlying the fashionable mix of Roman and canon law known as *ius commune*. In this model, women were inherently fragile, inferior to men, weaker of mind than men, only worthy of protection when acting honorably (however defined), properly under the power and aegis of a man, whether father or husband, and fulfilling their potential in a maternal role. This model appears paralyzing to modern eyes. But for medieval Christian women, instead of seeing ideological claims of women's limitations as a setback, there was opportunity: female Christian litigants fashioned the implications of such assumptions—that women natively needed to be protected, to be helped in order to maintain their proper domestic and familial roles, and needed to have their honorable reputations protected—into legal arguments that actually worked to their benefit.[75]

This is also true for Jewish women in Venetian Crete. Such advantageous reuse of sociolegal assumptions of womanhood took place despite that fact that, as Jews, they were not technically subject to canon law's assumptions about women, and as Venetian subjects, they were not technically subject to the *ius commune*, as Venice claimed its statutory law to be separate from this legal system identified with its sometimes nemeses, the papacy and the Holy Roman Empire. Nevertheless, no Italian (and indeed, no European) polity could entirely escape its effects. Venetian statutory law certainly evolved in the same Romano-Byzantine legal context; the *ius commune* was certainly taught in the law schools in Venice's *terraferma* towns, and Roman law jurists glossed Venetian law; and the same gender assumptions that obtained in the *ius commune* certainly shaped Venetian assumptions too.

Thus when Candiote women appeared to make their cases, they (and their legal teams) played on the court's sensitivity to the proper roles of women—particularly as wives meant to be protected by their husbands, and as mothers, who could only protect their children if their husbands protected them. They played on the pathos of a mistreated and unprotected wife. For example, though Abba Delmedigo spoke vaguely of "defects" his wife had, in a later iteration of this case in 1445 his wife, Potha, would successfully make the claim that, all the same, since he abandoned her (*dereliquisse*), left the island,

and took a second wife, he owed her separation alimony as long as they were still married.[76] In abandoning her, Abba had left his wife without protection, shirking his most important manly responsibilities.

This connection between abandonment and bigamy appears in three other cases. While Mina, the wife of Elia Catellan, spent six years litigating over the property of her husband—a rich businessman who had decamped to Chios and taken a second wife there—she too made a claim meant to appeal to the gendered assumptions of the ducal court.[77] Appearing in the ducal court in late summer 1423, she characterized her husband as a man who had abandoned her and kicked her out, such that he did not maintain her—a primary role of a husband. In asking for one of his homes to be given to her, she asked for it "so that she could maintain herself"—taking on an independence with which a well-married woman should not have to be burdened.[78] Five years later, seeking the revenue from the rent all of Elia's local homes, Mina's legal team emphasized that Elia did not provide for her at all (*nichil curavit de ipsam*), had totally abandoned her (*dereliquit totaliter*), and was living with his second wife in Chios. Moreover, Mina was very ill and thus had an "extreme need" for the revenue from the houses, even more now than ever before. An abandoned wife, without a husband to protect her, weakened because of her ill state, Mina made a compellingly pathetic claimant; the court indeed granted her the rental revenue from all of Elia's properties.[79]

Stamatini, whose husband abandoned her to take a second wife in Jerusalem, highlighted the "legitimacy" of their marriage, in which state and status she should properly still inhabit, in contrast to the painful position she was left in by her husband's abandonment: "living like a widow" (*vivere sicut vidum* [*sic*]). To be sure, Stamatini was explicitly concerned with losing her material support, the maintenance of which, as Joanne Ferraro has argued, constituted "the most important criterion for a good husband to meet."[80] Providing a great amount of detail, Stamatini's wealthy husband's brother (acting as the man's agent) claimed that the husband had already worked out an alimony agreement. Yet in making her case compelling, Stamatini had focused less on her material change and her inability to continue living up to the standard to which she had become accustomed but instead on the appearance of a change of status she did not merit: she now lived like a widow. The resolution satisfied both aims: the court granted Stamatini 150 hyperpera a year from her husband's estate.

While Stamatini's wealthy husband was willing to negotiate from his perch in Jerusalem by naming an agent, such was the not the case with Anastassu.

Twelve years after her husband, Lazaro, had abandoned her to move to the island of Naxos, in 1401 Anastassu told the court that while Lazaro had remarried and started a second family, she was destitute, hardly able to provide basic maintenance for her two marriage-aged daughters, much less dowries to set them up in marriages. Anastassu's emphasis on her inability to supply a dowry is not incidental: providing a dowry was a father's fundamental obligation. It was so important that Venetian statutory law guaranteed daughters of a man who died intestate, but had sons as well as daughters, a dowry appropriately sized for the family's social status.[81] Thus, in order to establish her own helplessness, Anastassu established her husband's negligence in his family role. Though Lazaro, unlike the previous bigamist, did not send an agent to negotiate with his wife, the ducal court could do something to ameliorate Anastassu's penury: Lazaro still owned a home in Candia, albeit a crumbling one, and if the court granted Anastassu the right to sell it and collect the revenue, she would have the means of supporting her daughters for at least some time.[82] The judges agreed.

In each of these legal separation cases, in which the wives claimed their husbands were guilty of abandonment and bigamy, the abandoned woman used the notion of her proper place and status—as a wife or mother, meant to be protected and maintained by her husband—to argue that the husband's behavior had upset her proper social and familial place. Each woman emphasized her own incapacity, as well as her inability to take care of herself in her current state. The call for material support was thus not generally seen by the judges as a sign of greed—although at least in Stamatini's case, her husband's agent hoped the court would—but rather as an obvious need, the fulfillment of which every married woman deserved. In these abandonment bigamy cases, we see the intersection of Jewish law and broader social values, both playing a role in the decision making: the bigamy itself was not illicit, as we have seen, and thus could not be the focus of argumentation. Rather, it was the abandoning of proper responsibilities in caring for their natively fragile wives that could not be tolerated. These proved effective arguments; in each of the four cases, the court found for the female Jewish litigant.

To be sure, a judgment in favor of the claimant was often not an end to the tale. After all, Mina had to continue fighting against her husband's agents for six years, perhaps a stressor that contributed to her illness. Moreover, a husband's legal team could appeal ad infinitum, or simply refuse to cooperate; the ducal court does not seem to have typically sent out enforcers to uphold their civil rulings.

One more case will suffice to demonstrate the types of gendered pathos built into the legal narratives, while also shedding light on another type of marital crisis faced by Candiote Jewish women. In late summer 1366, Hergina arrived in court claiming that her husband, Isaac Gracian, was a vagabond wastrel.[83] The spoiled son of a wealthy businessman named Joseph Gracian, Isaac had frittered away her enormous dowry, as well as an additional marriage gift known as the *dimissoria*, substantial real estate and other goods brought into the marriage by his wife, leaving her and her young son without so much as a home to live in. These real estate and movable property items were, of course, precisely the goods that a husband was supposed to protect, just as he was supposed to protect the wife. But she had been reduced to living with a poor aunt. In a deeply emotive parallel, Hergina compared her husband's behavior, squandering all her property while living his life erratically, *vivendo inordinate*, with her own pathetic, current predicament, in which she found herself living strictly (or "tightly," as on a tight budget) and miserably, *vivendo stricte et miserime*. The pathos of this tale reminds us that for Hergina, as for many female litigants in these situations, the court likely functioned both as a venue for publicly telling her side of the story and as a place to regain financial security.

The claim that a husband misused a dowry was not unusual in Candia, just as it was common across Mediterranean locales.[84] In another case, a lawsuit that ran from 1451 to 1454, we hear of a young couple who had been betrothed, at which point the parents of the bride-to-be, Hestera Capsali, handed over a very large dowry worth 3,500 hyperpera. In short order, the ostensible groom and his father used the money, which was meant to be safeguarded by the groom but never spent, to pay off their debts. Hestera's mother, a wealthy widow connected to an elite Jewish family, appeared in court to represent her daughter.[85]

But in contrast, Hergina, the wife of the wastrel Isaac, appears to have had no family able to defend her or take part in the suit. Nor could she sue the actual target of her ire, her husband, who seems to have been missing or off the island—perhaps hiding from debtors. Instead, Hergina appeared in court in August 1366 to sue her father-in-law, Joseph. Hergina clearly held Joseph responsible for the misbehavior of his son, but the man claimed he could not afford to repay his daughter-in-law. Unconvinced by Joseph's pleading, the court demanded that he pay a significant amount of money over the course of the following year, including a large payout of 800 hyperpera identified as her *dimissoria*, the bride's "bequest" given to the husband on top of the dowry to administer but not to own. Not divorced, but no longer in penury, Hergina was now able to begin to rebuild a life for herself and her son.

Cribbing a Christian Script: Adopting Categories of Canon Law

In the early fifteenth century, Eudochia Crusari came to ask for the same type of legal separation funds as many of the women addressed in this chapter had petitioned for. But unlike those whose husbands had abandoned them for other lands, other wives, or other gambling rooms, Eudochia's problem was quite the opposite: an all-too-present husband who had become so abusive, she claimed, that she feared for her very life. In April 1418, Eudochia argued that her husband, a surgeon named Monache Crusari, acted toward her with *sevitia et crudelitas*: brutality and cruelty. Eudochia recorded that the "most cruel hatred" (*crudellissimo odio*) expressed by her husband made her unable to live with him because she feared for her life.[86] Jealous and suspicious, he had even accused her of committing adultery before the state prosecutor. This panel had found her innocent of any adultery charge, but her husband continued to mistreat her. Eudochia asked the court to order Monache to give her a portion of her dowry, worth 400 hyperpera, in a yearly stipend, so that she could support herself. In a typical defense presented by his Christian lawyer (Eudochia had spoken for herself), Monache blamed his wife for the discord between them; he also noted she was welcome to come back home and that he was ready to treat her well. Indeed, he countersued, seeking to be absolved of the separation petition entirely.

But the court was convinced by Eudochia's well-constructed complaint, and after its investigation, it ordered Monache to pay an annual living stipend of 40 hyperpera to his estranged wife, paid in two increments of 20 hyperpera each, in addition to other goods for her own use. This settlement was financial, but like many of the judgments made for Jewish (and other) women in state courts, the awarding of money accomplished broader goals. Public judgments always did some public emotional work, notifying broader society of the separation. For Eudochia, the public "work" accomplished by the settlement appears far more significant: the award of a separation stipend legitimated her claims of her husband's cruelty, put his alleged behavior in the public sphere in which he worked, and forcefully acted as an announcement of her independence. Eudochia's settlement did much of the difficult social work of a nasty divorce.

Eudochia's claims regarding her husband's behavior look remarkably similar to the approaches taken by unhappy Latin wives across late medieval

Christendom. Indeed, it seems likely that the case built by Eudochia and her team (though we do not know who assisted her) intentionally sought to play on this similarity. Some of the very claims Eudochia used in arguing that her husband was cruel to her, particularly *sevitia* (cruelty; brutality; also spelled *saevitia*) and *odio* (hatred, particularly a mortal hatred that made a wife fear for her life), were the ones Christian ecclesiastical courts and their jurists began to accept as legitimate grounds for Christian legal marital separation in the thirteenth century.[87] Her choice of words, echoed in similar claims made by a number of Jewish women in the Cretan court, reflects a conscious appeal to a vocabulary familiar to Christian judges.[88] Using a script familiar to Christians in an unexpected setting, Eudochia could skillfully and subtly press the judiciary to react in the way she wanted. This is not to say that Jewish law did not consider domestic violence legitimate grounds for divorce; it did in many circumstances.[89] But Eudochia's choice of words here reflects a conscious strategy that would add strength to her case against a surgeon, a man in the employ of the judiciary itself and thus in a position of power.

Traditional rabbinic grounds for legitimate divorce almost always located fault in the wife. As Avraham Grossman has noted, "we search in vain" in the Talmud "for any comments about a bad husband and the way to free oneself of him."[90] The secular court provided Jewish women with the opportunity to do precisely this: tell their tale of the "bad husband." Indeed, these are constructed narratives, as all courtroom narratives are—and not simply because the text we have is mediated and translated through a Latin notary, although this fact must not be discounted. Joanne Ferraro has stressed the narrative and trope-oriented nature of claims made by women (and men) when litigating marriage: "Rather than read the self-descriptions of deposing husbands and wives as reflections of their actual experiences, we may view them as appropriations from a cultural repository of stories that became synthesized as personal narratives."[91]

To be sure, none of this goes to say that Eudochia and other women in Crete and elsewhere who used this language were simply performing. Howard Adelman has written about the very real abuse against wives visible in a number of early modern Italian rabbinic sources. There is no reason to think these late medieval Cretan Jewish women were not subject to some of the same mistreatment.[92] Nevertheless, the particular words used by women and their defenders were carefully chosen, the result of strategizing sessions with their legal teams, or perhaps approaches learned by watching other claimants use these terms and arguments in their own cases made before the open-air court in the Plateia.

Fascinatingly, as Adelman illustrates, this concept of *sevitia*—the Latin term that conveyed a level of cruelty considered above and beyond the bounds of acceptability—not only was adopted by women who sought their freedom from abusive marriages in secular court but by the sixteenth century would even permeate rabbinic discourse. That is to say, in the sixteenth century, "almost every rabbinic *responsum* on wife-beating in Italy contained terms for cruelty, *ahzariut*. This not only differentiated the behavior from less severe, sanctioned physical chastisements, but conveyed the Catholic notion of *saevitia*, savagery," that threshold level of cruelty at which canon law demanded a Catholic wife be given protection and separation.[93] The rabbis would use the term in the same way, to express a level of abuse that could not be condoned within the confines of Jewish marriage. But while Adelman sees a borrowing of terms from one educated legal elite to another, the case of Crete illustrates the way that women themselves could marshal this language and deploy it for the sake of their own protection, without having to wait for apparently ineffective rabbinic intervention.

We do not know if women like Eudochia tried religious paths first. But whether or not she had, by April 1418 she had decided that the rabbinic court and other community networks could not help her. Unlike a *beit din*—which not only had no enforcement power but also, perhaps, would not wish to upset an important member of Jewish society accused by his wife—Venice's court could assist women like Eudochia in making the most of a miserable situation. Perhaps the judgment of 40 hyperpera per year would act as a first step toward divorce; perhaps she would remain in her separated status for the rest of her life. But in either case, she could now afford to live away from her abusive husband without relying on the charity of sympathetic friends or family. If the language of canon law could help her achieve this goal, it would become one of the weapons she, a Jewish woman, was willing to wield.

In considering Jewish use of arguments inflected with the language of canon law, it is worth stressing the fact that the ducal court willingly accepted such claims from Jewish women. That the court would do so is not obvious. In the second half of the nineteenth century, a woman who came before the Hapsburg Supreme Court in Vienna—another court that promised Jews (as well as Catholics and Protestants) that their religious law would obtain in marriage and divorce cases—tried a similar approach. She petitioned for a separation on the grounds that her husband was abusive and threatened her life. By now such language is familiar to us; though the hearing was held and recorded in German, these terms are those that permit legal separation in canon law.

It was obvious to the Habsburg judges that this was the intent of using such words, as it likely was for the ducal court on Crete. But, as Ellinor Forster has noted, "the Supreme Court [in Vienna] argued quite formally that these were grounds only Catholic spouses could refer to," and the Jewish woman's claim was dismissed.[94] But in the far more flexible milieu of Venetian law, the line between legal claims and social assumptions blurred. Technically, the Venetian court was not responsible for basic Catholic separation claims. But as jurisdiction over marriage crises increasingly overlapped between the ecclesiastical and Venetian state courts, the language of abuse and honor seeped out of the ecclesiastical sphere into broader social conversation, just as broader social realities had informed ecclesiastical courts' decision making.[95] Even Jews, then, could use these assumptions to their benefit—just as these assumptions likely worked their way into Jewish attitudes toward marriage itself.

Gendering Marriage Claims: Women, Men, and the Discourse of Honor

In being the primary initiators of lawsuits specifically about their marital welfare, Jewish women acted similarly to their non-Jewish counterparts. The greater rate of women initiating marriage suits is a phenomenon scholars of Christian women have also identified, although Latin Christian women generally had to petition for legal separation in the ecclesiastical court system.[96] Nevertheless, this was not a pariah act for Jews, forcing them to act like Christians, out of the normative boundaries of the Jewish community. Many of the female litigants were members of elite Jewish families who clearly did not deem it out of bounds to seek resolution in the secular courts. We find no evidence that the families of these women thought it inappropriate for them to enter into this venue; some likely paid their daughters' court fees.

In fact, the twenty-five or so cases of women suing over marital crises paint a portrait of a group of women comfortable with their use of the secular judiciary, who had learned how to navigate the Cretan legal system, its vocabulary, and its sensitivities. Female Jewish litigants wielded the power of the secular court not by forgetting about their Jewish customs and Jewish attitudes toward marriage but rather by bringing arguments that wove together insider (Jewish) claims alongside secular—and even canon law–inflected—strategies. In the use of these dual strategies, the legal realm became another locus of Jewish integration, by choice, into the wider social fabric and an opportunity for knowledge sharing in both directions.

Jewish women were able to shape their narratives by using two modes of argumentation: the language of Jewish law, and the vocabulary and themes common to the larger Mediterranean community, particularly the Latin world, which ascribed (and circumscribed) proper gender roles and proper treatment of women, who were understood as inferior, weak, and in need of support and protection.

Men also used these two tools. We have already witnessed male litigants claiming the jurisdiction of Jewish law, as did the agent of Elea Mavristiri's father, trying to get out of a large fine for breaching a contract. He claimed that Jewish law and the court's promise of its jurisdiction meant that the case should be thrown out. Though the court did not accept the agent's claim in this case, in a number of others—including the two cases we have seen in which bigamists were accused of kicking their first wives out of their homes in order to take second wives—the judges indeed agreed with the male defendants that they had the right to behave in ways deemed unacceptable for Christians because Jewish law allowed them to do so. Thus the bigamists were allowed to engage in bigamy—despite the fact that this was an act considered both spiritually sinful and temporally criminal by the Venetian state.

Just as Jewish women were able to make the strange bedfellows of Jewish law and Romano-canon law come together to create compelling legal narratives, Jewish men also made claims based on a broader discourse of Mediterranean attitudes about women's roles, abilities, and rights. In particular, Jewish men—like their non-Jewish counterparts—called upon the legal and social assumption that only a respectable woman deserved the remedies that law could provide her. Honor was so important to states with laws influenced by the *ius commune* that to be recognized as a victim of rape, a woman had to be known as having a good reputation—that she was *honesta*. By undermining a woman's reputation, her honor, one could undermine her right to legal protection. In the medieval Mediterranean, not only those accused of rape but many other men involved in litigation, too, marshaled claims of dishonor to build their defense or plaint.[97] The husbands of unhappily married Jewish women in Crete wielded the same weapon.

In fact, we have already seen a number of claims made by Candiote men using tropes of dishonorable behavior and bad reputation to undermine their wives' claims or bolster their own. The bigamist Lazaro Vetu's defense, that his wife acted "entirely indecently" and was a thief, must fall into this narrative catchall. So does Solomon Astrug's attempt to derail Elea Mavristiri's rights to her divorce money by calling her an annoying, troublesome, burdensome wife who engaged in attacks. On the other side of the ledger are those who promote their own honorable behavior: as the bigamist Joseph Missini attempted to arbitrate a compromise with his unhappy wife, he promised that in her new, separate home, he would treat her "honorably and appropriately."

Perhaps most poignantly, undermining credibility through claims of dishonorable behavior was the aim of Monache Crusari, the surgeon whose wife, Eudochia, sued for legal separation, claiming his abusive behavior left her fearing for her very life. In attempting to undermine his wife's claim, he had accused her of adultery, a behavior deemed by all to undermine a woman's honor. She could not be trusted to give truthful accountings of his behavior, he claimed, because she was not an honorable woman. The court, however, had been unconvinced and, after investigation, had found any claims to infidelity unfounded. Because Eudochia's reputation and honor remained intact, she retained the moral authority to frame her marriage as abusive. As a result, she received her alimony and right to live apart from her husband.

If Monache Crusari's attempt to discredit his wife by questioning her sexual propriety failed, as did a number of these other examples, this was not always the case. In early 1416, Parnas Buchi petitioned the court to relieve him of alimony payments. He claimed that he should not have to pay provisions to his wife of less than four years, Saphira, which he had been ordered to pay at some unknown point in the past.[98] The plaintiff asserted that it was his wife who decided that they could no longer live together, and in a reversal of typical gender claims, Parnas said that Saphira forced him to move out of the house that she had brought into the marriage. But Saphira's desire for a separation was not Parnas's only complaint about his wife. Instead, as a rationale for his request to end his payments to her, Parnas challenged Saphira's behavior: she constantly acted inappropriately, wandering around the city every day, at all hours, and even entering strange (Gentile?) homes.[99] An honorable woman was a woman who stayed modestly close to home; what could she be doing in public, inside unfamiliar homes?

In contrast, Parnas fashioned himself into a sympathetic character, concerned with the humiliation his wife was causing him, as he simultaneously tried to save her from herself. Indeed, language of honor and shame—both his and hers—pervades this entry. Throughout his complaint, Parnas emphasized that he had always acted toward his wife with a consideration of her honor (*pro honorando ipsam*) and that he treated her with as much honor as possible (*semper tractavit ipsam honorifice ultra posse*). Her misbehavior, he argued, not only brought shame to him (*in dedecus dicti Parne*) and undermined her honor (or perhaps modesty) (*contra honestatem dictem Saphire*), but it even upset the honor and law of Venice herself (*contra honorem et ordinamentum dicti regiminis*)! The implications of a woman's honor did not just rest with her; a woman's honor coincided with, supporting or undermining, male honor and the honor of the state.[100]

Parnas Buchi also stressed previous attempts at reconciliation, and their failure at the hands of his wife. This 1416 case record intimates that the Venetian court had gotten involved in Saphira's activities once before at an unknown date, when it attempted to press Saphira into returning to her marriage and its duties. But this time, this goal could not be met; there was no hope of reconciliation, owing to Saphira's intractable behavior. The Latin words chosen to record her behavior are striking: she acts with *perversitas* (perversity) and *temeritas* (rashness), and is *duritia* (stubborn) and *obstinata* (obstinate).[101] There was no hope; her behavior could not be "corrected." Parnas was totally inculpable; Saphira was "in culpa"—at fault.[102]

In choosing to present himself as the blameless, honor-bound, ever-striving husband, Parnas was using familiar language to undermine his wife's reputation before this sensitive judiciary. In consistently undermining her honor, as it intersected with his reputation and the glory of the state, Parnas engaged a typical trope. A woman worthy of the court's protection had to be a woman of good *fama*, good reputation, which centered on her good status in the public eye. But as Carol Lansing has noted, "there was disagreement over what defined a woman as *inhonesta*" in Mediterranean courts.[103] So Parnas, who did not have direct evidence of his wife's indiscretions, covered all of his bases: her behavior was too public (wandering in the city), too private (entering strange homes), too sexually immodest, too unresponsive to her husband, and too intractable despite legal intervention—not to mention too inappropriate for a good Venetian subject!

Like his female coreligionists who had engaged with tropes familiar from a canon law–inflected social context, Parnas and his legal team had not chosen his words lightly. The claim that Saphira left because of her rashness and caprice must remind us of the canon law principle that a woman who leaves her husband of her own rashness (*temeritas*) must be returned to him, essentially no matter what claims she makes—even, for example, if she claims the couple is related at an unacceptable level of consanguinity. Only proof of cruelty—which Parnas went out of his way to reject—would give a wife the right not to return to her husband.[104] This is not to say that Parnas was making a canon law argument. Indeed, he was not trying to get Saphira to come home but rather to show the court that she did not deserve the legitimate alimony of a good wife. Rather, the point here is that the severity and familiarity of the terms Parnas chose would have been particularly effective as part of his strategy of defaming Saphira before the Catholic-minded court.

Saphira's short defense assists us in understanding how she and her legal team understood the game Parnas was playing. Saphira admitted that she did not want Parnas in her house, but she stressed that this house was her own—freely possessed by her above and beyond her dowry.[105] Her rights to the house were clear, and she had not acted unwifely in asserting them. Next, she rejected the assertion made in the complaint that she had thrown out belongings that Parnas had left in the house, items that would ostensibly show his intent to return, were he allowed. Instead, she claimed, Parnas had taken every last item with him when he left; he left nothing but a single pair of boots.[106] As Parnas claimed over and over again that he had worked to reconcile, Saphira attempted to convince the court that her husband had not tried to make sustained and serious efforts at reconciliation.

Finally, on the matter of her reputation, she simply announced that she was a *bona femina de corpore sua*, a strange formulation meaning that, as a "good woman," her "goodness" (read: honor and reputation) applied to her body as well. In short, she had not acted inappropriately with her body, confirming for the reader that all those who heard him understood Parnas's reference to her wandering into strange homes as an allegation against her sexual propriety, perhaps even prostitution. But she did not bring any character witnesses and did not try—or perhaps was not allowed to try—to establish her good reputation. Perhaps Parnas was right: maybe she did not have one. Fundamentally we cannot move beyond the narrative performed here. All we can say for certain is that the defamation of character worked. Indeed, in the end, the judges of the ducal court found for Parnas in this case, virtually repeating his own language in their sentence: Parnas had made honest attempts at reconciliation; Saphira had acted with obstinacy and rashness.

* * *

Parnas's assertions against his wife now make sense in the broader realms of Mediterranean legal and social norms. They must also be contextualized in their Jewish circumstance. That is to say, from the perspective of Jewish law, the necessity for such a case seems a bit strange. If Saphira were embarrassing him so greatly, why could not Parnas simply divorce his wife? The answer seems to lie in their finances. A Jewish man's right to divorce his wife also signified that, except under very limited circumstances, he had to pay out the *ketubbah* penalties equal to the dowry price plus additional moneys. Parnas, however, argued that he was a poor man (*Parna qui est pauper*) who lived hand to mouth, making only what he earned from work (*vivit de die in diem de labore et industria sua*). Perhaps we should take Parnas's claim to be a working man seriously: Buchi family members were known as pious scribes of Jewish texts, not as part of a great business family. But Parnas's brother served as *condestabulo*, a position one would imagine would not fall to a truly poor man.[107]

No matter his own wealth, Saphira—a daughter of the elite Angura family—had brought an extensive dowry into the marriage, and it would be no stretch to imagine that he married her for this reason. Though the amount is not recorded in the case registers, a betrothal contract preserved in the notarial registers from May 1412 lists a dowry of 2,500 hyperpera in cash.[108] The dowry also included real estate. On top of this, Saphira continued to live a comfortable lifestyle in the extra-dotal home she had brought into the marriage. In contrast, Parnas claimed that his poverty prevented him even from paying his wife's normal provisions (although apparently he could pay court fees), and it was to escape this responsibility that he began this round of litigation. For Jewish men, as for Jewish women, the Jewish mechanisms of divorce could not provide all solutions to the reality of family life, especially if you were not wealthy.

This apparent wealth disparity suggests a subtle corrective to the current understanding of male dominance in Jewish marriage. The notion that men held decidedly unequal power in late medieval marriages, in a Christian context as well, "has been a powerful force in shaping historians' interpretations of marriage" in this period.[109] Scholars have identified two elements of marriage across Christendom that enabled and supported this male control: first, the fact of his control over her dowry; second, the legal control over the woman (the *patria potestas*) that was transferred from the father to the husband.[110] These obtained for Jewish subjects of Venice as well.[111] Moreover, the normative power assigned to men in Jewish law—the exclusive ability to end a marriage, for example—has illustrated for scholars the dominant male role in such relationships. But as this case makes clear, these factors were not insurmountable for some women—especially quite wealthy ones. Nor did they protect all men. Saphira's home, from which she expelled Parnas, had come with her at the time of her marriage. But because it was extra-dotal, the house did not fall under Parnas's control along with the rest of the dowry. By holding the rights to a home, Saphira could wield power within the confines of her marriage. Moreover, the fact of Parnas's control over Saphira's dowry meant that he was mandated to pay for her provisions, so that he could not obtain complete control over his finances. Finally, no matter the normative element of *potestas*, Saphira's behavior makes clear that legal power did not equal control on the ground; Parnas could not mandate Saphira's comings and goings, nor could his status as her husband empower him to correct her. Despite the claims for male dominance so often made, marital control was never unidirectional. What such a man could do, however, was take back social power by undermining his wife's reputation and public honor.

* * *

Legal anthropologists have rightly warned those reading case records that the material presented is partial, and intentionally so. "In any culture we must expect some disparity between the form in which a dispute appears in court and the 'real' substance of the quarrel which gives rise to it," writes Simon Roberts. Those choosing to bring their disputes before judges understood, and understand, that they must present an argument in a way the court is "prepared to hear it."[112] An intuitive understanding of the complexity of marriage, as compared to, say, a property dispute, enables us to recognize that, in the cases explored above, we are not simply getting only one of side of the story; we are likely not even getting an entire side of the story.

Yet what does become clear is that, in developing complex and compelling narratives, the Jews of Candia—and particularly female litigants initiating lawsuits against husbands or their families—not only culled arguments from their own unique pool of possible legal logic but shared tropes of pathos and honor with Christians. In doing so, they demonstrated three important modes of cultural sharing: first, a shared knowledge of the ways in which broader society developed legal arguments, including claims most familiar from a specifically canon law context; second, a willingness and ability to share concepts of Jewish law before a Catholic audience; and third, what appears to be an already shared set of values related to gender, gender hierarchy, and the importance and role of honor and reputation, for both men and women.

While it may seem obvious that Jewish disputes and disputants functioned little differently from their Christian neighbors, the idea that Jewish marriage could function as a node of cross-confessional contact remains a fairly new assertion among scholars of medieval Jewish life. Jewish autonomy over Jewish marriage in the Middle Ages has been little questioned both in the historical record and in the historiography, until quite recently. As Rebecca Lynn Winer has articulated, "it has been a commonplace of Jewish history that marriage and inheritance in particular were almost the last bastions of Jewish life uncontaminated by the practices of the Christian majority. There, Jewish identity and tradition remained stable."[113] A number of studies, however, have questioned this assumption by demonstrating how family law did indeed act as a locus of acculturation among some medieval and early modern Jewish women: decisions about inheritance and the dowry portion reflect nontraditional choices outside the realm of normative Jewish practice.[114]

To be sure, nontraditional choices made by Candiote Jews does not mean that these individuals intended to, or did, step beyond the acceptable bounds of normative Jewish society. The women who chose to dispute over marriage in the ducal court were certainly not community outsiders but oftentimes members of Candia's Jewish elite families, suing elite husbands and their families. In litigating like this, rather than leaving the bounds of acceptability, these Jewish women—and men—helped shape the bounds of normative Jewish behavior; they helped construct a Jewish community in which outside institutions and outside society were not foils but instead provided tool kits ready to be utilized for the benefit of individual members of the community—and, as we have seen, often for the benefit of women, whose position vis-à-vis Jewish law and society often left them marginalized and without much clear agency. As Tommaso Astarita has argued for village litigants in the Kingdom of Naples, when a group is able to incorporate local traditions and social structures into their sovereign court cases, they can maintain for themselves some amount of agency while simultaneously acquiescing to the formalized court system.[115] By choosing Venice's courtroom, Jewish women did not have to choose between the *ritus iudeorum* and the promise of a more malleable, hopefully enforceable justice; they could have both.

Yet, as in every dispute, to quote Thomas Kuehn, "more was at stake and more was in play than law."[116] The *ritus iudeorum*, at first glance primarily a category important for its legal power, under careful analysis appears as a multifunctional tool by which emotionally laden disputes could be translated into norms that Jewish disputants could wield more effectively in a secular court. A real benefit of claiming jurisdiction of Jewish law, then, was that it empowered the claimant (or, much less frequently, the defendant) to define halacha according to her (or his) own understanding and thus potentially shape the judicial outcome more effectively. As such, Jewish law could be brandished in this fight, but another weapon could be chosen in its place: the language of honor and honesty, in the case of Parnas Buchi; claims of violence or impoverishment as with Eudochia Crusari and Hergina Gracian; or the emphasis on upholding valid and binding contracts, as in many others.

In a significant way, these Jewish and "secular" approaches did not fundamentally diverge but tended toward agreement on a great many social assumptions. A central point of convergence lay at precisely the node we have addressed here: women's modesty and the court. Venetian statutory law made an assumption that should remind us of the words of Solomon ibn Adret, who had claimed women did not go to either Jewish or secular courts because of "modesty." Tucked into an article about a widow's ability to recapture real estate from her dowry, the Venetian Statutes note that "a woman under her husband's protection, because of her modesty, feels ashamed to bring claims in front of the public judges."[117] This is not a legal order, forbidding women to come. To the contrary, it is a normative moral statement about how women act. Medieval Christian social norms assumed that a good woman had no interest in undermining her modesty or had any interest in performing male roles.[118] Jewish social norms generally assumed the same; we may reread Ibn Adret's statement in such a light. As such, just as for their Christian neighbors, for Jewish women entering the secular realm the consilient gender hierarchy could work for their benefit, as they portrayed themselves as victims, good and reputable women in need of support, willing to forego public modesty (though not honor) out of desperation—a portrayal effective in both Jewish and Christian religious communities represented in the audience.

Jews were not "just performing" what they thought the Christian judges would find convincing. The public nature of the court—its role as court of public opinion alongside the court of official note—suggests that the performance had to convince Christians and Jews alike. Joanne Ferraro has claimed that accusations made against men and women in sixteenth-century Venetian marriage trials "constitute an important index of community standards," telling us as much about the society in which the litigants lived as about the judges themselves.[119] The public nature of the ducal court, out in the central square of Candia, further suggests the importance of convincing Christians and Jews alike—those who regularly attended the judiciary for entertainment and gossip, as we know many did. If Daniel Lord Smail is correct that a major reason late medieval people chose to consume state justice can be found in the ability to publicly humiliate their opponents before their community of peers, we may speculate that the Jewish women of Candia hoped the public enumeration of their husband's bad behaviors would not only convince the judges to grant them financial remuneration but would shame the family of the errant husband—perhaps humiliating them enough to compel them to act against him on her behalf.

The aftermath of the dowry case initiated by Hergina, the wife of the wastrel Isaac Gracian, offers a case in point. Hergina had aired her grievances against her husband to her father-in-law in August 1366. A few months later, Joseph was called before the court again to make amends for some of his son's debts. In this case, Joseph admitted outright that he had raised a negligent and evil-doing son (*homo dissolutus et faciebat sinistre facta sua*).[120] Joseph, it seems, felt effectively shamed by his son's behavior, and the public rendering of Isaac's misdeeds spoke not only to the judges who had awarded Hergina large sums of maintenance money but also to him. Concerns for honor and protection of women were just as much part of the Jewish community's discourse as was the concern for upholding Jewish law.

* * *

In Candia's atmosphere of shared gender values, shared notions of honor, and a sense of comfort in sharing information about law, we witness a Jewish community trusting the Venetian judicial institution to ascertain enough data to judge fairly (or at least, beneficially) but remaining neutral and extracommunal enough to allow litigants to shape the definitions of Judaism. How far did this confidence in consuming colonial justice go? It would be one thing to identify individual Jewish trust in the system. It may be quite another to see the very leaders of Venetian Crete's Jewish community, the men responsible for ensuring autonomy for the *kehillah*, bringing in the Venetian government to intervene in intra-Jewish affairs. But this, too, became a norm among the community of Candia, and it is this institutional use of Venetian justice and intervention that concerns us in the next chapter.

Chapter 6

Inviting the State into the *Kahal*

In the autumn of 1406, the leadership of the Candiote Jewish community came together to pass a short set of statutes for its flock.[1] These five wide-ranging rules empowered the cantor to call for the beginning of Sabbath within the Judaica; set rules for the supervision of kosher animal slaughter by communally beholden slaughterers, butchers, and inspectors; and enabled the cantor to protect the ritual bath. It also set up a penalty for those officials who were not fulfilling their duties, banning them from service for six months. This is a set of ordinances that reflects the authors' sense of autonomous rule over the Jewish community's time (Sabbath), institutions (the slaughterhouse), officials (e.g., kosher butchers), and spaces (the entrance to the ritual bath), all conceived of as entities separate from the society outside the Jewish Quarter's walls. In the final line of the *taqqanah*, in fact, the authors articulate that these ordinances are the things that allow the Jews to live in Gentile society, apparently by acting as a protective fence not unlike the Judaica walls themselves: "And we have made these ordinances which, through them, we live among the nations."[2] It is a discourse of separation but also an assertion of the independent authority of the Jewish leaders, here defined as "the teachers and the masters of Torah . . . and the rest of the respected ones," whom the *condestabulo* gathered to create and publish these rules.

Why was autonomy important for the Jewish leaders of Venetian Crete? Beyond questions of simple authority and power, the claim of autonomy over Jewish communities had broader implications—implications that stood at the very heart of the legitimacy of the *kehillah* project. Over the course of the Middle Ages, authoritative rabbis set out a philosophy of Jewish life under non-Jewish sovereignty. At the heart of this philosophy was a corporate communal institution—the *kehillah*/*kahal* (used interchangeably in primary sources, as here)—which, in mimicking other corporate entities of the Middle Ages (the scholarly university, the guild, and the confraternity, to name just three), could obtain rights to some amount of internal self-governance from the sovereign. No one imagined that this self-governance would be all-encompassing.[3] But like other corporate entities, the *kahal* was entitled to make its own guiding bylaws and ordinances, and in the Jewish incarnation was born the *taqqanah*, the Hebrew statutory ordinance genre we have seen in play in Candia from only a few decades after Venetian rule took hold.

From the Jewish theorists' perspectives, however, this corporate institution was a sort of state within a state. The *kahal* was meant to be a purveyor and enforcer of a Jewish public law. Solomon ibn Adret, the authoritative Catalan halachic authority (whose opinions were sought by Candia's leadership), regularly referred to this task as "tikkun ha-medinah," literally "fixing [or ordering] the polity"—with the polity in question being the *kehillah*.[4] Modern scholars of the medieval *kehillah* have taken this language seriously. As Daniel J. Elazar has written, the *kehillah* "was virtually a Jewish city-state" and its liaison to the sovereign state (as in the person of the *condestabulo*) was handling its "foreign affairs."[5] In this autonomous-state model, the right to pass *taqqanot* is the product of a rereading of the *kahal* either as a *beit din*, a Jewish court with legislative authority, or (per Ibn Adret) another political unit with legislating rights, akin to a king or a high court.[6] The fact that an actual king (or other ruler) held the actual legislative cards remained absent from much of this theoretical discussion.

In his epistolary opinions, Solomon ibn Adret wrote stridently about the need for Jewish *kehillah* institutions across Christendom to retain as much autonomy as possible. Autonomy and legitimacy were, for him, two sides of the same coin—giving up autonomy meant forfeiting legitimacy at the same time.[7] One of the key tenets of maintaining this self-sufficiency was the principle of dealing with internal grievances internally. In short, no intra-Jewish fights should play out in a secular court but must rather be settled by Jewish judges and arbiters. Because legitimacy only came with autonomy, the halachic implications were enormous. He stridently wrote that if Jews do seek recourse for internal matters with the non-Jewish court, "you void all the *takkanot* of the community; and the customs [*minhagam*] of the communities are Torah."[8] For Ibn Adret, recourse to the secular court undermined and invalidated the internal Jewish set of communal ordinances, and because these ordinances attained the status of halacha (since custom becomes Torah), the undermining of the *taqqanot* was a grave sin.[9]

Ibn Adret's forceful assertions must be taken in context. Clearly, the Jews of Venetian Crete did not deem what they did personally—suing one another in the secular court—a violation of this ban. And to be sure, the Jewish leadership of Candia was highly aware that any corporate power they held ultimately came from—and could be limited by—the Venetian colonial government. Indeed, at the end of the entry in *Taqqanot Qandiya* that lists decrees made by the community leaders in 1406, the authors of the ordinance explicitly state that they empower community leaders to address emergencies "only if the will of the authority," that is to say, the ducal administration, "agrees to this."[10] Yet even here, the assumption remains that, from the perspective of the Jewish elites, intracommunal matters—if not intrapersonal matters—should stay inside the walls of the Judaica; intervention only occurs when the Venetian sovereign demands it.

A close reading of the prologue to this very same *taqqanah* from 1406, however, complicates even this issue of the extent and vector of Venetian involvement in the higher levels of Jewish communal life. The ordinance opens with the roster of the current elected leadership committee. These decrees were established during the tenure of "our *parnas* in this year, the leader of our community, a man of faith, Rabbi Malkiel Casani, the *condestabulo*, and his councillors, *chosen in the assembly, men of repute*,[11] our teacher and rabbi Shemarya Delmedigo, and the honored rabbi Isaiah Cohen Balbo, and the honored rabbi Elijah Missini, may they live."[12]

The names of the *condestabulo* and his three *hashvanim* are not surprising; the Casani, Delmedigo, Balbo, and Missini families long shared power with a few other clans. But the *taqqanah* reports that this roster does not reflect the original group of men chosen at the beginning of the current tenure cycle. Originally, Jeremiah Capsali was named *hashvan*, and Isaiah Balbo was not: "But when there was a marriage agreement between him [*capsali*] and the above-mentioned teacher and rabbi Shemarya [Delmedigo], some of our community became angry since they thought that it was not appropriate for two in-laws in one ministration together, and so the authority [i.e., the Venetian colonial government], may God protect it,[13] decreed one of the two to leave, as you can see in the notebook of decisions of the *cancellaria*."[14] While the Jewish community accepted that a small number of elite families would consistently hold the leadership positions, there was a limit to what could be tolerated. Two men, joined by their children's marriage, would share—whether by necessity or plan—certain goals and interests that could blind them to the common good. Now legally related, the two men could no longer be counted on to balance each other's self-interest.

Importantly, the discontent did not remain to be resolved within the confines of the Jewish community leadership, or the *kehillah* at all. Instead, the ducal court became involved and ruled that one man must step down. Balbo replaced Capsali for the cycle. However much our ordinance writer (the *condestabulo* Casani himself, according to a note among the signatures)[15] desired to show these men in a good light—after all, "the abovementioned honored men, quite good in ethics, did not go against this judgment" of the ducal court—the fact that the Jews involved the colonial government hints that the backstory of this event was far more complicated and bitter than the ordinance writer was willing to admit overtly. Perhaps a group of Jews sought an internal solution to this seemingly internal matter: one of the two in-laws must recuse himself. But each refused, and, so it would seem, the *condestabulo* Malkiel Casani declined or was unable to convince either of them to step down. What is certainly clear is that with no more internal recourse, the unnamed agitators sought justice in the secular court. And indeed the ducal court supported them. The ordinance then turns to the good values and strong leadership of this new four-man council, ignoring the wider implications of this coup.

This is an admittedly extreme case. I have not found other examples of the state entering into the election decisions of the *kahal*'s ruling council. But the underlying principle—that it is legitimate for leadership elites of the Jewish community in Candia to solve problems wholly internal to the *kahal*'s institutions and mandates through recourse to the ducal administration and its court—can be found in a wide variety of moments in the fourteenth and fifteenth centuries. In fact, when Venice intervened in the inner workings of Jewish institutional life in Candia, it was generally the result of the state being invited in by leadership elites—that is to say, either by current leaders or by members of other elite families, some of whom likely would hold office for the *kahal* at other times. Indeed, it seems likely that when the *taqqanah* from 1406 mentions "some of our community" who opposed the concurrent tenure of two in-laws, it refers to others from these same leadership elite families. Litigation against fellow Jews at the secular judiciary became the primary mode of inviting in such intervention.

It is undoubtedly true that some of this litigation was initiated by Jews unhappy with the *kahal* for various reasons; the court certainly acted as a venue for elites who felt (at least temporarily) disenfranchised from intracom-munal power or mistreated by the community structure (often embodied in the person of the *condestabulo*). Often, however, it was the *condestabulo*, in his official capacity, who initiated lawsuits, particularly against Jews who refused to pay the corporate tax, the collection of which was a primary responsibility of the *kahal*. But these fights over tax money were often also over bigger social questions of group identity and belonging. Likewise, disputes about syna-gogue rights—questions of ownership of synagogue seats and rights to syna-gogue leadership—also mesh financial interests with questions of belonging, honor, and the meaning of leadership. By airing disputes over these issues in the ducal court, Jewish leadership elites—and at least one former member of the leadership elite—invited Venice to act as arbiter and decisor for the kinds of institutionally internal fights that Jewish theorists had intended should stay decidedly "in-house." In some cases, the slippery slope these thinkers feared was realized: giving over arbitration rights led to long-term loss of decision-making abilities for the same elite leadership.

The *Condestabulo* in Court

As the primary representative of the Jewish community and the main liaison between the community and the Venetian government, the *condestabulo* nat-urally played an intermediary role. Generally a lay leader, he had allegiance to his flock. In the political philosophy of the *kehillah*, the liaison between the community and the state (often called a *shtadlan*, a term unfamiliar in the Cretan context) had as his "main function . . . to protect Jewish rights."[16] But the *condestabulo* also had responsibilities to the Venetian government that rec-ognized his authority. This right to authority carried a particular awkwardness with it, since the *condestabulo* acted as a quasi-official of the Venetian state in his role as tax collector, responsible for the gathering of the Jewish taxes levied on the community as a whole.

In articulating the acceptable relationship between the *kahal* and a Gen-tile sovereign, the influential Ashkenazi rabbi Meir of Rothenburg (Maharam, d. 1293) recognized that one of the major nodes of this relationship centered on taxation. In fact, in considering whether a king should be allowed to force the *kahal* to pay money he deemed was owed to him by an individual Jew, the Maharam confirmed that, in the case of a land or poll tax, a *kahal* could be forced to pay for Jews who had not contributed.[17] Maimonides, furthermore, was familiar with the situation in which a Jew was appointed to collect this royal tax: "If a king fixes a tax . . . and appoints to collect it on his behalf an Israelite known to be a trustworthy person who would not add to what was ordered by the king, this collector is not presumed to be a robber."[18]

Yet Maimonides also realized that there would be some members of the Jewish community who would refuse to pay: "Moreover," he writes, "if one avoids paying such a tax, he is a transgressor, for he steals the king's property, whether the king be a heathen or an Israelite."[19] He did not, however, explain how such a trustworthy tax collector should go about recovering funds from the recalcitrant Jew. In Candia, the *condestabulo* at times chose to pursue these fellow Jews through litigation in the Venetian court system. He was not the only party to such tax litigation; members of the Jewish community also appeared in court, holding their *condestabulo* responsible for tax pressure they deemed unfair.

Taxation and the Definitions of Membership

The *condestabulo* certainly saw litigation within the colonial justice system as a way to force members of the community to pay their piece of the impost pie. But this was not their only motivation; sometimes money could act as a currency of dispute with implications beyond the financial, entering in the realm of identity and status definition. A dispute between the Jewish leadership and a nonpaying member of the *kehillah* (and later, his son) that continued heatedly for almost forty years offers a particularly illustrative case in point. In April 1401, three men, namely David, the son of the late Moses, Alchana de Negroponte, and Lazaro Vetu, all identified as *condestabuli* of the Jews of Candia, brought suit against a Jewish agent for Elia Mosca, a successful Jewish businessman who had refused to take part in paying the Jewish taxes levied communally on the Jews of Candia.[20] Elia Mosca himself had left Candia, and the *condestabuli* (like the unhappy women in the previous chapter) were looking to Elia's agent as a man who could speak for him—and who held his Cretan purse strings.

The courtroom complaint records the dispute as follows: though Elia came from Negroponte, he had married and bought a home in Candia. As such, he should participate in the communal taxation burden of 4,000 hyperpera that the Jews of the city had to pay at that time. The agent defended Elia with the claim that his client was only a foreigner (*peregrinus*) and stranger in Candia, and did not have a home in the city. The judges, however, were not convinced, and in this case they found for the *condestabuli*: they ordered Elia to pay a portion of the Candiote Jewish tax.

The Venetian court did indeed sometimes exempt nonresidents, including Jews, from local taxation, often after the Jewish leadership had aggressively pursued them for payment. In 1391, the ducal court granted Maria, the widow of Hosea Theotonicus, an exemption from the Jewish tax because she was actually a resident of Venice, despite the fact that she had lived on Crete. The court explained that she should not be taxed as long as she did not own any property on the island.[21] In a parallel case from 1412, a Jewish member of the Capsali family resident in Rethymno extracted himself from the *geta* (watch-duty) tax in Candia based on the same principle—that he possessed no property in Candia.[22] The *condestabuli*'s argument in the Mosca case, then, relied in part on this principle: Mosca, in fact, did own real estate (a home) in Candia, claimed the *condestabuli*. Moreover, against his assertion that he had no real social place within the local Jewish community, the *condestabuli* countered that, in fact, he had married a local woman.

The court register does not record any more data in the aftermath of the judgment against Elia Mosca.[23] In May 1438, however, almost forty years after the original case, Aaron Mosca—the son of the now late Elia—appeared before the ducal court in Candia requesting a tax exemption.[24] Neither he nor his late father, he explained to the duke and his two councillors, really counted as Candiote Jews. Though they both resided in Candia, as Aaron continued to do after his father's death, they were actually from the island of Negroponte, where the family's land, assets, and main business remained. Nevertheless, he related, he was forced to pay various Jewish taxes on Candia, as well as back home in Negroponte. On that island, "we are taxed, and we have paid and pay the imposts, the *geta* tax, and the *angaria* taxes."[25] Therefore, he continued, he should not have to pay taxes since "one should not suffer" these Jewish taxes twice.[26] As his father's heir and trustee, he was responsible not only for his own taxes but for all of the years of backpay for when his father did not pay the Candiote Jewish tax (suggesting that the judgment of his father's case did not render the older man ready to hand over the money). He requested an exemption for his own and his father's back taxes in Candia, so that he could limit his financial suffering.

Despite Aaron's claim that he had been unfairly burdened by double taxation, the current *condestabulo*, Solomon de Potho, arrived to testify against Mosca using the same argument his predecessors had taken up four decades before. Though Aaron's petition did not rely on the original claims of property and connections, Solomon argued along the same lines as his predecessors, asserting that Aaron had truly become part of the community: like his father, he had married a wife in Candia, and—most importantly—he owned a home on the island. In truth, other evidence suggests that the Moscas had indeed sunk deep roots in Candia.[27] It comes as little surprise then that the court sided again with the *condestabulo*, and Mosca was ordered to pay the Jewish taxes both in Candia and in Negroponte (where he also owned property), both for himself and for his late father. Aaron's claim against the injustice of double taxation had been undermined by the parallel logic of the Jewish communal leaders: as long as the Moscas were legitimate members of Candia's Jewish community, they could not claim to be from (or "only" from) Negroponte.

On a basic level, the court's decision rested on a simple principle of proof of intentional settlement, through ownership and social connections. Over the course of arguments, however, we are able to sense the nonlegalistic elements of this case, particularly the intense discord between a member of the Jewish flock and its leadership. The pitting of the Mosca family against the Jewish leadership underscores the awkward position of a leader; though we might expect him to seek methods to protect his flock from the financial exploitation of the Venetian government, instead he marshaled the instruments of Venetian power in Crete to force them to pay.

The rancor is evident; in his complaint, Aaron told the court that he was motivated to seek this official exemption because, a number of years earlier, the leader of the Jewish community, the *condestabulo*, had harassed (*molestebat*) an agent for his father. Recently, he explained, he himself had been harassed by the current *condestabulo*. In each case, the Moscas were badgered by the Jewish communal leader because of their refusal to pay the Jewish taxes in Candia. We see from other evidence that the Jewish leadership used this type of pressure in other cases of nonpayment of taxes. For example, the ruling that protected the Venetian Jew Maria from paying Candiote Jewish taxes also stressed that Maria's son-in-law, her agent, should not be harassed anymore (*non molestetur amodo in ante*) for her money—ostensibly the impetus for her suit in the ducal judiciary. In his role as tax collector, the *condestabulo* at times felt compelled to pressure his own flock to the extent that they experienced it as harassment—quite a different image from that traditional view of the *condestabulo* as protector of his flock of Jews.

It seems that in Candia, as in most locations across Christian and Muslim lands, with a few exceptions, the government's choice of Jewish leader "was an extension of their preexisting communal offices."[28] The Jews chose their leader, and the government gave him the added imprimatur of a semigovernmental functionary. We have no reason to think this was otherwise in Candia; the names of the *condestabuli* listed in *Taqqanot Qandiya* suggest that the town's elite Jewish families continued to hold this role in high esteem and that the community respected this office as their own, internally chosen leader.

But the external authority granted to the leader appears to have become an important part of the job. While the first *condestabulo* to appear by name in Hebrew sources of *Taqqanot Qandiya*, David, son of Judah, mentioned in the reforming ordinances from March 1363, is called both *condestabulo* and *nasi*, reflecting his external and internal authority, most later *taqqanot* simply call Candia's current leader a *condestabulo*.[29] This dual role as religious leader (if not rabbi, like Elia Capsali, then lay upholder of religious rules and values) and civil liaison—and sometime enforcer of the Venetian regime—made the office of *condestabulo* one that inherently produced tension vis-à-vis members of his community.

The Jews of Candia were not the first to experience this tension. As Kenneth Stow remarked when evaluating modes of communal Jewish leadership in the Middle Ages, "this union of externally appointed and internally chosen leaders was not an ideal one," neither in the former Carolingian lands where a royally appointed Episcopus Judaeorum was also a *parnas*, an internal Jewish leader, nor in England, where the Presbyter or "Jews' Priest" filled the same role.[30] The English case illustrates for Stow the worst problems of this duality of roles: "The Episcopus and his ilk could be made to coerce the Jewish community against its will, and against its best interest. This occurred most visibly in England in the thirteenth century when the kings began to demand from the Jews abusive taxes and to use the Presbyter as their chief collectors."[31]

Likewise, in Candia, the last decades of the fourteenth and the fifteenth centuries were characterized by a steep increase in Jewish imposts to be paid as a community rather than individually. In 1386, the government demanded 1,000 hyperpera annually from its Candiote Jews, which was over 200 hyperpera more than any impost before that date.[32] Over the course of the following years, Venice tried to sharply raise this amount. In 1389, the attempt to raise the Jewish obligation to 3,500 hyperpera sparked a large and successful outcry, after which the Venetian senate agreed that the Jews as a whole "only" had to pay 2,000 hyperpera each year.[33] But in the years before Mosca's case, the Venetian government—struggling to pay for the wars against Genoa and the Turks—had raised the Jews' total tax level per annum to an exorbitant 4,000 hyperpera.[34] This time, no appeal was successful; the Jews of the city of Candia had to come up with this exceptionally large amount of money every single year.

Perhaps in this light, the harassment of Mosca's father's agent and Mosca himself appears to be a desperate act by a sympathetic leader trying to protect the rest of his flock. In the Mosca case, the reclamation of many years of back taxes was undoubtedly a significant motivating component in this case, and certainly in its longevity over years and multiple generations; obtaining that money would lighten the load on the rest of Candiote Jewry immensely. Furthermore, Venice's own desire to collect as much of its mandated amount as possible made the secular court an obvious ally for the *condestabuli*.

On another level, however, the fight over the Mosca family's tax payments represents a wider internal struggle within the Jewish community, beyond financial questions. This dispute was not only about money but about the right of the *condestabulo* to define the parameters of his community—who was "in" and who was "out." We see this concern, for example, in the repetition of *taqqanot* that stress that the *condestabulo* and his councillors alone have the right to excommunicate someone, that is, to literally expel him from within the ranks of the community.[35] But the *condestabulo*'s attempts at policing the borders of community were fraught for both the leaders and for those people who would have rather decided their own communal affiliations. *Taqqanot* regarding rules for excommunication seem to indicate that the Jewish leadership feared not only that community members would ignore their bans but also, more frighteningly, that they would compose their own writs of excommunication, sidelining the official leadership and their authority.[36] In the case of the Moscas, we witness an individual and then his son taking part in an attempt to define their own group identity. Father and son were undoubtedly Jews, but their decision to affiliate with the Candiote Jewish community—whether one would be part of the official *kehillah kedoshah*—should be their own choice, the Moscas claimed. This struggle over back pay on communal taxes can also be read, then, as a battle over the question of who was empowered to decide group membership.

The competing assertions of communal belonging were part of an internal power struggle. Yet they played out in a decidedly extracommunal venue—one that provided special benefits to the *condestabuli* who brought the initial suit. As we have seen, the Venetian legal environment allowed the claimants to set out their own religiolegal definitions in the courtroom. We may see a similar principle in play here: the Jewish community leadership set out its own definitions of official membership as having deep ties to the city through multiple measures of permanence, through real estate ownership and through marriage to a local wife. The defendant was, by nature of the proceedings, forced to answer according to a rubric foisted upon him, unable to express his views of belonging or unbelonging. His own definitions became moot. By actively initiating the case before the Venetian court, the *condestabuli* put themselves in the position of power by creating and controlling the tenor of the debate. While this did not universally ensure success, it seems that it was often an effective tactic.

* * *

As we have seen, the Jewish tax burden increased dramatically toward 1400. To be precise, however, we cannot associate the difficult role of the *condestabulo* and the awkward problem of individuals attempting to find loopholes to avoid communal taxation solely with the heavier taxes of the fifteenth century. Rather, the tax implications of other individuals' behaviors—such as losing members on the rolls to emigration—complicated the relationship between leadership and flock even a century before. Around 1300, a Jewish family emigrating from Candia to Negroponte was made to promise that, despite the move, they would still pay their fair share of the collective Jewish tax in Candia.[37] Nor was this tension limited to the world of Venetian dominions; as Elka Klein has noted, fights between Jewish communities and Jewish individuals over taxation regularly made their way to the Aragonese royal court in the thirteenth century.[38]

Tensions between the Jewish leadership and its flock over taxes did not solely revolve around issues of migration and mobility. A ruling from the early fourteenth century regarding a house in the Jewish Quarter suggests that the link between the Jewish community leader's awkward position and the vicissitudes of all types of Venetian taxation was already in place.[39] In 1319, Herini, the widow of Abraham, brought a suit against the current *condestabulo*, Lazaro Balbo. Herini claimed that her late husband had bought a house from another Jew, Samaria. This house, at least when owned by Samaria, was exempted from the *geta* tax. When Herini and her now dead husband took possession of the home, they were not given the same exemption, but she claimed they should have been. Now in court, Herini sought to have the exemption reinstated.

Herini did not bring this case as a complaint against the state. Instead, she treated the *condestabulo* as the victimizer and expected that only a court ruling against him could reinstate her house's exemption. There is no other reason

Balbo would have been brought to court; he was not directly affiliated with either the buyer or seller of the aforementioned house. Instead, he appeared as a representative of the state tax engine. And, indeed, it appears that at least Herini believed his power was quite widespread, that is, that the ducal court could not exempt her but that rather it could only compel the *condestabulo* to exempt her.

Apparently well versed in the tax code, the *condestabulo* defended his position by arguing that this sort of exemption was attached to a person, not a place. When the house was sold, the right to an exemption absented itself along with the former owner. That homeowner could have formally transferred the exemption if the house had been given as a gift; but since Herini and her husband bought the house, the exemption could not apply to them.[40] The court was convinced by the *condestabulo*'s argument and found that the claimant would indeed be compelled to pay the *geta* tax. As in the case of Aaron Mosca, the *condestabulo* sat uncomfortably between the flock he was meant to protect and the Venetian government that sought to earn significant income by taxing it. We can certainly sympathize with the claimant, whose logical argument could have been easily supported by the leader of her community; in the case, the *condestabulo* himself recognized a potential loophole by which she could have received the tax break. But we may also see the pattern informing the *condestabulo*'s decisions; the communal nature of taxation may have forced him to weigh one individual's tax break against the many others among whom this increased burden would have to be spread.

Condestabulo as Individual and Leader

The complex interests of the Jewish community leaders stemmed not only from their dual roles within the confines of the job but also from a second tension: their goals as leaders alongside their individual financial and familial interests. For a number of elites, the colonial courtroom became a site for expressing this tension between individual interests (usually financial) and the interests of the community. Certainly the Mosca family's case must be read through this lens.

But there was no clear dividing line between the elites who put their interests first and other elites who recognized the needs of the community. Rather, this same attempt to limit personal financial loss, even at the expense of the community as a whole, can be seen in the behaviors of the very same leading men who would act as *condestabuli* and councillors. In 1428, for example,

members of the Casani family came before the duke to demand that a *carta*
given to their ancestor in 1274 be honored, protecting them from paying certain Jewish taxes, whether the *dacia* or the *angaria*, two of the categories of
collective taxation imposed on Jews.[41] On an individual basis, of course, this
tax exemption appeared to be a boon. Yet, as in the case of Aaron and his
father, one man's advantage put a larger burden on the rest of the community,
which had to compensate for the Casanis' exemption by spreading out his per
capita tax to the rest of the community.

The position of Jewish doctors was particularly problematic, since physicians and surgeons who received salaries from the ducal government were
exempted from taxes. For *condestabuli* who were also doctors, in particular,
this tension was particularly apparent. A year after Aaron Mosca's case, in
1439, the Jews of Crete were forced to take on a significant portion of the war
debt, above and beyond their usual (and now heavier) annual taxes, in the
form of 4,000 ducats per annum for three years.[42] In the same year, the Jews
were ordered to give 3,000 measures of wheat, again above and beyond their
heavy annual impost.[43] In the aftermath of this order, many Jews attempted
to evade the tax either by utilizing the doctor's exemption, whereby physicians and surgeons of the state were exempted from the Jewish taxes, or by
somehow acquiring exemption documents.[44] As we saw in Chapter 3, many
Jewish doctors worked at least part of the time for the colonial government
as medical experts and expert witnesses, and in this semiofficial capacity they
were given tax exemptions. These doctors were even freed from the wheat tax
imposed in January 1439, as established in a case regarding the Jewish physician Hemanuel de Rodo.[45]

As Jewish doctors were among the community's most affluent, when they
were exempted, the burden necessarily fell to those less equipped to pay. Salo
Baron considered Candiote Jewish doctors who accepted the tax exemption to
be guilty of "abuse."[46] Nevertheless, if these doctors were harming the Jewish
community, they were often the same men who ran it. In 1438, for example,
Magister Solomon, a physician, and Magister Moses, a surgeon, were listed
as current *condestabuli* of the Jewish *universitas*. They also acted as petitioners
"for themselves and for the other salaried doctors" (ostensibly the Jewish ones)
in a judgment that resulted in the reaffirmation of Jewish doctors' exemption
from all taxes levied on the Jews.[47] This exposes another level of the tension
Jewish community leaders must have experienced between their varying allegiances: personal, familial, and communal. For the *condestabuli* involved in
the Mosca case, securing the Mosca family's portion of the Jewish tax would

lighten the burden for the rest of the city's Jews; for other community leaders, such as the doctors appealing in 1438, the ability to evade the Jewish tax, even if to the detriment of the rank and file, was too financially significant personally to set aside.

This particular crisis, however, was tempered by circumstances outside the control of the Candiote *kehillah*. In 1441, two years after the initial war-debt order, and ostensibly as a direct result of it, Venice revoked the medical exemption once and for all. The Senate in the metropole heard about the inability to collect the money from maritime Jews and offered a complaint that purports to be sympathetic to the plight of the rest of the Jews: with all of the rich (*potentes*) Jews claiming exemptions, the burden had fallen squarely and painfully on the shoulders of the less wealthy. Of course, this sympathy had its limits; the Senate was unwilling to lighten the collective weight, as the war still needed to be funded. Instead, the Senate chose to revoke all exemptions from all Jews—including doctors—in the Stato da mar.[48] Though we do not know if a Jew brought the initial complaint to the Senate, it is inconceivable that the disparity between those who were exempted and those who were obligated to pay did not create animosity within the corporate body of the Jews. Ironically, then, the end of the exemption may have at least removed one source of internal tension as Venice's exploitative tax program could become a weight equally felt by all Jews, doctors and others alike.

* * *

To be sure, as I have already intimated, other communities in the medieval world experienced some of the same tensions that faced the community of Candia—financial pressures, and particularly the tension surrounding corporate taxation policy. In thirteenth-century Barcelona, a document formulary offering a template for taxation reallocation expresses the common lament of Jews suffering from a state-imposed tax burden:

> We the elders and leaders and heads of the community of such and such a city [say]: so it was that for our sins and for the sins our generation . . . suffering multiplied from the heaviness of the penalties and the magnitude of taxation and the burden of all sorts of labor services imposed upon us daily . . . for our enemies have placed their yoke upon us; this one says, bring your [land] taxes, and this one says, bring your poll taxes, . . . and thus the members of our community

became fewer in the city, until for our sins we remained, a few of many . . . and the taxes that used to be imposed on all of our compatriots rebounded upon the heads of those who remained, until they could no longer bear them.[49]

The document's placement inside a formulary suggests that the author of this work, Judah Bartzeloni, believed it had wide applicability, at least in Spain, but perhaps beyond the peninsula as well. Throughout Europe, medieval state-building was accompanied by highly organized tax systems, and corporate associations like Jews were targeted.

But this theoretical case from Barcelona reflects an expectation quite at odds with what Candiote Jews experienced. In the next section of Bartzeloni's formula, the "elders and leaders and heads" of the Jewish community sought to negate the state burden by internally reallocating and redistributing the money owed. Internal reorganization among the Jews could solve external problems, claims this document, and there was no need to involve the secular authorities. In fact, in the Spanish case, the template for reallocation warns its signatories not to "mention anything about this assessment to the rulers."[50] In Crete, however, we have witnessed the *condestabulo* seeking to uphold the current allocation system and pressing for payment those burdened Jews who sought legal loopholes. Even those who held the position of *condestabulo* were willing to access the power of the secular court to enforce this system. Nevertheless, when concerned with personal and familial interest, these same men and their families would not hesitate to seek their own exemptions from the communal tax. In Candia, taxation became for the leadership an awkward example of complicated loyalties perhaps unforeseen by theoreticians such as Bartzeloni.

The Duke in the Synagogue

Although it remains noteworthy that the leader of the Jewish community chose to involve a medieval state in the inner workings of his *kahal*, taxation is a topic that fundamentally links the *kahal* with the sovereign state. Yet it is not solely in these liminal zones of the *kahal's* institutional responsibilities where we see leadership elites inviting in state intervention. In fact, in a number of cases, we witness these community leaders asking for ducal arbitration in the workings of the central institution of the *kahal*: the synagogue.

Money is the medium of civil litigation, and there was money involved in synagogue life. The line between religious and family interests can often be little separated from questions of property and ownership. Such is the lesson learned from a short entry in the ducal court records about a fight over a seat. Although the very curt court record betrays few of the details—neither the defendant nor the arguments made in the case are preserved—the essential narrative is made clear in the judgment from December 1439 that Michiel Sacerdos "should be able to stand and sit in the priests' synagogue, called Chochanitico, in the place in which his late father, Samuel, stood and sat."[51] According to Michiel, the seat he claimed had belonged to his father, Samuel, who obtained it when his own father, Joste, had bequeathed it to him. The duke and his councillors apparently agreed; the family seat belonged—legally—to Michiel.

The strange fight over a seat in the synagogue has its origins in Jewish tradition. The idea of establishing a consistent spot to pray in both while sitting and standing, known as a *maqom qavuah* (lit. "established location"), stems from a number of Talmudic discussions that find biblical precedent for the concept.[52] Medieval commentators, including Solomon ibn Adret, explained that a fixed prayer spot helped focus the mind for prayer and created an atmosphere of seriousness in the synagogue.[53]

With regard to Michiel, however, it seems that his distress over his fixed prayer location stemmed not only from a religious concern but from a point of familial honor. His family, members of the priestly class, had attended this priestly synagogue for at least three generations. This spot had likewise been used by the men in the family for three generations. We cannot know more than this, as no parallel court entries record the backstory of this case.

To be sure, this was not simply a question of honor; it was also a question of money. Although in the modern world the *maqom qavuah* is generally a social convention, in some medieval communities, the chosen seat was owned outright. It could even be bequeathed as part of an estate, as Rabbi Samuel Ascandrani had bequeathed his synagogue seat to his heir in thirteenth-century Barcelona. Because his heir was a daughter, a woman named Bonadona, who obviously could not sit among men in the sex-segregated synagogue space, it is clear that this bequest had financial value (listed alongside his real estate and vineyard in a Jewish court hearing) and that Bonadona was never intended to become an actual user of the seat.[54] Yet when Bonadona became concerned about provisions in her father's bequests, she turned to Solomon ibn Adret and his Jewish court and asked for a review of her father's will. In contrast, Michiel

Sacerdos—an elite member of Cretan Jewish society, if we can judge by his name, family longevity in this prominent synagogue, and financial where-withal to own a synagogue seat—bypassed the Jewish authorities entirely, comfortably asking the ducal court to make decisions about the internal life of the synagogue, in the guise of a dispute over ownership. The state was happy to intervene and forced the issue, compelling the leadership of the synagogue, which ostensibly did not want Michiel in that seat, to comply with its directive. So much for corporate self-governance.

The Crisis of the Cantors

This was not the only time the state intervened in the very workings of a Candiote synagogue, nor was this the most egregiously dangerous—at least from the perspective of some of Crete's rabbinic minds. Although Rabbi Moses Capsali (1420–95) had left his home in Crete to study in the *yeshivot* of Ashkenaz, and then to lead the Jewish community in Constantinople, he remained for the Candiote leadership a source of rabbinic wisdom and advice, and they often turned to him to answer particularly thorny questions of law and ethics.[55] Collected among *Taqqanot Qandiya* is a responsum written by Moses Capsali in the summer of 1458, addressed to the heads of Candia's community (including a relative, Eliezer Capsali), who had requested from him an opinion. The topic was a crisis in the office of *hazzan*, literally cantor, but a position that in reality was more akin to chief executive of an individual synagogue.[56] Each synagogue had a *hazzan* who appears to have been a powerful force in the microcosm of that building and its subcommunity of Jews. In explaining the query his responsum sought to address, Capsali recounted that the Venetian government had somehow become involved in the selection of a *hazzan* in one of the city's synagogues: "And you asked about the issue of the cantor who was appointed silently [or: violently/aggressively; *be-alimut*] by the patrician [*ha-partamim*] rulers of the lands and the ministers of the states, and was not appointed by the seven good-men of the city according to the law and the custom of our holy fathers, the sages of Candia, may their memories be a blessing."[57]

Capsali expressed his horror at such a situation. Yet he targeted his ire not at the Venetian government that had stepped into an area of Jewish semiautonomous rule. Rather, he blamed Jewish men: "How did men arise in your midst who would violate the covenant of commandment [mitzvah] and the laws, *new people who have recently come, whom your ancestors could not have imagined?*" This last phrase was an expression he borrowed from Deuteronomy

32:17, which incidentally seems to have been a favorite—he used the same words to denigrate Jews who had brought innovations in Jewish divorce.[58] Although in this case Capsali did not articulate the identities of the "newcomers," he claims that they were a group apart from the traditional leadership of Candia who wrote the inquiry; those traditional leaders, he must have assumed, would be precisely the ones who would closely hew to the ways of the Candiote sages. From the view of Capsali's responsum, practices in which Candiote Jews allowed Venice to interfere in their internal communal life were a new problem in the late 1450s, sparked by new troublemakers.

But it could be solved with swift action. By way of resolving the conflict, Capsali ordered the community leaders to publicly demand that the *hazzan* step down. If he refused, they should impose upon him a social ostracism and isolation akin to excommunication. According to a note appended to the letter, community leader Moses Casani read Capsali's missive aloud at a gathering of the community, an act of shaming that quickly convinced the *hazzan* to step down. Capsali's solution had worked, or so it seemed: the insiders would shame the outsiders, and life would return to "normal."

This conclusion, however—that is to say, the treatment of this problem as a one-and-done crisis speedily resolved—needs a bit of contextualization, starting with a bit more reading within *Taqqanot Qandiya* itself. The *taqqanah* immediately preceding Moses Capsali's letter, the final ordinance from the collection passed in early spring 1363, suggests that the problem of external intervention in the naming of cantors was not a new problem at all.[59] The laconic entry records:

> Furthermore, let it be known that it is not permitted for those seeking the cantorship to take it by means of violent Gentiles [*goyim almim*],[60] whether by pleas or threats, or through decrees from harsh lords [*adonim qashim*]. For this is not the law of Moses and Jewish custom [*ke-da'at mosheh ve-yehudit*],[61] and [the one seeking office] should not be *accepted by the multitude of his brothers*[62] and he should not approach the holy [sanctuary] to become the cantor since he has not done good for his people, *for the prosecutor cannot become the defense attorney.*[63]

By the 1360s, therefore, the Jewish leadership was already faced with the prospect of external intervention in the naming of synagogue cantors, spurred by the candidate for cantor himself. Unlike in Moses Capsali's letter from almost a century later, this earlier ordinance does not explicitly identify the Venetian government itself; we are not told to which violent Gentiles or to which harsh lords the *taqqanah* is hinting. And, as is typical with both the genre of *taqqanot* in general and those from Candia is particular, we are given no specific details to inform us about the context—about the crisis—in which such an ordinance was passed. Clearly, from the point of view of the 1363 ordinance, and from Capsali's angry epistle a century later, such a request for Venetian intervention was not an acceptable use of the state judicial apparatus. A line was crossed when a Candiote elite sought synagogue election through such means.

But if such behavior disgusted one part of the rabbinic leadership and their lay allies, the Hebrew sources hide the layers of meaning and complicity in such behavior. Indeed, if we broaden our scope beyond *Taqqanot Qandiya* to include the vantage point of the ducal court records, an even more detailed picture appears—one that sheds light on the sorts of circumstances in which elite Jews chose to involve the ducal court in their internal election processes. Despite the ordinance from 1363, a case inviting the duke's input on the naming of a *hazzan* had come before the ducal court in 1374, and another suit on the same topic was heard in 1411. Sure enough, the disputes involved not newcomers but members of the communal elite. In the early fifteenth-century case, the litigant was a man whose parents had built the very synagogue in which he wished to act as *hazzan*.

In this later case, from October 1411, Tam Belo, son of the late Chai, brought suit against the current *condestabulo*, Shabbetai Casani, over the election of the *sacerdos* of the Stroviliatiko (ostensibly the same as the Seviliatiko) synagogue.[64] Though *sacerdos* literally means "priest," it is clearly used in this context to refer to the position of *hazzan*, cantor, who served the synagogue in a leadership role that must have appeared to the court as similar to the role of a priest in a church. In his petition, Tam explained that in order to name a new *sacerdos* at any synagogue in Candia, the current *condestabulo* and his councillors were mandated to choose seven men who would then become the formal electorate with the power to appoint a new *sacerdos*; the elected cantor would then hold his position for two years. Once he completed his two years, he could not hold the position again for four years. This reference to the proper modes of election, based on an electorate of seven men, recalls Moses Capsali's assertion that seven "good men" of the city should choose the *hazzan* but offers more particulars.

In making his case, Tam called upon a precedent and historical memory from a previous lawsuit brought in 1374. He notes that, as a result of the previous lawsuit, the duke and his councillors had explicitly confirmed this communal practice of having a two-year tenure, a four-year mandatory break, and a panel of seven electors. Moreover, the ducal government threatened anyone who dared transgress this system with a hefty enough fine of twenty-five hyperpera. But it was not enough for the Jewish leadership of Candia to have this ducal court judgment. Nor was it enough to rely on an internal *taqqanah*. Instead, according to Tam Belo's testimony, the Jewish leadership had a Latin notary formulate a legally binding contract in 1374, applicable to all current and future communal leaders.

Tam, a member of the Stroviliatiko (i.e., Seviliatiko) synagogue—and not just a member but part of the elite family that built it, as he stated in his petition—claimed that if one were to properly follow the rules, he himself was supposed to be named the newest cantor, with all the concomitant (though unnamed) benefits.[65] But he had been prevented from taking his rightful post when the *condestabulo* and his councillors improperly intervened and refused him the position. Faced with this impediment, Tam brought his case before the secular court.

Ironically, at least as far as Tam represented his case, he was asking the Venetian government to intervene in order to demand that the Jewish communal organization remain both internal and fair—that is to say, that the Jewish community follow its own rules! According to Tam, the *condestabulo* and his councillors were the ones guilty of improper intervention in the election of the *hazzan*, and in doing so they were not only defying "the customs of the fathers" (to paraphrase one of Moses Capsali's favorite expressions) but simultaneously defying Venetian law. For Tam, Jewish custom in Candia and Venetian law were not in opposition but rather in agreement; it was only the Jewish leadership that refused to uphold them both. The secular court could be the enforcement arm for an authentic upholding of community custom (so claimed the plaintiff) when the internal leadership refused to follow its own rules.

* * *

The circumstances surrounding this court case offer important insight into government involvement in the community's internal Jewish life beyond just one suit. It highlights the recourse of the Jewish leadership to the secular authority and its notarial arm as a means of legitimating its own internal agreements—a practice apparently deemed unproblematic. This fact sheds light on the methods of electing officials that had been spelled out in the Hebrew *taqqanot* during the reforms of 1363. In a decree titled "An ordinance [lit. fence] for the election of seven good-men [*tovei*] of the community," the signatories of the reforms declared that upon the election of a new *condestabulo* (no councillors are mentioned, though a number of lines of the manuscript are illegible), the new leader chooses seven "important men from the good men of the community." Their role, according to the Hebrew decree, was "to uphold and strengthen that which the community sets in place and decrees, on all of the issues which are for the need of this community, and to fix and to straighten every obstinate and crooked thing which it [i.e., the *kahal*] may do which is outside the laws of the community during his [i.e., the *condestabu-lo's*] tenure."[66] During each *condestabulo's* time in office, then, the *kahal* also formed a larger board of seven who were meant to uphold and enforce (in whatever unspecified way) the communal rules and decrees. Though this ordinance does not indicate that these are the same seven called to name synagogue cantors, it certainly seems likely.

Although this structure of choosing communal officials appears to be an internal process, the final line of this *taqqanah* hints otherwise. As in the Hebrew act from 1406 discussed at the opening of this chapter, the role of the Venetian government is written into the ordinance itself: "And according to this set-up should this topic be dealt with forever, *until the spirit be poured upon us from on high.*[67] And only if the will of our lords, the duke and the captain and his advisors (may their glory be raised), is [in agreement] with this [plan]."[68] At first glance, this may seem like a commonplace statement intended to appease the colonial government, but without active implication. The events of 1374 as outlined in the Latin court case, however, hint otherwise: that the active interference of the Venetian government suggested in the Hebrew ordinance was intended to be, and was, real. Eleven years after the decree of 1363, the somewhat vague organization and election principles set down in this ordinance were made more detailed because of government intervention, verified in a Venetian courtroom, and notarized in a Latin legal instrument. Some elite Jews had asked Venice to intervene; at that point, the ducal court had confirmed the practice of creating an electoral council of seven men and had pressed the Jewish leadership to make it official in a Latin notarized contract—which they did. It was this contract that gave Tam the confidence to ask the ducal court to intervene in his own situation in 1411. The ducal court was asked to spell out consequences for noncompliance, a financial penalty backed up by the colonial government itself. Venice's theoretical "glory" evolved into a literal enforcement power in the form of a significant penalty for those who do not observe "that which the community sets in place and decrees."

The final judgment in Tam's court case of 1411, however, also suggests the ways in which the acceptance of some amount of intervention could become a slippery slope. Instead of choosing to side either with the *condestabulo* or with Tam, the court provided a compromise solution in which it further inserted itself into the decision-making process. Undermining the agreement made in 1374, by which the *condestabulo* was empowered to choose the seven men of the electorate, the duke and his councillors decreed the following: when a new cantor was to be chosen in the Stroviliatiko synagogue, the *condestabulo* at that time was given the right to choose three electors, while Tam and his brother (apparently as the first family of the synagogue) would choose another three. This accounts for six men. The duke decreed that these six should attempt to reach an agreement, but if they could not agree, a final elector should be chosen. Here we see the most blatant change: this final elector, the tiebreaker, would be chosen by the colonial government.

This final sentence thus showcases the possible extent of government intervention and its effect on both the institutional leadership and other Jews. Instead of serving as a powerful enforcement arm for already established internal policies, the intervention of the court actually undermined the independent corporate decision-making power of the Jewish community. Refusing to side with the official leader of the community, the ducal court chose a compromise resolution that empowered itself to the detriment of the Jewish community on all sides. It is clear that Tam's family and the *condestabulo's* company had differences of opinion over whom to elect as cantor; it is likely that this division would continue in future years. A split vote would be more than probable. By establishing itself as the body empowered to choose a final elector, the colonial government had given itself the deciding vote in the internal election process of the Jewish community. It does not surprise us, then, that in a list of the accomplishments of some of the *condestabuli* of the Jewish community of Candia, Shabbetai Casani is remembered for "acting regarding the *hazzanim*, that they will be under the authority of the *condestabulo* and his councilors."[69] The official leadership council of Candia was clearly very unhappy with the outcome of this trial and worked to prevent it from happening again in the future.

Broader Implications: The Synagogue Crisis and Conversion

In the intervening years between Tam Belo's lawsuit in 1411 and Moses Capsa-li's angry responsum of 1458, we hear nothing on the matter from the official record of *Taqqanot Qandiya*. But the ducal court record suggests one more way in which local administrative control over synagogues could be contested and, in doing so, could create the space for Venetian intervention—much to the long-term chagrin and pain of the Jewish community. In this case, a lawsuit from 1421, once again a person claiming his supposed family rights to a synagogue came before the ducal court, and once again Shabbetai Casani was called as defendant.[70] But in this case, the plaintiff was not exactly a member of the Jewish community. He was Francesco Trivisano, identified as "olim iudeus, nunc christianus": formerly a Jew, now a Christian. In the case record, Francesco is immediately identified as the son of a late Jew named Parna. This reference is not typical; generally a convert's Jewish family is not directly named. But the reason for this unusual identification quickly becomes clear: it was precisely his connection to his old family that Francesco wanted to publicize. Indeed, Francesco claimed that in the 1260s—about a century and a half earlier—a group of Jews had come together to buy a synagogue building from a certain Venetian nobleman and that by the 1330s, the synagogue had been held by Francesco's great-grandfather, a certain Parna. Then it was in his grandfather Elia's hands. But somehow, Francesco noted, now it was in the hands of Shabbetai Casani. Francesco's suit aimed at recovering the syna-gogue for himself, as the legitimate descendant of Parna and Elia. Ostensibly, Francesco saw a financial windfall in the synagogue, though how, precisely, he might profit from taking over the building remains vague.

In legal terms, the suit started as a petition to force Shabbetai to produce notarial records to show that the Casani family had a legal right to possession of the synagogue. Indeed, Shabbetai produced record after record to show that there had been an official transfer in 1407 to Shabbetai's father—with proper license granted by the Venetian judges responsible for inheritance law.[71] But Francesco continued to press the case, claiming fraudulent dealings and deceptive practices and records. He further argued that the synagogue land was part of a military feudatory (one of the mechanisms of noble land distri-bution in Crete) and that it was wholly forbidden for Greeks and Jews to hold feudatory land. He then outlined other reasons why Jews should not be able to hold the land and building.

In defending himself, Shabbetai Casani cited legal precedent and claimed that the synagogue was not actually his. Rather, it belonged to the *universitas iudeorum*—it belonged to the *kahal* as a whole; he simply held it in a sort of legal mechanism, which is how Francesco's relatives also had held it. Regarding the question of Jews on feudatory land, he said, the entire Jewish Quarter and the third of the city of Candia where the Greeks live is all technically (*de iure*) feudatory land. He also he noted that if Francesco had rights to the synagogue, then so did his three siblings—a brother and two sisters—ostensibly still members of the Jewish community. Moreover, Shabbetai noted, the person who holds the synagogue is actually the person who also runs it, officiating and governing. Is that what the new Christian Francesco hoped to do?

As a convert, Francesco tried to actively play both sides of his identity. On the one hand, he claimed his right to a synagogue building because of his Jewish past. He listed his Jewish ancestors, proudly connecting himself with them, at least as far as their material concerns go. They owned the synagogue, and he was still their rightful heir, and thus he should have possession of the synagogue too. But then he turned the tables. His own Jewish ancestors held the synagogue, but no Jew should actually be allowed to hold this synagogue at all. Only he—once a Jew, now a Latin—could properly hold this synagogue on military feudatory land. The convert from Judaism to Christianity tried to use the court as a place to assert both the rights afforded to him as a member of a Jewish family and the rights afforded to him as a new Christian.

Importantly for our discussion of Venetian intervention in Jewish self-rule, the court actually did find for Francesco, nullifying the contracts Shabbetai had shown. We know nothing about what this meant for the synagogue in the long run; indeed, the register of the suit never identified the synagogue, its name, or its precise location. We must assume that this land and synagogue were lost to the Jewish community from here forward. In this case, it was not a current member of the Jewish community whose choice to litigate in Venice's civil court ended up undermining Jewish self-governance but a former member of the same elite whose litigative choice removed from the Jewish community some of the very land it had owned, and one of the very centers of communal religious life. But in helping define the ways in which use of the ducal court could promote Venetian intervention, this case suggests that the overlapping jurisdictions of ownership, overlapping modes of legal claims, and the liminal space between Jewish and non-Jewish members of the community created further space for Venice to enter—when invited.

Excommunication: Choosing Extreme Intervention

The only real social tool that a *kehillah* could wield, excommunication, was and remains a prime symbol of Jewish communal autonomy. It was the social enforcement tool par excellence that Jewish communities could use to sway the behavior of a recalcitrant member. As we saw with Capsali's *hazzan*, excommunication could indeed work and could prevent the effects of state intervention from influencing the community. But the pull to involve the Venetian state in intra-elite disputes became so strong that even this emblem of autonomy ended up in government hands. In fact, it seems that over the course of the fifteenth and sixteenth centuries, the Jewish leadership chose to hand over to the duke the right to approve Jewish excommunication.

When read alone, a strange, short record in the Latin court registers dated to 1409 seems to tell the opposite story.[72] This entry records that seven members of the Jewish community—men whose names are familiar as Jewish community leaders, and also identified as residents of the Jewish Quarter—came before the duke and "humbly explained" that "the Jewish Quarter was being corrupted by the vices of adultery." Moreover, they explained that "according to their rite and habits, it was expedient to cautiously admonish the adulterers in order that they would refrain" from the adultery. In this case, such admonitions seem to have failed. In fact, the seven men explain that they have come before the duke to request permission to follow the mandate of the Law of Moses (here, the *lex moisis*) and excommunicate the adulterers. The duke and his councillors evaluated the case, the entry records, and adjudicated that these men should be allowed to make an excommunication order.

If such a Latin court entry makes one suspect that the colonial government had mandated Jewish petitions before permitting intra-Jewish excommunication, an entry in *Taqqanot Qandiya* from 1527—over a century later—seems to tell a different story. In a catchall ordinance mostly dealing with synagogue-related problems (lack of attendance, inappropriate closure), Elia Capsali includes an intervention regarding excommunication. Borrowing his great-uncle Moses Capsali's favorite phrase, he blames "new people recently come" for a bad turn of events: some Candiote Jews were carelessly excommunicating their fellow Jews for even minor wrongs. "Therefore we have agreed," then *condestabulo* Capsali writes, "that no man will be allowed to excommunicate except if he gets permission first from the town-crier [*makhriz*] of our sovereign." Capsali further mandates that the town crier (likely identified with the Venetian *gastaldo*) should instruct the petitioner regarding how to go about undertaking the excommunication and should instruct him on which synagogue to use for the formal announcement.[73]

Was such behavior new in the sixteenth century? Or was the petition about excommunicating adulterers from 1409 the beginning of a process of handing over the power of excommunication to the Venetian colonial government? Further investigation of *Taqqanot Qandiya* suggests that we ought to read this evolution as Capsali did: in reference to tensions between the official leadership council and other elites in Candia. Among the very first ordinances from 1228 is an entry forbidding anyone to call excommunications on anyone "without the permission of the appointed leaders and with the advice of the officers [*sarim*] and wise men [*hakhamim*]."[74] In the fourteenth-century revision of these *taqqanot*, the officer with the power to permit excommunications is more specific—the *condestabulo* in office at the time—as are the guilty parties: members of various synagogues (and perhaps elites specific to those synagogues) who close down the synagogue during prayer time to call the excommunication.[75] Clearly the tendency for those other than the current leaders to engage in excommunication was not new in the sixteenth century.

A far longer entry on this matter is found among the reforming ordinances of 1363, some forty years before the first excommunication petition brought before the Venetian court appears. Here, those accused of arbitrarily engaging in excommunication explicitly include the *hazzanim* of individual synagogues. The process for excommunicating also becomes even more specific: a person wanting to excommunicate a fellow Jew must first appeal to the seven elected "good men" of the city. These seven men must decide whether or not to approve the excommunication, and they must also instruct the petitioner on how to go about calling the ban: "and do not veer right or left from all that they will instruct him."[76]

It must be these seven men, then, who appear before the duke in 1409 to request ducal imprimatur for their excommunication. Seen in this light, it appears that internal controls had failed; elite members of individual synagogues (including *hazzanim*) had proven unwilling to limit their acts of excommunication to those approved by the official *kehillah* board. The authority of the *condestabulo* did not limit these acts, and if we read the 1409 case as a further step past the reforming ordinance of 1363, neither was the board of seven "good men" powerful enough to control those choosing to excommunicate on their own. By 1409, then, the seven men, likely in consultation with the *condestabulo*, had decided to bolster their own power by bringing in the authority of the Venetian government to further intervene. We do not know

what happened between 1409 and 1527, when Elia Capsali recorded for posterity that all excommunication petitions must be approved by a representative of
the Venetian government.[77] Could Venice have pushed the Jewish community
to formalize its petitioning system? Could Venice have forced the *kehillah* to
hand over its chief tool of social control? Perhaps, but that is not what Capsali
says. Rather, at least in its most explicit and straightforward interpretation, the
taqqanah tells us that it was the choice of Capsali's council of elite community
leaders. In seeking a mechanism to retain control and not allow other elites
from asserting their power, they requested Venetian intervention in this most
serious of acts.

* * *

A short court record from the end of the period under study here suggests just
how common it became for Jewish community leadership to air the *kahal*'s
institutional dirty laundry before the Venetian judiciary. In September 1451,
Mioche (son of Moses) Delmedigo sued Solomon, son of the late Potho, over
236 hyperpera Mioche claimed Solomon owed him. But this was not the result
of a business deal gone sour. Rather, Mioche had served as *condestabulo* of
the Jewish community in the recent past but had not received the salary he
claimed had been promised: 236 hyperpera for his time in office. Solomon, on
the other hand, was the current *condestabulo*, and in his official capacity as the
head of the *kahal*, and ostensibly as the holder of the communal purse strings,
he was called to defend the claims of nonpayment.[78] For Mioche Delmedigo,
his own need to pay the bills—or at least his need for his efforts to be recognized through promised remuneration—far exceeded any sense that intralead-
ership squabbles over the *kahal* should remain internal to the community.

For the men who were both community leaders and private individuals
with personal concerns, extracommunal interests created a significant tension.
The notion of a tension between the individual interests of the Jewish elite and
the needs of the community as a whole has been woven into many parts of this
study. Elia Capsali surely sought to promote his friendship with the duke of
Crete to aid his community, but the personal benefits he could obtain should
not be ignored. Joseph Missini, whose last will illustrates that he cared deeply
for his community of Jews in Crete and beyond, was also willing to marshal
the malleable secular court system to maintain his bigamous marriage. Judah
de Damasco leveraged his role as a doctor to maintain a Greek Orthodox
mistress, while also serving the Jewish community in a formal function. In

each of these cases, the tensions between elite families' individual and community interests played out in the end in the arena of the ducal court, not within the framework of the Jewish communal organization. It was a venue in which those pursuing their individual interests could seek protection from the community's will, and where the community leadership in their official capacity could push individuals to recognize wider communal interests. The same individuals, depending on the situation, could find themselves on either side of this interest divide.

The men who led the Jewish community of Candia were part and parcel of broader Candiote society, individuals with personal, familial, and economic interests. Yet in general terms, they still acted—effectively, it seems—for the communal cause. This duality of focus presents quite a different picture than the one usually assigned to medieval rabbinic and communal leadership, whom we tend to perceive as halachic first. In this historiographic narrative, their relationship to secular legal culture is relegated to the world of *dinah de-malkhutah dinah*—that is to say, a necessary evil that reflects the reality of living as a minority in a non-Jewish society. But as this study has illustrated throughout, premodern Jewish axes of identity were more complicated, and many premodern Jews felt deep affiliation and social connection with their so-called host societies. Likewise, the legal culture of places like the Venetian empire was not a social factor ignored or begrudgingly accepted by Jews but actively adopted and utilized by them. It was part of an overlapping world of jurisdictions, and the turn to the Venetian colonial courts was as natural—if not more so—than turning inward and dealing with disputes amongst the *kahal* itself. The implications of this complex set of identities, affinities, and institutional interests were equally as important for those desiring and enacting leadership as they were for those concerned with their own personal financial and juridical lives.

Crete's Jewish Renaissance Men in Context

In the aftermath of the successful Ottoman conquest of Constantinople in 1453, Byzantine refugees flooded Candia. By migrating to Crete, they were seeking to hold onto their Greek identity—a choice that seems ironic considering the vociferous anti-Venetian sentiments that exploded from time to time on the island. These newcomers would join and help produce the cultural flourishing we now call the Cretan Renaissance. Crete, already a cosmopolitan financial center, would become a hub of artistic and literary creativity expressed in a style defined by its fusion of Greek and Latin sensibilities, an approach deemed central to the Renaissance project.[1]

Crete's Jews, in their own ways, took part in this cultural flourishing. Indeed, two native sons of the Jewish community would put Candiote Jewry on the map in a new way in this period. Scion of the famed family we have witnessed traveling from Germany to Negroponte and then to Crete, Elia Delmedigo would spend the late fifteenth century working in Latin in Italy— explaining Aristotelian and Averroistic philosophy to Italy's Christian Hebraists in person, through translations into Latin, and in his own Latin compositions—before returning to Crete to lead the Candiote *kehillah* and to write his own Hebrew work of Jewish-Averroistic fusion, the *Behinat Hadat* (or "Examination of Religion"). Admired by Jews and Christians alike, an expert in philosophy as well as Talmud, Elijah Cretensis, as some knew him, would embody the new Renaissance Jew.[2]

A child when Elia Delmedigo led the Jewish community in Crete, Elia Capsali, whom we met in Chapter 1 taking a stroll in 1540s Candia, would emerge as a historian, rabbi, community leader, and the most important son of Candia's greatest Jewish family. Capsali also would bridge the cultural gap between Jewish and secular modes of learning. He would write histories in a way not much attended to before this period—histories not of the Jewish people alone but of Venice itself (*Divrei ha-yamim le-malkhut Venezia*, 1517) and of the Ottoman Empire (*Seder Eliyahu Zuta*, 1523). Like his older relative (for Capsali was also a Delmedigo, on his mother's side) who had fused Jewish and "Greek" thought into one philosophical approach, the younger Elia would weave the story of the Jews into a broader history, attentive to doges and Ashkenazi immigrants, sultans and Sephardi refugees, contemporary history and its parallels to the Hebrew Bible.[3] Capsali, like Delmedigo, consciously situated himself in overlapping thought-worlds as he did in overlapping political worlds—just like he made sure to build a relationship with his "dear friend," the duke of Crete. In their interests and expertise, intersecting realms and complex creative outlets, Capsali and Delmedigo each characterize the Jewish Renaissance man who fit so easily in the Cretan cultural world after 1453.

As much as each of these men—and the other renaissance men in their circles[4]—must be seen as a product of the world after the fall of Constantinople, they cannot be read outside the context of their community's previous centuries of history, when Venetian Crete existed side by side with a reduced but still viable Byzantine Empire.[5] Indeed, as this study has illustrated, the Jews of Venetian Crete lived as part of the wider colonial society in Venetian Candia and participated in—both absorbing and contributing to—that cultural and social milieu. Although the Jewish Quarter offered a sense of privacy and autonomy, its location and open access suggest that the *kehillah* space offers analyzers of the community a sort of synecdoche of Jewish life. The Judaica was a neighborhood enmeshed within the city grid, not a locked ghetto—not even following the walling in of the quarter, a process that, in any event, took over a century to complete.

Like Jewish life across the city, the Judaica's importance lay neither in its actual separation from nor in its physical openness to the broader society. Rather, the essential significance of the Judaica stems from the way the community's Jews interpreted its meaning. A contradictory space in many ways, the Judaica could contain both the drive to self-segregate and protect and the need to welcome in outsiders, whether Candiote Christians or Jews from suspect villages. Likewise could individual Jewish inhabitants of Candia's Judaica live comfortably between multiple realities and values. Medieval Candiote Jews could be worldly and provincial, isolated and inviting, halachic and law-breaking, and these opposing qualities could often be found within individual Jews—elite leaders, wealthy women, and low-status people alike.

That is to say, the reality of interaction did not prevent the Jews of Candia from experiencing a sense of safety as a result of their ability to hold their own neighborhood. Indeed, the Judaica's relative locational isolation in a corner of the city and its growing set of walls enabled the community's leadership to feel a sense of ownership over the neighborhood and its environs. This perceived control over the space sparked a desire to control what occurred within, from who could sell food on the street to how to relate to the sound of monastic prayer bells ringing next door. In reality, though, the individual Jews who lived within the walls made their own decisions, without constant concern for the leadership's directives. They bought and sold food that they deemed acceptable, they cavorted with Jewish prostitutes (or prostituted themselves) within Jewish-owned buildings, they left the quarter on Sabbath precisely when their leaders told them they should be in synagogue. To be sure, many Jews lived within the acceptable bounds of Jewish life in the Judaica, and these breaches of the leadership's rules do not demonstrate anarchy or chaos within its confines. But in contrast to the typical view of medieval Jewish communities as homogenous, rule abiding, and community minded, Jewish behavior in Candia suggests a community with diverse approaches to community and Judaism, with individuals weighing communal interests against their own and often choosing their own utility over the official party line. Even members of the leadership class, scions of wealthy and prestigious families destined to hold office in the *kehillah*'s corporate organization, could exist on both sides of the divide—on one hand, signing the very ordinances that promoted self-segregation, control of the Judaica, and community-minded values while simultaneously, on the other hand, working quite outside the system, whether by building intimate relations with Candia's Christians or by inviting in secular institutions and officials of the colonial state to intervene and make judgments about intra-communal affairs.

Part of this diversity of approaches to Jewish life and identity stemmed from local factors: the very ethnic and ideological heterogeneity of the Jews of Candia, their easy mobility across the Mediterranean, and their sense that they could benefit from the Venetian system of law, justice, and policy. Though mostly of Romaniote origin, even those who came from old Jewish families long on the island held differing allegiances, whether to their Ashkenazi rabbis or their familial traditions, to Kabbalistic mysticism or rationalist philosophy. These very tensions would produce some of the most interesting Jewish thinkers of the fifteenth and sixteenth centuries, in the persons of Elia Delmedigo and Elia Capsali. While the creativity and scholarly output of these two men put them on the historical map far more clearly than their ancestors, those who came before them set the stage for the culturally cosmopolitan, intellectually interwoven views these men would disseminate.

* * *

One of the most visible ways that Candia's Jews intersected with, learned about, and integrated themselves into the city's wider social milieu and institutional structures was through their regular visitation of, litigation at, and professional employment through the colonial judiciary, especially the duke's highest court held in the open air of the Plateia, the city's central square and nerve center. Whether by choosing to watch court cases unfold on Saturday morning instead of attending Sabbath services, by suing family members or business partners or Jewish leaders in the same courts, or working as medical experts for the court system, many of Candia's Jews engaged with the judicial system and its ideologically tinged brand of justice throughout their lives. Even poor Jews who could not afford the court fees would encounter the justice system if they were wounded and needed to be evaluated, if they defaulted on debt, or if they were suspected of criminal activity. The ducal court was the quintessential Cretan institution known across the Mediterranean (including to Boccaccio), and Jewish residents of Candia were not left out of its social importance simply by dint of their religious affiliation.

Far from experiencing the justice system as a mode of colonial oppression, Candia's Jews understood the judiciary as a tool that could be marshaled for their own interests, whether group concerns or individual interests that went against those of their coreligionists, as a group or as individuals. It was a locus of empowerment for a surprisingly broad set of Jewish subgroups, including the leadership itself, those questioning the leadership's authority, and even women. That the secular courtroom became for them an important venue for intra-Jewish fighting does not suggest that the Jews were disconnected from Candia and simply using its institutions for the sake of convenience, disputing among themselves because they were not part and parcel of the broader society. Rather, their choice to play out intracommunal disputes in the sovereign court, and the ways in which they undertook the task, suggests just how deeply tied into Candiote society these Jews felt, for they framed their disputes according to Venetian sensibilities and statutes, while reframing Jewish law in terms a Catholic, patrician judge could understand.

The ways in which Jewish individuals—from unhappy spouses, to angry neighbors, to *condestabuli*—made use of colonial justice certainly tells us a great deal about the competing interests of the Jews in question and about their self-conception as part of the Venetian imperial enterprise. But even more so, it suggests a corrective to a common scholarly assumption about the relationship between medieval Jewish communities and the sovereign governments under which they lived. Expressing a scholarly commonplace, Robert Bonfil wrote: "The Jewish public, always and everywhere, saw itself through its communities as subject to Jewish law alone for the determination of its parameters and identity."[6] This theory holds that individual Jews "sought solutions to all questions, both public and private, within this normative system," that is, within the *kehillah*. It further suggests that these answers would be dictated through "subjugation to *halakhah*," as understood and translated for the people by the official "quasi-municipal organizational frameworks." Underlying this assumption is the idea that premodern Jews saw themselves primarily as part of a semiautonomous community and that for all castes within Jewish society, identity was tied up far more with the community than with their individual needs and concerns.

In Candia, at least, the model of easy subjugation to the will of the Jewish leadership does not meet the reality of the evidence. To be sure, a reading of elite Hebrew sources alone undoubtedly leaves this impression. As Uriel Simonsohn has noted in his discussion of Jewish and Christian use of early Islamic courts, "the principle of autonomous units based on confessional affiliation was best realized in the minds of those who sought to implement them—namely, the religious elites—and not necessarily in the lives of their communities."[7] Scholars of Jewish history have often assumed the validity of the rabbinic voice as a spokesman for all Jews and therefore have read rabbinic sources as true for all Jews. In many ways, the rabbis cannot be understood this way; they represent a set of elite power brokers who do not speak for the whole but rather seek to manage and stand for the whole. Communal ordinances that have served as evidence for these arguments must be interrogated for the under-the-surface tensions between the leadership (the authors of these ordinances) and their "public." We must move beyond a wholesale reliance on these sources and not simply allow Jewish voices to supply evidence on the unity of Jewish communities.

When we put Jewish sources into conversation with others, such as the Latin court documents explored here, a different picture comes to light. Throughout the sources from the fourteenth and fifteenth centuries, whether written from a Jewish or a Venetian point of view, we witness Jews using the apparatus of the colonial government as a way to express individual agency, often in opposition to the Jewish corporate entity and its leadership. Individual choice was a feature of this premodern community. Whether it stemmed from a rejection of the ineffectual and unenforceable nature of the Jewish court or from a conscious decision to access Venice's perhaps less-biased (toward individual Jews) and indubitably more regular court, Jews thought and acted outside the frame of their relationship to the *universitas iudeorum*. Indeed, we are witness to a variety of suits between two Jewish people that had nothing to do with the litigants qua members of the Jewish community. Rather, family ties, connections from within the spatial confines of the Judaica, and coreligionist business partnerships are the reason that Jews were suing other Jews.

These were not issues that destabilized the semiautonomous *kehillah* structure in Candia. Issues of importance to the community—both those that were intended to uphold the leadership's status quo and those in which members of the community hoped to unsettle the current circumstances of rule—were not simply kept inside what Bonfil called the "normative system" of Jewish institutional structures. Intracommunal fights were played out in the public venue, without the involvement of a *beit din* but with decided intervention of the duke and his councillors. Despite the seemingly incongruous venue, the religious leadership maneuvered through the secular court as part of their mandate to maintain control over the Jews of Crete and to maintain a status quo in terms of the identity markers of their supposed flock. Likewise, those who were unsatisfied were no less able to push back against the leadership's power in this public space, particularly when they saw that power becoming too concentrated or unfairly wielded.

* * *

Despite the focus on individuality, elite Jewish access to the halls of power was at times certainly a real boon to the community as a whole. At times, the community's leadership acted as liaisons, successfully speaking on behalf of the whole community, for example to protect them from unfair taxation. At other moments, Venetian support undoubtedly offered the Jewish leadership an important and powerful ally, one whose authority and legitimacy in the eyes of all those on Crete strengthened the position of a potentially flaccid *condestabulo*—even when his opponent was one of the Jewish flock. As such, the common image of a semiautonomous community engaging with the sovereign ruler only through an appointed and approved liaison is incomplete, if not simply incorrect. The role and reality of this liaison must be revisited. Moreover, for those not in leadership positions, access to Venice's ducal court proved to be a means of asserting control within the Jewish milieu. At times, the use of the courts resigned the leaders to a position of sheer impotence, unable even to control those things that were meant to be squarely within their purview, such as issues related to synagogue life.

The implications for our understanding of premodern Jewish individual agency are great. Every (sufficiently well-to-do) member of the Jewish community had access to an arbitrating power outside the framework of the Jewish community. The ducal court enabled those inside the box of a supposedly corporate entity to act independently. In some sense, the ducal court represents a defanging of the power of the *universitas iudeorum*, whose right to internal self-rule was at least in theory part of Venice's concession to its subject Jews. In moments when corporate power weakened, individual agency could find a voice. As such, we must reconsider the notion that medieval Jewish "power" existed only as a product of the structures of self-government. It is not that the *kehillah* did not have institutional authority; rather, the reality of legal pluralism offered the Jews of Candia alternative modes of power beyond the confines of the corporate body. And indeed, the *kehillah* structure itself could benefit from the intervention of the state, giving up some of its supposed autonomy for the sake of an ultimately more enforceable system. When we look beyond a set of moral judgments that deems autonomy the highest ideal, and when we recognize the overlapping worlds in which individual Jews and Jewish communities could take part, we can begin to see a different picture of the reality of Jewish life—and life for many inhabitants—in the late medieval Mediterranean.

An Epilogue: Ever After

The earliest origins of Jewish settlement on Crete remain somewhat murky. In the centuries before Venetian rule, we catch only glancing references in the writings of Philo, Josephus, and Christian authors and in letters from the Cairo Genizah.

But the end of this story of continuous Jewish life on the island—like much of European Jewish life—is tragically transparent. In late May 1944, three years after Nazi occupation of the island, Crete's remaining Jews—mostly residents of Khania (Venetian Canea), which had become the center of Jewish life on the island—were rounded up and imprisoned. Numbering just under three hundred, these Jews were herded a few weeks later onto a Greek freighter, the *Tanais* ("Danae"), along with Greek and Italian prisoners of war. The ship left port at Heraklion (formerly Candia), heading to a Polish concentration camp. On 9 June, a British submarine, unaware of the human prisoners aboard, torpedoed the ship in the dead of night. None of the prisoners survived. Only about twenty-five Cretan Jews, those who had managed to evade the roundup and those who had fled in advance, lived to see the liberation of Crete in October 1944, mere months later.[8] Thus ended almost two thousand years of Jewish daily life—millennia of loves and life cycles, prayers and market visits, family feuds and litigation, holiday meals and hide-tanning and philosophy—on this Mediterranean island.

Perhaps one day there will be vibrant Jewish life again on Crete. In the 1990s, the son of a Cretan Orthodox father and a Turkish Jewish mother took it upon himself to rebuild the synagogue at Khania. Despite financial challenges and two arson attacks in 2010, Nikos Stavroulakis (1932–2017, of blessed memory, who passed away shortly before this book was completed) managed to rebuild the Etz Hayyim synagogue, stock it with a library, and act as its spiritual director until his death. Khania has once again become a place associated with its Jewish past, and perhaps a renewed Jewish present.

Heraklion, Venice's city of Candia, however, has little trace of its Judaica and its Jewish past. The remnants of the last Venetian-era synagogue were bombed in World War II, bulldozed, and covered over. A park overlooking the blue waters of the Mediterranean and a museum lie on the old Jewish Quarter's foundations. The Historical Museum of Crete holds the last vestiges of the material evidence for Jewish life from Candia: a stone inscription from one of the synagogues ("believed to have stood in the same area as the Historical Museum of Crete," notes the accompanying sign), a stone relief of the crest of "Don Shaltiel Hen," and some headstones from the now vanished cemetery.[9] At least the historic models of the city under Venetian rule clearly mark out the Jewish Quarter. And a picture of the *Tanais*, the cargo ship upon which Crete's last Jewish community met its fate, also hangs on the wall.

Nevertheless, neither the community's abrupt, tragic end nor the limited memory of Jewish Candia in Greek spaces can efface the reality of Jewish life's vitality and continuity on Crete before World War II, and particularly through the Ottoman period. Although the centuries studied in this book characterize one of the golden ages of Jewish life on Crete, the community continued to thrive even after the death of its favorite son Elia Capsali around 1550. Despite challenges in the late sixteenth and seventeenth centuries, the Jewish community in Venetian Candia remained active and sizable. Capsali's successors continued to add to his collection of historical and legal documents, *Taqqanot Qandiya*, for another generation. Jewish literary, philosophical, and artistic production—that particular creative interaction of local and foreign, mystical and rational, specifically Jewish and that which was not—continued in Candia.[10] Business partners and family members continued to appeal to Venetian justice.

As the Ottoman advance threatened more and more of Venice's holdings by the sixteenth century, Crete became the only real remaining bulwark in the eastern Mediterranean. This anxiety did not escape the Jews of Candia, not least because the Greek population occasionally took out its fears of the Turks on them, as they did in an act of mob violence in 1538. Only Venetian military intervention at the last moment rescued those under attack.[11] In the 1570s Venice sent Giacomo Foscarini to Crete as *provveditore*, charging him with any and all powers that might help protect the island and prepare it for Ottoman incursions. Jews (and too-friendly Jewish-Christian interactions) became one of his particular targets, though he was certainly not the "Jew-baiter" scholars once imagined.[12]

More poignant struggles, it seems, came from the continued immigration of Jews to the island, in particular baptized Sephardim who immigrated to Crete in order to return to Judaism.[13] Nevertheless, unlike in other parts of the Stato da mar and the Ottoman Empire, Crete's Jewry did not divide into two separate communities of Romaniotes and Sephardim. Romaniote tradition remained dominant through the end of Venetian rule. New Jewish immigrants did, however, spark the need for more living space, and in the second half of the sixteenth century, as Venice built fortifications beyond the original city walls, Jews were allowed to settle west of the traditional Jewish Quarter, south of Dermata Bay.[14]

Jewish life continued on Crete, even as Venetian rule gave way to Ottoman. By 1646, the growing Jewish community in Khania had survived a siege and, along with the Jews of Rethymno, began to adapt to a new ruler: by that year, the Ottomans held the entire western part of the island. Candia would hold out until 1669, suffering perhaps the longest siege in European history. The Jewish Quarter witnessed a great deal of the fighting; Venetian batteries were placed on the Judaica's seawalls, making that neighborhood a particular target and site of destruction.[15] As the Siege of Candia progressed to its end, most inhabitants—including Jews—fled the city to seek haven, temporary or permanent, especially in other Venetian territories. Hundreds of Jews settled on the island of Zakynthos (Zante), where an explicitly "Cretan" synagogue was founded in 1699.[16]

But the Ottomans were eager to repopulate "Kandiye" (they essentially maintained the Venetian name), and they were keen on attracting Jews willing to settle and invest in the economic life of the city. Jews were allowed to buy property anywhere in Kandiye, no longer limited to the Jewish Quarter. Taking advantage of the glut of abandoned property left by fleeing Venetian Christians, Jewish settlement extended outward from the traditional Jewish Quarter toward the eastern districts.[17] By the 1690s, the Jewish population of the city seems to have recovered; an Ottoman tax census from 1693 reports 126 Jewish adult male taxpayers; a report from the French botanist Joseph Pitton de Tournafort from six years later counts a far larger number: a thousand Jews in the city (though likely including temporary merchants).[18]

Immediately after the end of the Ottoman siege, with a new sovereign in charge of Crete, the island's Jews also returned to another old habit: litigating and disputing against fellow Jews in the sovereign court. Turkish records dated to 1671—only two years after Venice surrendered and abandoned Candia—tell of two Jewish business partners seeking a resolution over jointly owned property before the Ottoman Muslim *qadi* (judge).[19]

What else they and their fellow Jews disputed in these courts remains unknown. The extent and contours of this Ottoman-era litigation by Jews in the *qadi* court—a new phase of Jewish engagement with colonial justice—remains a subject primed for its own investigative storyteller.

Notes

A NOTE ON USAGE

1. Frederic C. Lane and Reinhold C. Mueller, *Money and Banking in Medieval and Renaissance Venice*, vol. 1 (Baltimore: Johns Hopkins University Press, 1985), 296, 416.

2. See Lane and Mueller, *Money and Banking*, 296n28.

3. Lane and Mueller, *Money and Banking*, 297.

4. Among other locations in the text, ducats appear in a Hebrew contract recorded within *Taqqanot Qandiya* dated from 1530; the penalty for noncompliance is 50 *ducati*. *TQ* no. 83, p. 100. Elia Capsali mentions that his ancestor Elijah Delmedigo (active in the late fifteenth century) had collected a large amount of money, close to 100 florins ("prahim," meaning flowers, a literal translation), for a scheme to build kosher ovens that never came to anything. *TQ* no. 102, p. 134. Grossi are mentioned in *TQ* no. 43, p. 35, from 1363, also translated quite literally in Hebrew as "gdolim," i.e., "large ones."

5. For example, the Venetian government fines Joseph Missini (active at the end of the fourteenth century and the first decade of the fifteenth) 100 *dinarim*. *TQ* no. 46, p. 40.

INTRODUCTION

1. *TQ* no. 32, pp. 20–22, quote on p. 21.

2. *TQ* no. 32, p. 20.

3. *TQ* no. 32, p. 21.

4. For a classic scholarly view on "informing," or *mesirah*, still useful despite later studies, see David Kaufman, "Jewish Informers in the Middle Ages," *Jewish Quarterly Review*, o.s. 8 (1896): 217–38.

5. *TQ* no. 43, pp. 34–36, quote on p. 35.

6. *TQ* no. 46, p. 40.

7. For an overview on the genre of *taqqanot*, its historical development, and some examples, see Elliot N. Dorff and Arthur I. Rosett, *A Living Tree: The Roots and Growth of Jewish Law* (Albany: SUNY Press, 1988), 402–20.

8. See Menachem Lorberbaum, *Politics and the Limits of Law: Secularizing the Political in Medieval Jewish Thought* (Stanford, CA: Stanford University Press, 2001),

99–100. Lorberbaum notes the romanticism of the vision of autonomy as set forth in *taqqanot*, especially as put forth by Louis Finkelstein in his highly influential work, *Jewish Self-Government in the Middle Ages* (New York: Jewish Theological Seminary of America, 1924).

9. *TQ* no. 46, p. 40.

10. *TQ* no. 31, pp. 19–20.

11. On the St. Tito revolt, see Sally McKee, *Uncommon Dominion: Venetian Crete and the Myth of Ethnic Purity* (Philadelphia: University of Pennsylvania Press, 2000), 133–67.

12. Michael Angold, *The Fall of Constantinople to the Ottomans: Context and Consequences* (London: Routledge, 2014), 97.

13. A number of article-length studies have been undertaken on the Jews of Crete, most notably Joshua Starr, "Jewish Life in Crete Under the Rule of Venice," *Proceedings of the American Academy for Jewish Research* 12 (1942): 59–114, which attempts a synthesis. Starr, however, had access neither to the full Hebrew nor to ducal sources from Candia. Also important is Zvi Ankori, "Jews and the Jewish Community in the History of Mediaeval Crete," in *Proceedings of the Second International Congress of Cretological Studies* (Athens: N.p., 1968), 3:312–67. More recently, David Jacoby's numerous articles on the Jews of Crete have fleshed out elements of the picture, particularly in the realm of economics and their social implications. Among the most important of these studies are David Jacoby, "Jews and Christians in Venetian Crete: Segregation, Interaction, and Conflict," in *"Interstizi": Culture ebraico-cristiane a Venezia e nei suoi domini dal Medioevo all'Età Moderna*, ed. Uwe Israel, Robert Jütte, and Reinhold C. Mueller (Rome: Edizioni di Storia e Letteratura, 2010), 243–79; idem, "Quelques aspects de la vie juive en Crète dans la première moitié du XVe siècle," in *Actes du Troisième Congrès international d'études crétoises* (Rethymnon, 1971), vol. 2 (Athens: N.p., 1974), 108–17; idem, "Rofim ve-kirurgim Yehudiim be-Kritim tahat shilton Venetzia" [Jewish Doctors and Surgeons in Crete Under Venetian Rule], in *Culture and Society in Medieval Jewry: Studies Dedicated to the Memory of Haim Hillel Ben-Sasson*, ed. Menachem Ben-Sasson, Robert Bonfil, and Joseph Hakar (Jerusalem: Zalman Shazar Center, 1989), 431–44; idem, "Venice and the Venetian Jews in the Eastern Mediterranean," in *Gli Ebrei e Venezia, secoli XIV–XVIII*, ed. Gaetano Cozzi (Milan: Edizioni Comunità, 1987), 29–58; and idem, "Venice, the Inquisition and the Jewish Communities of Crete in the Early Fourteenth Century," *Studi veneziani* 12 (1970): 127–44. Nevertheless, a thorough analysis of the ducal court records has remained a lacuna, and the present study takes up one angle of this analysis by focusing on Jews in the sources.

14. In the aftermath of the Ottoman conquest of Candia in 1669, Venice negotiated a treaty whereby its chancellery archives could be safely taken back to the metropole, and they eventually were included in the state archives, the Archivio di Stato, Venezia, in the Campo dei Frari. On the structure and reorganization of these materials, see Ernst Gerland, *Das Archiv des Herzogs vom Kandia im K. Staatsarchiv zu Venedig* (Strassburg: Karl J. Trubner, 1899); and Maria Francesca Tiepolo, "Note sul riordino degli archivi del Duca e dei notai di Candia nell'Archivio di Stato di Venezia," *Thesaurismata* 10 (1973): 88–100.

15. For the period in question, the relevant *buste* (envelope-boxes, the primary unit of organization at the ASV) of Sentenze are b. 26 (1364–1436) and b. 26 bis (1437–55). The relevant *buste* of Memoriali are b. 29 (1318–64), b. 29 bis (1366–83), b. 30 (1386–95), b. 30 bis (1395–1413), b. 30 ter (1415–25), b. 31 (1428–40), and b. 32 (1443–90).

16. No Greek or Hebrew notarial registers from this period survive, though their existence echoes in the Latin materials. A person utilizing a Latin notary did not necessarily patronize that notary exclusively, or even a notary only in a single language.

17. Other registers, not included in this count, contain testamentary (last will) materials; for part of the period under study here, these wills have been edited and collected by Sally McKee, *Wills from Late Medieval Venetian Crete, 1312–1420*, 3 vols. (Washington, DC: Dumbarton Oaks, 1998). There were likely more notaries working in the capital city of Candia whose registers are lost; other notaries worked in the other Venetian cities, such as Canea, Rethymno, and Sitia.

18. Important announcements were made by an official town crier, and the contents of those announcements were recorded and are known as *banni*. For the time period relevant to this project, I have used the first two registers of b. 15, covering 1356–74 and October 1425–October 1427. (The next register does not begin until 1469.)

19. *TQ* no. 46, pp. 39–42.

20. MS. Heb 28°7203. For the Sassoon collection, see David Solomon Sassoon, ed., *Ohel Dawid: Descriptive Catalogue of the Hebrew and Samaritan Manuscripts in the Sassoon Library, London* (London: Oxford University Press, 1932), 1:349–57.

21. No edition in any other language has been published, although a short section of the earliest ordinances was translated in Finkelstein, *Jewish Self-Government*, 265–75.

22. On Artom and Cassuto's plans for the never-to-materialize volume 2, which aimed to give the historical and religiolegal background to *Taqqanot Qandiya*, see *TQ*, introductory pp. x–xi.

23. See John L. Comaroff and Jean Comaroff, *Ethnography and the Historical Imagination* (Boulder, CO: Westview Press, 1992), xi; Diane Owen Hughes, "Toward Historical Ethnography: The Notarial Records and Family History in the Middle Ages," *Historical Methods Newsletter* 7 (1974): 61–71; Michael Dietler, *Archaeologies of Colonialism: Consumption, Entanglement, and Violence in Ancient Mediterranean France* (Berkeley: University of California Press, 2010), 50. For the basic tenets of modern ethnography, see Clifford Geertz, "Thick Description: Toward an Interpretive Theory of Culture," in *The Interpretation of Cultures* (New York: Basic Books, 1973), 3–20.

24. *TQ* no. 18, pp. 9–10.

25. In recent decades, a number of scholars have taken up the approach of placing in conversation premodern Jewish sources and secular sources that deal with Jews with excellent results. For example, see Elka Klein, *Jews, Christian Society, and Royal Power in Medieval Barcelona* (Ann Arbor: University of Michigan Press, 2006); Birgit Klein, *Wohltat und Hochverrat: Kurfürst Ernst von Köln, Juda bar Chajjim und die Juden im Alten Reich* (Hildesheim: G. Olms, 2003).

26. See David Nirenberg, *Communities of Violence: Persecution of Minorities in the Middle Ages* (Princeton, NJ: Princeton University Press, 1996), 11.

27. In this historiographic dichotomy, Jewish life under Muslim rule was far easier, more successful, and marked by a fundamental tolerance of Jews by Islamic rulers and their people. Cohen's *Under Crescent and Cross* unpacked the assumptions of this methodological approach, illustrating not only that Jewish life under Muslim rule could not be painted in such a rosy shade but that contemporary concerns had informed much of this analysis of the Middle Ages. Mark Cohen, *Under Crescent and Cross: The Jews in the Middle Ages*, 2nd ed. (Princeton, NJ: Princeton University Press, 2008), esp. chap. 1, "Myth and Countermyth," 3–16.

28. For example, see David Biale, ed., *Cultures of the Jews*, vol. 2, *Diversities of Diaspora* (New York: Schocken Books, 2006), esp. pp. xix–xii.

29. Jacoby, "Venice, the Inquisition"; Nickiphoros I. Tsougarakis, *The Latin Religious Orders in Medieval Greece, 1204–1500* (Turnhout: Brepols, 2012), 158, 161.

30. For an excellent discussion of the historiographical trends regarding *convivencia* as it applies to debates over medieval Iberian Jews, see Klein, *Jews, Christian Society, and Royal Power*, 13–16.

31. For Iberia, see Yom Tov Assis, "Yehudei Sepharad be-arkhaot ha-goyim (ha-mayot ha-13 ve-ha-14)" [Spanish Jews in Gentile Courts (Thirteenth and Fourteenth Centuries)], in *Tarbut ve-khevra be-toldot Yisrael be-yemei ha-beinayim* [Culture and Society in Jewish History in the Middle Ages], ed. Robert Bonfil, Menachem Ben-Sasson, and Joseph Hakar (Jerusalem: Zalman Shazar Center, 1989), 390–430. For Provence, see Joseph Shatzmiller, "Halikhatam shel yehudim l'arkhaot shel goyim be-Provanz be-yemei ha-beinayum" [Jews Going to Gentile Courts in Provence in the Middle Ages], in *Divrei ha-kongress ha-olami ha-khamishi l'madaei ha-yahadut* [Proceedings of the Fifth World Congress of Jewish Studies), ed. Pinchas Peli and Avigdor Shin'an (Jerusalem: Ha-Igud ha-'olami le-mada'e ha-Yahadut, 1973), 2:375–81.

32. On women in court, see Elka Klein, "Public Activities of Catalan Jewish Women," *Medieval Encounters* 12 (2006): 48–61. For a discussion of how Jewish recourse to secular litigation has been treated too narrowly by modern scholars, see Klein, *Jews, Christian Society, and Royal Power*, 153–54. Despite evidence of this reality, scholars have continued to toe the rabbinic line, assuming that Jews for the most part upheld the prohibition.

33. Uriel Simonsohn, *A Common Justice: The Legal Allegiances of Christians and Jews Under Early Islam* (Philadelphia: University of Pennsylvania Press, 2011).

34. See, for example, the very title of Avraham Grossman's work *Pious and Rebellious: Jewish Women in Medieval Europe*, trans. Jonathan Chipman (Waltham, MA: Brandeis University Press, 2004).

35. Much of this new literature on medieval Jewish women centers on family life but also steps beyond it to attest to Jewish-Christian encounters between women. See Elisheva Baumgarten, *Mothers and Children: Jewish Family Life in Medieval Europe* (Princeton, NJ: Princeton University Press, 2004). Also see Shalom Sabar, "Childbirth and Magic: Jewish Folklore and Material Culture," in *Cultures of the Jews*, vol. 2, *Diversities of Diaspora*, ed. David Biale (New York: Schocken Books, 2006), 369–420.

36. In this, I build on the concepts developed in Klein, "Public Activities."

37. Starr, "Jewish Life," 63.

38. For a revisionist study accused of such rose-tinted rereading, see Jonathan Elukin, *Living Together, Living Apart: Rethinking Jewish-Christian Relations in the Middle Ages* (Princeton, NJ: Princeton University Press, 2007).

39. See Benjamin Ravid, "The Legal State of the Jews in Venice to 1509," *Proceedings of the American Academy for Jewish Research* 54 (1987): 169–202, esp. 173–81.

40. For one view of this foundational moment in light of broader Venetian needs, see Robert Finlay, "The Foundation of the Ghetto: Venice, the Jews, and the War of the League of Cambrai," *Proceedings of the American Philosophical Society* 126 (1982): 140–54.

41. On the complications of hard-and-fast identity markers, especially in colonial environments, see Frederick Cooper, *Colonialism in Question: Theory, Knowledge, History* (Berkeley: University of California Press, 2005), 9.

42. For the phrase "axes of identity," see Daniel Jütte, "Interfaith Encounters Between Jews and Christians in the Early Modern Period and Beyond: Toward a Framework," *American Historical Review* 118 (2013): 382.

43. For this view, see Jacob Katz, *Tradition and Crisis: Jewish Society at the End of the Middle Ages*, trans. Bernard Dov Cooperman (Syracuse, NY: Syracuse University Press, 2000), 3. This is a relatively recent (and second) translation of a text originally published in Hebrew as *Masoret u-mashber: He-hevrah ha-yehudit be-motsa'ei yemei ha-benayim* (Jerusalem: Mosad Bialik, 1958). Also see this view fleshed out in Jacob Katz, *Jewish Emancipation and Self-Emancipation* (Philadelphia: Jewish Publication Society, 1986), esp. viii.

44. Across the Mediterranean, for the most part, the challenges wrought by internal Jewish heterogeneity are only taken seriously for the post-expulsion world and beyond. On the Dutch case, see Miriam Bodian, *Hebrews of the Portuguese Nation: Conversos and Community in Early Modern Amsterdam* (Bloomington: Indiana University Press, 1997), esp. 125–31. For a case study on Ashkenazi-Sephardi tensions in seventeenth-century Hamburg, see Dean P. Bell, "Jews, Ethnicity, and Identity in Early Modern Hamburg," *TRANSIT* 3 (2007): 1–16. In the eastern Mediterranean, tensions between Sephardi newcomers and Romaniote locals in the Ottoman Empire after the expulsion have elicited significant work. On the tensions between Sephardim and Romaniotes after 1492, and Sephardi cultural imperialism, see Esther Benbassa and Aron Rodrigue, *Sephardi Jewry: A History of the Judeo-Spanish Community, 14th–20th Centuries* (Berkeley: University of California Press, 1999), 11–16. On the problems of "Sephardization," a triumphalist imposition of the Sephardi rite on locals, see Minna Rozen, *The History of the Jewish Community of Istanbul: The Formative Years, 1453–1566* (Leiden: Brill, 2002), esp. 87–92.

45. For an important sociological approach delineating how minority groups relate to the majority groups in a given society, see Steve Rytina and David L. Morgan, "The Arithmetic of Social Relations: The Interplay of Category and Network," *American Journal of Sociology* 88 (1982): 88–113.

46. Klein, *Jews, Christian Society, and Royal Power*, 153.

47. Daniel Lord Smail has argued that the late medieval and early modern periods witnessed two apparently contradictory but in fact symbiotic changes: (1) the state became more

interested in dealing with corporate groups (e.g., holding kin groups responsible for the misdeeds of an individual), and (2) people asserted their individualism more explicitly and fluidly. Smail suggests the move toward assertion of the self (characterized by allying with groups by choice, not by blood, i.e., factionalism) stemmed from a reaction to the governmental push toward the corporate: "Individualism, here, was not the handmaiden of the state but, instead, a mode of resistance." Daniel Lord Smail, "Factions and Vengeance in Renaissance Italy: A Review Article," *Comparative Studies in Society and History* 38 (1996): 789.

48. James Harvey Robinson, *New History: Essays Illustrating the Modern Historical Outlook* (New York: Macmillan, 1912). Robinson's ideas were built on and developed in the now far more famous work of E. H. Carr, *What Is History?* (New York: Vintage Books, 1961).

49. While scholars continue to debate many aspects of the Fourth Crusade, primarily when Byzantium actually became the target, and how much "blame" should be ascribed to Venice in this whole endeavor, scholars do not tend to question the exceptional impact of the Fourth Crusade on the balance of power in the Mediterranean.

50. In 1124, during the Siege of Tyre, Venetian forces helped secure Crusader control of all Levantine ports north of Ascalon and ensured their own commercial dominance in these ports. For the story of the growth of the Venetian naval and commercial empire before the Fourth Crusade, see the concise discussion by the father of Venetian maritime history, Frederic C. Lane, *Venice: A Maritime Republic* (Baltimore: Johns Hopkins University Press, 1973), 31–36.

51. David Jacoby, "Creta e Venezia nel contesto economico del Mediterraneo orientale sino alla metà del Quattrocento," in *Venezia e Creta: Atti del convegno internazionale di studi Iraklion-Chanià, 30 settembre–5 ottobre 1997*, ed. Gherardo Ortalli (Venice: Istituto veneto di scienze, lettere ed arti, 1998), 74; Donald M. Nicol, *Byzantium and Venice: A Study in Diplomatic and Cultural Relations* (Cambridge: Cambridge University Press, 1988), 81, 85–86. The earliest record of individual Venetian merchants trading on Crete of which Nicol is aware is dated 1111. For this document, see Raimondo Morozzo della Rocca and Antonino Lombardo, eds., *Documenti del commercio veneziano nei secoli XI–XIII* (Rome: Sede dell'Istituto, 1940), 1:35–36.

52. Freddy Thiriet, *La Romanie vénitienne au Moyen Age: Le développement et l'exploitation du domaine colonial vénitien, XIIᵉ–XVᵉ siècles* (Paris: Editions E. de Boccard, 1975 [1959]), 105–6; McKee, *Uncommon Dominion*, 22.

53. Lane, *Venice*, 43.

54. Thiriet, *La Romanie vénitienne*, 145. On the fourteenth-century Cretan agrarian economy and trade in Cretan-produced goods, see Mario Gallina, *Una società colonial del trecentro: Creta fra Venezia e Bysanzio* (Venice: Deputazione di storia patria per le Venezie, 1989), esp. chaps. 2 and 3.

55. Thiriet, *La Romanie vénitienne*, 95; David Jacoby, "Candia Between Venice, Byzantium, and the Levant: The Rise of a Major Emporium to the Mid-Fifteenth Century," in *The Hand of Angelos: An Icon Painter in Venetian Crete*, ed. Maria Vassilaki (Farnham, Surrey: Lund Humphries, 2010), 38.

56. Angeliki Laiou, "Venetians and Byzantines: Investigations of Forms of Contact in the Fourteenth Century," *Thesaurismata* 22 (1992): 33.

57. Lane, *Venice*, 99.

58. Monique O'Connell, *Men of Empire: Power and Negotiation in Venice's Maritime State* (Baltimore: Johns Hopkins University Press, 2009), 94. On the Avogaria, see p. 84.

59. According to Thiriet, the trip from Candia to Venice in the summer during the fourteenth century was eighteen to twenty-five days. Thiriet, *La Romanie vénitienne*, 188.

60. "Beyond-the-Sea" (Oltremare) was a common name for the eastern Mediterranean territories. Originally signifying "what Europeans then called the region in which the Crusaders were founding states in Syria and Palestine," it then became something of a catchall term for overseas colonies, a Venetian synonym for the region known as the Stato da mar. Lane, *Venice: A Maritime Republic*, 32. Also see Benjamin Arbel, "Colonie d'oltremare," in *Storia di Venezia dalle origini alla caduta della Serenissima*, vol. 5, *Il Rinascimento: Società ed economia*, ed. Alberto Tenenti and Ugo Tucci (Rome: Instituto della encyclopedia italiana, 1996), 947–85.

61. Elisabeth Crouzet-Pavan, *Venice Triumphant: The Horizons of a Myth*, trans. Lydia G. Cochrane (Baltimore: Johns Hopkins University Press, 2002), xiv.

62. Around 1300, the island was divided into four north-south units, each utilizing one of Crete's main cities (Candia, Rethymno, Canea, and Sitia) as a local capital. Thiriet, *La Romanie vénitienne*, 125; Chryssa Maltezou, "The Historical and Social Context," in *Literature and Society in Renaissance Crete*, ed. David Holton (Cambridge: Cambridge University Press, 1991), 17–47. For a clear explication of the wider governmental structure and apparatus of Venetian Candia, focusing on the fourteenth century, see Johannes Jegerlehner, "Beiträge zur Verwaltungsgeschichte Kandias im XIV. Jahrhunderts," *Byzantinische Zeitschrift* 13 (1904): 435–79, esp. 444–46.

63. Jacoby, "Candia Between Venice, Byzantium, and the Levant," 45. Also see idem, "Creta e Venezia," 103. First constructed around 1282, then rebuilt after the earthquake of 1303, the arsenal functioned not only as a shipyard but also as a warehouse for defense-related material such as weapons and timber. On the first century of Venetian rule, see the straightforward narrative history by Silvano Borsari, *Il dominio veneziano a Creta nel XIII secolo* (Naples: F. Fiorentino, 1963), which addresses political, economic, social, and religious history. Jews, however, are absent from these discussions. ·

64. Increasing emphasis on viniculture in the fifteenth century made the island the prime exporter of the much-beloved fortified wine known to the English as Malmsey, or more technically as Malvasia, vine-stocks of which were first brought to the island around the 1330s. Jacoby, "Candia Between Venice, Byzantium, and the Levant," 41.

65. For more on Cretan slavery, see Charles Verlinden, "La Crète, debouché et plaque tournante de la traite des esclaves aux XIVᵉ et XVᵉ siècles," in *Studi in onore di Amintore Fanfani* (Milan: Giuffrè, 1962), 3:591–669.

66. Jacoby, "Creta e Venezia," 75–76; Jacoby, "Candia Between Venice, Byzantium, and the Levant," 39.

67. Though Crete's role as a way station lessened in 1345 with direct trade between the west and Egypt reinstated, the capture of Famagusta (Cyprus) by the Genoese in 1374 would restore Candia to its position as the main stopover on the Venice-Alexandria and Venice-Beirut routes. This political situation would remain to Crete's advantage through

the period under study here; the Venetian capture of Famagusta in the late fifteenth century would redirect a significant amount of Crete's traffic to that more easterly port. Nevertheless, much of the period under study here constitutes what David Jacoby has considered Candia's peak as a major emporium. Jacoby, "Candia Between Venice, Byzantium, and the Levant," 43–45.

68. Such is the conclusion of Monique O'Connell in her work on patrician administrators of the Stato da mar. See her *Men of Empire*, esp. pp. 9–11.

69. The ideological nature of the modern scholarly claim for sharp segregation stems in part from Greek nationalist scholarship that desires to see the period of Venetian rule (like Arab rule before) as nothing but a long period of persecution of the rightful inhabitants of Crete, i.e., the Greek Orthodox. See, e.g., Theocaris E. Detorakis, *History of Crete*, trans. John C. David (Iraklion, Crete: N.p., 1994), who sees the centuries of Venetian rule as nothing but "another long period of irksome oppression" (145) and thus highlights the only important element of this period as the "Cretan Resistance" movement (153–71). Even Detorakis, however, has to admit that the first half of the fifteenth century, until the fall of Constantinople, was a high point of economic and social stability (171).

70. On the inability to squarely divide Latins and Greeks in Crete, see McKee, *Uncommon Dominion*, 57–132, esp. 99. On the Veneto-Latins, see 133–67.

71. See, for example, the very title of the excellent collection edited by Benjamin Arbel, Bernard Hamilton, and David Jacoby, *Latins and Greeks in the Eastern Mediterranean After 1204* (London: Frank Cass, 1989). The volume does indeed discuss Jews, Mongols, and others but frames the major conversation as one that engages with Latin-Greek tensions.

72. McKee, *Uncommon Dominion*, 6.

73. For a particularly influential formulation of this division, see Albert Memmi, *The Colonizer and the Colonized*, trans. Howard Greenfield (Boston: Beacon, 1965), originally published in French in 1957.

74. As mentioned above, in the case of the St. Tito revolt. In addition, in the late fifteenth century, a Jew named David Mavrogonato uncovered and reported an anti-Venetian conspiracy by Greeks and was awarded for his loyalty. See David Jacoby, "Un agent juif au service de Venise: David Mavrogonato de Candie," *Thesaurismata* 9 (1972): 68–96.

75. For poignant critiques of Memmi, which are also fundamental studies in historically applied postcolonial theory, see Cooper, *Colonialism in Question* (esp. p. 17); Eve Troutt Powell, *A Different Shade of Colonialism: Egypt, Great Britain, and the Mastery of the Sudan* (Berkeley: University of California Press, 2003).

76. For a recent assessment of the state of the field and a call to articulate the "Jewish Imperial Turn" as a unique and relevant approach, see Ethan Katz, Lisa Leff, and Maud Mandel, eds., *Colonialism and the Jews* (Bloomington: Indiana University Press, 2017), esp. the editors' very useful introduction (1–28).

77. A number of scholars made this move already in the 1970s; see R. I. Burns, *Medieval Colonialism: Postcrusade Exploitation of Islam Valencia* (Princeton, NJ: Princeton University Press, 1975); Joshua Prawer, *The Crusaders' Kingdom: European Colonialism in the Middle Ages* (New York: Praeger, 1972). More recently, premodernist scholars have aggressively,

intentionally, and fruitfully marshaled the language and theories of postcolonial studies in work spanning the gamut of subjects, from the Greek Mediterranean to medieval medicine. For just a few examples: Irad Malkin, "Postcolonial Concepts and Ancient Greek Colonization," *Modern Language Quarterly* 65 (2004): 341–64; Nadia Altschul, "Postcolonialism and the Study of the Middle Ages," *History Compass* 6 (2008): 588–606; Dietler, *Archaeologies of Colonialism*; Iona McCleery, "What Is 'Colonial' About Medieval Colonial Medicine? Iberian Health in Global Context," *Journal of Medieval Iberian Studies* 7 (2015): 151–75.

78. Giovanni Boccaccio, *The Decameron*, trans. G. H. McWilliam (New York: Penguin Books, 1995 [1972]), 317.

79. On this historiography of flexibility on the Iberian frontier, see Heath Dillard, *Daughters of the Reconquest: Women in Castillian Town Society, 1100–1300* (Cambridge: Cambridge University Press, 1990), on female agency and public life; and Jonathan Ray, *The Sephardic Frontier: The "Reconquista" and the Jewish Community of Medieval Iberia* (Ithaca, NY: Cornell University Press, 2008), which looks at the social and economic mobility made available to Jews on the Iberian frontier.

80. Boccaccio, *Decameron*, 313.

81. For some important works on Venetian justice, see Stanley Chojnacki, "Crime, Punishment, and the Trecento Venetian State," in *Violence and Civil Disorder in Italian Cities, 1200–1500*, ed. Lauro Martines (Berkeley: University of California Press, 1972), 184–228; the corpus of work of Gaetano Cozzi, especially "Authority and Law in Renaissance Venice," in *Renaissance Venice*, ed. J. R. Hale (London: Faber and Faber, 1974), 293–345, and idem, ed., *Stato, società e giustizia: Nella repubblica veneta (sec. XV–XVIII)* (Rome: Jouvence, 1980); and Edward Muir, "The Sources of Civil Society in Italy," *Journal of Interdisciplinary History* 29 (1999): 379–406. Also see the work of Dennis Romano, including "Equality in Fifteenth-Century Venice," *Studies in Medieval and Renaissance History* 6 (2009): 125–45; Guido Ruggiero, *Violence in Early Renaissance Venice* (New Brunswick, NJ: Rutgers University Press, 1980). A scholarly interest in this topic can already be spotted in the early twentieth century in Melchiorre Roberti, *La magistrature giudiziare veneziane* (Padua: Tipografia del Seminario, 1907).

82. James E. Shaw, *The Justice of Venice: Authorities and Liberties in the Urban Economy, 1550–1700* (Oxford: Oxford University Press, 2006), 19. For a pioneering work on the malleability of the medieval justice system for the social and emotional needs of those utilizing the civil courts, see Daniel Lord Smail, *The Consumption of Justice: Emotions, Publicity, and Legal Culture in Marseille, 1264–1423* (Ithaca, NY: Cornell University Press, 2003).

CHAPTER I

1. Capsali recounts elements of this walk in *TQ* no. 102, pp. 131–38. He calls Capello his "beloved dear" friend on p. 133.

2. Maria Georgopoulou, *Venice's Mediterranean Colonies: Architecture and Urbanism* (Cambridge: Cambridge University Press, 2001), 82–84.

3. McKee, *Uncommon Dominion*, 152.

4. *TQ* no. 18, p. 10.

5. Crete after 1453 (and especially after 1510, for hitherto unexplained reasons) became the locus of an artistic and literary explosion as Constantinopolitan literati, philosophers, and painters fled their home following the conquest and encountered Venetian cultural trends. For literary trends, see David Holton, ed., *Literature and Society in Renaissance Crete* (Cambridge: Cambridge University Press, 1991); for visual arts in context, especially icon painting, see Maria Vassilaki, ed., *The Hand of Angelos: An Icon Painter in Venetian Crete* (Farnham, Surrey: Lund Humphries, 2010). The Jewish community was in no way quarantined from this Cretan Renaissance, as it is known; the philosophical and Latin writings of Elia Delmedigo (1458–93) and the histories of Elia Capsali should be read as part of this trend. On the philosophy of Delmedigo, who tutored Pico della Mirandola, see Harvey J. Hames, "Elia del Medigo: An Archetype of the Halachic Man," *Traditio* 56 (2001): 213–27.

6. Jacoby, "Candia Between Venice, Byzantium, and the Levant," 43.

7. Jacoby, "Candia Between Venice, Byzantium, and the Levant," 45.

8. On cheese, see David Jacoby, "Cretan Cheese: A Neglected Aspect of Venetian Medieval Trade," in *Medieval and Renaissance Venice*, ed. Ellen E. Kittell and Thomas F. Madden (Urbana: University of Illinois Press, 1999), 49–68.

9. McKee, *Uncommon Dominion*, 24.

10. McKee, *Uncommon Dominion*, 59, 90–91.

11. The census counted nearly fourteen thousand (84 percent) middle-class Greeks, Armenians, and non-noble Italians; 964 Venetian nobles (5.7 percent); and 950 Jews (5.6 percent).On this census, see Stephen Margaritis, *Crete and the Ionian Islands Under the Venetians* (Athens: Liontiadis, 1978), 52–53; Georgopoulou, *Venice's Mediterranean Colonies*, 284–85n28.

12. These numbers apparently do not include enslaved people who worked as domestics, artisans, and farmhands. On slavery in Candia, see Sally McKee, "Greek Women in Latin Households in Fourteenth-Century Crete," *Journal of Medieval History* 19 (1993): 229–49, and idem, "Domestic Slavery in Renaissance Italy," *Slavery & Abolition* 29 (2008): 305–26.

13. Lane, *Venice*, 19.

14. McKee, *Uncommon Dominion*, 91–92.

15. One indication comes from an Italian Jewish traveler who visited the city of Candia in 1481. He reported 600 Jewish households in the city of Candia—approximately 2,500 to 3,000 individuals, assuming about four or five members per household. Meshullam of Volterra, *Masah Meshullam Mi-Voltera be-Eretz Yisrael be-shnat 241 (1481)* [The Journey of Meshullam of Volterra in the Land of Israel in the Year 241 (1481)] ed. Avraham Yaari (Jerusalem: Mosad Bialik, 1948), 82. Salo Baron considered this an exaggeration and instead preferred an estimate given by a Venetian administrator in 1577, who counted approximately 700 Jews in the city. Salo W. Baron, *A Social and Religious History of the Jews*, vol. 17, *Byzantines, Mamluks, and Maghribians* (New York: Columbia University Press, 1980), 71. The administrator's own approximation seems to be too low, however, considering that only six years later a more exacting census revealed 250 more Jewish inhabitants than he

had guessed. To be sure, neither estimate provides a basis for reckoning the population in the century surrounding 1400.

16. When we collect the names of Jews mentioned during this century in *Taqqanot Qandiya*, the legal records of the ducal court, Sally McKee's published wills, and just a few of the notarial registers, already 833 individual Jews resident or working in Candia materialize from the sources. Of these 833 individuals, 230 are female, and the remaining 603 are male—a proportion that makes sense in light of the male-centered Hebrew sources and the predominance of males in the professional spheres. We can safely assume that at least 1,000 Jewish people—women left unmentioned in the sources first among them but also Jews too poor to take part in the city's financial and litigative life—called Candia home.

17. See Chapter 2 for further discussion of Jewish engagement with the city's economic life.

18. Notarial contracts shed light on these positions. In 1380, the teacher Melchiel Alamanus contracted to teach Jewish subjects to a boy named Moyses Carvuni in Melchiel's home, for which the tutor earned twenty hyperpera a year. Another Jewish teacher received usage of two homes in the Jewish Quarter for teaching another student for one year beginning in 1386. This latter man, Solomon de Iocuda, may have run an actual elementary school for Jewish boys. Mentioned in McKee, *Uncommon Dominion*, 120.

19. For just one example, in a 1432 will, a wealthy Jewish testator bequeathed to her Jewish servant girl, Esther, some goods and cash from the mistress's home where Esther had served for most of her life. Jacoby, "Venice and the Venetian Jews," 45; idem, "Quelques aspects," 114–15.

20. See Chapters 2 and 5 for more on women's activities. Also see Rena Lauer, "Jewish Women in Venetian Candia: Negotiating Intercommunal Contact in a Premodern Colonial City, 1300–1500," in *Religious Cohabitation in European Towns (10th–15th Centuries)*, ed. John Tolan and Stéphane Boissellier (Turnhout: Brepols, 2015), 293–309.

21. The clock was installed on the bell tower in 1463. Georgopoulou, *Venice's Mediterranean Colonies*, 85.

22. Elia Capsali wrote his famed historical chronicle of the Ottoman Empire, titled *Seder Eliyahu Zuta* [The Order of Elijah the Younger], in 1523, during a bout of plague on Crete. But he had also written an earlier historical work on the history of Venice, *Divrei ha-Yamim le-Malkhut Venezia* [The Chronicle of the Kingdom [*sic*] of Venice] in 1517. On Capsali, and particularly his self-conscious construction of himself as a historian, see Meir Benayahu's Hebrew-language monograph *Rabi Eliyahu Kapsali, ish Kandiya: Rav, manhig, ve-historiyon* [Rabbi Elijah Capsali of Candia: Rabbi, Leader, and Historian] (Tel Aviv: Center for Diaspora Studies of Tel Aviv University, 1983); Aleida Paudice, *Between Several Worlds: The Life and Writings of Elia Capsali* (Munich: M-Press, 2010); Robert Bonfil, "Jewish Attitudes Toward History and Historical Writing in Pre-Modern Times," *Jewish History* 11 (1997): 7–40; Martin Jacobs, "Exposed to All the Currents of the Mediterranean: A Sixteenth-Century Venetian Rabbi on Muslim History," *AJS Review* 29 (2005): 33–60; and Aryeh Shmuelevitz, "Capsali as a Source for Ottoman History, 1450–1523," *International Journal of Middle East Studies* 9 (1978): 339–44.

23. In his *Seder Eliyahu Zuta*, he wrote of his own memories of the impact of the Spanish expulsion. On Capsali's sources and their difficulties, see Shmuelevitz, "Capsali as a Source for Ottoman History," 340–41.

24. Philo Judaeus, *Legatio ad Gaium*, 36:282; Josephus Flavius, *The Life of Josephus Flavius*, 76.

25. On the church historian, see Starr, "Jewish Life," 59. For inscriptions, see Stylianos V. Spyridakis, "Notes on the Jews of Gortyna and Crete," *Zeitschrift für Papyrologie und Epigraphik* 73 (1988): 171–75.

26. Spyridakis, "Notes," 172–75.

27. See David Jacoby, "The Jews in the Byzantine Economy (Seventh to Mid-Fifteenth Century)," in *Jews in Byzantium: Dialectics of Minority and Majority Cultures*, ed. Robert Bonfil et al. (Leiden: Brill, 2012), 230. A Hebrew letter from the tenth or eleventh century suggests that Jewish tanners were already at work on Crete by that time. Nicholas de Lange, ed., *Greek Jewish Texts from the Cairo Genizah* (Tübingen: Mohr-Siebeck, 1996), 21–27, no. 4.

28. For this pre-Venetian community and the pre-Venetian nature of the Jewish Quarter, see Ankori, "Jews and the Jewish Community," esp. 327–39 and 350–54.

29. Parnas is an unusual personal name, which led at least one scholar to suggest that Parnas should be read here as a title, with the man's first name missing (Nathan Porges, "Elie *Capsali* et sa Chronique de Venise," *Revue des études juives* 78 [1924]: 25). Artom and Cassuto (see *TQ* no. 12, p. 7, n. 13), however, believe Parnas was the man's actual first name. Their assertion is supported by evidence from research in the ducal archives, which illustrates that a significant number of other Candiote Jews also were called Parnas, including Parnas tu Setu, Parnas Buchi (see Chapter 5), Parnas Calopo, and others. Feminized versions, Pernatissa (also Parnatissa) and Parnaza, also appear among Crete's Jewish women. Other men named Parnas Capsali are also attested in the Latin records, ostensibly the descendants of the thirteenth-century signatory: one lived in the late fourteenth and early fifteenth centuries, and another, this man's grandson, was active in the middle of the fifteenth century.

30. In particular, see Jacoby, "The Jews in the Byzantine Economy," esp. 222–33.

31. The Venetians (in Latin and Venetian) and the Jews (in Hebrew) both used the term "Candia" interchangeably for the city and for the whole island. Both also used "Crete" for the island. *TQ* no. 13, p. 6.

32. *TQ* no. 2, p. 3.

33. *TQ* no. 13, p. 7.

34. This manuscript of Capsali's collection found its way into David Solomon Sassoon's famed collection, and is now held in Israel's National Library as Ms. Heb. 28°7203. See Sassoon, *Ohel Dawid*, 1:349–57.

35. For the classic narrative account, see Salo W. Baron, *The Jewish Community, Its History and Structure to the American Revolution* (Philadelphia: Jewish Publication Society, 1948).

36. See Chapter 4.

37. Jacoby, "Venice and the Venetian Jews," 38. For a case regarding Jewish-owned buildings in the Judaica intended to house the community's poor, see ASV Duca di Candia, b. 30 ter, r. 30, fol. 18v (22 November 1415).

38. See Chapter 6 for a fuller discussion of the role of the community head, the *condestabulo*, as tax collector.

39. In thirteenth-century Burgos, for example, the *aljama*, as the Jewish corporate organization was called in Iberia, was empowered to fine those guilty of "assault and vilification." David Biale, *Power and Powerlessness in Jewish History* (New York: Schocken Books, 1986), 79. Biale quotes the English translation of Yitzhak Baer's work: Fritz (Yitzhak) Baer, *The History of the Jews in Christian Spain*, trans. Louis Schoffman (Philadelphia: Jewish Publication Society, 1961), 1:235.

40. Most famously, by reading the Book of Jonah in Greek (though written in Hebrew letters) on Yom Kippur. Starr, "Jewish Life," 100; see idem, *The Jews in the Byzantine Empire, 641–1204* (Athens: Verlag der "Byzantinisch-Neugriechischen Jahrbücher," 1939), 212, for a comprehensive list of references to this practice.

41. Hippolyte Noiret, ed., *Documents inédits pour servir à l'histoire de la domination vénetienne en Crète de 1380 à 1485* (Paris: Thorin & fils, 1892), 26–27 (25 May 1389).

42. Noiret, *Document inédits*, 71 (10 September 1395), and n. 1, which points to the immigration of Jews expelled from Venice on 27 August 1394. Starr here follows Noiret's assertion: Starr, "Jewish Life," 77.

43. Jacoby, "Quelques aspects," 110, 110n10.

44. The sale of the finials is recorded in *TQ* no. 88, pp. 109–10 (undated, but apparently in the 1530s). The previous ordinance suggests the ubiquity of the problem; Jews from Coron and Patras had been kidnapped, and the Candiote community contributed three ducats to their ransom (*TQ* no. 87, pp. 108–9, dated 29 October 1533). For the sale of Capsali's library, see Umberto Cassuto, *I manoscritti palatini ebraici della Biblioteca apostolic vaticana e la loro storia* (Vatican City: Biblioteca apostolica vaticana, 1935).

45. For example, *TQ* no. 35, pp. 25–26; *TQ* no. 41, p. 33; *TQ* no. 43, pp. 34–36. All of these reference and deal with Jewish-Christian business relations. For a more extensive discussion of Jewish-Christian relations, see Chapters 2 and 3.

46. In the Jewish context, the ban was a harsh social alienation with consequences in every area of economic, religious, and emotional life.

47. Joshua Starr has outlined the evolution of the Jewish leadership council over the course of the fourteenth and fifteenth centuries in his seminal synthetic essay on the Jews of Venetian Crete. Starr, "Jewish Life," 101–2.

48. For the dating of Rabbi Tzedakah's revisions, see *TQ*, introduction, p. 8. For the *condestabulo*, see *TQ* no. 22, p. 13.

49. *TQ* no. 24, p. 13.

50. *TQ* no. 25, p. 14.

51. See BT Megillah 26a–b.

52. *TQ* no. 31, p. 19. It is unclear whether these positions were innovations or whether only their explication was new.

53. *TQ* no. 50, p. 46.

54. Starr, "Jewish Life," 102.

55. For example, in a ducal decree from 1454 instructing the Jews to give the government a very large forced loan of 5,900 ducats, the duke specifically addresses the *condestabulo* (at that time, another member of the Capsali clan named David) and his three *camerarii*. The number of these advisors suggests that these are one and the same as the *hashvanim* mentioned in *Taqqanot Qandiya*. ASV Duca di Candia, b. 26 bis, r. 11, fols. 56r–v (24 October 1454).

56. The documents listed include divorce writs, marriage contracts and *ketubbot* (listed separately), halachic decisions, letters (of certification) to be sent abroad regarding kosher wine, cheese, and scouring (*hag'alah*, ostensibly the process of kashering vessels), and any other documents deemed necessary at the time. *TQ* no. 69, p. 71.

57. *TQ* no. 31, p. 19, and see esp. nn. 15 and 16.

58. *TQ* no. 32, pp. 20–22.

59. Georgopoulou, *Venice's Mediterranean Colonies*, 54.

60. Meshullam of Volterra notes Jewish shops along the Ruga in 1481. See Meshullam of Volterra, *Masah Meshullam*, 82. Though Jews could not live on the Ruga Maistra from the late fourteenth century onward, they were still entitled to rent storefronts and warehouses outside the Judaica. See, e.g., ASV Duca di Candia, b. 11, fragment 11/2, fol. 69v (27 April 1391), in which a Christian is given permission to rent to Jews three of his stalls situated near (but outside) the Jewish Quarter, which can be used as storage and retail venue. The Christian owner was required to ensure that the tenants did not live or sleep overnight in the stalls, on pain of fines imposed on both tenant and owner. Also referenced and edited in Georgopoulou, *Venice's Mediterranean Colonies*, 200n52.

61. ASV Duca di Candia, b. 15 (Bandi), fol. 79v, no. 109 (23 July 1361) and f. 104v, no. 26 (10 April 1363). Also referenced in Georgopoulou, *Venice's Mediterranean Colonies*, 76, with the complete text of the proclamation accompanying n. 7 (pp. 293–94).

62. Such is the primary focus of the ordinance in which Capsali describes this walk. *TQ* no. 102, pp. 132–33.

63. This archway was erected and decorated in 1390, according to Georgopoulou, *Venice's Mediterranean Colonies*, 194. The source that mentions the building of this "arcum de novo positum pro signo confinium Judaice" is attested in 1390 or 1391, though Santschi misdates it to 1370. See Elisabeth Santschi, "Contribution à l'étude de la communauté juive en Crète vénitienne au XIVe siécle, d'après des sources administratives et judiciaires," *Studi Veneziani* 15 (1973): 189.

64. Ankori, "Jews and the Jewish Community," 332. Ankori notes that this Stenón still existed as a narrow lane in modern Iraklion through 1963. When he returned in 1966, however, he discovered that the whole street had been razed as part of the grounds of a hotel built in the area of the Jewish Quarter.

65. Georgopoulou, *Venice's Mediterranean Colonies*, 198.

66. Ankori, "Jews and the Jewish Community," 324; Georgopoulou, *Venice's Mediterranean Colonies*, 192.

67. The Jewish Quarter, according to Lorenzo, "nella più bella parte della città, sopre di mare, con case et stabili belissimi." Quoted in Georgopoulou, *Venice's Mediterranean Colonies*, 199n48.

68. Maria Georgopoulou, *The Meaning of the Architecture and the Urban Layout of Venetian Candia: Cultural Conflict and Interaction in the Late Middle Ages* (PhD diss., UCLA, 1992) (Ann Arbor: UMI Dissertation Services, 1995), 321.

69. Starr, "Jewish Life," 98.

70. ASV Duca di Candia, b. 30 ter, r. 32, fols. 151r–154r (27 February 1421).

71. For 1369, see *TQ* no. 50, p. 46; for 1406, see *TQ* no. 52, p. 52; for 1424, see *TQ* no. 59, p. 61.

72. *TQ* no. 85, p. 107. Some evidence suggests at least five synagogues by 1500. See Zvi Ankori, "The Living and the Dead: The Story of Hebrew Inscriptions in Crete," *Proceedings of the American Academy for Jewish Research* 38 (1970–71): 19n25. See also Georgopoulou, *Venice's Mediterranean Colonies*, 196–97.

73. For 1369, see *TQ* no. 50, p. 46; for 1518, see *TQ* no. 72, p. 76.

74. *TQ* no. 57, p. 58 (1435). Similar language positing the importance of the Synagogue of the Priests for community meeting appears during the tenure of a *condestabulo* named Elijah Missini a decade earlier; see *TQ* no. 59, p. 61.

75. *TQ* no. 62, p. 64.

76. To assess ethnic origin of the Jewish community, I use toponymic surnames, onomastic suffixes, and postnominal toponymics. Although scholars before me have noted that the Jews of Crete came from a diverse set of origins, the prosopographical analysis of the Jews of Candia bears out the complex makeup of the community and the arrival of newcomers after the Black Death with more specificity. For example, Simon Marcus, "Herkev ha-yishuv ha-yehudi ba-'i kritim biyemei ha-shilton ha-venetsiani" [The Composition of the Jewish Community on the Island of Crete in the Days of Venetian Rule] *Sinai* 60 (1967/68): 63–76.

77. Four of Anatoli Casani's poems appear in Leon Weinberger, *Jewish Poets in Crete* (Cincinnati: Hebrew Union College Press, 1985), 25–37.

78. Jacoby, "Venice and the Venetian Jews," 45; idem, "Quelques aspects," 114–15.

79. Sephardi Jews likely made up the largest subminority in Candia after the Romaniotes. Of the 833 Jews mentioned in the sources, 23 are identified as coming from Iberia or as the children of those who came from there; when a regional affiliation is specified, we see that Jews came from Portugal and Majorca but especially Catalonia (representing 15 of the 23). In addition to these 23, the Astruc (Astrug) family, which rose to prominence in the community soon after their arrival by the mid-fourteenth century (see below), appear to have come from Catalonia and represent another 23 individuals. Closely behind the Sephardim in numbers, another 18 Jews can be identified as having German origin, as specified by the designation Theotonicus, Allemanus, Tedescho, or, in *Taqqanot Qandiya*, Ashkenazi. In addition to these, we have the members of the Delmedigo family with Ashkenazi origins (see below), who count another 23 individuals among the total 833.

80. On the common migratory effect of the Black Death on Jews, see Samuel K. Cohn Jr., "The Black Death and the Burning of Jews," *Past and Present* 196 (2007): 3–36, esp. 1.

81. On the Pestpogrom, see, e.g., Karl Heinz Burmeister, *Der Schwarze Tod: Die Juden-verfolgungen anlässlich der Pest von 1348/49* (Göppingen: Jüdisches Museum, 1999); František Graus, *Pest-Geissler-Judenmorde: Das 14. Jahrhundert als Krisenzeit* (Göttingen: Vandenhoeck und Ruprecht, 1987); Alfred Haverkamp, "Die Judenverfolgungen zur Zeit des Schwarzen Todes im Gesellschaftsgefüge deutscher Städte," in *Zur Geschichte der Juden im Deutschland des späten Mittelalters und der frühen Neuzeit*, ed. Alfred Haverkamp (Stuttgart: A. Hierse-mann, 1981), 27–93. On Wenceslas IV's debt cancellation, see the classic work, Arthur Süss-mann, *Die Judenschuldentilgung unter König Wenzel* (Berlin: Lamm, 1906).

82. David Nirenberg, *Communities of Violence: Persecution of Minorities in the Middle Ages* (Princeton, NJ: Princeton University Press, 1996).

83. Anna Foa, *The Jews of Europe After the Black Death*, trans. A. Grover (Berkeley: University of California Press, 2000), 84.

84. For the classic account of the massacres of 1391 in Iberia, see Baer, *The History of the Jews in Christian Spain*, 2:95–169.

85. Foa, *The Jews of Europe*, 88–89.

86. Robert Bonfil, *Jewish Life in Renaissance Italy*, trans. Anthony Oldcorn (Berke-ley: University of California Press, 1994), 19–20. Ariel Toaff sees an increase in anti-Jewish behavior in Umbria in the second half of the fifteenth century and connects it to the found-ing of the Monti di Pietà, though some anti-Jewish activity also took place between 1320 and 1450; see Ariel Toaff, *Love, Work, Death: Jewish Life in Medieval Umbria*, trans. Judith Landry (Oxford: Littman Library, 1996), 106 (table 5.1), 118–19. For a set of local studies on Jews on the Venetian mainland territories in the fifteenth century, see Gian Maria Varanini and Reinhold C. Mueller, eds., *Ebrei nella Terraferma veneta del Quattrocento* (Florence: Firenze University Press, 2005).

87. Nurit Ben-Aryeh Debby, "Jews and Judaism in the Rhetoric of the Popular Preachers: The Florentine Sermons of Giovanni Dominici (1356–1419) and Bernardino da Siena (1380–1444)," *Jewish History* 14 (2000): 188–89.

88. Bonfil, *Jewish Life*, 20–21.

89. The right to lend in the city evolved over the course of the 1360s through the 1380s. See Reinhold C. Mueller, "Les prêteurs juifs de Venise au moyen âge," *Annales ESC* 30 (1975): 1277–1302; idem, "The Jewish Moneylenders of Late Trecento Venice: A Revisitation," *Mediterranean Historical Review* 10 (1995): 202–17; David Jacoby, "Les Juifs à Venise du XIV\u1d49 au milieu du XVI\u1d49 siècle," in *Venezia centro di mediazione tra oriente e occidente*, ed. Hans-Georg Beck, Manoussos Manoussacas, and Agostino Pertusi (Florence: L. S. Olschki, 1977), 1:163–216; and Eliyahu Ashtor, "Gli inizi della comunità ebraica a Venezia," *La rassegna mensile di Israel* 44 (1978): 683–703.

90. Benjamin Ravid, "The Venetian Government and the Jews," in *The Jews of Early Modern Venice*, ed. Robert C. Davis and Benjamin Ravid (Baltimore: Johns Hopkins Uni-versity Press, 2001), 5.

91. Ravid, "The Venetian Government and the Jews," 5.

92. On this controlling of Jewish settlers, known as the *herem hayishuv*, see the classic English work, Louis I. Rabinowitz, *The Herem Hayyishub: A Contribution to the Medieval*

Economic History of the Jews (London: Golston, 1945). On the phenomenon and its decline in medieval Champagne, see Emily Taitz, *The Jews of Medieval France: The Community of Champagne* (Westport, CT: Greenwood Press, 1994), 45–46, 74–75, 128–29.

93. On Byzantine policy regarding Jewish quarters, see David Jacoby, "Les quartiers juifs de Constantinople à l'époque byzantine," *Byzantion* 37 (1967): 178–83. On the 1325 residential limitations, see Starr, "Jewish Life," 63, and Jacoby, "Venice and the Venetian Jews," 37. For the 1391 ruling, see ASV Duca di Candia, b. 30, r. 22. fols. 105v–106v (24 June 1391). For the rule of 1450, see Georgopoulou, "Mapping Religious and Ethnic Identities," 483, and see 497n58.

94. Noiret, *Documents inédits*, 297–98.

95. Occasionally, however, Jews did manage to secure this privilege, as the case of Grissono, son of Salomone, demonstrates. A Jewish shipowner of Sicilian origin who lived in Rethymno in the 1410s, Grissono did obtain a special dispensation to trade even with Venice itself. See Eliyahu Ashtor, "New Data for the History of Levantine Jewries in the Fifteenth Century," *Bulletin of the Institute of Jewish Studies* 3 (1975): 78–79. Also mentioned in Francesco Apellániz, "Venetian Trading Networks in the Medieval Mediterranean," *Journal of Interdisciplinary History* 44 (2013): 176.

96. David Jacoby, "Pèlerinage médiéval et sanctuaires de Terre Sainte: La perspective vénitienne," *Ateneo Veneto* 173 (1986): 45.

97. Jacoby, "Venice and the Venetian Jews," 47.

98. On Jewish taxation on Crete, see Baron, *A Social and Religious History of the Jews*, vol. 17, *Byzantines, Mamluks, and Maghribians*, 61, and Starr, "Jewish Life in Crete," 77–80. For the embassy of 1389, see Noiret, *Documents inédits*, 13 (25 February 1387) and 26 (25 May 1389). For the impost of 4,000 hyperpera, see ASV Duca di Candia, b. 26, r. 6, fol. 102v (?1430). For the added wheat tax, see ASV Duca di Candia, b. 31, r. 40, fol. 119r (11 January 1439), in which the Jews are ordered to pay 3,000 measures, while the island's feudatories pay 2,000 measures, the citizens in the city pay 2,000, and the burghers pay 2,500. The clerics are told to pay a token 400 measures. Also see Chapter 6 for discussion of the implications of this taxation on the inner workings of the community and its leadership.

99. Jacoby, "Venice and the Venetian Jews," 36.

100. Jacoby, "Quelques aspects," 110, 110n10. On this subject, see also David Jacoby, "Les Juifs vénitiens de Constantinople et leur communauté du XIIIᵉ au milieu du XVᵉ siècle," *Revue des études juives* 131 (1972): 404 for a corrective regarding taxation.

101. As noted by Jacoby, "Venice and the Venetian Jews," 33–34.

102. Jacoby, "Venice and the Venetian Jews," 35–36. In this last case, in 1402, some Jews were permitted to send money from the metropole to the colonies, including Crete, on state galleys for a fee of 2 percent. Ibid., 49.

103. On the rise of Famagusta, see Benjamin Arbel, "Traffici marittimi e sviluppo urbano a Cipro (secoli XIII–XVI)" [Maritime Traffic and Urban Development in Cyprus (13th–16th Centuries)], in *Città portuali del Mediterraneo*, ed. Ennio Poleggi (Genoa: SAGEP Editrice, 1989), 89–94. Also of interest is Benjamin Arbel, "Maritime Trade in Famagusta During the Venetian Period (1474–1571)," in *The Harbour to All This Sea and*

Realm: Crusader to Venetian Famagusta, ed. Michael J. K. Walsh, Tamas Kiss, and Nicholas Coureas (Budapest: Central European University, 2014), 91–103.

104. Charalampos Gasparis, ed., *Franciscus de Cruce: Notarios ston Chandaka, 1338–1339* (Venice: Hellenic Institute for Byzantine and Post-Byzantine Studies, 1999), no. 216, pp. 165–66. Also noted by David Jacoby, "The Jewish Communities of the Byzantine World from the Tenth to the Mid-Fifteenth Century: Some Aspects of Their Evolution," in *Jewish Reception of Greek Bible Versions: Studies in Their Use in Late Antiquity and the Middle Ages*, ed. Nicholas de Lange, Julia G. Krivoruchko, and Cameron Boyd-Taylor, Text and Studies in Medieval and Early Modern Judaism 23 (Tübingen: Mohr Siebeck, 2009), 179.

105. McKee, *Wills*, no. 648, p. 820 (3 December 1358)

106. ASV Duca di Candia, b. 32, r. 44, fol. 2r (23 July 1447), in which his children settle his estate.

107. On the Iberian origins of the name Astruc, see Fritz Baer, *Die Juden im christlichen Spanien*, vol. 1, *Urkenden und Regesten*, I. Aragonien und Navarra (Berlin: Akademi-Verlag, 1929), 1101–2.

108. ASV Duca di Candia, b. 29 bis, r. 15, fols. 63v–65v (7 March 1368). This relationship and its end will be discussed more fully in Chapter 5. For his second marriage, see ASV Duca di Candia, b. 29 bis, r. 15, fol. 73v (30 March 1368). He also adopted his new wife's young daughter.

109. The notarial registers of Egidio Valoso (ASV Notai di Candia, b. 13) and Nicolo Tonisto (ASV Notai di Candia, b. 273) both testify to Solomon's active moneylending business in the 1360s through the 1380s. We also witness him renting out his real estate (see ASV Notai di Candia, b. 273 [not. N. Tonisto], fol. 78r [15 January 1388]) and buying grain (see ASV Notai di Candia, b. 273 [not. N. Tonisto], fol. 86r [26 February 1388]).

110. ASV Duca di Candia, b. 30, r. 22, fols. 106r–v (undated but possibly from 1391).

111. Solomon's own son signed a *taqqanah* in 1435, and another apparent descendant did the same in 1439. Meir Astruc, son of the late Solomon, signed in 1435. *TQ* no. 57, pp. 57–58. Shalom Astruc, the son of Shabbetai, signed in 1439. *TQ* no. 76, pp. 83–85. The relationship between this Shalom and the patriarch Solomon Astruc remains unclear to me, since none of Solomon's known children is named Shabbetai (or the Latin Sabatheus). It is possible, then, that (1) Solomon came to Candia with an otherwise unknown relative, (2) the manuscript has mistaken the signatory's father's name, or (3) these men are not related but Shalom comes from another Astruc family that arrived after 1391.

112. Solomon b. Mordechai Astruc is recorded as *condestabulo* on 4 Sivan 5206 according to the Jewish calendar, which falls in 1446 on the Julian calendar. *TQ* no. 60, p. 63.

113. For some fifteenth-century examples of the same phenomenon, see Jacoby, "Quelques aspects," 111–12.

114. Antonino Lombardo, ed., *Imbreviature di Pietro Scardon* (Turin: Editrice libraria italiana, 1942) [hereafter *Pietro Scardon*], no. 45 (8 February 1271).

115. McKee, *Wills*, no. 743, pp. 935–36 (4 May 1378).

116. *de melioribus iudeis theotonicis habitatoribus in Candide.*

117. ASV Duca di Candia, b. 30, r. 22, fol. 77v (4 April 1391).

118. On German Jews' migration to northern Italy and the Veneto, see Angela Möschter, *Juden in venezianischen Treviso (1389–1509)* (Hannover: Hahnsche Buchhandlung, 2008); Ariel Toaff, "Gli insediamenti ashkenaziti nell'Italia settentrionale," in *Gli ebrei in Italia*, ed. Corrado Vivanti (Storia d'Italia 11) (Turin: Einaudi, 1996), 155–71; Alessandra Veronese, "Mobilità, migrazioni e presenza ebraica a Trieste nei secoli XIV e XV," in *Scritti in onore di Girolamo Arnaldi offerti dalla Scuola nazionale di studi medioevali*, ed. Andrea Degrandi and Ovidio Capitani (Rome: Istituto storico italiano per il Medio Evo, 2001), 545–82.

119. Starr, "Jewish Life," 77.

120. On this debate, see Brian Ogren, *Renaissance and Rebirth: Reincarnation in Early Modern Italian Kabbalah* (Leiden: Brill, 2009), esp. chaps. 1–2.

121. According to his son Saul, Moses Cohen Ashkenazi was "of Ashkenazic stock who had joined the exile of Jerusalem in Spain, currently dwelling on the slopes of the isle of Candia," as quoted in Aviezer Ravitzky, "The God of the Philosophers Versus the God of the Kabbalists: A Controversy in Fifteenth-Century Crete (Heb MSS Vatican 105 and 254)," in *Studies in Jewish Manuscripts*, ed. Joseph Dan and Klaus Herrmann (Tübingen: Mohr Siebeck, 1999), 140. An extant letter from Rabbi Judah Obernik of Mestre to Moses hints at his previous residence in Venice and his father's continued presence there. Ephraim Kupfer, "Le-demut ha-tarbutit shel yahadut ashkenaz ve-hakhameha be-me'ot ha-14-15" [Concerning the Cultural Image of German Jewry and Its Rabbis in the Fourteenth and Fifteenth Centuries], *Tarbiz* 42 (1972/73): 129.

122. For the classic views of the Delmedigo family, see Abraham Geiger, *Kevutsat ma'amarim*, ed. Samuel Abraham Poznanski (Warsaw: Tushiyah, 1910), 285–96; and Moritz Steinschneider, "Candia: Cenni di storia letteraria," *Mosè: Antologie Israelitica* 3 (1880): 282.

123. Judah and Shemarya Delmedigo, the sons of Elia, and identified as "di Nigroponte," first appear in ASV Duca di Candia, b. 29 in 1359. By October 1359 Judah was already a legal resident of Candia and had already loaned money to a fellow Jew, now dead. Judah sued the dead man's family to recover his money. ASV Duca di Candia, b. 29, r. 12, fol. 8r (3 October 1359), and fols. 14r–16r (17 October 1359). In 1360, both brothers were forbidden from leaving Candia because of pending litigation. ASV Duca di Candia, b. 29, r. 12, fols. 66v–67r (9 March 1360).

124. For this dating of the Allemaniko synagogue, see Starr, "Jewish Life," 98.

125. As noted by Kupfer, "Le-demut ha-tarbutit," 126.

126. See Isaac Barzilay, *Yoseph Shlomo Delmedigo (Yashar of Candia)* (Leiden: Brill, 1974), 86–87.

127. *TQ* no. 85, p. 107.

128. On the sewer project, see ASV Duca di Candia, b. 30 bis, r. 29, fol. 60v (20 November 1411).

129. *TQ* no. 102, p. 132.

130. *TQ* no. 50, p. 48.

131. McKee, *Wills*, no. 743, pp. 935–36 (4 May 1378).

132. ASV Duca di Candia, b. 32, r. 42, fol. 18v (27 November 1444).

133. *TQ* no. 76, p. 85.

134. See *TQ* no. 61, p. 63, where a new method of checking the head of a slaughtered animal is explicitly connected to Ashkenaz, and the audience is told that Moses Capsali brought this new practice back from Germany when he returned from his studies there.

135. Potha Plumari, a resident of Candia, mentions in her will that her mother, Cali, resides in Belvedere in 1319. McKee, *Wills*, no. 336, p. 445 (24 June 1319). A Jewish doctor named Moses lived in Belvedere in 1373. ASV Duca di Candia, b. 29 bis, r. 16, fol. 10r (1 February 1373). Occasionally Jews living in other villages or fortress towns appear in the record. The Jewish businessman Abraham (Avragha), son of the late Zacha Bufalo, lived in Castro Chilie. See Salvatore Carbone, ed., *Pietro Pizolo notaio in Candia* (Venice: Il Comitato, 1978–85) [hereafter *Pietro Pizolo*], vol. 2, no. 763 (24 May 1304).

136. Among those living in Castro Bonifacio we find: a doctor, Magister Elia, who was active in 1373 (ASV Duca di Candia, b. 29 bis, r. 17, fol. 16v [9 September 1373]) and may or may not be the same man as the salaried Jewish surgeon Elia Crusari active three decades later (e.g., ASV Duca di Candia, b. 30 bis, r. 26, fol. 1r [9 September 1401]); the doctor Elia Lago (e.g., ASV Duca di Candia, b. 30 ter, r. 30, fol. 162r [18 January 1417]); the doctor Joseph (Joste) Gracian (e.g., ASV Duca di Candia, b. 30 ter, r. 30, fol. 177r [27 February 1417]); and Judah (Jocuda) Balbo (ASV Duca di Candia, b. 31, r. 40, fol. 137r [19 April 1439]).

137. ASV Duca di Candia, b. 31, r. 40, fol. 137r (19 April 1439).

138. ASV Duca di Candia, b. 30 ter, r. 32, fol. 9v (21 October 1419). The ducal court could not find the perpetrators.

139. Starr, "Jewish Life," 64n16. Evidence for the attack comes from Laurentius de Monacis, *Chronicon de rebus Venetis ab urbe condita ad annum MCCCCIV* (Venice: Ex typographia Redmondiniana, 1758), 179, 186. The surviving Jewish sources make no mention of the attack.

140. For Carfocopo, see ASV Duca di Candia, b. 29 bis, r. 16, fol. (55)53r (5 July 1369); e.g., see ASV Duca di Candia, b. 31, r. 36, fol. 153r (1 August 1429).

141. ASV Duca di Candia, b. 26, r. 3, fol. 158r (12 August 1370).

142. ASV Duca di Candia, b. 29 bis, r. 17, fol. 13r (2 May 1373). Another injured Jew from Castronovo, Samaria Calopo, appears in the record in 1417. ASV Duca di Candia, b. 30 ter, r. 30, fol. 162v (27 January 1417).

143. *Iudei morantes in Castronovo*. ASV Duca di Candia, b. 29 bis, r. 19, fol. 53v (2 September 1382).

144. Benjamin Arbel, "Jews and Christians in Sixteenth-Century Crete: Between Segregation and Integration," in *"Interstizi": Culture ebraico-cristiane a Venezia e nei suoi domini dal Medioevo all'Età Moderna*, ed. Uwe Israel, Robert Jütte, and Reinhold C. Mueller (Rome: Edizioni di Storia e Letteratura, 2010), 283.

145. Michael Malchisedech of Canea owned a house in the Candiote Judaica, which, at the turn of the fourteenth century, he was renting to another Jew. ASV Duca di Candia, b. 30 bis, r. 25, fols. 34r–35r (19 February 1400). Michael Antiqui acquired a pair of apartments in a two-floor building in Candia, which he rented out to other Jews, as well as two pairs of

apartments in Rethymno. (These apartments became a point of contention among his heirs after his death in 1453 or 1454.) ASV Duca di Candia, b. 26 bis, r. 11, fol. 46r (16 July 1454).

146. See ASV Duca di Candia, b. 30 bis, r. 29, fols. 137v–138r (30 May 1412), for Moses Capsali, resident of Rethymno. ASV Duca di Candia, b. 30 ter, r. 30, fol. 65v (? June 1416) records a Ligiachus Capsali of Rethymno and a Sabatheus Capsali "de Rodo." Ankori notes that Delmedigo descendants lived in Khania (Canea) in the nineteenth century. Ankori, "Jews and the Jewish Community," 320.

147. ASV Duca di Candia, b. 26, r. 5, fols. 63v–64r (18 March 1427).

148. McKee, *Wills*, no. 638 (vol. 2, p. 809).

149. ASV Duca di Candia, b. 29 bis, r. 16, fol. (32)31r (29 February 1369). Though the text clearly reads Pilopotamo, it may be a mistake by the scribe who intended to write Milopotamo, the name of a village known from other sources.

150. For Jews from other communities in Crete signing ordinances during the period under study, see *TQ* no. 51, p. 50 (Eliezer son of Rabbi Gershom, of Rethymno; 1428); and *TQ* no. 52, p. 52 (Eliezer son of Rabbi Gershom, of Rethymno; Judah son of Moses from Rethymno; 1406). *TQ* no. 48, pp. 44–46, records a *taqqanah* regarding kosher slaughterers and cantors from Rethymno dated to 1362, which was adopted by the Candiote community in 1385–86.

151. ASV Duca di Candia, b. 32, r. 44, fol. 168r (11 February 1449).

152. The Byzantines lost Negroponte following the Fourth Crusade. While the island as a whole came under Venetian colonial rule only in 1390, Venice began to influence the island in the early thirteenth century when its Veronese ruler gave over significant power to the Venetian *bailo* who represented La Serenissima's interests. See John B. Bury's classic studies "The Lombards and Venetians in Euboia (1205–1303)," *Journal of Hellenic Studies* 7 (1886): 309–52; "The Lombards and Venetians in Euboia (continued)," *Journal of Hellenic Studies* 8 (1887): 194–213; "The Lombards and Venetians in Euboia (1340–1470)," *Journal of Hellenic Studies* 9 (1888): 91–117.

153. On the Jews of Venetian Negroponte, see David Jacoby, "The Demographic Evolution of Euboea Under Latin Rule, 1205–1470," in *The Greek Islands and the Sea*, ed. Julian Chrystomides, Charalambos Dendrinos, and Jonathan Harris (Camberley, Surrey: Porphyrogentius, 2004), 131–79. Also see Silvano Borsari, "Ricchi e poveri nelle comunità ebraiche di Candia e Negroponte (secc. XIII–XVI)," in *Ricchi e poveri nella società dell'oriente greco-latino*, ed. Chryssa Maltezou (Venice: Hellenic Institute of Byzantine and Post-Byzantine Studies, 1998), 211. For one marriage contract, see Mario Chiaudano and Antonino Lombardo, eds., *Leonardo Marcello, notaio in Candia, 1278–1281* (Venice: Il Comitato, 1960) [hereafter *Leonardo Marcello*], nos. 109–10, pp. 43–44.

154. In March 1360, Judah Delmedigo (Jacuda del Medico) is identified as "judeo di Nigroponte." He and his brother Samargia are ordered not to leave the island pending the resolution of a financial agreement gone wrong with members of the Kalergi family. ASV Duca di Candia, b. 29, r. 12, fols. 66v–67r (9 March 1360). The matter was apparently resolved quickly, since both acts were canceled on 12 March.

155. In her 1379 will, Parnatissa tu Carteru names her son-in-law, "Samerya de Rodo," now living in Candia, as her sole executor; see McKee, *Wills*, no. 705, p. 892 (11 March 1379). The same man appears as the procurator for Liacho (Ligiachus) Mavristiri, a Candiote Jew resident in Rhodes. ASV Duca di Candia, b. 30, r. 20, fols. 8v–9v (6 February 1386). For more on Mavristiri, see McKee, *Uncommon Dominion*, 71, 184–88. As compared to Crete, Rhodes offered lower trade duties, as noted by Apellániz, "Venetian Trading Networks," 178. Samuel, the son of Candiote community leader and Jewish representative to Venice Joseph Missini, was for a time betrothed to a fabulously wealthy Rhodian girl named Jocheyna. ASV Duca di Candia, b. 30, r. 22, fols. 33r–34r (11 July 1390).

156. In February 1300, two Jews, Joseph (Iosep) Gavio and Isaac Ligon, both residents of Barcelona, made a nautical *colleganza* (joint-venture agreement) before a notary in Candia, noting that two Majorcan Jews, Abramo Bono and Aymbrano Xulel, would actually travel on the ship bound for Sardinia and Tunis. *Pietro Pizolo*, no. 60 (13 February 1300). In the same month, another Barcelona native, the Jew Isaac Gracian, received an interest-free loan from the Candiote Jew Sambatheus, son of the late David, with the understanding the Gracian might soon leave Crete for Alexandria. *Pietro Pizolo*, no. 101 (26 February 1300). A Roman Jew named Meble took a loan in Crete in 1306 that he had to repay in Alexandrian currency, in Alexandria, after he traveled there on a Catalan merchant's boat, as recorded in the notarial register of Angelo de Cartura, no. 487 (8 April 1306), as edited in Alan M. Stahl, ed., *The Documents of Angelo de Cartura and Donato Fontanella: Venetian Notaries in Fourteenth-Century Crete* (Washington, DC: Dumbarton Oaks, 2000).

157. On the Alexandria trade in general, see Francesco Apellániz, "Collaboration des réseaux marchands à Alexandrie (XIVᵉ–XVᵉ siècles)," in *From Florence to the Mediterranean and Beyond: Studies in Honor of Anthony Molho*, ed. Diogo Ramada Curto et al. (Florence: L. S. Olschki, 2009), 2:581–99, esp. 585–91. In the second decade of the fifteenth century, two Candiote Jews (including one from the Capsali family) are among the most active of all Venetian-affiliated merchants, and Jews remain important in the sources through the 1440s; see Apellániz, "Venetian Trading Networks," 176, and table 1; idem, "Collaboration," 588–89. Apellániz recognizes the need for a more comprehensive study of Crete's Jewish traders in Alexandria, especially in the period after the 1440s. On the Venetian-Alexandrian wine trade, see Georg Christ, *Trading Conflicts: Venetian Merchants and Mamluk Officials in Late Medieval Alexandria* (Leiden: Brill, 2012), 167–74, and for the place of Cretan traders, see 170–72. Also see Benjamin Arbel, "The 'Jewish Wine' of Crete," in *Μονεμβάσιος Οἶνος, Μονοβας(ι)ά–Malvasia*, ed. Elias Anagnostakes (Athens: National Hellenic Research Foundation, 2008), 81–88.

158. David Jacoby, "The Jews of Constantinople and Their Demographic Hinterland," in *Constantinople and Its Hinterland: Papers from the Twenty-Seventh Spring Symposium of Byzantine Studies, Oxford, April 1993*, ed. Cyril Mango and Gilbert Dagron (Aldershot: Varorium, 1995), 229; Jacoby, "The Jewish Communities," 177. After 1453, Jewish traders took on an even larger role in the Venetian-Ottoman trade; see Benjamin Arbel, *Trading Nations: Jews and Venetians in the Early-Modern Eastern Mediterranean* (Leiden: Brill, 1995), 13, 83–86.

159. Those who visited or lived in Jerusalem include Cardina, only known to us as the *filiastra* (stepdaughter?) of a wealthy female testator named Chaluda Balbo, who was in Jerusalem (*est in Yerusalem*) when a will bequeathing her ten hyperpera was drawn up in the 1370s. McKee, *Wills*, no. 97, p. 127 (no date; from its placement it must date to the early 1370s). A number of older Cretan Jews left for the Holy Land with the explicit understanding that they did not have too long to live and would be buried there: McKee, *Wills*, no. 137, pp. 174–75 (12 October 1340). This remained a common enough practice into the seventeenth century: Chryssa Maltezou, "From Crete to Jerusalem: The Will of a Cretan Jew (1626)," *Mediterranean Historical Review* 10 (1995): 189–201. Others lived there during more youthful years. A middle-aged member of the Capsali clan lived in Jerusalem in 1405: ASV Duca di Candia, b. 31, r. 41, fols. 40r–v (27 January 1440). Around the turn of the fifteenth century, a wealthy Candiote Jew named Samuel moved to Jerusalem permanently, abandoning his wife in Candia—and marrying a second wife bigamously in Jerusalem, whence he had no plans to return: ASV Duca di Candia, b. 30 bis, r. 27, fols. 53r–54r (16 September 1406).

160. For this will, written for a Jew named Salachaya, see McKee, *Wills*, no. 511, pp. 650–51 (6 April 1348); for Chaluda Balbo's will: McKee, *Wills*, no. 97, p. 127 (no date; from its placement it must date to the early 1370s).

161. *TQ* no. 76, pp. 83–84.

162. *TQ* no. 32, pp. 21.

163. *TQ,* no. 89, p. 110.

164. *TQ* no. 85, p. 103.

165. *TQ* no. 36, pp. 26–27; *TQ* no. 37, pp. 27–28.

166. *TQ* no. 37, p. 27 is concerned with the Castronovan Jews' "secret" selling of unapproved dairy; the Candiote Jews are treated as passive dupes. *TQ* no. 36, p. 26 quietly but equally implicates Candia's Jews in this behavior, this time regarding unapproved meat.

167. Solomon Torchidi of Candia contracted for his son Samaria to marry Cherana, the daughter of Isaac Gaytani of Castronovo. Gaytani's daughter brought with her a significant dowry, including 300 hyperpera and an additional 25 hyperpera for a home. ASV Notai di Candia, b. 2 (not. Michele Calergi), fol. 43r (15 July 1451).

168. For the epistle-cum-ordinance from 1567, see *TQ* no. 108, pp. 143–44. Here, the Candiote leadership is horrified that the local religious leadership in Castronovo saw fit to take it upon themselves to excommunicate a member of the community on the first day of the holiday of Shavuot. The Candiote leadership reminds the people of Castronovo that only Candia's rabbis have that right—given to them by Venice itself—and that their behavior, if continued, would provoke a wholesale excommunication of Castronovo's Jews. The bad behavior of the Jews of Castronovo is explicitly contrasted with the behavior of good Jews: those from Candia, Rethymno, and Castro (or Castel) Bonifacio.

169. In previous scholarship, I claimed that this refers to Castile in Spain. I no longer believe this to be true, as *Taqqanot Qandiya* generally refers to Spain as Sepharad, as above with Abraham Tofer.

170. *TQ* no. 47, p. 43.

171. *TQ* no. 47, p. 44.

172. The irony increases when one considers that Ashkenazi approaches to its own tradition and custom were deeply conservative and claimed aversion to innovation—and had been since at least the tenth century when Ashkenazi communities established themselves in the Rhineland. See David Malkiel, "Renaissance in the Graveyard: The Hebrew Tombstones of Padua and Ashkenazic Acculturation in Sixteenth-Century Italy," *AJS Review* 37 (2013): 334n3 for an extensive literature on the phenomenon.

173. *TQ* no. 45, pp. 36–39.

174. See Chapter 6 for more on this.

175. *TQ* no. 61, p. 63.

176. The manuscripts are: MS Vat. ebr. 247 (1324); MS Oxford Hunt. 561 (1375); MS Parma 2286 (1395); Roma Cas. 2847 (1395); MS Leiden Cod. Or. 4751 (1397); MS Moscow Guenzburg 362 (1400); MS Vatican Barb. Or. 82 (1407); MS Parma 2473 (1408); MS Moscow Guenzburg 906 (1414); MS Vat. ebr. 345 (1451); MS Vat. ebr. 249 (1452); MS Vat. ebr. 225 (1458); MS Vat. ebr. 187 (1463); MS Vat. ebr. 257 (1469); MS Paris BnF heb. 919 (1481–85); MS Vat. ebr. 171 (1493). In addition, MS Vat. ebr. 254 and 105 record the two sides of the aforementioned 1466 metempsychosis debate between Moses Ashkenazi and Michael Balbo. (For full bibliographic information, see the bibliography.)

177. See Rena Lauer, "Cretan Jews and the First Sephardic Encounter in the Fifteenth Century," *Mediterranean Historical Review* 27 (2012): 131.

178. Referenced in Starr, "Jewish Life," 105.

179. Data I have collected from legal, notarial, and Hebrew sources have uncovered Joseph's family, including his parents, Chaim and Cali Missini, siblings Ligiacho and Cherana, alongside their spouses and families, two wives who both seem to be named Channa, and two children, Crussana (and her family) and Samuel (who died before marrying).

180. I thank David Jacoby for suggesting Messinia as a possible origin point for this name. Messinia is the region of the Peloponnese in which Venice's port city holdings of Coron and Modon can be found.

181. *TQ* no. 46, p. 40. The year of Missini's service as *condestabulo* is unclear, only identified as during the rule of "the duke Bembo." A number of Bembo family members, however, served as dukes of Crete, and in addition, the list of known dukes is incomplete. It is possible though uncertain that Missini held his office when Leonardo Bembo was duke in late 1405 through 1407.

182. The record of the Senate's decision following the hearing in which Joseph Missini, along with fellow Cretan Jews Sabatheus Retu (or perhaps, Vetu) and Melchior (probably Melchiele) Cassani, argued for a reduction in taxes is edited in Noiret, *Documents inédits*, 26 (25 May 1389). In this fascinating case, three Venetian noblemen, including a former duke of Crete, testify to the truth of the Jews' claims that the Jews had been an enormous help to the Venetians during the war and that recent plague had stripped the Jewish community of its high numbers. The senate agreed to reduce the tax.

183. See Chapter 5. ASV Duca di Candia, b. 30 bis, r. 26, fols. 18v–19v (27 October 1401).

184. For the cases in which parts of this testament are recopied, see ASV Duca di Candia, b. 30 ter, r. 31, fols. 17r–18v (18 October 1417); b. 26 bis, r. 8, fols.7v–8r (1 October 1437); and b. 31, r. 40, fols. 14r–15r (1 October 1437). The will was written up by Giovanni Catacalo on 14 August 1411. The original will does not survive in the extant register of Catacalo (ASV Notai di Candia, b. 24), which unfortunately covers only parts of 1389. For these funds to support poor boys and girls, see the portion of the will copied in ASV Duca di Candia, b. 30 ter, r. 31, fols. 17r–18r (18 October 1417). Missini's family had a tradition of such generosity at death. Joseph's own sister Cherana, writing a will during a difficult pregnancy in 1373, bequeathed funds for the writing of three *Vetera Testamenta* (whether this meant Torah scrolls or codices we cannot know). She also left money for "poor Jewish orphan girls" to be married. McKee, *Wills*, no. 762, p. 954 (25 December 1373). Other wealthy Candiote Jews did the same, though Missini's amounts are larger than is typical, for example in funding one girl's wedding a year for twelve years and funding twelve boys' education for twelve years. For another example, Anastassia, the wife of the wealthy spice merchant Judah Balbo, stipulated in her will that fifty hyperpera were to be used in the first year after her death to help marry off poor Jewish girls. See McKee, *Wills*, no. 463, pp. 595–96 (24 June 1334).

185. *Quod vadat in manibus doctorum iudeorum theotonicorum et francigenorum qui fuerint ibi.* This is the language of the will as paraphrased in ASV Duca di Candia, b. 30 ter, r. 31, fol. 17v.

186. Israel died, leaving Crussana a widow. She remarried, this time to a Jew with an apparently Italian name: Ottaviano Bonavita. See ASV Duca di Candia, b. 30 ter, r. 32, fols. 8v–9r (16 October 1419).

187. See Chapter 5. Also see Rena Lauer, "In Defence of Bigamy: Colonial Policy, Jewish Law, and Gender in Venetian Crete," *Gender & History 29* (2017): 570–88.

188. For an ordinance warning Jewish landlords about mistreating and evicting their tenants, see *TQ* no. 29, p. 16; for examples of intra-Jewish landlord/tenant litigation, see Chapter 6. Also see Georgopoulou, *Venice's Mediterranean Colonies*, 197–98.

CHAPTER 2

1. *TQ* no. 33, p. 22. The quote is a paraphrase of Lamentations 4:16, and in remaining faithful to the verse, the text becomes a bit redundant.

2. *TQ* no. 33, p. 23.

3. *TQ* no. 94, p. 115.

4. David Jacoby, "Les Juifs de Byzance: Une communauté marginalisée," in *Marginality in Byzantium*, ed. Chryssa A. Maltezou (Athens: Goulandri-Horn Foundation, 1993), 142–43.

5. Jacoby, "Jews and Christians," 276.

6. Meshullam of Volterra, *Masah Meshullam*, 82. Parallel laws and customs would be spotted by visitors in Rhodes and in the Venetian holdings of Corfu, Zante, and Famagusta. Jacoby, "Jews and Christians," 276.

7. Kenneth Stow, *Jewish Dogs: An Image and Its Interpreters: Continuity in the Catholic-Jewish Encounter* (Stanford, CA: Stanford University Press, 2006), 23. See also Maurice Kriegel, "Un trait de psychologie sociale: Le Juif comme intouchable," *Annales ESC* 31 (1976): 72–97.

8. Stow, *Jewish Dogs*, 20.

9. *TQ* no. 74, p. 79. Quote from Isaiah 64:5.

10. *TQ* no. 41, p. 33. The quote is a slightly awkward paraphrase and play on the first half of Lamentations 4:1, which reads, "How the gold has become dim, how has the most fine gold changed."

11. Arbel, "The 'Jewish Wine' of Crete," 88.

12. ASV Duca di Candia, b. 30 ter, r. 35, fols. 27r–32r (3 September 1424).

13. Lax attitudes toward Jewish consumption of Christian-produced wine are well attested in the northern Italian sphere. See, e.g., Toaff, *Love, Work, Death*, 74–79.

14. ASV Duca di Candia, b. 30 ter, r. 35, fols. 27r–v reports that the nuns (*calogree*) who were there "immediately closed the gate of the monastery lest the youths [i.e., the attackers] enter and kill the Jew" (*statim clauserunt ostium monasterii ne dicti iuvenes intravent et occiderent istum judeum*). Later witnesses say that the nuns let in two of the Jewish men to hide there.

15. ASV Duca di Candia, b. 30 ter, r. 35, fol. 31v.

16. ASV Duca di Candia, b. 30 ter, r. 35, fol. 31v. *Georgius Turcopulo cucurit post ipsos agoziatos.*

17. According to one witness, one robber yelled, "male vaditis, canes." ASV Duca di Candia, b. 30 ter, r. 35, fol. 31r.

18. *Leonardo Marcello*, no. 110 (25 April 1279).

19. Paola Ratti Vidulich, ed., *Duca di Candia: Bandi (1319–1329)* (Venice: Il Comitato, 1965), p. 156, no. 392 (15 January 1325).

20. ASV Duca di Candia, b. 29, r. 10, fol. 7v (20 October 1350); ASV Duca di Candia, b. 29, fol. 5r (30 September 1359).

21. The record of the acquisition and sale of this feudal holding can be found in four acts: ASV Notai di Candia, b. 101 (not. G. Gerardo), fols. 302v (17 May 1331), 302v (17 May 1341), 302v–303r (17 May 1341), and 303r (18 May 1341). These acts are edited in McKee, *Uncommon Dominion*, 184–87, and discussed on p. 71.

22. For the ship co-ownership, see Antonino Lombardo, ed., *Zaccaria de Fredo, notaio in Candia (1352–1357)* (Venice: Il Comitato, 1968) [hereafter *Zaccaria de Fredo*], nos. 61, 66, 71, and 72 (16–18 September 1352). Also mentioned in David Jacoby, "Greeks in the Maritime Trade of Cyprus Around the Mid-Fourteenth Century," in *Cipro-Venezia: Communi sorti storiche* (Atti del simposio internazionale, Atene, 1–3 marzo 2001), ed. Chryssa Maltezou (Venice: Hellenic Institute, 2002), 59–83. For the legal advisors, see ASV Duca di Candia, b. 26, r. 3, fol. 121r (27 November 1368). As recorded in this case, the hiring contract is dated 13 July 1368. The Latin, Facino di Molino, and the Jew, Liacho Sacerdoto, were later sued together by the woman, Elea Mavristiri, for lack of benefit. See Chapter 5. On the masons, see Chryssa Maltezou, "Métiers e salaires en Crète vénitienne (XVe siècle)," *Byzantinische Forschungen* 12 (1987): 326.

23. Gaetano Pettenello and Simone Rauch, eds., *Stefano Bono, notaio in Candia, 1303–1304* (Rome: Viella, 2011) [hereafter *Stefano Bono*], no. 290 (20 September 1303).

24. *Zaccaria de Fredo*, no. 94 (20 April 1357).

25. *Pietro Scardon*, no. 253 (20 April 1271).

26. *Stefano Bono*, no. 55 (17 May 1303).

27. ASV Duca di Candia, b. 29 bis, r. 17, fol. 44v (26 February 1378). In a tantalizing record from 1371, a case between two Christian members of the de Rippa family, a Jewish woman named Jani appears on the witness list, though her testimony does not survive. ASV Duca di Candia, b. 29 bis, r. 17, fol. 35v (20 November 1371).

28. Jacoby, "Jews and Christians," 268.

29. Ricardo Court, "*Januensis ergo mercator*: Trust and Enforcement in the Business Correspondence of the Brignole Family," *Sixteenth Century Journal* 35 (2004): 997.

30. Court, "*Januensis ergo mercator*," 995–96.

31. Francesca Trivellato, *The Familiarity of Strangers: The Sephardic Diaspora, Livorno, and Cross-Cultural Trade in the Early Modern Period* (New Haven, CT: Yale University Press, 2009), 9–11.

32. Trivellato, *The Familiarity of Strangers*, 16.

33. I am grateful to Dr. Ethan Katz for suggesting the language of "reflective" and "generative" trust.

34. This reevaluation of the social implications of moneylending is part of a scholarly revision most famously articulated by Joseph Shatzmiller in *Shylock Reconsidered: Jews, Moneylending, and Medieval Society* (Berkeley: University of California Press, 1990).

35. A few other examples of this ubiquitous practice: Moses Nomico lent the *borgo*-based goldsmith Leone Villari 11.5 hyperpera without interest (*Pietro Scardon*, no. 219, 9 April 1271); Potho, son of Parna de Hebraam, gave an interest-free loan of 150 measures of wheat to the Christian Marcus Zanbom (*Leonardo Marcello*, no. 222, 6 September 1280); the widow Archondissa, a businesswoman involved in the kosher wine trade, gave a number of interest-free loans to Christian men from both the outlying villages and Candia who do not seem to be involved in her other business dealings (*Stefano Bono*, no. 351 [16 August 1303] and no. 402 [17 October 1303]); the Jew Samuele Atalioti gave an interest-free loan of 60 hyperpera to Michael Cabuso, of the *borgo*, to be paid back in goods (ASV Notai di Candia, b. 2 [not. M. Calergi], fol. 8r [27 February 1449]); the Jew Mordechai Man (?) gave 15 hyperpera as an interest-free loan to George Copio (ASV Notai di Candia, b. 2 [not. Francesco Avonale], fol. 37r [2 April 1451]). Interest-free loans, of course, did not mean collateral-free, and sometimes these loan documents specify pawns. Let us note that Jews did not always give their fellow Jews such good terms: the Jewish lender Eudochia, daughter of Lago, gave a loan of 13 hyperpera to her coreligionist Cali Casani but had her agree both to pay interest and to leave goods in pawn (ASV Notai di Candia, b. 13 [not. E. Valoso], fol. 20r [22 April 1370]).

36. *Leonardo Marcello*, no. 100 (21 April 1279).

37. ASV Notai di Candia, b. 273 (not. Nicolo Tonisto), fol. 80r (23 January 1388).

38. Elite, i.e., identified as "ser." For an example from 1370, see ASV Notai di Candia, b. 13 (not. Egidio Valoso), fol. 33r. For the 1380s, see ASV Notai di Candia, b. 273 (not. Nicolo Tonisto), including fols. 78r, 82v, and 90v.

39. The suit is mentioned in a contract in ASV Notai di Candia, b. 273 (not. Nicolo Tonisto), fol. 82v (10 February 1388). The angry creditor is the Jewish Solomon Astrug, a well-known moneylender and real estate investor.

40. William Chester Jordan, "Jews on Top: Women and the Availability of Consumption Loans in Northern France in the Mid-Thirteenth Century," *Journal of Jewish Studies* 29 (1978): 56.

41. To be sure, even in other parts of Christendom in which Christian debtors tended to choose favorite Jewish lenders, the volatile combination of religious difference and economic dependency did not always explode into hatred. See, e.g., Hannah Meyer, "Gender, Jewish Creditors and Christians Debtors in Thirteenth-Century Exeter," in *Intersections of Gender, Religion and Ethnicity in the Middle Ages*, ed. Cordelia Beattie and Kirsten A. Fenton (Houndmills: Palgrave Macmillan, 2011), 112.

42. Such a mandate is made even more remarkable by the fact that the Crusader kingdom's merchant court also assumed that the lender was responsible for securing the guarantor for the borrower. For these laws from the *Assises de la Cour des Bourgeois*, see A. A. Beugnot, ed., *Recueil des historiens des croisades: Lois, vol. II* (Paris: Imprimerie Royale, 1843), 53–56.

43. *TQ* no. 5, p. 4.

44. *TQ* no. 23, p. 13.

45. *TQ* no. 35, pp. 25–26.

46. *TQ* no. 43, pp. 34–36.

47. On the prohibition against "informing" in its medieval context, see Elena Lourie, "Mafiosi and Malsines: Violence, Fear, and Faction in the Jewish Aljamas of Valencia in the Fourteenth Century," in *Crusade and Colonisation: Muslims, Christians, and Jews in Medieval Aragon* (Hampshire: Variorum, 1990), 69–102.

48. *Pietro Pizolo*, no. 849 (3 September 1304).

49. ASV Duca di Candia, b. 26 bis, r. 27, fols. 63r–v (5 November 1406). The court of first instance that found for Spathael was the *di proprii* (for Latins), not the *di prosopi* (for Jews and Greeks).

50. For example, when Moses Carlion, a Jew and former *daciarius olei* (collector of a tax on oil imports), fought against the current, Christian holder of the same position, the spat had nothing to do with their difference in religion but over who had the rights to collect the tax at the end of Moses' tenure. ASV Duca di Candia, b. 30 bis, r. 26, fols. 179r–v (23 July 1403).

51. On the Jewish Exchequer, an office set up to record, control, and perhaps protect Jewish credit in the century before the expulsion of 1290, see the entries "Exchequer of the Jews" and "Exchequer of the Jews, Plea Rolls of," in *The Palgrave Dictionary of Medieval Anglo-Jewish History*, ed. Joe Hillaby and Caroline Hillaby (Houndmills: Palgrave Macmillan, 2013), 130–34. For an extensive account of current historiographic understanding of the

office, see the introduction to the latest edition of the Plea Rolls in Paul Brand, ed., *Plea Rolls of the Exchequer of the Jews* (London: Jewish Historical Society of England, 2005), 1–51.

52. Simon Roberts, "The Study of Dispute: Anthropological Perspectives," in *Disputes and Settlements: Law and Human Relations in the West*, ed. John Bossy (Cambridge: Cambridge University Press, 1983), 4.

53. ASV Notai di Candia, b. 273 (not. Nicolo Tonisto), fols. 74v–94v (1 January–23 March 1388).

54. ASV Notai di Candia, b. 273 (not. Nicolo Tonisto), fols. 76v–93v (10 January–8 March 1388).

55. ASV Notai di Candia, b. 13 (not. Egidio Valoso), fols. 17r–42v (3 April–28 August 1370).

56. ASV Notai di Candia, b. 24 (not. Giovanni Catacalo), fols. 2r–v (18–20 May 1389).

57. Giovanni Catacalo's surviving registers cover only May 1389 through May 1391 (ASV Notai di Candia, busta 24). Even a quick perusal shows him to have been favored by Jewish businessmen and moneylenders of the elite Candiote houses, including Lazaro, son of Judah Balbo; Melchiel Casan (later *condestabulo*); and Jacob "Tam" Belo (discussed in Chapter 6).

58. ASV Duca di Candia, b. 30 ter, r. 32, fols. 69v–72v (25 July 1425?).

59. For another example of his business dealings with Christians, in which Protho Spathael acted as a guarantor for the Latin Nicolas Geno when the latter borrowed a hundred hyperpera from a Jewish creditor, see ASV Notai di Candia, b. 23 (not. Andrea Cocco), fol. 6r (28 July 1400). For his Jewish leadership, see *TQ* no. 46, p. 40: Protho Spathael as *condestabulo* served during the ducate of "messer Donado," likely Andrea Donato (1447).

60. Elisabeth Santschi, "Affaires pénales en Crète vénetienne (1407–1420)," *Thesaurismata* 13 (1976): 72. There is evidence that the Inquisition sought relapsed converts who had fled to Crete in the 1320s, but our evidence regarding this case comes exclusively from the canonist Oldrado de Ponte of Avignon. See Starr, "Jewish Life," 64.

61. ASV Duca di Candia, b. 30 ter, r. 32, fol. 71r (? July 1420).

62. ASV Duca di Candia, b. 30 ter, r. 32, fol. 71v (? July 1420).

63. Members of the Delmedigo family, especially Aba son of Liacho, Alcana son of Aba, Moyses son of Aba, Samargia son of Aba, and Moyses son of Judah, particularly favored Michele Calergi in the first half of the 1450s. See his surviving registers: ASV Notai di Candia, b. 2 (not. Michele Calergi). There appears to be a significant amount of overlap, however, between the Jews who patronized Calergi and those who patronized Francesco Avonale in the same period, and whose registers are stored in the same box at the ASV as Calergi's registers. For Avonale, see ASV Notai di Candia, b. 2 (not. Francesco Avonale).

64. *TQ* no. 102, pp. 131–38.

65. For a concise discussion of the rise of compulsory Jewish quarters, see Benjamin Ravid, "All Ghettos Were Jewish Quarters, but Not All Jewish Quarters Were Ghettos," *Critical Inquiry* 10 (2008): 5–24. He notes in particular fourteenth-century trends toward limiting and delimiting Jewish residence in Germany, France, and Iberia; see pp. 8–11.

66. Georgopoulou, *Venice's Mediterranean Colonies*, 193.

67. For the senatorial order of 1334, see Spyridonos Theotokés, *Thespismata tes Vene-tikes gerousias, 1281–1385* (Athens: Grapheion Demosieumaton Akademias Athenon, 1936), 1:43 (no. 35). The order to confine the Jews to this bounded area is edited by Georg Martin Thomas, *Commission des Dogen Andreas Dandolo für die Insel Creta vom Jahre 1350* (Munich: Verlag der K. Academie, 1877), 185. Also see Starr, "Jewish Life," 63, esp. n. 15; and Geor-gopoulou, *Venice's Mediterranean Colonies*, 193.

68. ASV Duca di Candia, b. 30, r. 22, fols. 105v–106v (24 June 1391).

69. For this event, see Georgopoulou, "Mapping Religious and Ethnic Identities," 483.

70. *TQ* no. 18, p. 10.

71. That medieval Jewish quarters were a product of both externally imposed atti-tudes and internally constructed self-segregation has become something of a commonplace among scholars, as has the notion that these two factors functioned simultaneously without apparent contradiction. For one analysis of this approach, see Ravid, "All Ghettos Were Jewish Quarters."

72. Jacoby, "Jews and Christians," 273.

73. Jacoby, "Jews and Christians," 256.

74. *TQ* no. 31, p. 19.

75. *TQ* no. 18, p. 10. The manuscript section in which the 1228 version of this ordi-nance appears is damaged and completely illegible.

76. *TQ* no. 30, p. 18.

77. *TQ* no. 54, p. 53.

78. *TQ* no. 38, p. 28.

79. See Ankori, "Jews and the Jewish Community," 330. On the meaning of sound within a Jewish community, see Robert Bonfil, "Sounds and Silence," in *Jewish Life in Renaissance Italy*, 233–42.

80. The Dominican monastery was probably established during the reign of a Domin-ican archbishop, Giovanni Querini, whose tenure spanned 1247–52. Georgopoulou, *Venice's Mediterranean Colonies*, 136. On the effect of preachers such as Vincent Ferrer, and of Pope Benedict XII's 1415 papal bull that called for Jewish residential segregation, on Italian (and thus Italian-sphere) policies, see Ravid, "All Ghettos Were Jewish Quarters," 11–12.

81. Georgopoulou, *Venice's Mediterranean Colonies*, 194.

82. Georgopoulou, *Venice's Mediterranean Colonies*, 201.

83. ASV Duca di Candia, b. 30, r. 22, fols. 105v–106 v (undated; 1391?).

84. Noiret, *Documents inédits*, 133 (30 May 1402).

85. Jacoby, "Jews and Christians," 261. Jacoby cites evidence for the continued pur-chase and residence outside the Jewish quarters of Rethymno, a town on the northwestern coast of the island, as well as in Castronovo and Bonifacio, closer to Candia.

86. Georgopoulou, *Venice's Mediterranean Colonies*, 196.

87. Georgopoulou, *Venice's Mediterranean Colonies*, 194, 196.

88. ASV Duca di Candia, b. 32, r. 44, fols. 176r–v (6 March 1449).

89. *Non debeant ire ad iudaicam candide per aliqua causa*. The only hint of the cir-cumstances of this restraining order comes from the final segment of the verdict, where the

three men are also instructed not to harm Ser Johannes Suriano, an *advocatus*, or Maria Christiana, a former Jew.

90. *TQ* no. 31, p. 19, and see esp. nn. 15, 16.

91. For one example among many, see *Stefano Bono*, no. 480 (5 November 1303), in which the Jew David Villara hires two Christian masons, Thomas Alberigo and Thomasinus Tanoligo, to build three walls and three gates at his house.

92. *TQ* no. 53, pp. 52–53. This entry in the *taqqanot* is not dated and is presented not as a statute but as a narrative, labeled "A Thing That Happened in the *Kehillah Kedoshah* of Candia for the Protection of Milk." Meir Ashkenazi is likely the father of the surgeon Malkiel (Melchiele Theotonicus), active and visible in both the ducal records and the *taqqanot* (see *TQ* 50, p. 48) in the 1360s, thus putting his father's activities sometime in the midfourteenth century.

93. A further assertion of power through the control of the dairy trade can be found in *TQ* no. 55, pp. 54–56.

94. *TQ* no. 41, p. 33.

95. *TQ* no. 74, pp. 78–80.

96. *TQ* no. 74, p. 80.

97. Elisabeth Santschi, "Contrats de travail et d'apprentissage en Crète vénetienne au XIVᵉ siècle d'après quelques notaires," *Revue Suisse d'Histoire* 19 (1969): 50. Mentioned in Jacoby, "Jews and Christians," 268–69.

98. ASV Duca di Candia, b. 15, r. 1, fol. 118r (25 January 1365).

99. For a number of examples in which a Christian owned a home that he rented to a Jew: *Pietro Scardon*, no. 358 (29 May 1271), in which Marcus Bernardo de Lassiti, a resident of Candia, rents a piece of land with a building on it for one year to the Jew Sambatheus, son of the late Moyses, for the low price of 1.5 hyperperon (whether this home was inside the Judaica or not is unclear); *Stefano Bono*, no. 265 (10 September 1303), in which Eleazaro Balbi and Potha Cummani, Jews, rent the house owned by Marinus Quirino of Candia for 12.5 hyperpera a year; *Pietro Pizolo*, no. 798 (16 July 1304), in which Giovanni Corner rents (it seems, actually, re-rents) his home in the "campo iudee," which is "next to the city wall" to the Jew Ligiacho Lago for up to twenty-nine years at a rate of 2 hyperpera per year; the next month, the same Corner rents a nearby home to the Jew Elia Vilara for 2.5 hyperpera per annum (*Pietro Pizolo*, no. 824, 6 August 1304).

100. For Hemanuel Jalina, see Sally McKee, "Women Under Venetian Colonial Rule in the Early Renaissance," *Renaissance Quarterly* 51 (1998): 43; Jacoby, "Jews and Christians," 277.

101. ASV Duca di Candia, b. 30, r. 23, fols. 20v–21v (2 December 1393). For more on Joseph Missini, see Chapters 1 and 5.

102. ASV Duca di Candia, b. 29, r. 12, fols. 2r–v (27 November 1358).

103. Another member of the family, Nicolò Gradenigo, owned a home in the Jewish Quarter around 1300, in addition to feudatory land elsewhere on the island, but he rented it out to Jewish tenants. See *Pietro Pizolo*, vol. 1, no. 309 (27 March 1300). In this contract he rents the home to Podha, widow of Avragha (Abraham).

104. ASV Duca di Candia, b. 30, r. 23, fols. 20v–21v (2 December 1393).

105. As the Jewish community is instructed as part of the 1363 reforms, in *TQ* no. 38, p. 28.

106. *TQ* no. 102, p. 135.

107. *TQ* no. 36, pp. 26–27; *TQ* no. 37, pp. 27–28.

108. *TQ* no. 74, p. 79.

109. Richard Sennett, *Flesh and Stone: The Body and the City in Western Civilization* (New York: W. W. Norton, 1994), 237. Quoted in Benjamin Ravid, "How 'Other' Really Was the Jewish Other? The Evidence from Venice," in *Acculturation and Its Discontents: The Italian Jewish Experience Between Exclusion and Inclusion*, ed. David N. Myers et al. (Toronto: University of Toronto Press, 2008), 43–44.

CHAPTER 3

1. The ducal court's case against Judah de Damasco appears in ASV Duca di Candia, b. 30 ter, r. 31, fols. 222r–228r (18 July 1419). This case is also mentioned in the town crier's rolls: ASV Duca di Candia, b. 15, r. 3, fol. 15r, no. 17 (18 January 1427). The aspects of the case pertaining to criminal justice are discussed by Elisabeth Santschi in "Affaires pénales," 63–69. David Jacoby deals with Judah's case in the context of familial dynasties of doctors in his "Rofim v'kirurgim yehudiim be-Kritim tahat shilton Venetzia." Scholarly attention to Jewish doctors in Crete (and in Venetian Corfu) can already be identified in the nineteenth century; see Eliakim Carmoly, *Histoire des médecins juifs ancien et modernes* (Brussels: Imprimerie de H. Bourland, 1844), 1:135–39.

2. The first record of Judah de Damasco's return to his official position dates to 16 September 1429 (ASV Duca di Candia, b. 31, r. 36, fol. 177v), though he may have gone back to work earlier. There is a source lacuna here: the ducal court registers are lost from the dates between 8 April 1425 (the end of busta 30 ter) and 20 April 1428 (the beginning of busta 31).

3. ASV Duca di Candia, b. 30 ter, r. 31, fol. 226v (23 July 1419).

4. The image of the dog will be discussed further. It has been addressed at length by Kenneth Stow in *Jewish Dogs*. For the judge's claim of bestiality, see pp. 18–19.

5. On this notion of peripheral figures taking part in meaningful cross-confessional relationships, see Stow, "Jews and Christians: Two Different Cultures?" 32n5.

6. Judah de Damasco's prolific work for the Venetian colonial administration is attested throughout the ducal court records. The earliest record of Judah in the Duca di Candia series dates to 15 December 1401, when Judah along with his brother Nathan are listed as two wound evaluators of note (ASV Duca di Candia, b. 30 bis, r. 26, fol. 25v).

7. See the testimony of Costa Guna (or Guva), inhabitant of the *borgo*, who articulates this connection most explicitly: ASV Duca di Candia, b. 30 ter, r. 31, fols. 226r–v (23 July 1419).

8. The acts in which doctors testified that a given patient should be rendered "out of mortal danger" list not only the three (or more) wound evaluators but also the doctor who

cared for the patient during his/her illness. For example, the records indicate that Nathan de Damasco personally treated a spectrum of patients, from Latin elites (ASV Duca di Candia, b. 30 bis, r. 29, fols. 232v–233r. [23 January 1413]) to wounded slaves (ASV Duca di Candia, b. 30 ter, r. 30, fol. 62v [2 June 1416] for one slave patient, and fol. 63r [3–4 June 1416] for two more slaves in his care).

9. We do not have nearly as detailed information for locations outside of Candia. Two Jewish physicians (*physicos*) from Canea, Solomon and Isaac, appear in the court record from 1395, as they come to testify that a Candiote patient who was in danger of death, and who had come to Canea before leaving the island, was out of mortal danger before he left their care. ASV Duca di Candia, b. 30, r. 23, fol. 99r (5 May 1395).

10. McKee, *Uncommon Dominion*, 51–52, 98.

11. Joseph Shatzmiller, *Jews, Medicine, and Medieval Society* (Berkeley: University of California Press, 1994), 1.

12. Shatzmiller, *Jews, Medicine, and Medieval Society*, 112–15.

13. On wound-evaluating doctors in the judiciaries of Italy, see Michel Ascheri, "'*Concilium sapientis*' perizia medica e '*res judicata*': Diritto dei '*dottori*' e istituzione comunale," in *Proceedings of the Fifth International Congress of Medieval Canon Law*, ed. Stephen Kuttner and Kenneth Pennington (Vatican City: Biblioteca apostolica vaticana, 1980), 533–79; Edgardo Ortalli, "La perizia medica a Bologna nei secoli XII e XIV: Normativa e practica di un istituto giudiziario," *Deputazione di storia patria per le provincie di Romagna: Atti e memorie* 17–19 (1969): 223–59; Guido Ruggiero, "The Cooperation of Physicians and the State in the Control of Violence in Renaissance Venice," *Journal of the History of Medicine and Allied Sciences* 33 (1978): 156–66. Toaff notes the occasional use of Jewish municipal doctors in an expert witness capacity in Umbria; Toaff, *Love, Work, and Death*, 225–26. For Provence, with an emphasis on Jewish wound evaluators, see Joseph Shatzmiller, *Médecine et justice en Provence médiévale: Documents de Manosque, 1262–1348* (Aix-en-Provence: Publications de l'Université de Provence, 1989), esp. pp. 27–43. For a microhistorical example, see Andrée Courtemanche, "The Judge, the Doctor, and the Poisoner: Medieval Expertise in Manosquin Judicial Rituals at the End of the Fourteenth Century," in *Medieval and Early Modern Ritual: Formalized Behavior in Europe, China, and Japan*, ed. Joëlle Rollo-Koster (Leiden: Brill, 2002), 105–23. In that article, Courtemanche also cites examples of this sort of wound evaluator in Germany and Dijon (115n25).

14. Shatzmiller, *Jews, Medicine, and Medieval Society*, 23.

15. Shatzmiller, *Jews, Medicine, and Medieval Society*, ix. *Ciroicus* is the local Venetian-inflected back-formation. It consistently replaces the standard Latin *cirurgicus*, surgeon, using the root of the Venetian *ceròico*.

16. On medieval Jewish doctors and formal licensing processes, see Cecil Roth, "The Qualifications of Jewish Physicians in the Middle Ages," *Speculum* 28 (1953): 838–43. Andrée Courtemanche makes a similar point in "The Judge, the Doctor, and the Poisoner," 109n16.

17. The court records only occasionally mention Jewish affiliation with the *collegium*, though it appears that anyone granted the title of *magister* and employed as a wound evaluator held membership in the collegium. Explicit reference to the medical college occurs

sometimes in extenuating or unusual circumstances but simply seems dependent on a given notary's inclination. For example, in an unusual act from 1395, Nathan de Damasco (Judah's brother), referred to as *iudeum medicum cirurgicum di colegio*, had taken care of (and placed on the list of those whose wounds were potentially fatal) a Jewish victim of an assault who had left Candia for Canea and then left the island. Because the patient left Candia, he could not be evaluated and taken off the list (*videri non poterat per collegium medicorum*), but Nathan and his father, Joste, come to testify that they had seen him before he left and that he was out of danger of death. Once again, the two men are explicitly named as "medicos cirurgicos de collegio," further establishing for bureaucratic posterity their authority to testify about this absent patient. ASV Duca di Candia, b. 30, r. 23, fol. 99r (5 May 1395). However, the notary of the same register then proceeds to note that a number of doctors, Jewish and otherwise, are *medicos de colegio* without suggesting a clear reasoning. See b. 30, r. 23, fol. 105v (14 June 1395), where the Jewish doctor Elia Gadinelli is *cirurgicus de colegio*, and fol. 109v (21 June 1395), in which Cosmas Rosso and Elia Gadinelli are *medicos cirurgicos de colegio*.

18. The ducal court acts record the confirmation of Magister Elias, *fisicus*, to the position of salaried doctor of a feudatory in 1366 (ASV Duca di Candia, b. 29 bis, r. 15, fol. 16v [17 November 1366]). In 1454, Magister Salamone, son of the late Magister Monachem, *fisicus*, held an official salaried position with one of the feudatories of Candia, though he decided not to seek a renewal of this position at the end of his contract. In order to end his tenure, he had to formally submit his intention before the ducal court (ASV Duca di Candia, b. 26 bis, r. 11, fol. 23r [8 April 1454]).

19. ASV Duca di Candia, b. 26 bis, r. 11, fol. 23r (8 April 1454).

20. As the case of Lazaro suggests, the state's involvement in conferring authority worked both ways: to bolster a career and to destroy it. In a similar case, Elia Gadinelli, a surgeon who had been working as a wound evaluator for the ducal court since 1393, was officially forbidden from taking care of any more wounds in December 1411, when his eyesight was deemed too poor for proper evaluation. ASV Duca di Candia, b. 30 bis, r. 29, fol. 61r (7 December 1411). For other doctors who are explicitly paid a salary by the state, see two acts on ASV Duca di Candia, b. 31, r. 40, fol. 67v (24 July 1438 and 14 April 1439), which mentions state salaries for the physician Magister Solomon (son of Magister Monachem), the surgeon Magister Moses (son of Magister Joseph), and the surgeon Stamatinus Gadinelli.

21. Courtemanche, "The Judge, the Doctor, and the Poisoner," 115.

22. "cum magna industria et labore": ASV Duca di Candia, b. 30 bis, r. 29, fols. 232v–233r (23 January 1413). For a similar case between doctor and patient in which no Jew was involved, see McKee, *Uncommon Dominion*, 98.

23. See the decidedly unclear testimony of George Vlagho (ASV Duca di Candia, b. 30 ter, r. 31, fols. 224r–v), who appears all too eager to share conversations he had with friends. When those friends are deposed, however, they never affirm George's stories. George Vlagho claims that upon seeing Costas Guna in the church: *interrogavit ipsum quid fecerat de differentia quam habebet cum Jocuda medico de aliquibus ovibus viri condam dicte Marule, venditis dicto Coste per dictum Jocudam, et ipse Costas respondit, non potui facere*

aliquie, quia vendidit dictas oves aliis, dicens de ipso Jocuda et adiuvat ipsam Marulam, et iste dixit sibi, quare adiuvat ipsam? Et ipse Costas respondit, nescis quare, quia habet agere cum ipsa Marula carnaliter, sed non dixit isti si erat gravida nec iste curavit interrogare ipsum.

24. Shatzmiller posits the former in *Jews, Medicine, and Medieval Society*, 91. A series of bans put forth by church councils, beginning with the Council of Trier in 1227, threatened Christian consumers of Jewish medicine with excommunication. See Toaff, *Love, Work, and Death*, 220n24.

25. Shatzmiller, *Jews, Medicine, and Medieval Society*, 92.

26. Toaff, *Love, Work, and Death*, 215–18.

27. Toaff, *Love, Work, and Death*, 225.

28. On fugitives in Venice, see Cozzi, "Authority and Law in Renaissance Venice," 293–95.

29. Jacoby, "Venice and the Venetian Jews," 35. Benjamin Arbel, however, questions the evidence for such an assertion based on this linguistic distinction. See Arbel, "Jews and Christians in Sixteenth-Century Crete," 285.

30. Mueller, "The Status and Economic Activity of Jews," 64.

31. Ashtor, "New Data for the History of Levantine Jewries in the Fifteenth Century," 72.

32. Jacoby, "Venice, the Inquisition," 134–35.

33. On the complicated category of "citizenship" in a Venetian metropolitan and colonial context, and the difficulty of obtaining this status, see Reinhold Mueller, *Immigrazione e cittadinanza nella Venezia medievale* (Rome: Viella, 2010), esp. 18–32.

34. See Mueller, *Immigrazione*, 13. On the scholarly debate between Eliyahu Ashtor, Reinhold Mueller, and David Jacoby on the question of Jewish citizenship in Crete, see Eliyahu Ashtor, "Ebrei cittadini di Venezia?" *Studi Veneziani* 17–18 (1975–76): 145–56; Mueller, "The Status and Economic Activity of Jews," 69; and David Jacoby, "Le-Ma'amadam shel ha-yehudim be-moshavot Venetzia biyemei ha-beinayim" [The Status of Jews in the Venetian Settlements During the Middle Ages], *Zion* 28 (1962): 65–67. Jacoby's meticulous rereading of the sources convincingly shows that two individuals were given citizen-like economic privileges but never attained the legal status of Venetian citizen. Jacoby, "Venice and the Venetian Jews," 34.

35. See Jacoby, "Le-Ma'amadam," 65–67. In contrast, Mueller, *Immigrazione*, 49–55.

36. Mueller, "The Status and Economic Activity," 68. Also addressed in Jacoby, "Le-Ma'amadam," 58–59. The original offer of incentives can be found in two locations: ASV Commemoriali, r. 5, fol. 37; and Senato Misti, r. 26, copia, fols. 245v–246v (21 June 1353).

37. Jacoby, "Venice and the Venetian Jews," 34.

38. On the wider work of the Avogaria di Comun (and its members, the Avvogadori di Comun), see Lane, *Venice*, 100. Also see Cozzi, "Authority and Law," 309.

39. On the role of the Quarantia as the highest appeals court, alongside their responsibility to prepare legislation on coinage and finances, see Lane, *Venice*, 96.

40. The appeal is addressed by Jacoby, "Rofim v'kirurgim yehudiim be-Kritim tahat shilton Venetzia," 441. On the complicated methods of voting among the judges of the

Quarantia that could create the situation described above, see Horatio Forbes Brown, *Studies in the History of Venice* (New York: E. P. Dutton, 1907), 1:311–12.

41. ASV Duca di Candia, b. 15, r. 3, fol. 15r, no. 17 (18 January 1427).

42. ASV Duca di Candia, b. 31, r. 36, fol. 177v (16 September 1429). Judah and two Jewish colleagues, the physician Magister Monachem and the surgeon Moyses, son of the late Magister Joste, testify that a victim is out of danger of death.

43. O'Connell, *Men of Empire*, 75. This is addressed further below.

44. Dennis Romano, "Equality in Fifteenth-Century Venice," *Studies in Medieval and Renaissance History* 6 (2009): 131. For examples from 1205 and 1229, see Gisella Graziato, ed., *La promissioni del doge di Venezia dale origini alla fine del Duecento* (Venice: Il Comitato, 1986), esp. 5, 16.

45. Lane, *Venice*, 97.

46. Arbel, "Colonie d'oltremare," 979. Cozzi argues that, in the early sixteenth century, notions of equality gave way to the concept of authority. This, in turn, led to changes in the Venetian justice system and its hierarchy. See Cozzi, "Authority and Law," 317–19.

47. Romano, "Equality in Fifteenth-Century Venice," 130–31. Dennis Romano has counted the uses of terms related to equality (*equalitas, equales, equaliter, inqualitas*, and their Venetian equivalents) in the mid-fifteenth century and discovered that, in the reign of Doge Francesco Foscari alone (1423–57), these terms "were used more than one hundred times in laws passed by the Great Council, Senate, and [the Council of] Ten. Its use far exceeds that of terms such as *unanimitas*," which had previously been identified as the "ultimate expression of Venetian political ideals." On the concept of *unanimitas* as the republican ideal par excellence, see Margaret L. King, *Venetian Humanism in an Age of Patrician Dominance* (Princeton, NJ: Princeton University Press, 1986), esp. 92–105. The difference here, it seems to me, is that *unanimitas* became the ideal most typically expressed by Venetian humanist writers. In legal and political texts, equality stood in first position.

48. Chojnacki, "Crime, Punishment, and the Trecento Venetian State," 197, 201, 224, 194.

49. Romano, "Equality in Fifteenth-Century Venice," 130.

50. Lane, *Venice*, 95.

51. O'Connell, *Men of Empire*, 78.

52. Gaetano Cozzi, "La politica del diritto nella repubblica di Venezia," in *Stato, società e giustizia: Nella repubblica veneta (sec. XV–XVIII)*, ed. Gaetano Cozzi (Rome: Jouvence, 1980), 69.

53. Brown, *Studies in the History of Venice*, 1:312.

54. Noiret, *Documents inédits*, 13–14. On the rich Jews, p. 13: "per insulam sunt quamplures Judei cum maximo havere et valde divites."

55. On this taxation, see Starr, "Jewish Life," 77.

56. This judgment is recorded in Noiret, *Document inédits*, 26–27.

57. On the patrician conviction that Jews were essential to Venice's economy, see Cozzi, "Authority and Law," 333–34.

58. Baron, *A Social and Religious History of the Jews*, vol. 17, *Byzantines, Mamluks, and Maghribians*, 62, where he notes an important caveat: this ruling did not set a long-standing precedent. In 1485 the doge of Venice, Giovanni Mocenigo, explicitly stated that "no Jew and Jewess shall be able to free themselves from some *angaria*, except through accepting baptism."

59. Noiret, *Documents inédits*, 358; also referenced in Freddy Thiriet, *Régestes des delibe-rations du Sénat de Venise concernant la Romanie* (Paris: Mouton & Co., 1961), 3:29.

60. *cum suis sagacitatibus et astutiis, ac cum suis verbis cautelosis.*

61. *ad vendendum ius et iusticiam, officia et beneficia nostri dominii insule Crete.*

62. ASV Duca di Candia, b. 31, r. 40, fols. 114r–v (26 January 1439).

63. ASV Duca di Candia, b. 31, r. 39, fol. 149r (22 February 1437).

64. ASV Senato mar, r. 4, fols. 120v–121r (11 May 1452), summarized in Thiriet, *Régestes*, 1:175, no. 2887.

65. ASV Duca di Candia, b. 29 bis, r. 19, fols. (13)60r–(15)62r (10 November 1382).

66. Paola Ratti Vidulich, ed., *Duca di Candia: Bandi (1319–1329)* (Venice: Il Comitato, 1965), no. 35 [48] (28 June 1314).

67. Jacoby, "Venice, the Inquisition," 135.

68. For the role of Gradenigo and the timeline of the case, see Starr, "Jewish Life in Crete," 66–67. Note that Starr believed there were two different accusations in the early 1450s, one the lamb crucifixion and one a host desecration. It seems far more likely that this is one and the same event and, indeed, that there was no host desecration libel involved. See Ariel Toaff, *Pasque di sangue: Ebrei d'Europa e omicidi rituali*, 2nd ed. (Bologna: Il Mulino, 2008), 50–54. Nevertheless, on the supposed host desecration element, see Miri Ruben, *Gentile Tales: The Narrative Assault on Late Medieval Jews* (Philadelphia: University of Pennsylvania Press, 2004), esp. 115–16, where she briefly deals with the Cretan case addressed here as a host desecration, the import of which she deems to be further evidence that "an accusation that was aborted could nonetheless cause a great deal of pain and suffering" (115).

69. See colophon to MS Vat 249.

70. For a comprehensive, if traditional and Christianocentric, view of the blood libel claim, see Darren O'Brien, *The Pinnacle of Hatred: The Blood Libel and the Jews* (Jerusalem: Magnes Press, 2011). On the blood libel in Ashkenaz (including the German cases and Blois), see Israel Yuval, *Two Nations in Your Womb: Perceptions of Jews and Christians in Late Antiquity and the Middle Ages*, trans. Barbara Harshav and Jonathan Chipman (Berkeley: University of California Press, 2006), 135–204, esp. 159ff. Yuval's view finds the origin of the blood libel in Jewish-Christian contacts, though he in no way "blames" the Jews for it. For another, highly influential view that reads Jews as disconnected from the Christian accusation, see Gavin Langmuir, *Toward a Definition of Antisemitism* (Berkeley: University of California Press, 1990), 195–298, which also addresses the earliest English ritual murder accusations on 209–62. For an account of the continuation and new significance of the blood libel in early modern Germany, see Ronnie Po-chia Hsia, *The Myth of Ritual Murder: Jews and Magic in Reformation Germany* (New Haven, CT: Yale University Press, 1988). On the role of the blood libel in the expulsion of Jews from England and France, see Sophia

Menache, "Faith, Myth, and Politics: The Stereotype of the Jews and Their Expulsion from England and France," *Jewish Quarterly Review*, n.s. 73 (1985): 351–74.

71. Noiret, *Documents inédits*, 244–47; Starr, "Jewish Life," 85. Regarding the new limit on interest, most loans after this do follow a 10 percent rate plus pawns. Nevertheless, notarial registers, particularly those of Giorgio Mendrino, illustrate that some Jews gave variable interest loans of up to 12 percent still in the 1440s. For example, see ASV Notai di Candia, b. 30 (not. Giorgio Mendrino), fols. 1v (24 November 1441), 3r (3 December 1441), 6v (7 January 1442).

72. For France, see William Chester Jordan, *The French Monarchy and the Jews: From Philip Augustus to the Last Capetians* (Philadelphia: University of Pennsylvania Press, 1989), 30–31. For Aragon, see Yom Tov Assis, *Jewish Economy in the Medieval Crown of Aragon, 1213–1327: Money and Power* (Leiden: Brill, 1997), 38–40.

73. Noiret, *Documents inédits*, 245–46, 264–65. The debt crisis was indeed overwhelming, and the commission of just three men was unable to deal with all of the 1,970 cases that it was supposed to resolve. After two years (in May 1418), only 138 out of 1,970 cases had been resolved, and the commission was renewed for another two years; in June the compromise scheme was reiterated (Noiret, *Documents inédits*, 265–66). Unfortunately we do not know about a final resolution to the crisis, although by August 1420 the remaining debtors had again fled the island, and the Senate again sought a compromise resolution (Noiret, *Documents inédits*, 274–76). Starr's account of these events ("Jewish Life," 85) offers a decidedly lachrymose reading, highlighting the changing interest rates and underplaying, in my opinion, the unusual compromise solution.

74. Noiret, *Documents inédits*, 322–23; Starr, "Jewish Life," 86.

75. *quod omnes pecunie in quibus tenentur dictis Judeis sunt prode prodium et usure usurarum.*

76. Noiret, *Documents inédits*, 425–26; Starr, "Jewish Life," 86.

77. Robert C. Stacey, "The English Jews Under Henry III," in *The Jews in Medieval Britain: Historical, Literary, and Archeological Perspectives*, ed. Patricia Skinner (Woodbridge, Suffolk: Boydell, 2003), 52–53.

78. Stacey, "The English Jews," 54.

79. Noiret, *Documents inédits*, 360.

80. For reference to a Jewish tax farmer collecting the impost on imported oil, the *daciarius olei*, in dispute with his successor, see ASV Duca di Candia, b. 30 bis, r. 26, fols. 179r–v (23 July 1403). On Jewish access to tax-farming positions, and their continuity in Venetian times from Byzantine precedents, see David Jacoby, "From Byzantium to Latin Romania: Continuity and Change," *Mediterranean Historical Review* 4 (1989): 14–15.

81. In the early fourteenth century, a Jew named Sambathinus, son of the late Moyses, had acted as *messetarius*; he appears in a town crier's proclamation of 1321. See Vidulich, *Duca di Candia*, no. 316 (3 November 1321).

82. *per Antistitem Ecclesie consueverit annis singulis populum ammoneri, quod nullus audeat per medium Judei, sub pena excommunicationis, mercatum aliquod contrahere ullo modo.*

83. *tum quia evangelica ammonitione docemur non esse bonum sumere panem filiorum et dare canibus Judeis, scilicet, qui varios modo exquirunt ad suggendum sanguine Christianorum.*

84. The Vulgate Matthew 15:26 reads: *non est bonum sumere panem filiorum et mittere canibus.*

85. Stow, *Jewish Dogs*, esp. 3–7, 15–22.

86. For this imagery used by contemporary Italian clergy, see Bonfil, *Jewish Life in Renaissance Italy*, 23; Ariel Toaff, *The Jews in Medieval Assisi, 1305–1487: A Social and Economic History of a Small Jewish Community in Italy* (Florence: L. S. Olschki, 1979), 61. Both quoted in Stow, *Jewish Dogs*, 28.

87. Noiret, *Documents inédits*, 359–60. Almost the whole Senate voted yes (*de parte omnes alii*), except for three men who voted against (*de non 3*) and five who abstained (*non sincere 5*).

88. *Dictus ordo sit honestus et laudabilis Deo et mundo et utilis christianis qui exercebunt illum officium.*

89. *Judei perfidi sunt privati omni officio et beneficio christianorum.*

90. For a typical example of the assumed meaning of the term "pragmatism" as applied to the Venetian state, see Photis Baroutsos, "Venetian Pragmatism and Jewish Subjects (Fifteenth and Sixteenth Centuries)," *Mediterranean Historical Review* 27 (2012): 227–40.

91. Arbel, "Jews and Christians in Sixteenth-Century Crete," 281.

92. ASV Duca di Candia, b. 31, r. 36, fol. 177v (16 September 1429).

93. ASV Duca di Candia, b. 31, r. 37, fols. 34r (26 January 1430), 55v (1 March 1430), 66r (20 March 1430), 97r (31 May 1430), and 103r (16 June 1430); ASV Duca di Candia, b. 32, r. 44, fol. 82v (5 September 1448).

94. ASV Duca di Candia, b. 32, r. 42, fol. 18v (27 November 1444).

95. ASV Duca di Candia, b. 26 bis, r. 10, fol. 206r (27 September 1451).

96. ASV Duca di Candia, b. 32, r. 42, fols. 64r–v, 65r–66v (30 June 1445).

CHAPTER 4

1. Vidulich, *Duca di Candia*, no. 304 [69] (14 July 1321).

2. *TQ* no. 10, p. 5.

3. On the other hand, this list of people may be those for whom the litigant is responsible to ensure a peaceful Sabbath.

4. While the impetus for the creation of medieval Jewish communal organizations across Europe and North Africa stemmed from the same historical phenomena as contemporary corporate associations, such as the ubiquitous guilds and confraternities that sprang up in the Christian world, the rabbis couched their *kahal*'s origins in Talmudic terms. For the rabbis—concerned to not overstep the biblical prohibition against creating new laws—the authority of Jewish townspeople to make decisions about their own communal life, produce ordinances, and enforce them came via canonical passages in the Babylonian

Talmud: BT Gittin 36b authorized the power of the Jewish court; BT Yebamot 30b authorized townspeople to organize and enforce functions that were indisputably necessary, for example, defense and charity; and BT Baba Batra 7b–9a allowed occupational corporations, such as butchers and bakers, to make group statutes and enforce them. See Yacov Guggenheim, "Jewish Community and Territorial Organization in Medieval Europe," in *The Jews of Europe in the Middle Ages (Tenth to Fifteenth Centuries)*, ed. Christoph Cluse (Turnhout: Brepols, 2004), 76. Though the rulings that set out a theory of a semiautonomous Jewish corporate organization were often formulated inside responsa to particular questions, the rulings were intended to—and indeed did—carry weight beyond the confines of the specific case. For more on this political philosophy, see Lorberbaum, *Politics and the Limits of Law*, esp. pp. 95–96.

5. See Rena Lauer, "Jewish Law and Litigation in the Secular Courts of the Late Medieval Mediterranean," *Critical Analysis of Law* 3 (2016): 114–32.

6. See, for example, a mainstream modern Orthodox perspective that argues that such behavior was never acceptable: Simcha Krauss, "Litigation in Secular Courts," *Journal of Halacha and Contemporary Society* 2 (1982): 35–53.

7. See Elena Lourie, "Mafiosi and Malsines," in Lourie, *Crusade and Colonisation: Muslims, Christians, and Jews in Medieval Aragon* (Hampshire: Variorum, 1990), 69.

8. Ibn Adret is here paraphrased by Lorberbaum, *Politics and the Limits of Law*, 99. The original responsum can be found in Solomon ibn Adret, *Responsa* (Bnei Brak: Sifriyati, 1981), 2:290.

9. Baron, *A Social and Religious History of the Jews*, vol. 17, *Byzantines, Mamluks, and Maghribians*, 48.

10. For a concise, traditional view of the Ashkenazi rejection of secular litigation except in rare circumstances, see Bernard Rosensweig, *Ashkenazi Jewry in Transition* (Waterloo, Ontario: Wilfrid Laurier University Press, 1975), 81–83. For Spain, see Assis, "Yehudei Sepharad be-arkhaot ha-goyim," 399–430. For Jews in Provençal courts, see Shatzmiller, "Halikhatam shel yehudim l'arkhaot shel goyim be-Provanz be-yemei ha-beinayim."

11. For an optimistic overview of Jewish agency and autonomy, see Biale, *Power and Powerlessness in Jewish History*, 77–83.

12. See Simonsohn, *A Common Justice*. For a discussion of the recent explosion of scholarship on this topic, see Oded Zinger, "Women, Gender, and Law: Marital Disputes According to Documents from the Cairo Geniza" (PhD diss., Princeton University, 2014), 116–18.

13. *TQ* no. 10, p. 5.

14. O'Connell, *Men of Empire*, 76.

15. An entry from the senate's records from 1339 spells out part of the system regarding the courts *di propio* and *di petizion*: three Venice-based judges would be sent and paired with three local Latin judges on Crete, and four Venetian officers of the night would also be chosen and sent to Candia. Thiriet, *Régestes*, 40, no. 90 (2 April 1339). On the roles of these courts, see McKee, *Uncommon Dominion*, 27–28.

16. For example, Venice's infamous Officers of the Night, mentioned even by Shakespeare in *Othello* (I.I.180), were known for using torture to seek confessions. On the

functions of this Venetian police court, see Roberti, *La magistrature giudiziare veneziane*, 1:206–9.

17. O'Connell, *Men of Empire*, 78.

18. Jewish customary law will be addressed below and especially in Chapter 5. On Byzantine customary law upheld in Venice's Cretan courts for the Greek Orthodox population, see Chryssa Maltezou, "Byzantine 'Consuetudines' in Venetian Crete," *Dumbarton Oaks Papers* 49 (1995): 269–80.

19. David Jacoby, "Multilingualism and Institutional Patterns of Communication in Latin Romania (Thirteenth–Fourteenth Centuries)," in *Diplomatics in the Eastern Mediterranean, 1000–1500: Aspects of Cross-Cultural Communication*, ed. Alexander D. Beihammer, Maria G. Parani, and Christopher D. Schabel (Leiden: Brill, 2008), 42.

20. ASV, Notai di Candia, b. 2 (not. Francesco Avonale), fol. 3r (4 February 1450). Evidence from the ducal court also suggests that some adversaries chose to seek arbitration, though we do not know many details about this process. See, for instance, ASV Duca di Candia, b. 30 bis, r. 27, fols. 94r–v (? March 1406), in which two Jewish men (Elia Mosca and Judah son of the late Octaviano) had sought arbitration. Unhappy with the results, one of the men appealed in the ducal court. The ducal court annulled the arbiter's conclusions.

21. ASV Duca di Candia, b. 29, r. 12, fol. 23r (7 November 1359).

22. *TQ* no. 10, p. 5.

23. ASV Duca di Candia, b. 30 bis, r. 26, fol. 91v: *certam quantitem piperis et aliquos panos [sic] et libros judaicos*. The date has been erased by water damage, but its placement in the register suggests that the case is from May 1402. Similar sources of discord appear in litigation between Jews and Christians. For such a case in which payment for a shipment of cloth is the central concern, see ASV Duca di Candia, b. 26, r. 5, fols. 63v–64r (18 March 1427).

24. ASV Duca di Candia, b. 31, r. 37, fol. 107r (1 August 1430).

25. ASV Duca di Candia, b. 31, r. 37, fol. 107v (12 June 1430).

26. ASV Duca di Candia, b. 30 bis, r. 25, fols. 41v–42r (10 June 1400). Protho Spathael is known to have owned a number of homes, a fact that is referred to both in this case and in others. His involvement in real estate and his obvious wealth and power are further described here: ASV Duca di Candia, b. 30 bis, r. 25, fols. 108v–109r (24 March 1401). In its final judgment, the court sided with Protho, and Liacho was ordered to fix the wall within fifteen days; they reconfirmed Liacho's right to build a balcony but stressed to him the need to be more careful when doing so. But Protho did not entirely win his case; at some point during the year after the original case, the court ordered Protho to dismantle the light-blocking home extension, which covered the street in between their homes. ASV Duca di Candia, b. 30 bis, r. 25, fol. 123r (undated).

27. ASV Duca di Candia, b. 30bis, r. 28, fols. 33v–34r. No date recorded; placement in the register suggests February 1409.

28. ASV Duca di Candia, b. 30 bis, r. 28, fols. 21v–22v (12 November 1408).

29. ASV Duca di Candia, b. 30 bis, r. 29, fols. 35r–37r (27 October 1411).

30. ASV Duca di Candia, b. 30 bis, r. 20, fols. 40v–41v (27 October 1411).

31. For example, right before Isaiah's death, in 1406, he served as *hashvan* of the community; *TQ* no. 52, p. 51.

32. ASV Duca di Candia, b. 26, r. 5, fol. 62r (30 January 1427); ASV Duca di Candia, b. 31, r. 37, fols. 102v–103r (15 May 1430). Also b. 31, r. 37, fols. 214v–215r (10 December 1433).

33. ASV Duca di Candia, b. 32, r. 42, fols. 64r–66v; r. 43, fols. 26v–28r, 34v–37r, 38v–40r, 52v–53v. Dated respectively: 30 June 1445, 22 November 1445, 26 November 1445, 14 December 1445, 15 December 1445, 19 January 1446.

34. On this document and its relevance in the context of Islamic courts, see Simonsohn, *A Common Justice*, 175.

35. Klein, *Jews, Christian Society, and Royal Power*, 151–61.

36. By way of just a few examples of what is a very large historiography: Maya Shatzmiller, interested in the ways that fights over Muslim females' property rights played out in fifteenth-century Granadan courtrooms, notes the ubiquity of women in her sources: 95 percent of her case records have at least one female actor. Maya Shatzmiller, *Her Day in Court: Women's Property Rights in Fifteenth-Century Granada* (Cambridge, MA: Harvard University Press, 2007), 1. Sue Sheridan Walker has noted that "the frequency with which women used the law courts and bureaucratic tribunals of the king, the church, and the town is one of the striking features of medieval England." Sue Sheridan Walker, introduction to *Wife and Widow in Medieval England*, ed. Sue Sheridan Walker (Ann Arbor: University of Michigan Press, 1993), 1.

37. For example, as Judith Baskin articulates the rabbinic notion of women's domestic sphere and their influence on marriage roles: "The framers of rabbinic Judaism discouraged a female presence in the communal realms of worship, study, and governance. Rather, rabbinic social policy directed women's energies to domestic activities to provide for their husband's and children's needs; women are praised for modest and self-sacrificing behavior that enables their husbands and sons to achieve success in the public domain." But while Baskin readily admits that late antique women's behavior probably did not square with this Talmudic ideal, she does insist that the rabbis' "prescribed patterns . . . became increasingly normative for Jewish life in general" during the Middle Ages. Baskin, "Medieval Jewish Models of Marriage," in *The Medieval Marriage Scene: Prudence, Passion, Policy*, ed. Sherry Roush and Cristelle L. Baskins (Tempe: Arizona Center for Medieval and Renaissance Studies, 2005), 1–2. In an admittedly extreme example, undoubtedly influenced by the elite Muslim social context in which he lived, the late twelfth-century philosopher and legalist Maimonides claimed that modest Jewish women should not be seen on the street more than once a month. Maimonides, *Mishnah Torah, Hilkhot Ishut* 13:11.

38. Cited in Klein, "Public Activities of Catalan Jewish Women," 49.

39. As Yom Tom Assis and Elka Klein have both illustrated, Jewish women regularly brought suit in Gentile courtrooms across the Iberian Peninsula, including in Aragon, Castile, and Navarre. Assis, "Yehudei Sepharad be-arkhaot ha-goyim," 422–23. Klein deals extensively with women in court in her "Public Activities." Joseph Shatzmiller has likewise uncovered Jewish women litigating in Provence. For example, see "Halikhatam shel yehudim l'arkhaot shel goyim be-Provanz be-yemei ha-beinayim," 380.

40. *TQ* no. 17, p. 9.

41. *TQ* no. 74, p. 80.

42. *TQ* no. 99, p. 125.

43. A meeting of rabbis recorded in *TQ* no. 76, p. 83, dated to 1439, may refer to a *beit din*, but on the other hand, it may simply relate to a meeting of the city's Jewish elders without any litigants.

44. In a recent study of Jewish (and Christian) use of early Islamic courts, Uriel Simonsohn argues that three main factors drove Jews in that context into the sovereign's courtroom, and not to the Jewish rabbinical court: "the weakness of Jewish judicial institutions; the advantages inherent in the Islamic judiciary; and environmental causes, namely, factors that derive from life within a Muslim majority." We may find it useful to modify and apply these three categories to the case of Cretan Jews, but they do not constitute a comprehensive list. Simonsohn, *A Common Justice*, 174.

45. Amnon Linder, "The Legal Status of Jews in the Byzantine Empire," in *Jews in Byzantium: Dialectics of Minority and Majority Cultures*, ed. Robert Bonfil et al. (Leiden: Brill, 2012), 162.

46. Linder, "The Legal Status of Jews," 207–12.

47. *TQ* no. 14, pp. 7–8.

48. *TQ* no. 14, p. 7.

49. *TQ* no. 14, p. 8.

50. Ecclesiastes 10:8. As a rabbinic code word for a transgressor or lawbreaker, see for reference BT *Bava Kamma* 60b and Avoda Zara 27b, among other locations. Also see Ze'ev W. Falk, "Jewish Law and Medieval Canon Law," in *Jewish Law in Legal History and the Modern World*, ed. Bernard S. Jackson (Leiden: Brill, 1980), 90.

51. *TQ* no. 6, p. 4 (from 1228); *TQ* no. 22, p. 13 (dated between 1300 and 1363); *TQ* no. 27, pp. 14–15 (from 1336).

52. *TQ* no. 82, p. 99. The Hebrew records the official as the "makhriz," the crier or herald, who must be the Venetian *gastaldo*, as the public crier was known.

53. For example, ASV b. 15, r. 1, fol. 133v (24 March 1367), in which the Jew Liacho (Ligiachus), son of Vetu, and a Christian accomplice, Marcus Veto, were convicted, jailed "in the prison of the castle" (*in carcerem castelli*), and then escaped from prison. The *gastaldo* was instructed to alert Candia's residents, including the Jews, that anyone found protecting the fugitives would serve time in prison as well.

54. This phenomenon is addressed in the discussion of marriage lawsuits in Chapter 5.

55. Jacoby, "Multilingualism and Institutional Patterns of Communication," 42.

56. Elisabeth Santschi, "Procès criminels en Crète vénetienne (1354–1389)," *Thesaurismata* 7 (1970): 83.

57. One may think of a case from Ferrara, in which a fight between two Jewish bankers in 1507 was not brought before the rabbinical court for twelve years. This represents an extreme case for certain, but it is indicative of the irregular and erratic schedule one faced when seeking Jewish justice. See Elliott S. Horowitz, "Families and Their Fortunes: The

Jews of Early Modern Italy," in *Cultures of the Jews*, vol. 2, *Diversities of Diaspora*, ed. David Biale (New York: Schocken Books, 2002), 292.

58. *TQ* no. 14, p. 8.

59. Codified into a comprehensive civil code only in 1242 at the behest of Doge Jacopo Tiepolo, the five volumes of law plus an appendix on court procedure would become the "fundamental nucleus," the foundational document in the canonization of Venetian legislation, although it would be added to and adjusted through the fifteenth century. On the effect of Crete on this statutory law code, see Maltezou, "Byzantine 'Consuetudines,'" 271; Cozzi, "La politica del diritto," 21–22, 28–29.

60. This judge's oath of office from the Capitularium was first published in Gerland, *Das Archiv des Herzogs*, 93–98. It is also referenced in O'Connell, *Men of Empire*, 77; McKee, *Uncommon Dominion*, 27–30; and Maltezou, "Byzantine 'Consuetudines,'" 271.

61. Cozzi, "La politica del diritto," 22.

62. Muir, "The Sources of Civil Society in Italy," 394. Nevertheless, of course, statutes, customary law, and precedents did technically provide the body of Venetian jurisprudential material.

63. Cozzi, "La politica del diritto," 23. On Venice's relationship to Roman law, see Mario Ascheri, *The Laws of Late Medieval Italy (1000–1500)* (Leiden: Brill, 2013), 276–78, 329–30.

64. Venice's approach to office, judiciary and otherwise, tended toward the patrician amateur and away from any sort of professional bureaucratic corps. See Lane, *Venice*, 98.

65. Shaw, *The Justice of Venice*, 12.

66. Shaw, *The Justice of Venice*, 18.

67. Edward Muir, "Was There Republicanism in the Renaissance Republics? Venice After Agnadello," in *Venice Reconsidered: The History and Civilization of an Italian City State*, ed. John J. Martin and Dennis Romano (Baltimore: Johns Hopkins University Press, 2002), 146.

68. Shaw, *The Justice of Venice*, 11.

69. James C. Scott, *Weapons of the Weak: Everyday Forms of Peasant Resistance* (New Haven, CT: Yale University Press, 1985). On the medieval courtroom as a weapon of another "weak" population, women, see Carol Lansing, "Conflicts over Gender in Civil Courts," in *The Oxford Handbook of Women and Gender in Medieval Europe*, ed. Judith M. Bennett and Ruth Mazo Karras (Oxford: Oxford University Press, 2013), 123–24.

70. On rural populations on the mainland, see Muir, "The Sources of Civil Society in Italy," 398–99. On the parallel phenomenon in the Stato da mar, see O'Connell, *Men of Empire*, 75.

71. Horowitz, "Families and Their Fortunes," 292. Also see Alexander Marx, "A Jewish Cause Célèbre in Sixteenth-Century Italy," in *Studies in Jewish History and Booklore*, ed. Alexander Marx (New York: JTS, 1944), 107–54.

72. Thomas Kuehn, *Law, Family, and Women: Toward a Legal Anthropology of Renaissance Italy* (Chicago: University of Chicago Press, 1991), 73. In a small Jewish community such as Candia, it would be difficult to find a Jewish judge who was not somehow invested in the outcome, whether for religious or social reasons.

73. Lauren A. Benton, *Law and Colonial Cultures: Legal Regimes in World History, 1400–1900* (Cambridge: Cambridge University Press, 2002), 41.

74. Benton, *Law and Colonial Cultures*, 41.

75. See the conclusion to Wendy Davies and Paul Fouracre, eds., *The Settlement of Disputes in Early Medieval Europe* (Cambridge: Cambridge University Press, 1986), 234. Quoted in Kuehn, *Law, Family, and Women*, 99.

76. Smail, *The Consumption of Justice*, 3–24.

77. Smail, *The Consumption of Justice*, 33–34.

78. McKee, *Uncommon Dominion*, 152, 24.

79. The Shekhinah is the manifestation of the Divine Presence on earth. The synagogue is understood as a central place where the Shekhinah can dwell, as it did in the Temple in Jerusalem.

80. *TQ* no. 18, p. 9.

81. Job 9:26; here indicating swiftness.

82. *TQ* no. 18, p. 10.

83. Krauss, "Litigation in Secular Courts," 44–46.

84. The first formulation of this maxim can be found in BT Gittin 9b, in which Shemuel argues that when Jews live under a non-Jewish sovereign, all secular transactions, i.e., those necessitating deeds, should be dealt with according to the secular authority's law. (His argument contrasts with the first opinion, which rejects the use of secular instruments entirely.)

85. Amos Funkenstein, *Perceptions of Jewish History* (Berkeley: University of California Press, 1993), 157.

86. Funkenstein, *Perceptions of Jewish History*, 157–58.

87. Quoted in translation by Lorberbaum, *Politics and the Limits of Law*, 132. The original can be found in Nissim b. Reuben Gerondi, *Teshuvot ha-Ran: Responsa of R. Nissim b. Reuben Gerondi*, ed. Leon A. Feldman (Jerusalem: Shalem Institute, 1984), 2:14.

88. Howard Tzvi Adelman, "Jewish Women and Family Life, Inside and Outside the Ghetto," in *The Jews of Early Modern Venice*, ed. Robert C. David and Benjamin Ravid (Baltimore: Johns Hopkins University Press, 2001), 143–65.

89. Adelman, "Jewish Women," 149.

90. Adelman, "Jewish Women," 150.

91. Adelman, "Jewish Women," 150.

92. *TQ* no. 82, p. 99.

93. ASV Duca di Candia, b. 30 ter, r. 30, fol. 20r (10 December 1415). Ferer's daughter Astruga, the children's mother, had died just prior to this naming of the *tutoria*; her husband had died a few years before.

94. Borsari, "Ricchi e poveri," 221–22. Jewish serfs are attested on Negroponte from the Byzantine period on. See, for example, a case in which the eleventh-century emperor Constantine IX Monomachos granted fifteen formerly free Jewish families to a monastery on Chios as serfs. Linder, "The Legal Status of Jews," 208. Jewish ownership of Jewish serfs, however, seems to be an unusual phenomenon, and as Baron has remarked on this case,

"pending further clarification by some new documents, it must be regarded as a singular exception." Baron, *A Social and Religious History of the Jews*, vol. 17, *Byzantines, Mamluks, and Maghribians*, 14–15.

95. That the Venetian system was known widely to benefit Jews can be seen by the fact that, by the thirteenth century, Byzantine Jews sought shelter under the banner of La Serenissima. In the years following the recapture of Constantinople from the Latins in 1261, tempted by the promise of exemption from Byzantine taxes and jurisdiction, Jews who were previously imperial subjects sought the title of Venetian (and to, be sure, Genoese) national. The Palaeologan emperor Andronicus II (r. 1282–1328) "complained that numerous Venetian Jewish craftsmen" working in Constantinople "were in fact imperial subjects from the provinces who, after settling in the city, had obtained Venetian status there." Jacoby, "The Jews of Constantinople," 229. To be sure, part of the Jewish decision making in this situation was economic; for those working with fur and hides, at least, Venetian subjects were fully exempted from imperial taxation, while Byzantine subjects were not. Jacoby, "Venice and the Venetian Jews," 39. Nonetheless, it seems clear that those who sought Venetian nationality believed that the overarching picture of life under Venetian sovereignty was more pleasant, in more ways than just economic, than under the emperor's rule.

96. Klein, *Jews, Christian Society, and Royal Power*, 153, 155–58.

CHAPTER 5

1. Elea's extant ducal court cases take place between 1359 and 1382, and appear in ASV Duca di Candia, b. 26, 29, and 29 bis.

2. ASV Duca di Candia, b. 29 bis, r. 19, fols. (13)60r–(15)62r (10 November 1382): *et imponatur dicte Marie perpetuum silentium in premissis.*

3. For this evolution, see Lois C. Dubin, "Jewish Women, Marriage Law, and Emancipation: A Civil Divorce in Late-Eighteenth-Century Trieste," *Jewish Social Studies*, n.s. 13 (2007): 65–92.

4. This limitation is already spelled out explicitly as the majority opinion in Mishnah Gittin 1:5, further discussed in TB Gittin 10b. See Leo Landman, *Jewish Law in the Diaspora: Confrontation and Accommodation* (Philadelphia: Dropsie College, 1968), 15.

5. Attested in Ashkenaz. See Grossman, *Pious and Rebellious*, 246, citing the Mordechai's commentary on TB Gittin.

6. Dennis Romano has noted that "noble legislators generally viewed women as deserving the same right to legal equity as men," both when bringing civil suit and when tried for illicit activity. Romano, "Equality in Fifteenth-Century Venice," 143–44.

7. Cited in Klein, "Public Activities," 49.

8. Vidulich, *Duca di Candia*, no. 304 [69] (14 July 1321).

9. For an introduction to this concept, see Roderick Phillips, *Putting Asunder: A History of Divorce in Western Society* (Cambridge: Cambridge University Press, 1988), 13–15.

For a fuller accounting of the development of this phenomenon in canon law, see Giuliano Marchetto, *Il divorzio imperfetto: I giuristi medievali e la separazione dei coniugi* (Bologna: Il Mulino, 2008). On the application of this mechanism of separation in ecclesiastical courts, see Silvana Seidel Menchi and Diego Quaglioni, eds., *Coniugi nemici: La separazione in Italia dal XII al XVIII secolo* (Bologna: Il Mulino, 2000) for the Italian sphere, and Charles Donahue Jr., *Law, Marriage, and Society in the Later Middle Ages* (Cambridge: Cambridge University Press, 2007) for English ecclesiastical courts.

10. See below. On Venice and its connection to the development of the new medieval Roman-law-inflected *ius commune*, see Mario Ascheri, *The Laws of Late Medieval Italy (1000–1500)* (Leiden: Brill, 2013), 276–78, 329–30.

11. TB Kiddushin 2a.

12. Michael S. Berger, "Two Models of Medieval Jewish Marriage: A Preliminary Study," *Journal of Jewish Studies* 52 (2001): 61.

13. Berger, "Two Models," 61–62.

14. For a fuller discussion of marriage practices, including the stipulations of the *ketubbah*, see Judith Baskin, "Medieval Jewish Models of Marriage," in *The Medieval Marriage Scene: Prudence, Passion, Policy*, ed. Sherry Roush and Cristelle L. Baskins (Tempe: Arizona Center for Medieval and Renaissance Studies, 2005), 2–3.

15. TB Yevamot 89a; Ketubot 11a; Berger, "Two Models," 62. To be sure, the financial implications of marriage were real for Jews and Christians alike, and the Jewish marriage contract undoubtedly shared characteristics with betrothal agreements among Christians. For a foundational work on the place of economic considerations in medieval marriage, see Anthony Molho, *Marriage Alliance in Late Medieval Florence* (Cambridge, MA: Harvard University Press, 1994).

16. Mishnah Gittin 9:10 and Mishnah Ketubbot 7:6. The widely accepted ban of Rabbeinu Gershom of Mayence in the eleventh century limited this further, forbidding a man to divorce his wife without her consent. Berger, "Two Models," 76. Nevertheless, the acceptance of this decree in Candia was limited. See Lauer, "In Defence of Bigamy."

17. TB Ketubbot 71a.

18. ASV Duca di Candia, b. 26, r. 3, fol. 158r (12 August 1370).

19. ASV Duca di Candia, b. 26, r. 5, fols. 69v–70r (1 July 1417?): *scriptum in lingua ebraycha et ex altram in latinam.*

20. See Guido Ruggiero, *The Boundaries of Eros: Sex Crime and Sexuality in Renaissance Venice* (Oxford: Oxford University Press, 1985), 27.

21. Quoted here in a trial from 1401, discussed below, and used to declare bigamy legal for Jews. ASV Duca di Candia, b. 30 bis, r. 26, fols. 18v–19v (27 October 1401): *Judei possunt facere secundum ritus eorum.*

22. On this accommodation, its limits, its comparison to other Jewish policies across Christendom, and the implication for the exchange of knowledge of Jewish law between Jews and Crete's Catholic judges, see Rena Lauer, "Jewish Law and Litigation in the Secular Courts of the Late Medieval Mediterranean," *Critical Analysis of Law* 3 (2016): 114–32.

23. For this case, see ASV Duca di Candia, b. 29, r. 12, fols. 23r–25r (7 November 1359).

24. ASV Duca di Candia, b. 29, r. 12, fol. 24r: *Lex moisi erat divina, secundum quam iudei regebantur in matrimoniis suis et dominatio temporalis debebat iudeos regere, videlicet eorum leges et ritus, vigore quorumdam previligiorum proprialium que habebet universitas iudeorum.*

25. ASV Duca di Candia, b. 29, r. 12, fol. 25r.

26. On marital law in Iberian courtrooms, see Assis, "Yehudei Sepharad be-arkhaot ha-goyim," 422. Also see Elka Klein, *Jews, Christian Society, and Royal Power in Medieval Barcelona* (Ann Arbor: University of Michigan Press, 2006), 153–61. Vittore Colorni has noted two exceptional cases in the Italian sphere (Sicilian Malta in 1416 and Venetian Feltre in 1578) in which Jewish men were given explicit permission to marry second wives (by the king and a bishop, respectively) because of extenuating circumstances, such as prolonged absence and infertility. But these are true exceptions to the rules of normal juridical decision making, and not the typical response. Vittore Colorni, *Legge ebraica e leggi locali* (Milan: Giuffrè, 1945), 194.

27. In at least one case, a court in Aragonese Girona came to a decision after discussing the halachic ramifications of a marriage with Rabbi Solomon ibn Adret himself (despite his own prohibition of Jewish use of courts!) and Rabbi Aharon Halevi de na Clara, two of the major halachists of their generation. Assis, "Yehudei Sepharad be-arkhaot ha-goyi," 422. See also Yom Tov Assis, *The Golden Age of Aragonese Jewry: Community and Society in the Crown of Aragon, 1213–1327* (London: Littman Library of Jewish Civilization, 1997), 311–14, for further examples and discussion.

28. ASV Duca di Candia, b. 30 bis, r. 27, fol. 54r (16 September 1406): *in hac questione considerari debent dato prius sacramento secundum legem iudeorum.*

29. ASV Duca di Candia, b. 30 bis, r. 27, fol. 98v (14 April 1407).

30. ASV Duca di Candia, b. 30 bis, r. 27, fol. 98v (14 April 1407).

31. ASV Duca di Candia, b. 30 bis, r. 28, fol. 54v (7 May 1409): *discrepant a ritibus xristianorum.* See below.

32. See below.

33. ASV Duca di Candia, b. 26 bis, r. 9, fols. 41v–42r (3 April 1443); ASV Duca di Candia, b. 32, r. 43, fol. 14r (4 November 1445). There are many men named Abba Delmedigo on Crete; this is Abba the son of Moses.

34. During the same period, while involved in another court case regarding the Jewish community organization, he is identified as having become *camerlengus* (a Latin translation of *hashvan*) of the Jewish community. ASV Duca di Candia, b. 32, r. 42, fol. 18v (27 November 1444).

35. On reputation as a legal tool, see, e.g., Marie Kelleher, "Later Medieval Law in Community Context," in *The Oxford Handbook of Women and Gender in Medieval Europe*, ed. Judith M. Bennett and Ruth Mazo Karras (Oxford: Oxford University Press, 2013), 141–42. Also see the collection of essays in Thelma Fenster and Daniel Lord Smail, eds., *Fama: The Politics of Talk and Reputation in Medieval Europe* (Ithaca, NY: Cornell University Press, 2003), especially Thomas Kuehn, "*Fama* as a Legal Status in Renaissance Florence," in *Fama: The Politics of Talk and Reputation in Medieval Europe*, ed. Thelma Fenster and Daniel Lord Smail (Ithaca, NY: Cornell University Press, 2003), 27–46.

36. See TB Ketubbot 72b–73b. For a discussion of the relevant rabbinic sources, see Aviad Hacohen, *The Tears of the Oppressed: An Examination of the Agunah Problem: Background and Halakhic Sources* (Jersey City: Ktav Publishing, 2004), 23–33.

37. ASV Duca di Candia, b. 26 bis, r. 9, fols. 41v–42r (3 April 1443).

38. ASV Duca di Candia, b. 32, r. 43, fol. 14r (4 November 1445). By late 1451, Abba was remarried to a woman named Conortis, who seems to have worked with him on his various moneylending and business ventures. ASV Notai di Candia, b. 2 (not. Michele Calergi), fol. 45v (16–20 September 1451), 52v (20 December 1451).

39. For just one example, see Shona Kelly Wray, "Instruments of Concord: Making Peace and Settling Disputes Through a Notary in the City and Contado of Late Medieval Bologna," *Journal of Social History* 43 (2009): 733–60.

40. Joanne M. Ferraro, *Marriage Wars in Late Renaissance Venice* (Oxford: Oxford University Press, 2001), 123.

41. ASV Duca di Candia, b. 26 bis, r. 10, fol. 35v (10 October 1447).

42. Here called the *more iudaico* and *more abraico*.

43. TB Ketubbot 47b–48a; Berger, "Two Models," 65–66.

44. Berger, "Two Models," 67.

45. For a few pre-twelfth-century cases in which Jewish women were able to "initiate" (to varying degrees) divorce with the help of the rabbinic court, and the push to stop this behavior in the twelfth century, see Dubin, "Jewish Women, Marriage Law, and Emancipation," 69–70.

46. Ferraro, *Marriage Wars*, 9.

47. Ferraro, *Marriage Wars*, 70. For more on the importance of consummation in the making of a legally valid Christian marriage, and Gratian's formulation, see Marchetto, *Il divorzio imperfetto*, 43–52 (for Gratian); 67–80 (in other jurists' formulations). For an evolution in the attitude toward divorce in the case of nonconsummation, see 207–31.

48. For the Venetian case, see Ferraro, *Marriage Wars*, 9. For a wider canon law approach to this so-called *divortium quoad thorum*, see Marchetto, *Il divorzio imperfetto*, 253–60.

49. ASV Duca di Candia, b. 29, r. 12, fol. 41r (3 December 1359).

50. ASV Duca di Candia, b. 29, r. 13, fol. 2(35v) (3 November 1360).

51. This case appears in two records, both in the *Memoriali* (longer court records), as ASV Duca di Candia, b. 29 bis, r. 15, fols. 63v–65r (7 March 1368), and in the *Sentenze* (shorter judgment records), as ASV Duca di Candia, b. 26, r. 3, fols. 85v–86r (7 March 1368).

52. The Venetian *exagium*, or *saggio*, as measured for precious metals (the so-called *saggio sottile*), weighed 1/72 of a Venetian pound, or a sixth of a Venetian ounce. Scholars debate the exact weight of the medieval *saggio*, but all estimates fall between four and five grams. See the comparative table of scholarly estimates in Hans Ulrich Vogel, *Marco Polo Was in China: New Evidence from Currencies, Salts, and Revenues* (Leiden: Brill, 2013), 474.

53. *mulieribus adduntur secundum ritum iudeorum, prout continebatur in quadam scriptura catasticata.*

54. On the legal category of *minhag*, see Dorff and Rosett, *A Living Tree*, 421–34.

55. *mulieribus ebreis adduntur secundum ritum iudeorum.*

56. ASV Duca di Candia, b. 26, r. 3, fol. 121r (27 November 1368). As recorded in this case, the hiring contract is dated 13 July 1368.

57. *contra consuetudinem iudaice candide.* For this case, see ASV Duca di Candia, b. 30 bis, r. 26, fols. 18v–19v (27 October 1401). For an in-depth discussion of this case and its Jewish and Venetian contexts, see Lauer, "In Defence of Bigamy."

58. Kuehn, *Law, Family, and Women,* 19.

59. The notary records that Joseph first said that the rabbis permit bigamy for marriage with nieces and other relatives (*sicut est in accipiendo neptem filiam fratris, amitam et germanam consanguineam*), women the Mishnah explicitly forbids to be taken in levirate marriage because of close degrees of consanguinity (Mishnah Yebamot 1:1).

60. ASV Duca di Candia, b. 30 bis, r. 26, fol. 19r: *hoc fecit secundum legem moisis et secundum ritus judeorum qui semper fuerunt observati et adpresens observantur in pluribus partibus mundi, unde non est solus qui ad presens sit ad hanc conditionem cum etiam quotidie nuptie fiant inter eos marioris? admirarum quam sit habere duas uxores sicut est in accipiendo neptem filiam fratris, amitam et germanam consanguineam et uxores olim fratrum suorum et huiusmodi accipere autem duas uxores multum magistrum? est concessum, et specialiter quando Iudeus non habet filium masculum et sit extra spem habendi filium masculum cum aliqua uxore quam teneat. In quo causa est adpresens dictus Josteff* (reading unclear at points). Sadly for Joseph Missini and his dreams of a son, his new wife also could not produce a male heir for him. A fight over his inheritance from 1437 indicates that when he died, likely in 1411, his only direct heir was a daughter, Ghrussana. She, in turn, gave birth to a daughter, interestingly enough named Channa (also spelled Ghana) but who was known by the nickname "Sclavuna." ASV Duca di Candia, b. 26 bis, r. 8, fols. 7v–8r (1 October 1437).

61. The Talmud, and confirmed by Rabbi Gershom himself as well as Rashi, allowed bigamy in case of barrenness. Grossman, *Pious and Rebellious,* 71.

62. Elimelech Westreich, *Temurot be-ma'amad ha-ishah be-mishpat ha-'ivri: Masa ben masorot* [Transitions in the Legal State of the Wife in Jewish Law: A Journey Among Traditions] (Jerusalem: Hebrew University Magnes Press, 2002), 200–201.

63. It should be noted that, though this ban is traditionally attributed to Gershom, and known by his name, some scholars consider the connection between the man and the ban spurious, attached to his name later because of his prominence. See Grossman, *Pious and Rebellious,* 70–71.

64. Solomon ibn Adret notes in his responsa that the ban of Gershom "did not spread throughout our borders." Responsa of Rashba, 3:446. For a discussion of Spanish bigamy that takes into consideration both Jewish and secular archival sources, see Yom Tov Assis, "'Herem de-rabbeinu Gershom' ve-nisuei kefel be-Sepharad" ["The Excommunication of Rabbeinu Gershom" and Bigamous Marriage in Spain], *Zion* 46 (1981): 251–77. On Provence, see Grossman, *Pious and Rebellious,* 87–88.

65. M. A. Friedman, *Ribui nashim be-Yisrael: Mekorot hadashim me-genizat Kahir* [Jewish Polygyny: New Sources from the Cairo Genizah] (Jerusalem: Bialik Institute, 1986), 34, 36, 42, 43, and sources mentioned there.

66. Thomas Kuehn has noted that it was very common for each side in a dispute to offer evidence of competing, and often convincing, norms in late medieval courts. Kuehn, *Law, Family, and Women*, 97.

67. ASV Duca di Candia, b. 30 bis, r. 26, fols. 19r–v: *Magnificus dominus Albanus Baduario et eius consilium noluerunt causis superis allegatis, quod ad vocum? se impedirent in dicto facto, que Judei possunt facere secundum ritus eorum* [reading unclear].

68. ASV Duca di Candia, b. 30 bis, r. 28, fol. 54r (7 May 1409).

69. To be sure, contemporary American law, for example, permits certain religious beliefs and rituals that would otherwise be banned (such as the right of members of the Native American Church to ingest hallucinogenic peyote, otherwise an illegal, controlled substance). Nevertheless, let us not confuse the medieval state's choices regarding legal toleration with American constitutional rights. That Jewish rights would be upheld even when in diametric opposition to Christian religious values remains a fascinating and unusual circumstance.

70. William Carew Hazlitt, *The Venetian Republic: Its Rise, Its Growth, and Its Fall, 421–1797*, vol. 2 (London: Adam and Charles Black, 1900), 505–6.

71. To be sure, we should not overestimate the Venetian aversion to bigamy. At least since 1289, the government treated bigamy as a civil offense, not a religious one: in limiting the power of the Holy Office (Inquisition), which set down roots in Venice in 1289, the Maggior Consiglio demanded that "exemption may also be claimed for persons guilty of bigamy, blasphemy, usury, or necromancy, it being considered by the Government that, except in cases where a breach of the sacrament can be proved, these are merely secular offenses." Paraphrased in Hazlitt, *The Venetian Republic*, 395. Also see Lauer, "In Defence of Bigamy."

72. The central premise of Sara McDougall's first monograph, that bigamy was seen as a crisis in the late Middle Ages because it particularly threatened Christian identity, may help us understand why Jewish bigamy was less problematic for the Venetian court. Sara McDougall, *Bigamy and Christian Identity in Late Medieval Champagne* (Philadelphia: University of Pennsylvania Press, 2012).

73. Pnina Lahav, "Theater in the Courtroom: The Chicago Conspiracy Trial," *Law and Literature* 16 (2004): 381–474, esp. 392. Also see footnote 27: "Compared to the voluminous bibliography on law and literature, there has been little effort at theorizing the meaning of theater in the courtroom." Also see Adi Parush, "The Courtroom as Theater and the Theater as Courtroom in Ancient Athens," *Israel Law Review* 35 (2001): 118–68.

74. On law as culture, see the now classic work by Lawrence Rosen, *The Anthropology of Justice: Law as Culture in Islamic Society* (Cambridge: Cambridge University Press, 1989).

75. Marie Kelleher, *The Measure of Woman: Law and Female Identity in the Crown of Aragon* (Philadelphia: University of Pennsylvania Press, 2010), 11. See also idem, "Later Medieval Law," 138–39.

76. ASV Duca di Candia, b. 32, r. 43, fol. 13v (4 November 1445).

77. The first mention of the lawsuit, from 1422, simply mentions that Elia had "expelled" (*expullit*) Mina from Chios and that she had come to Candia, ostensibly where

the couple had started out. The court ordered Elia's agent to let Mina live in a house in the Judaica owned by Elia. But the agent did not hand over the house, leading to further litigation a year later. ASV Duca di Candia, b. 31 ter, r. 33, fol. 5v (27 July 1422).

78. ASV Duca di Candia, b. 31 ter, r. 34, fols. 51v–52r (3 August 1423).

79. ASV Duca di Candia, b. 31, r. 36, fol. 113r (2 December 1428).

80. Ferraro, *Marriage Wars*, 122.

81. Linda Guzzetti, "Women in Court in 14th-Century Venice: The Meaning of 'Equality' and 'Rationality' in Written Law and in Court," in *Gender Difference in European Legal Culture: Historical Perspectives*, ed. Karin Gottschalk (Stuttgart: Franz Steiner Verlag, 2013), 45.

82. ASV Duca di Candia, b. 30 bis, r. 25, fols. 98v–99r (14 January 1401).

83. ASV Duca di Candia, b. 29 bis, r. 15, fol. 7r–v (13 August 1366).

84. See Susan Mosher Stuard, "Brideprice, Dowry, and Other Marital Assets," in *The Oxford Handbook of Women and Gender in the Middle Ages*, ed. Judith M. Bennett and Ruth Mazo Karras (Oxford: Oxford University Press, 2013), 149; Ferraro, *Marriage Wars*, 135–54.

85. ASV Duca di Candia, b. 26 bis, r. 10, fols. 199v–200r (15 April 1451); ASV Duca di Candia, b. 26 bis, r. 11, fols. 25r–v (22 May 1454).

86. For the case between Eudochia Crusari and her husband, Monache, see ASV Duca di Candia, b. 30 ter, r. 31, fols. 90r–v (26 April 1418). Eudochia is recorded as saying that, *nullo modo potest conversari secum, sine suspitionem vite sue.*

87. Marchetto, *Il divorzio imperfetto*, 361–75.

88. For example, this language is also used by Arconda, who seeks relief from the abuse of her in-laws. In this case, the in-laws stand in as the power brokers in her marriage to a man who was powerless both in that he was under his father's *patria potestas* (noted explicitly in the record) and in that he was ill. ASV Duca di Candia, b. 30 bis, r. 25, fols. 141v–143r (31 May 1401) and fols. 145v–146r (23 June 1401).

89. Grossman, *Pious and Rebellious*, 212–30, 235, 239.

90. Grossman, *Pious and Rebellious*, 232.

91. Ferraro, *Marriage Wars*, 7. On the ways in which court records reflect constructed narratives, see Natalie Zemon Davis, *Fiction in the Archives: Pardon Tales and Their Tellers in Sixteenth-Century France* (Stanford, CA: Stanford University Press, 1987).

92. Howard Tzvi Adelman, "Law and Love: The Jewish Family in Early Modern Italy," *Continuity and Change* 16 (2001): 283–303, esp. 291–96.

93. Adelman, "Law and Love," 296.

94. Ellinor Forster, "Between Law, Gender and Confession: Jewish Matrimonial Law Provisions Against the Background of Catholic and Protestant Regulations in Austria, 18th-and 19th-Centuries," in *Gender Difference in European Legal Cultures: Historical Perspectives*, ed. Karin Gottschalk (Stuttgart: Franz Steiner Verlag, 2013), 102.

95. See Ferraro, *Marriage Wars*, 138.

96. Joanne Ferraro has noted a similar trend in fifteenth- and sixteenth-century Christian marriage litigation in Venice. "Married women, more often than married men, called upon established institutions to protect their welfare and interests." Ferraro, *Marriage Wars*, 8.

97. Carol Lansing, "Conflicts over Gender in Civic Courts," in *The Oxford Handbook of Women and Gender in Medieval Europe*, ed. Judith M. Bennett and Ruth Mazo Karras (Oxford: Oxford University Press, 2013), 125–28. Also see Kuehn, "*Fama* as a Legal Status in Renaissance Florence," 31–35.

98. ASV Duca di Candia, b. 30 ter, r. 30, fols. 27v–28v (14 January 1416). The date of the marriage is not indicated here, but a betrothal agreement is dated 23 May 1412: ASV Notai di Candia, b. 23 (not. Andrea Cocco), fol. 21r. We learn here as well that Saphira is a member of the elite Angura family, though her father died before her betrothal, and negotiations were undertaken by her mother, Chana. Recorded in May, the betrothal agreement mandates that the marriage take place before the following March.

99. ASV Duca di Candia, b. 30 ter, r. 30, fol. 27v: *videlicet a perversitate ipsius Saphira, que ibat vagabunda omni die et hora sicut volebat per civitatem et per domos alienas.*

100. This intersection of individual sexual behavior and state honor is attested among Venice's patrician class and in the broader medieval world. Late Roman law branded some men convicted of sexual crimes with *infamia*, a "legal taint" that made them "incapable of holding public office or exercising any position of trust or honor," alongside other legal disabilities. The eleventh-century canonists carried over this notion for many sexual offenses, including bigamy, rape, and homosexual relations. Here too *infamia* constituted "a deprivation of respectable status," which barred the guilty man from playing public leadership roles, among other acts that necessitated trustworthiness and reliability, including the right to "appear in court as a complainant or witness." James A. Brundage, *Law, Sex, and Christian Society in Medieval Europe* (Chicago: University of Chicago Press, 1987), 37–38, 207; Ruggiero, *Boundaries of Eros*, 19–23, 30–31. The fact that a Jew would claim that Jewish dishonor undermined state honor offers a tantalizing coda to such scholarship.

101. *Propter perversitatem duritiam et temeritatem*; later *propter duritiam et obstinatam voluntatem suam.*

102. Regarding Parnas: *Non processit ab ulla culpa; non sit in culpa aliqua.* In contrast, regarding Saphira: *est in culpa.*

103. Lansing, "Conflicts over Gender," 125.

104. See Marta Madero, "The Servitude of the Flesh from the Twelfth to the Fourteenth Century," *Critical Analysis of Law* 3 (2016): 145, for the decretal of Innocent III.

105. On such non-dotal assets brought into marriage by Italian brides, see Julius Kirshner, "Materials for a Gilded Cage: Non-Dotal Assets in Florence, 1300–1500," in *The Family in Italy*, ed. David I. Kertzer and Richard P. Saller (New Haven, CT: Yale University Press, 1991), 184–207.

106. *In dicta domo non remanserat nisi unum par stivalorum dicti Parne viri sui.*

107. For example, one Protho Buchi, son of Elia, appears as the scribe of the manuscript Mos 906. But Parnas's brother Protho Buchi, son of Samaria, was *condestabulo* and signed *TQ* nos. 60 (1424), 51 (1428), and 57 (1435).

108. ASV Notai di Candia, b. 23 (not. Andrea Cocco), fol. 21r (23 May 1412).

109. Kuehn, *Law, Family, and Women*, 198.

110. Kuehn, *Law, Family, and Women*, 198.

111. For a reference to a Jewish man controlled by his father's *patria potestas*, much to the chagrin of his unhappy wife, see ASV Duca di Candia, b. 30 bis, r. 25, fols. 141v–143r (31 May 1401) and fols. 145v–146r (23 June 1401).

112. Roberts, "The Study of Dispute," 20–22. Also quoted in Kuehn, *Law, Family, and Women*, 96.

113. Rebecca Lynn Winer, *Women, Wealth, and Community in Perpignan, c. 1250–1300* (Aldershot: Ashgate, 2006), 81.

114. Some of the important work of the late Elka Klein focused on this: "The Widow's Portion: Law, Custom and Marital Property Among Medieval Catalan Jews," *Viator* 31 (2000): 147–64; "Splitting Heirs: Patterns of Inheritance Among Barcelona's Jews," *Jewish History* 16 (2002): 49–71. Also see Stefanie B. Siegmund, "Division of the Dowry on the Death of the Daughter: An Instance in the Negotiation of Laws and Jewish Customs in Early Modern Tuscany," *Jewish History* 16 (2002): 73–106.

115. Tommaso Astarita, *Village Justice: Community, Family, and Popular Culture in Early Modern Italy* (Baltimore: Johns Hopkins University Press, 1999), esp. 52–53.

116. Kuehn, *Law, Family, and Women*, 99.

117. Stat. ven. 3:53: *Cum mulieri sub viro constitute propter ipsius pudicitiam verecundum sit conspectum publicorum iudicum in litigiis propulsare.* Quoted and translated in Guzzetti, "Women in Court," 46.

118. In the Roman jurist Ulpian's explanation for the basic prohibition from the *Senatus consultum velleianum* (a key Roman law provision limiting women's public power), which forbade women from assuming liability, doing business, or going to court on behalf of someone else, he notes that such behavior is both against female modesty and meant to shield women from performing the functions of males. This assumption, that good women would not want to do either of these things, was a basic legal and social assumption in the medieval Mediterranean—and likely rang true for most women. On Ulpian's comment, see Guzzetti, "Women in Court," 50.

119. Ferraro, *Marriage Wars*, 122.

120. ASV Duca di Candia, b. 29 bis, r. 15, fols. 15r–16r (quote on fol. 15v) (12 November 1366).

CHAPTER 6

1. *TQ* no. 52, pp. 51–52.

2. *TQ* no. 52, p. 52.

3. Even from a contemporary Jewish theorist's perspective, the medieval *kehillah*—that institution of communal self-government—existed at the pleasure of the sovereign state. See Lorberbaum, *Politics and the Limits of Law*, 112–13, for a responsum by Ibn Adret in which this reliance on the sovereign is made clear in both the question and the answer.

4. See Lorberbaum, *Politics*, chaps. 5 and 6.

5. Daniel J. Elazar, "The Kehillah," in *Kinship and Consent: The Jewish Political Tradition and Its Contemporary Uses*, 2nd ed., ed. Daniel J. Elazar (New Brunswick, NJ: Transaction

Publishers, 1997), 249. As Salo Baron noted, the idea of the Jewish "state within a state" was first levied as a complaint against Jewish communities in the eighteenth century: "Before that time, extensive Jewish self-government was universally accepted as the necessary and welcome complement to recognized religious disparity." Baron claimed that the "sort of little state" that was the *kehillah* was "non-political, but none the less quasi-totalitarian." Baron, *The Jewish Community*, 208. For another example, this one far more problematic in its wholesale acceptance of the internal Jewish narrative, see Irving Agus, *Rabbi Meir of Rothenburg*, 2nd ed. (New York: Ktav, 1970), 57: "The self-government of the German and French Jews, therefore, came into being because of their own ardent desire for freedom and independence, and not at all as a result of administrative expediency on the part of the secular government." Such adamant generalizations warrant further interrogation.

6. Gerald J. Blidstein, "Individual and Community in the Middle Ages: Halakhic Theory," in *Kinship and Consent: The Jewish Political Tradition and Its Contemporary Uses*, 2nd ed., ed. Daniel J. Elazar (New Brunswick, NJ: Transaction Publishers, 1997), 332–38.

7. Among their larger bodies of halachic writing, the Catalan Solomon ibn Adret and the Ashkenazi rabbi Meir of Rothenburg most comprehensively explicated both the legitimation of the corporate project and its practical applications. Lorberbaum, *Politics and the Limits of Law*, 95–96. Though both sets of writings probably influenced Cretan Jewry, as they did Jews across Christendom, Ibn Adret's opinions were especially sought by Candiote Jews, to whom he addressed at least two responsa. Starr, "Jewish Life," 105. These two responsa deal with questions regarding proper use of phylacteries and the use of an agent to sign a document. Another Cretan Jew, one Solomon of Candia, is addressed in a responsum written by the famed Nissim Girondi, also Catalan, in the mid-fourteenth century.

8. Quoted in translation in Lorberbaum, *Politics and the Limits of Law*, 98; italics in the original.

9. He also feared that such behavior would facilitate assimilation. See Lorberbaum, *Politics and the Limits of Law*, 99. The original responsum can be found in Solomon ibn Adret, *Responsa*, 2:290.

10. *TQ* no. 52, p. 52.

11. Numbers 16:2. Strangely, this verse actually refers to evil characters in the Bible: the community leaders who joined with Korah to rebel against Moses' authority.

12. *TQ*, no. 52, p. 51.

13. *Yarim qarnam*, literally "May He raise their horns."

14. *TQ* no. 52, p. 51.

15. *TQ* no. 52, p. 51.

16. Elazar, "The Kehillah," 249.

17. In other moments of (to him, unfair) demands for payment from an individual, the Jewish community should not be forced (at least, ethically) to pay. As translated in Michael Walzer, Menachem Lorberbaum, and Noam Zohar, eds., *The Jewish Political Tradition*, vol. 1, *Authority* (New Haven, CT: Yale University Press, 2000), 442.

18. *The Code of Maimonides, Book Eleven: The Book of Torts*, trans. H. Klein (New Haven, CT: Yale University Press, 1954), 108–10, as reprinted in Walzer, Lorberbaum, and Zohar, *Jewish Political Tradition*, 443.

19. *The Code of Maimonides*, 108–10, as reprinted in Walzer, Lorberbaum, and Zohar, *The Jewish Political Tradition*, 443.

20. ASV Duca di Candia, b. 30, r. 25, fols. 124v–125r (19 April 1401).

21. *Cum constiterit dictam iudeam non habere possessiones in creta.* ASV Duca di Candia, b. 30, r. 22, fol. 77v (4 April 1391).

22. ASV Duca di Candia, b. 30 bis, r. 29, fols. 137v–138r (30 May 1412).

23. We do learn, however, that Elia died before May 1417, when a creditor from Negroponte appeared at the ducal court seeking money Elia had owed him, and which the Curia Prosoporum, the court of first instance for Greeks and Jews, had already demanded be paid to him. ASV Duca di Candia, b. 30 ter, r. 30, fols. 220v–221r (11 May 1417).

24. This case is recorded very similarly in two locations: ASV Duca di Candia, b. 26 bis, r. 8, fols. 33v–34r; and b. 31, r. 40, fols. 58r–59r (5 May 1438).

25. Aaron (here spelled Acharon) came to court claiming the following: *patrus suus predictus et ipse Acharon erant et sunt de Negroponte in quo loco taxabantur et faciebant et faciunt imposiciones et geta ac engarias suas* (in the language of the b. 26 bis record). The impost was the general annual tax; the *geta* or *gettum*, according to Elisabeth Santschi, "is probably a corruption of guettus or guetus, which signifies the watch-duty tax: in effect, the Jews of Candia, as the other inhabitants of the city, had to participate in the guarding of the walls for their quarter." Santschi, "Contribution," 185 (translation mine). For the Jews in this period, the *geta* had seemingly become a monetary replacement tax and not an actual levy of man-hours. The *angaria* was an ad hoc labor tax, sometimes rendered by localities but not usually employed for the Jews of Candia.

26. It is worth noting that Mosca's claim, that his "visitor" status should afford him protection from local imposts, was not one that would carry weight throughout the medieval Jewish world. In fact, in many cities, including those in Germany and Iberia, Jewish communities demanded that temporary residents and visitors participate in communal obligations. To be sure, we cannot know if Mosca paid into any internal Jewish pots—for example, funds to pay for the marriages of poor orphans (a fund made known to us through bequests in wills)—but he certainly claimed to not be obligated to pay any of the Venetian-imposed taxes. On taxation levied on visitors by Jewish communities, see Baron, *The Jewish Community*, 12.

27. An entry in the court records from 1407 witnesses Elia Mosca, Aaron's late father, fighting another Jew over a contract they had made in 1400. ASV Duca di Candia, b. 30 bis, r. 27, fols. 94r–v (? May 1407). We see Aaron involved in local business in 1430, when he was trusted to manage money belonging to Latin noblemen in Candia. ASV Duca di Candia, b. 31, r. 37, fol. 82v (12 May 1430).

28. Kenneth Stow, *Alienated Minority: The Jews of Medieval Latin Europe* (Cambridge, MA: Harvard University Press, 1992), 164.

29. *TQ* no. 24, p. 13. The term *nasi*, literally a prince, was originally used by Jewish leaders supposedly descended from the Davidic line during the Babylonian captivity and resuscitated in the Middle Ages (along with the title *nagid* in Muslim lands) to indicate an internally accepted leader of a diasporic Jewish community. Like many titles used within

medieval Jewish communities, *nasi* could sometimes signify the title of a specific appointed or recognized leader and thereby bestow status (as in the Candiote context); however, in some medieval locales, the title could function as a general category of respected members of the community—a title, then, recognizing an already held social status, akin to *zaqen* (elder) or *tov ha'ir* (good man of the city). For a discussion of these titles and statuses, see Klein, *Jews, Christian Society, and Royal Power*, 65–67.

30. Stow, *Alienated Minority*, 160–61.

31. Stow, *Alienated Minority*, 161.

32. An overview of Jewish taxation of Crete can be found in Baron, *A Social and Religious History of the Jews*, vol. 17, *Byzantines, Mamluks, and Maghribians*, 61.

33. Published in Noiret, *Documents inédits*, 13 (25 February 1387) and 26 (25 May 1389).

34. ASV Duca di Candia, b. 26, r. 6, fol. 102v (?1430).

35. *TQ* nos. 6, 22, and 27 outline the limits to excommunication. In 43, we see this in practice, as the leadership rejects the use of excommunication in a particular case. In a number of other *taqqanot*, excommunication is threatened; see, e.g., nos. 68 and 70.

36. *TQ* no. 22, p.13.

37. Thiriet, *Régestes*, vol. 1, no. 194, p. 107. Mentioned in Borsari, "Ricchi e poveri," 211.

38. Klein, *Jews, Christian Society, and Royal Power*, 158.

39. Santschi, "Contribution," 185.

40. Summarized in Santschi, "Contribution," 185.

41. ASV Duca di Candia, b. 31, r. 26, fols. 109r–v (4 August 1428).

42. ASV Misti del Senato fol. 125r; partial text published in Noiret, *Documents inédits*, 387; referenced in Thiriet, *Régestes*, 3:70. The feudatories of Candia were also told to pay the same amount for three years.

43. ASV Duca di Candia, b. 31, r. 40, fol. 119r (11 January 1439), in which the Jews are ordered to pay 3,000 measures, while the island's feudatories pay 2,000 measures, the citizens in the city pay 2,000, and the burghers pay 2,500. The clerics are told to pay a token 400 measures.

44. Baron, *A Social and Religious History of the Jews*, vol. 17, *Byzantines, Mamluks, and Maghribians*, 59.

45. ASV Duca di Candia, b. 31, r. 40, fol. 115r (27 January 1439)—only sixteen days after the initial order for the wheat tax was announced.

46. Baron, *A Social and Religious History of the Jews*, vol. 17, *Byzantines, Mamluks, and Maghribians*, 59.

47. *Per se et aliis medicis salariatis.* ASV Duca di Candia, b. 26 bis, r. 8, fol. 38v (24 July 1438).

48. ASV Misti del Senato fol. 57r (5 September 1441). Referenced in Noiret, *Documents inédits*, 399, and in Thiriet, *Régestes*, 3:89.

49. As translated and quoted in Klein, *Jews, Christian Society, and Royal Power*, 41.

50. Klein, *Jews, Christian Society, and Royal Power*, 44.

51. ASV Duca di Candia, b. 31, r. 41, fol. 23r (3 December 1439).

52. TB Berakhot 6b and 7b; TJ Berakhot 4:4.

53. Solomon ibn Adret, *Pirushei ha-agadot,* Berakhot 6:2, edited by Getz in his *Sifre Ha-Rashba* (Jerusalem: Oraita, 1986).

54. See Joaqim Miret y Sans and Moïse Schwab, "Documents sur les juifs Catalans aux XIe, XIIe, et XIIIe siècles," *Révue des Études Juives* 68, no. 36 (1914): 188–97.

55. Moses Capsali, also discussed in Chapter 1, served in Constantinople as a community leader and later as official head rabbi of the city under Ottoman rule.

56. *TQ* no. 45, p. 37.

57. *TQ* no. 45, p. 37.

58. *TQ* no. 47, p. 43. Deuteronomy utilizes this expression to refer to false gods, an extremely negative association.

59. *TQ* no. 44, p. 36.

60. Borýsek reads this as "powerful Gentiles," but in light of the connotation of "ali-mut" in Capsali's entry, which likely pulls language from this 1363 *taqqanah,* I do not believe such a neutral translation is accurate. Martin Borýsek, "The Jews of Venetian Candia: The Challenges of External Influences and Internal Diversity as Reflected in Takkanot Kandiyah," *Al-Masaq* 26 (2014): 252.

61. A rabbinic expression found, inter alia, in Mishnah Ketubbot 7:6. The expression is chosen, it seems, to highlight that such behavior has violated legal and social norms within the Jewish community.

62. Esther 10:3.

63. This final expression is a rabbinic principle found, among other places, in TB Brachot 59a and TB Rosh Hashanah 26a, meaning that something done sinfully cannot then be used for pious means.

64. ASV Duca di Candia, b. 30 bis, r. 29, fols. 19v–21r (3 October 1411). From other evidence, this "Tam" can be identified as Jacob Belo, son of the late Chai. Tam is his nickname: see ASV Duca di Candia, b. 30 ter, r. 30, fols. 11v–13r (21 October 1415). He is dead by August 1437, when his widow appears in court; see ASV Duca di Candia, b 31, r. 40, fols. 5r–v (30 August 1437).

65. It seems likely that the Stroviliatiko synagogue is the same as the one mentioned in *Taqqanot Qandiya* as Seviliatiko and identified as the major synagogue (*beit ha-knesset ha-gadol*) in 1518. *TQ* no. 72, p. 76.

66. *TQ* no. 25, p. 14.

67. Isaiah 32:15.

68. *TQ* no. 25, p. 14.

69. TQ no. 46, p. 42.

70. ASV Duca di Candia, b. 30 ter, r. 32, fols. 151r–154r (27 February 1421).

71. The judges "di proprii" or, in Latin, the *iudicum proprii.*

72. ASV Duca di Candia, b. 30 bis, r. 28, fol. 61v (4 June 1409).

73. TQ no. 82, pp. 98–99.

74. TQ no. 6, p. 4.

75. TQ no. 22, p. 13.

76. TQ no. 27, pp. 14–15.

77. TQ no. 72, pp. 98–99.

78. ASV Duca di Candia, b. 26 bis, r. 10, fol. 206r (27 September 1451).

CONCLUSION

1. For the literature of this Cretan Renaissance, see Holton, *Literature and Society in Renaissance Crete*. For just one of the many studies on the revolutionary icon painting that defined this period, see Anastasia Drandaki, *The Origins of El Greco: Icon Painting in Venetian Crete* (New York: Onassis Foundation, 2009).

2. On Delmedigo as a Jewish thinker, see Harvey Hames, "Elia del Medigo: An Archetype of the Halachic Man," *Traditio* 56 (2001): 213–27, reprinted as "Elijah Delmedigo: An Archetype of the Halakhic Man?" in *Cultural Intermediaries: Jewish Intellectuals in Early Modern Italy*, ed. David B. Ruderman and Giuseppe Veltri (Philadelphia: University of Pennsylvania Press, 2004), 39–54. For a recent accounting of Delmedigo's philosophical approach in a broader context, see Michael Engel, *Elijah Del Medigo and Paduan Aristotelianism: Investigating the Human Intellect* (London: Bloomsbury, 2017).

3. Capsali's work on Ottoman history, *Seder Eliyahu Zuta* (Order of Elijah the Younger), has been edited and annotated in Hebrew: Eliyahu Capsali, *Seder Eliyahu Zuta*, ed. Aryeh Shmuelevitz, Shlomo Simonsohn, and Meir Benayahu, 3 vols. (Jerusalem: Ben Zvi Institute, 1975–77). Also see Shmuelevitz, "Capsali as a Source for Ottoman History," esp. p. 341 for Shmuelevitz's critique of what he sees as Capsali's overreliance on biblical parallels.

4. For a discussion of the impact of the circle of Jewish Candiote scholars in the late fifteenth and early sixteenth centuries, see Robert Morrison, "A Scholarly Intermediary Between the Ottoman Empire and Renaissance Europe," *Isis* 105 (2014): 32–57.

5. Continuity exists even on a literary level, argues Bonfil, who stresses Capsali's dependence on earlier literary forms in *Seder Eliyahu Zuta*. See Bonfil, "Jewish Attitudes Toward History and Historical Writing in Pre-Modern Times," 16–22. Nevertheless, both men are often treated without consideration of their Cretan connections. Bonfil dismisses the Cretan element in Delmedigo's thinking, highlighting instead the importance of Delmedigo's time in Padua and his family's Ashkenazi connection. Robert Bonfil, "A Cultural Profile," in *The Jews of Early Modern Venice*, ed. Robert C. Davis and Benjamin Ravid (Baltimore: Johns Hopkins University Press, 2001), 177. Harvey Hames recognizes the importance of contemporary debates in Crete (such as the 1466 fight over metempsychosis) but chalks up the tension to a "clash between different halakhic traditions, the Sephardi and the Ashkenazi," ignoring the Romaniote and local elements that informed Cretan Jewish life; see Hames, "Elijah Delmedigo," 41.

6. All quotes in this paragraph come from Robert Bonfil, *Rabbis and Jewish Communities in Renaissance Italy* (Oxford: Littman Library, 1990), 4–5.

7. Simonsohn, *A Common Justice*, 7.

8. On the sinking of the *Tanais*, its remembrance, and the controversy over the role of the British in bombing it, see Judith Humphrey, "The Sinking of the 'Danae' off Crete in June 1944," *Bulletin of Judaeo-Greek Studies* 9 (1991): 19–34.

9. Some of these (already in the museum in the late 1960s) are noted and discussed in Ankori, "Jews and the Jewish Community," 332–34.

10. For example, see illuminated *haggadot* discussed in Ilona Steiman, "Making Illuminated Haggadot in Venetian Crete," *Mediterranean Historical Review* 27 (2012): 161–73. On the natural philosophy and scientific works of the Cretan Jewish polymath Joseph Solomon Delmedigo (1591–1655), see Barzilay, *Yoseph Shlomo Delmedigo*.

11. Elia Capsali mandated an annual celebration known as the "Purim of Candia" after the Jews of the community (and particularly women and children) were saved from Greek mob violence by Venetian military intervention in 1538. The Greek mob apparently believed that Jews were harboring Turkish spies: *TQ* no. 99, pp. 118–28. Also see Elliott S. Horowitz, *Reckless Rites: Purim and the Legacy of Jewish Violence* (Princeton, NJ: Princeton University Press, 2006), 290–93.

12. Zvi Ankori, "Giacomo Foscarini and the Jews of Crete: A Reconsideration," *Michael: On the History of the Jews in the Diaspora* 7 (1981): 9–118.

13. *TQ* nos. 112 and 113, pp. 146–48.

14. This may have become a neighborhood for poorer Jews and perhaps for Karaites as well. Zvi Ankori, "From Zudecha to Yahudi Mahallesi: The Jewish Quarter of Candia in the Seventeenth Century," in *Salo Wittmeyer Baron Jubilee Volume*, vol. 1, ed. Saul Lieberman and Arthur Hyman (Jerusalem and New York: American Academy for Jewish Research and Columbia University Press, 1974), 112–19.

15. Ankori, "From Zudecha," 88.

16. Molly Greene, *A Shared World: Christians and Muslims in the Early Modern Mediterranean* (Princeton, NJ: Princeton University Press, 2000), 81–82.

17. Ankori, "From Zudecha," 92–95.

18. Greene, *A Shared World*, 96.

19. Ankori, "From Zudecha," 97–98.

Bibliography

UNEDITED ARCHIVAL SERIES

Venice, Archivio di Stato, Duca di Candia.
Venice, Archivio di Stato, Notai di Candia.

MANUSCRIPTS

Jerusalem, National Library of Israel, Heb. 28°7203.
Leiden, Universiteitsbibliotheek Leiden, Cod. Or. 4751.
Moscow, Russian State Library, Guenzburg 362.
Moscow, Russian State Library, Guenzburg 906.
Oxford, Bodleian Library, MS. Hunt. 561.
Paris, *Bibliothèque nationale de France, BnF heb. 919.*
Parma, Biblioteca Palatina, Parm. 2473 (De Rossi 428).
Parma, Biblioteca Palatina, Parm. 2286 (De Rossi 861).
Rome, Biblioteca Casanatense, Roma Cas. 2847.
Vatican City, Biblioteca Apostolica Vaticana, Barb. Or. 82.
Vatican City, Biblioteca Apostolica Vaticana, Vat. ebr. 105.
Vatican City, Biblioteca Apostolica Vaticana, Vat. ebr. 171.
Vatican City, Biblioteca Apostolica Vaticana, Vat. ebr. 187.
Vatican City, Biblioteca Apostolica Vaticana, Vat. ebr. 225, fols. 4–139.
Vatican City, Biblioteca Apostolica Vaticana, Vat. ebr. 247.
Vatican City, Biblioteca Apostolica Vaticana, Vat. ebr. 249.
Vatican City, Biblioteca Apostolica Vaticana, Vat. ebr. 254.
Vatican City, Biblioteca Apostolica Vaticana, Vat. ebr. 257.
Vatican City, Biblioteca Apostolica Vaticana, Vat. ebr. 345.

EDITED PRIMARY SOURCES

Allony, Nehemya. "Derekh la'asot haruzim le-David ibn Bilia" [The Way to Make Rhymes
by David ibn Bilia]. *Kovets 'al Yad* 6 (1966): 225–46.

Artom, Elias, and Umberto Cassuto. *Taqqanot Qandiya u'Zikhronoteha (Statuta Iudaeorum Candiae eorumque Memorabilia)*. Jerusalem: Mekize Nirdamim, 1943.

Beugnot, A. A., ed. *Recueil des historiens des croisades: Lois, vol. II*. Paris: Imprimerie Royale, 1843.

Boccaccio, Giovanni. *The Decameron*. Translated by G. H. McWilliam. New York: Penguin Books, 1995 [1972].

Capsali, Eliyahu. *Seder Eliyahu Zuta*. Edited by Aryeh Shmuelevitz, Shlomo Simonsohn, and Meir Benayahu. 3 vols. Jerusalem: Ben Zvi Institute, 1975–77.

Carbone, Salvatore, ed. *Pietro Pizolo notaio in Candia*. 2 vols. Venice: Il Comitato, 1978–85.

Chiaudano, Mario, and Antonino Lombardo, eds. *Leonardo Marcello, notaio in Candia, 1278–1281*. Venice: Il Comitato, 1960.

Contarini, Gasparo. *The Commonwealth and the Government in Venice*. Translated by Lewes Lewkenor. London: Iohn Windet for Edmund Mattes, 1599.

Delmedigo, Joseph Solomon. *Sefer Elim*. Edited by Moses Metz. Amsterdam: N.p, 1629.

Gasparis, Charalampos, ed. *Franciscus de Cruce: Notarios ston Chandaka, 1338–1339*. Venice: Hellenic Institute for Byzantine and Post-Byzantine Studies, 1999.

Graziato, Gisella, ed. *La promissioni del doge di Venezia dale origini alla fine del Duecento*. Venice: Il Comitato, 1986.

Joseph HaKohen. *Sefer Emeq Ha-bakha (The Vale of Tears), with the Chronicle of the Anonymous Corrector*. Edited by Karin Almbladh. Uppsala: Uppsala University, 1981.

Laurentius de Monacis. *Chronicon de rebus Venetis ab urbe condita ad annum MCCCCIV*. Venice: Ex typographia Redmondiniana, 1758.

Lombardo, Antonino, ed. *Imbreviature di Pietro Scardon*. Turin: Editrice libraria italiana, 1942.

———. *Zaccaria de Fredo, notaio in Candia (1352–1357)*. Venice: Il Comitato, 1968.

McKee, Sally. *Wills from Late Medieval Venetian Crete, 1312–1420*. 3 vols. Washington, DC: Dumbarton Oaks, 1998.

Meshullam of Volterra. *Masah Meshullam mi-Volterah be-Eretz Yisrael be-shnat 241 (1481)* [The Journey of Meshullam of Volterra in the Land of Israel in the Year 241 (1481)]. Edited by Avraham Yaari. Jerusalem: Mosad Bialik, 1948.

Morozzo della Rocca, Raimondo, and Antonino Lombardo, eds. *Documenti del commercio veneziano nei secoli XI–XIII*. 2 vols. Rome: Sede dell'Istituto, 1940.

Nissim b. Reuben Gerondi. *Teshuvot ha-Ran: Responsa of R. Nissim b. Reuben Gerondi*. Vol. 2. Edited by Leon A. Feldman. Jerusalem: Shalem Institute, 1984.

Noiret, Hippolyte, ed. *Documents inédits pour servir à l'histoire de la domination vénetienne en Crète de 1380 à 1485*. Paris: Thorin & fils, 1892.

Obadiah of Bertinoro. *Me-Italyah li-Yerushalayim: Igrotav shel R. Ovadyah mi-Bartenura me-Eretz Yisrael* [From Italy to Jerusalem: The Letters of Rabbi Obadiah of Bertinoro from the Land of Israel]. Edited by M. E. Artom and Abraham David. Ramat Gan: Bar Ilan University Press, 1997 [1988].

Pettenello, Gaetano, and Simone Rauch, eds. *Stefano Bono, notaio in Candia, 1303–1304*. Rome: Viella, 2011.

Solomon ibn Adret. *Responsa*. Vol. 2. Bnei Brak: Sifriyati, 1981.

———. *Sifre Ha-Rashba*. Edited by Menahem Getz. Jerusalem: Oraita, 1986.

Stahl, Alan M., ed. *The Documents of Angelo de Cartura and Donato Fontanella: Venetian Notaries in Fourteenth-Century Crete*. Washington, DC: Dumbarton Oaks, 2000.

Theotokés, Spyridonos. *Thespismata tes Venetikes gerousias, 1281–1385*. 2 vols. Athens: Grapheion Demosieumaton Akademias Athenon, 1936–37.

Thiriet, Freddy. *Régestes des deliberations du Sénat de Venise concernant la Romanie*. 3 vols. Paris: Mouton & Co., 1958–61.

Thomas, Georg Martin. *Commission des Dogen Andreas Dandolo für die Insel Creta vom Jahre 1350*. Munich: Verlag der K. Academie, 1877.

Vidulich, Paola Ratti, ed. *Duca di Candia: Bandi (1319–1329)*. Venice: Il Comitato, 1965.

SECONDARY SOURCES

Adelman, Howard Tzvi. "Jewish Women and Family Life, Inside and Outside the Ghetto." In *The Jews of Early Modern Venice*, edited by Robert C. David and Benjamin Ravid, 143– 65. Baltimore: Johns Hopkins University Press, 2001.

———. "Law and Love: The Jewish Family in Early Modern Italy." *Continuity and Change* 16 (2001): 283–303.

Agus, Irving. *Rabbi Meir of Rothenberg*. 2nd ed. New York: Ktav, 1970.

Altschul, Nadia. "Postcolonialism and the Study of the Middle Ages." *History Compass* 6 (2008): 588–606.

Ando, Clifford. *Imperial Ideology and Provincial Loyalty in the Roman Empire*. Berkeley: University of California Press, 2000.

Angold, Michael. *The Fall of Constantinople to the Ottomans: Context and Consequences*. London: Routledge, 2014.

Ankori, Zvi. "From Zudecha to Yahudi Mahallesi: The Jewish Quarter of Candia in the Seventeenth Century." In *Salo Wittmeyer Baron Jubilee Volume*, vol. 1, edited by Saul Lieberman and Arthur Hyman, 63–127. Jerusalem and New York: American Academy for Jewish Research and Columbia University Press, 1974.

———. "Giacomo Foscarini and the Jews of Crete: A Reconsideration." *Michael: On the History of the Jews in the Diaspora* 7 (1981): 9–118.

———. "Jews and the Jewish Community in the History of Mediaeval Crete." In *Proceedings of the Second International Congress of Cretological Studies*, 3:312–67. Athens: N.p., 1968.

———. "The Living and the Dead: The Story of Hebrew Inscriptions in Crete." *Proceedings of the American Academy for Jewish Research* 38 (1970–71): 1–100.

Apellániz, Francesco. "Collaboration des réseaux marchands à Alexandrie (XIVᵉ–XVᵉ siècles)." In *From Florence to the Mediterranean and Beyond: Studies in Honor of Anthony Molho*, edited by Diogo Ramada Curto, Eric Dursteler, Julius Kirshner, and Francesca Trivellato, 2:581–601. Florence: L. S. Olschki, 2009.

————. "Venetian Trading Networks in the Medieval Mediterranean." *Journal of Interdisciplinary History* 44 (2013): 157–79.

Arbel, Benjamin. "Colonie d'oltremare." In *Storia di Venezia dalle origini alla caduta della Serenissima*. Vol. 5, *Il Rinascimento: Società ed economia*, edited by Alberto Tenenti and Ugo Tucci, 947–85. Rome: Instituto della encyclopedia italiana, 1996.

————. "The 'Jewish Wine' of Crete." In *Μονεμβάσιος Οίνος, Μονοβας(ι)ά—Malvasia*, edited by Elias Anagnostakes, 81–88. Athens: National Hellenic Research Foundation, 2008.

————. "Jews and Christians in Sixteenth-Century Crete: Between Segregation and Integration." In *"Interstizi": Culture ebraico-cristiane a Venezia e nei suoi domini dal Medioevo all'Età Moderna*, edited by Uwe Israel, Robert Jütte, and Reinhold C. Mueller, 281–94. Rome: Edizioni di Storia e Letteratura, 2010.

————. "The Last Decades of Mamluk Trade with Venice." *Mamluk Studies Review* 8 (2004): 37–86.

————. "Maritime Trade in Famagusta During the Venetian Period (1474–1571)." In *The Harbour to All This Sea and Realm: Crusader to Venetian Famagusta*, edited by Michael J. K. Walsh, Tamas Kiss, and Nicholas Coureas, 91–103. Budapest: Central European University, 2014.

————. *Trading Nations: Jews and Venetians in the Early-Modern Eastern Mediterranean*. Leiden: Brill, 1995.

————. "Traffici marittimi e sviluppo urbano a Cipro (secoli XIII–XVI)" [Maritime Traffic and Urban Development in Cyprus (13th–16th Centuries)]. In *Città portuali del Mediterraneo*, edited by Ennio Poleggi, 89–94. Genoa: SAGEP Editrice, 1989.

Arbel, Benjamin, Bernard Hamilton, and David Jacoby, eds. *Latins and Greeks in the Eastern Mediterranean After 1204*. London: Frank Cass, 1989.

Ascheri, Mario. *The Laws of Late Medieval Italy (1000–1500)*. Leiden: Brill, 2013.

Ascheri, Michel. "'*Concilium sapientis*' perizia medica e '*res judicata*': Diritto dei '*dottori*' e istituzione comunale." In *Proceedings of the Fifth International Congress of Medieval Canon Law*, edited by Stephen Kuttner and Kenneth Pennington, 533–79. Vatican City: Biblioteca apostolica vaticana, 1980.

Ashtor, Eliyahu. "Ebrei cittadini di Venezia?" *Studi Veneziani* 17–18 (1975–76): 145–56.

————. "Gli inizi della comunità ebraica a Venezia." *La rassegna mensile di Israel* 44 (1978): 683–703. Reprinted in Eliyahu Ashtor, *The Jews and the Mediterranean Economy, 10th–15th Centuries*. London: Variorum Reprints, 1983, article IV.

————. "New Data for the History of Levantine Jewries in the Fifteenth Century." *Bulletin of the Institute of Jewish Studies* 3 (1975): 67–102.

————. "Prolegomena to the Medieval History of Oriental Jewry." *Jewish Quarterly Review* 50 (1959): 55–56, 147–66.

Assis, Yom Tov. *The Golden Age of Aragonese Jewry: Community and Society in the Crown of Aragon, 1213–1327*. London: Littman Library of Jewish Civilization, 1997.

————. "'Herem de-rabbeinu Gershom' ve-nisuei kefel be-Sepharad" ["The Excommunication of Rabbeinu Gershom" and Bigamous Marriage in Spain]. *Zion* 46 (1981): 251–77.

———. *Jewish Economy in the Medieval Crown of Aragon, 1213–1327: Money and Power*. Leiden: Brill, 1997.

———. "Yehudei Sepharad be-arkhaot ha-goyim (ha-mayot ha-13 ve-ha-14)" [Spanish Jews in Gentile Courts (Thirteenth and Fourteenth Centuries)]. In *Tarbut ve-hevra be-toldot Yisrael be-yemei ha-beinayim* [Culture and Society in Jewish History in the Middle Ages], edited by Robert Bonfil, Menachem Ben-Sasson, and Joseph Hakar, 390–430. Jerusalem: Zalman Shazar Center, 1989.

Astarita, Tommaso. *Village Justice: Community, Family, and Popular Culture in Early Modern Italy*. Baltimore: Johns Hopkins University Press, 1999.

Baer, Fritz (Yitzhak). *Die Juden im christlichen Spanien*. 2 vols. Berlin: Akademie-Verlag, 1929–36. English translation: *The History of the Jews in Christian Spain*. Translated by Louis Schoffman. Philadelphia: Jewish Publication Society, 1961–66.

Baron, Salo W. *The Jewish Community, Its History and Structure to the American Revolution*. Philadelphia: Jewish Publication Society, 1948.

———. *A Social and Religious History of the Jews*. Vol. 17, *Byzantines, Mamluks, and Maghribians*. New York: Columbia University Press, 1980.

Baroutsos, Photis. "Venetian Pragmatism and Jewish Subjects (Fifteenth and Sixteenth Centuries)." *Mediterranean Historical Review* 27 (2012): 227–40.

Barzilay, Isaac. *Yoseph Shlomo Delmedigo (Yashar of Candia)*. Leiden: Brill, 1974.

Baskin, Judith. "Medieval Jewish Models of Marriage." In *The Medieval Marriage Scene: Prudence, Passion, Policy*, edited by Sherry Roush and Cristelle L. Baskins, 1–22. Tempe: Arizona Center for Medieval and Renaissance Studies, 2005.

Baumgarten, Elisheva. *Mothers and Children: Jewish Family Life in Medieval Europe*. Princeton, NJ: Princeton University Press, 2004.

Bell, Dean P. "Jews, Ethnicity, and Identity in Early Modern Hamburg." *TRANSIT* 3 (2007): 1–16.

Bellomo, Manlio. *The Common Legal Past of Europe, 1000–1800*. Translated by Lydia G. Cochran. Washington, DC: Catholic University of America Press, 1995.

Benayahu, Meir. *Rabi Eliyahu Kapsali, ish Kandiya: Rav, manhig, ve-historiyon* [Rabbi Elijah Capsali of Candia: Rabbi, Leader, and Historian]. Tel Aviv: Center for Diaspora Studies of Tel Aviv University, 1983.

Benbassa, Esther, and Aron Rodrigue. *Sephardi Jewry: A History of the Judeo-Spanish Community, 14th–20th Centuries*. Berkeley: University of California Press, 1999.

Benton, Lauren A. *Law and Colonial Cultures: Legal Regimes in World History, 1400–1900*. Cambridge: Cambridge University Press, 2002.

Berger, Michael S. "Two Models of Medieval Jewish Marriage: A Preliminary Study." *Journal of Jewish Studies* 52 (2001): 59–84.

Betts, Raymond. *Assimilation and Association in French Colonial Theory, 1890–1914*. New York: Columbia University Press, 1960.

Biale, David, ed. *Cultures of the Jews*. Vol. 2, *Diversities of Diaspora*. New York: Schocken Books, 2006.

———. *Power and Powerlessness in Jewish History*. New York: Schocken Books, 1986.

Blidstein, Gerald J. "Individual and Community in the Middle Ages: Halakhic Theory." In *Kinship and Consent: The Jewish Political Tradition and Its Contemporary Uses*, 2nd ed., edited by Daniel J. Elazar, 327–70. New Brunswick, NJ: Transaction Publishers, 1997.

Bodian, Miriam. *Hebrews of the Portuguese Nation: Conversos and Community in Early Modern Amsterdam*. Bloomington: Indiana University Press, 1997.

Bonfil, Robert. "A Cultural Profile." In *The Jews of Early Modern Venice*, edited by Robert C. Davis and Benjamin Ravid, 169–90. Baltimore: Johns Hopkins University Press, 2001.

———. "Jewish Attitudes Toward History and Historical Writing in Pre-Modern Times." *Jewish History* 11 (1997): 7–40.

———. *Jewish Life in Renaissance Italy*. Translated by Anthony Oldcorn. Berkeley: University of California Press, 1994.

———. *Rabbis and Jewish Communities in Renaissance Italy*. Oxford: Littman Library, 1990.

Borsari, Silvano. *Il dominio veneziano a Creta nel XIII secolo*. Naples: F. Fiorentino, 1963.

———. "Ricchi e poveri nelle comunità ebraiche di Candia e Negroponte (secc. XIII–XVI)." In *Ricchi e poveri nella società dell'oriente grecolatino*, edited by Chryssa Maltezou, 211–22. Venice: Hellenic Institute of Byzantine and Post-Byzantine Studies, 1998.

Borýsek, Martin. "The Jews of Venetian Candia: The Challenges of External Influences and Internal Diversity as Reflected in Takkanot Kandiyah." *Al-Masaq* 26 (2014): 241–66.

Bourbou, Chryssi. *Health and Disease in Byzantine Crete (7th–12th Centuries AD)*. Farnham: Ashgate, 2010.

Brand, Paul, ed. *Plea Rolls of the Exchequer of the Jews*. London: Jewish Historical Society of England, 2005.

Brown, Horatio Forbes. *Studies in the History of Venice*. Vol. 1. New York: E. P. Dutton, 1907.

Brucker, Gene. *Giovanni and Lusanna: Love and Marriage in Renaissance Florence*. Berkeley: University of California Press, 1986.

Brundage, James A. *Law, Sex, and Christian Society in Medieval Europe*. Chicago: University of Chicago Press, 1987.

Burmeister, Karl Heinz. *Der Schwarze Tod: Die Judenverfolgungen anlässlich der Pest von 1348/49*. Göppingen: Jüdisches Museum, 1999.

Burns, R. I. *Medieval Colonialism: Postcrusade Exploitation of Islam Valencia*. Princeton, NJ: Princeton University Press, 1975.

Burrows, Mathew. "'Mission civilisatrice': French Cultural Policy in the Middle East, 1860–1914." *Historical Journal* 29 (1986): 109–35.

Bury, John B. "The Lombards and Venetians in Euboia (1205–1303)." *Journal of Hellenic Studies* 7 (1886): 309–52.

———. "The Lombards and Venetians in Euboia (continued)." *Journal of Hellenic Studies* 8 (1887): 194–213.

———. "The Lombards and Venetians in Euboia (1340–1470)." *Journal of Hellenic Studies* 9 (1888): 91–117.

Carmoly, Eliakim. *Histoire des médecins juifs ancien et modernes.* Vol. 1. Brussels: Imprimerie de H. Bourland, 1844.

Carpi, Daniel, ed. *Pinkas va'ad kahal kadosh Padovah* [Minutes Book of the Council of the Jewish Community of Padua, 1577–1630]. Jerusalem: Israel National Academy of Sciences and Humanities, 1973.

Carr, E. H. *What Is History?* New York: Vintage Books, 1961.

Cassuto, Umberto. *I manoscritti palatini ebraici della Biblioteca apostolic vaticana e la loro storia.* Vatican City: Biblioteca apostolica vaticana, 1935.

Chazan, Robert. *Medieval Stereotypes and Modern Antisemitism.* Berkeley: University of California Press, 1997.

Chojnacki, Stanley. "Crime, Punishment, and the Trecento Venetian State." In *Violence and Civil Disorder in Italian Cities, 1200–1500,* edited by Lauro Martines, 184–228. Berkeley: University of California Press, 1972.

Christ, Georg. *Trading Conflicts: Venetian Merchants and Mamluk Officials in Late Medieval Alexandria.* Leiden: Brill, 2012.

Clark, Patricia Ann. *A Cretan Healer's Handbook in the Byzantine Tradition: Text, Translation and Commentary.* Farnham: Ashgate, 2011.

Cohen, Jeremy. "The Jews as the Killers of Christ in the Latin Tradition: From Augustine to the Friars." *Traditio* 39 (1983): 1–27.

Cohen, Mark. *Under Crescent and Cross: The Jews in the Middle Ages.* 2nd ed. Princeton, NJ: Princeton University Press, 2008.

Cohn, Samuel K., Jr. "The Black Death and the Burning of Jews." *Past and Present* 196 (2007): 3–36.

Colorni, Vittore. *Legge ebraica e leggi locali.* Milan: Giuffrè, 1945.

Comaroff, John L., and Jean Comaroff. *Ethnography and the Historical Imagination.* Boulder, CO: Westview Press, 1992.

Conklin, Alice L. *A Mission to Civilize: The Republican Idea of Empire in France and West Africa, 1895–1930.* Stanford, CA: Stanford University Press, 1997.

Cooper, Frederick. *Colonialism in Question: Theory, Knowledge, History.* Berkeley: University of California Press, 2005.

Court, Ricardo. "*Januensis ergo mercator:* Trust and Enforcement in the Business Correspondence of the Brignole Family." *Sixteenth Century Journal* 35 (2004): 987–1003.

Courtemanche, Andrée. "The Judge, the Doctor, and the Poisoner: Medieval Expertise in Manosquin Judicial Rituals at the End of the Fourteenth Century." In *Medieval and Early Modern Ritual: Formalized Behavior in Europe, China, and Japan,* edited by Joëlle Rollo-Koster, 105–23. Leiden: Brill, 2002.

Cozzi, Gaetano. "Authority and Law in Renaissance Venice." In *Renaissance Venice,* edited by J. R. Hale, 293–345. London: Faber and Faber, 1974.

———. "La politica del diritto nella repubblica di Venezia." In *Stato, società e giustizia: Nella repubblica veneta (sec. XV–XVIII),* edited by Gaetano Cozzi, 15–152. Rome: Jouvence, 1980.

Crouzet-Pavan, Elisabeth. *Venice Triumphant: The Horizons of a Myth*. Translated by Lydia G. Cochrane. Baltimore: Johns Hopkins University Press, 2002.

Davies, Wendy, and Paul Fouracre, eds. *The Settlement of Disputes in Early Medieval Europe*. Cambridge: Cambridge University Press, 1986.

Davis, Natalie Zemon. *Fiction in the Archives: Pardon Tales and Their Tellers in Sixteenth-Century France*. Stanford, CA: Stanford University Press, 1987.

Davis, Robert C., and Benjamin Ravid, eds. *The Jews of Early Modern Venice*. Baltimore: Johns Hopkins University Press, 2001.

De Lange, Nicholas, ed. *Greek Jewish Texts from the Cairo Genizah*. Tübingen: Mohr-Siebeck, 1996.

Debby, Nurit Ben-Aryeh. "Jews and Judaism in the Rhetoric of Popular Preachers: The Florentine Sermons of Giovanni Dominici (1356–1419) and Bernardino da Siena (1380–1444)." *Jewish History* 14 (2000): 175–200.

Detorakis, Theocaris E. *History of Crete*. Translated by John C. David. Iraklion, Crete: N.p., 1994.

Dietler, Michael. *Archaeologies of Colonialism: Consumption, Entanglement, and Violence in Ancient Mediterranean France*. Berkeley: University of California Press, 2010.

Dillard, Heath. *Daughters of the Reconquest: Women in Castillian Town Society, 1100–1300*. Cambridge: Cambridge University Press, 1990.

Donahue, Charles, Jr. *Law, Marriage, and Society in the Later Middle Ages*. Cambridge: Cambridge University Press, 2007.

Dorff, Elliot N., and Arthur I. Rosett. *A Living Tree: The Roots and Growth of Jewish Law*. Albany: SUNY Press, 1988.

Drandraki, Anastasia. *The Origins of El Greco: Icon Painting in Venetian Crete*. New York: Onassis Foundation, 2009.

Dubin, Lois. "Jewish Women, Marriage Law, and Emancipation: A Civil Divorce in Late-Eighteenth-Century Trieste." *Jewish Social Studies*, n.s. 13 (2007): 65–92.

Duby, George. *Le chevalier, la femme, et le prêtre: La mariage dans la France féodale*. Paris: Hachette littérature générale, 1981. English translation: *The Knight, the Lady, and the Priest: The Making of Modern Marriage in Medieval France*. Translated by Barbara Bray. New York: Pantheon Books, 1983.

Elazar, Daniel J. "The Kehillah." In *Kinship and Consent: The Jewish Political Tradition and Its Contemporary Uses*, 2nd ed., edited by Daniel J. Elazar, 233–76. New Brunswick, NJ: Transaction Publishers, 1997.

Elukin, Jonathan. *Living Together, Living Apart: Rethinking Jewish-Christian Relations in the Middle Ages*. Princeton, NJ: Princeton University Press, 2007.

Engel, Michael. *Elijah Del Medigo and Paduan Aristotelianism: Investigating the Human Intellect*. London: Bloomsbury, 2017.

Falk, Ze'ev W. "Jewish Law and Medieval Canon Law." In *Jewish Law in Legal History and the Modern World*, edited by Bernard S. Jackson, 78–96. Leiden: Brill, 1980.

Fenster, Thelma, and Daniel Lord Smail, eds. *Fama: The Politics of Talk and Reputation in Medieval Europe*. Ithaca, NY: Cornell University Press, 2003.

Ferraro, Joanne M. *Marriage Wars in Late Renaissance Venice.* Oxford: Oxford University Press, 2001.

Finkelstein, Louis. *Jewish Self-Government in the Middle Ages.* New York: Jewish Theological Seminary, 1924.

Finlay, Robert. "The Foundation of the Ghetto: Venice, the Jews, and the War of the League of Cambrai." *Proceedings of the American Philosophical Society* 126 (1982): 140–54.

Foa, Anna. *The Jews of Europe After the Black Death.* Translated by A. Grover. Berkeley: University of California Press, 2000.

Forster, Ellinor. "Between Law, Gender and Confession: Jewish Matrimonial Law Provisions Against the Background of Catholic and Protestant Regulations in Austria, 18th- and 19th-Centuries." In *Gender Difference in European Legal Cultures: Historical Perspectives*, edited by Karin Gottschalk, 95–104. Stuttgart: Franz Steiner Verlag, 2013.

Freidenreich, David M. *Foreigners and Their Food: Constructing Otherness in Jewish, Christian, and Islamic Law.* Berkeley: University of California Press, 2011.

Friedman, M. A. *Ribui nashim be-Yisrael: Mekorot hadashim me-genizat Kahir* [Jewish Polygyny: New Sources from the Cairo Genizah]. Jerusalem: Bialik Institute, 1986.

Funkenstein, Amos. *Perceptions of Jewish History.* Berkeley: University of California Press, 1993.

Gallina, Mario. *Una società coloniale del Trecento: Creta fra Venezia e Bisanzio.* Venice: Deputazione di storia patria per le Venezie, 1989.

Geertz, Clifford. "Thick Description: Toward an Interpretive Theory of Culture." In *The Interpretation of Cultures*, 3–20. New York: Basic Books, 1973.

Geiger, Abraham. *Kevutsat ma'amarim.* Edited by Samuel Abraham Poznanski. Warsaw: Tushiyah, 1910.

Georgopoulou, Maria. "Mapping Religious and Ethnic Identities in the Venetian Colonial Empire." *Journal of Medieval and Early Modern Studies* 26 (1996): 467–96.

———. "The Meaning of the Architecture and the Urban Layout of Venetian Candia: Cultural Conflict and Interaction in the Late Middle Ages." PhD diss., UCLA, 1992.

———. *Venice's Mediterranean Colonies: Architecture and Urbanism.* Cambridge: Cambridge University Press, 2001.

Gerland, Ernst. *Das Archiv des Herzogs vom Kandia im K. Staatsarchiv zu Venedig.* Strassburg: Karl J. Trubner, 1899.

Gertwagen, Ruthi. "Geniza Letters: Maritime Difficulties Along the Alexandria-Palermo Route." In *Communication in the Jewish Diaspora: The Premodern World*, edited by Sophia Menache, 73–91. Leiden: Brill, 1996.

Gil, Moshe. *A History of Palestine, 634–1099.* Cambridge: Cambridge University Press, 1992.

Goitein, S. D. *A Mediterranean Society: The Jewish Communities of the Arab World as Portrayed in the Documents of the Cairo Geniza.* 6 vols. Berkeley: University of California Press, 1967–93.

Graus, František. *Pest-Geissler-Judenmorde: Das 14. Jahrhundert als Krisenzeit.* Göttingen: Vandenhoeck und Ruprecht, 1987.

Green, Monica H. "Conversing with the Minority: Relations Among Christian, Muslim, and Jewish Women in the High Middle Ages." *Journal of Medieval History* 34 (2008): 105– 18.

Greenblatt, Rachel. *To Tell Their Children: Jewish Communal Memory in Early Modern Prague*. Stanford, CA: Stanford University Press, 2014.

Greene, Molly. *A Shared World: Christians and Muslims in the Early Modern Mediterranean*. Princeton, NJ: Princeton University Press, 2000.

Grossman, Avraham. *Pious and Rebellious: Jewish Women in Medieval Europe*. Translated by Jonathan Chipman. Waltham, MA: Brandeis University Press, 2004.

Guggenheim, Yacov. "Jewish Community and Territorial Organization in Medieval Europe." In *The Jews of Europe in the Middle Ages (Tenth to Fifteenth Centuries)*, edited by Christoph Cluse, 71–91. Turnhout: Brepols, 2004.

Guzzetti, Linda. "Women in Court in 14th-Century Venice: The Meaning of 'Equality' and 'Rationality' in Written Law and in Court." In *Gender Difference in European Legal Culture: Historical Perspectives,* edited by Karin Gottschalk, 43–56. Stuttgart: Franz Steiner Verlag, 2013.

Hacohen, Aviad. *The Tears of the Oppressed: An Examination of the Agunah Problem: Background and Halakhic Sources*. Jersey City: Ktav Publishing, 2004.

Hames, Harvey J. "Elia del Medigo: An Archetype of the Halachic Man." *Traditio* 56 (2001): 213–27. Reprinted as "Elijah Delmedigo: An Archetype of the Halakhic Man?" in *Cultural Intermediaries: Jewish Intellectuals in Early Modern Italy*, edited by David B. Ruderman and Giuseppe Veltri, 39–54. Philadelphia: University of Pennsylvania Press, 2004.

Haverkamp, Alfred. "Jews and Urban Life: Bonds and Relationships." In *The Jews of Europe in the Middle Ages*, edited by Christoph Cluse, 55–67. Turnhout: Brepols, 2004.

———. "Die Judenverfolgungen zur Zeit des Schwarzen Todes im Gesellschaftsgefüge deutscher Städte." In *Zur Geschichte der Juden im Deutschland des späten Mittelalters und der frühen Neuzeit*, edited by Alfred Haverkamp, 27–93. Stuttgart: A. Hiersemann, 1981.

Hazlitt, William Carew. *The Venetian Republic: Its Rise, Its Growth, and Its Fall, 421–1797*. Vol. 2. London: Adam and Charles Black, 1900.

Herzfeld, Michael. *Cultural Intimacy: Social Poetics in the Nation-State*. New York: Routledge, 2004.

Hillaby, Joe, and Caroline Hillaby, eds. *The Palgrave Dictionary of Medieval Anglo-Jewish History*. Houndmills: Palgrave Macmillan, 2013.

Holton, David, ed. *Literature and Society in Renaissance Crete*. Cambridge: Cambridge University Press, 1991.

Horowitz, Elliott S. "Families and Their Fortunes: The Jews of Early Modern Italy." In *Cultures of the Jews*. Vol. 2, *Diversities of Diaspora*, edited by David Biale, 271–336. New York: Schocken Books, 2002.

———. " 'Hachnasat Kallah' in the Venetian Ghetto: Between Tradition and Innovation, and Between Ideal and Reality." *Tarbiz* 56 (1987): 347–72.

————. *Reckless Rites: Purim and the Legacy of Jewish Violence.* Princeton, NJ: Princeton University Press, 2006.

Hughes, Diane Owen. "Toward Historical Ethnography: The Notarial Records and Family History in the Middle Ages." *Historical Methods Newsletter* 7 (1974): 61–71.

Humphrey, Judith. "The Sinking of the 'Danae' off Crete in June 1944." *Bulletin of Judaeo-Greek Studies* 9 (1991): 19–34.

Hyams, Paul R. *Rancor and Reconciliation in Medieval England.* Ithaca, NY: Cornell University Press, 2003.

Innes, Matthew. "Charlemagne's Government." In *Charlemagne: Empire and Society*, edited by Joanna Story, 71–89. Manchester: Manchester University Press, 2005.

Jacobs, Martin. "Exposed to All the Currents of the Mediterranean: A Sixteenth-Century Venetian Rabbi on Muslim History." *AJS Review* 29 (2005): 33–60.

————. "Joseph Ha-Kohen, Paolo Giovio, and Sixteenth-Century Historiography." In *Cultural Intermediaries: Jewish Intellectuals in Early Modern Italy*, edited by David B. Ruderman and Giuseppe Veltri, 67–85. Philadelphia: University of Pennsylvania Press, 2004.

Jacoby, David. "Un agent juif au service de Venise: David Mavrogonato de Candie." *Thesaurismata* 9 (1972): 68–96. Reprinted in Jacoby, *Recherches sur la Méditerranée orientale*, no. XI.

————. "Byzantine Crete in the Navigation and Trade Networks of Venice and Genoa." In *Oriente e Occidente tra medioevo ed età moderna: Studi in onore di Geo Pistarino*, edited by Laura Balletto, 517–40. Genoa: G. Brigati, 1997. Reprinted in Jacoby, *Byzantium, Latin Romania, and the Mediterranean*, no. II.

————. *Byzantium, Latin Romania, and the Mediterranean.* Aldershot: Ashgate, 2001.

————. "Candia Between Venice, Byzantium, and the Levant: The Rise of a Major Emporium to the Mid-Fifteenth Century." In *The Hand of Angelos: An Icon Painter in Venetian Crete*, edited by Maria Vassilaki, 38–47. Farnham, Surrey: Lund Humphries, 2010.

————. *Commercial Exchange Across the Mediterranean: Byzantium, the Crusader Levant, Egypt, and Italy.* Aldershot: Ashgate/Variorum, 2005.

————. "Creta e Venezia nel contesto economico del Mediterraneo orientale sino alla metà del Quattrocento." In *Venezia e Creta: Atti del convegno internazionale di studi Iraklion-Chanià, 30 settembre–5 ottobre 1997*, edited by Gherardo Ortalli, 73–106. Venice: Istituto veneto di scienze, lettere ed arti, 1998. Reprinted in Jacoby, *Commercial Exchange Across the Mediterranean*, no. VII.

————. "Cretan Cheese: A Neglected Aspect of Venetian Medieval Trade." In *Medieval and Renaissance Venice*, edited by Ellen E. Kittell and Thomas F. Madden, 49–68. Urbana: University of Illinois Press, 1999.

————. "The Demographic Evolution of Euboea Under Latin Rule, 1205–1470." In *The Greek Islands and the Sea*, edited by Julian Chrystomides, Charalambos Dendrinos, and Jonathan Harris, 131–79. Camberley, Surrey: Porphyrogentius, 2004.

————. "The Encounters of Two Societies: Western Conquerors and Byzantines in the Peloponnesus After the Fourth Crusade." *American Historical Review* 78 (1973): 873–906. Reprinted in Jacoby, *Recherches sur la Méditerranée orientale*, no. II.

———. *La féodalité en Grèce médiévale: Les "Assises de Romanie."* Paris: Mouton, 1971.

———. "From Byzantium to Latin Romania: Continuity and Change." *Mediterranean Historical Review* 4 (1989): 1–44. Reprinted in *Latins and Greeks in the Eastern Mediterranean After 1204*, edited by Benjamin Arbel, Bernard Hamilton, and David Jacoby. London: Frank Cass and Co., 1989. Also reprinted in Jacoby, *Byzantium, Latin Romania, and the Mediterranean*, no. VIII.

———. "Greeks in the Maritime Trade of Cyprus Around the Mid-Fourteenth Century." In *Cipro-Venezia: Comuni sorti storiche* (Atti del simposio internazionale, Atene, 1–3 marzo 2001), edited by Chryssa Maltezou, 59–83. Venice: Hellenic Institute, 2002. Reprinted in Jacoby, *Latins, Greeks, and Muslims*, no. XII.

———. "The Jewish Communities of the Byzantine World from the Tenth to the Mid-Fifteenth Century: Some Aspects of Their Evolution." In *Jewish Reception of Greek Bible Versions: Studies in Their Use in Late Antiquity and the Middle Ages*, edited by Nicholas de Lange, Julia G. Krivoruchko, and Cameron Boyd-Taylor, 157–81. Text and Studies in Medieval and Early Modern Judaism 23. Tübingen: Mohr Siebeck, 2009.

———. "Jews and Christians in Venetian Crete: Segregation, Interaction, and Conflict." In *"Interstizi": Culture ebraico-cristiane a Venezia e nei suoi domini dal Medioevo all'Età Moderna*, edited by Uwe Israel, Robert Jutte, and Reinhold Mueller, 243–79. Rome: Edizioni di Storia e Letteratura, 2010.

———. "The Jews in the Byzantine Economy (Seventh to Mid-Fifteenth Century)." In *Jews in Byzantium: Dialectics of Minority and Majority Cultures*, edited by Robert Bonfil, Oded Irshai, Guy G. Stroumsa, and Rina Talgam, 219–55. Leiden: Brill, 2012.

———. "The Jews of Constantinople and Their Demographic Hinterland." In *Constantinople and Its Hinterland: Papers from the Twenty-Seventh Spring Symposium of Byzantine Studies, Oxford, April 1993*, edited by Cyril Mango and Gilbert Dagron, 221–32. Aldershot: Varorium, 1995. Reprinted in Jacoby, *Byzantium, Latin Romania, and the Mediterranean*, no. IV.

———. "Les Juifs à Venise du XIVᵉ au milieu du XVIᵉ siècle." In *Venezia centro di mediazione tra oriente e occidente*, edited by Hans-Georg Beck, Manoussos Manoussacas, and Agostino Pertusi, 1:163–216. Florence: L. S. Olschki, 1977. Reprinted in Jacoby, *Recherches sur la Méditerranée orientale*, no. VI.

———. "Les Juifs de Byzance: Une communauté marginalisée." In *Marginality in Byzantium*, edited by Chryssa A. Maltezou, 103–54. Athens: Goulandri-Horn Foundation, 1993. Reprinted in Jacoby, *Byzantium, Latin Romania, and the Mediterranean*, no. III.

———. "Les Juifs vénitiens de Constantinople et leur communauté du XIIIᵉ au milieu du XVᵉ siècle." *Revue des études juives* 131 (1972): 397–410. Reprinted in Jacoby, *Recherches sur la Méditerranée orientale*, no. XII.

———. *Latins, Greeks, and Muslims: Encounters in the Eastern Mediterranean, 10th–15th Centuries*. Farnham, Surrey: Ashgate, 2009.

———. "Le-Ma'amadam shel ha-yehudim be-moshavot Venetzia biyemei ha-beinayim" [The Status of Jews in the Venetian Settlements During the Middle Ages]. *Zion* 28 (1962): 24–69.

————. "Multilingualism and Institutional Patterns of Communication in Latin Romania (Thirteenth–Fourteenth Centuries)." In *Diplomatics in the Eastern Mediterranean,
1000–1500: Aspects of Cross-Cultural Communication*, edited by Alexander D. Beihammer, Maria G. Parani, and Christopher D. Schabel, 27–48. Leiden: Brill, 2008.

————. "Pèlerinage médiéval et sanctuaires de Terre Sainte: La perspective vénitienne."
Ateneo veneto 173 (1986): 27–58. Reprinted in Jacoby, *Studies on the Crusader States and
on Venetian Expansion*, no. IV.

————. "Les quartiers juifs de Constantinople à l'époque byzantine." *Byzantion* 37 (1967):
167–227. Reprinted in Jacoby, *Société et démographie à Byzance et en Romanie latine*,
no. II.

————. "Quelques aspects de la vie juive en Crète dans la première moitié du XVᵉ siècle." In *Actes du Troisième Congrès international d'*études crétoises (Rethymnon, 1971),
2:108–17. Athens: N.p., 1974. Reprinted in Jacoby, *Recherches sur la Méditerranée orientale*, no. X.

————. *Recherches sur la Méditerranée orientale du XIIᵉ au XVᵉ siècle: Peuples, sociétés, écon-
omies*. London: Variorum Reprints, 1979.

————. "Rofim ve-kirurgim yehudiim be-Kritim tahat shilton Venetzia" [Jewish Doctors and
Surgeons in Crete Under Venetian Rule]. In *Culture and Society in Medieval Jewry: Stud-
ies Dedicated to the Memory of Haim Hillel Ben-Sasson*, edited by Menachem Ben- Sasson,
Robert Bonfil, and Joseph Haker, 431–44. Jerusalem: Zalman Shazar Center, 1989.

————. *Société et démographie à Byzance et en Romanie latine*. London: Variorum, 1975.

————. *Studies on the Crusader States and on Venetian Expansion*. Northampton: Variorum, 1989.

————. "Venice and the Venetian Jews in the Eastern Mediterranean." In *Gli Ebrei e Venezia,
secoli XIV–XVIII*, edited by Gaetano Cozzi, 29–58. Milan: Edizioni Comunità, 1987.
Reprinted in Jacoby, *Studies on the Crusader States and on Venetian Expansion*, no. X.

————. "Venice, the Inquisition and the Jewish Communities of Crete in the Early Fourteenth Century." *Studi veneziani* 12 (1970): 127–44. Reprinted in Jacoby, *Recherches sur
la Méditerranée orientale*, no. IX.

Jegerlehner, Johannes. "Beiträge zur Verwaltungsgeschichte Kandias im XIV. Jahrhunderts." *Byzantinische Zeitschrift* 13 (1904): 435–79.

Jordan, William Chester. *The French Monarchy and the Jews: From Philip Augustus to the Last
Capetians*. Philadelphia: University of Pennsylvania Press, 1989.

————. "Jews on Top: Women and the Availability of Consumption Loans in Northern
France in the Mid-Thirteenth Century." *Journal of Jewish Studies* 29 (1978): 39–56.

Jütte, Daniel. "Interfaith Encounters Between Jews and Christians in the Early Modern
Period and Beyond: Toward a Framework." *American Historical Review* 118 (2013):
378–400.

Kagan, Richard. *Lawsuits and Litigants in Castile, 1500–1700*. Chapel Hill: University of
North Carolina Press, 1981.

Katz, Ethan, Lisa Leff, and Maud Mandel, eds. *Colonialism and the Jews*. Bloomington:
Indiana University Press, 2017.

Katz, Jacob. *Jewish Emancipation and Self-Emancipation.* Philadelphia: Jewish Publication Society, 1986.

———. *Tradition and Crisis: Jewish Society at the End of the Middle Ages.* Translated by Bernard Dov Cooperman. Syracuse, NY: Syracuse University Press, 2000.

Kaufman, David. "Jewish Informers in the Middle Ages." *Jewish Quarterly Review*, o.s. 8 (1896): 217–38.

Kelleher, Marie. "Later Medieval Law in Community Context." In *The Oxford Handbook of Women and Gender in Medieval Europe*, edited by Judith M. Bennett and Ruth Mazo Karras, 133–47. Oxford: Oxford University Press, 2013.

———. *The Measure of Woman: Law and Female Identity in the Crown of Aragon.* Philadelphia: University of Pennsylvania Press, 2010.

King, Margaret L. *Venetian Humanism in an Age of Patrician Dominance.* Princeton, NJ: Princeton University Press, 1986.

Kirshner, Julius. "Materials for a Gilded Cage: Non-Dotal Assets in Florence, 1300–1500." In *The Family in Italy*, edited by David I. Kertzer and Richard P. Saller, 184–207. New Haven, CT: Yale University Press, 1991.

Klein, Birgit. *Wohltat und Hochverrat: Kurfürst Ernst von Köln, Juda bar Chajjim und die Juden im Alten Reich.* Hildesheim: G. Olms, 2003.

Klein, Elka. *Jews, Christian Society, and Royal Power in Medieval Barcelona.* Ann Arbor: University of Michigan Press, 2006.

———. "Public Activities of Catalan Jewish Women." *Medieval Encounters* 12 (2006): 48–61.

———. "Splitting Heirs: Patterns of Inheritance Among Barcelona's Jews." *Jewish History* 16 (2002): 49–71.

———. "The Widow's Portion: Law, Custom and Marital Property Among Medieval Catalan Jews." *Viator* 31 (2000): 147–64.

Kolsky, Elizabeth. *Colonial Justice in British India.* Cambridge: Cambridge University Press, 2010.

Krauss, Samuel. *Studien zur byzantinisch-jüdischen Geschichte.* Vienna: Verlag der Israel-Theol. Lehranstalt, 1914.

Krauss, Simcha. "Litigation in Secular Courts." *Journal of Halacha and Contemporary Society* 2 (1982): 35–53.

Kriegel, Maurice. "Un trait de psychologie sociale: Le Juif comme intouchable." *Annales ESC* 31 (1976): 72–97.

Kuehn, Thomas. "Fama as Legal Status in Renaissance Florence." In *Fama: The Politics of Talk and Reputation in Medieval Europe*, edited by Thelma Fenster and Daniel Lord Smail, 27–46. Ithaca, NY: Cornell University Press, 2003.

———. *Law, Family, and Women: Toward a Legal Anthropology of Renaissance Italy.* Chicago: University of Chicago Press, 1991.

Kupfer, Ephraim. "Le-demut ha-tarbutit shel yahadut Ashkenaz ve-hahameha be-me'ot ha-14-15" [Concerning the Cultural Image of German Jewry and Its Rabbis in the Fourteenth and Fifteenth Centuries]. *Tarbiz* 42 (1972/73): 113–47.

Lahav, Pnina. "Theater in the Courtroom: The Chicago Conspiracy Trial." *Law and Literature* 16 (2004): 381–474.

Laiou, Angeliki. "Venetians and Byzantines: Investigations of Forms of Contact in the Fourteenth Century." *Thesaurismata* 22 (1992): 29–43.

Landman, Leo. *Jewish Law in the Diaspora: Confrontation and Accommodation.* Philadelphia: Dropsie College, 1968.

Lane, Frederic C. *Venice: A Maritime Republic.* Baltimore: Johns Hopkins University Press, 1973.

Lane, Frederic C., and Reinhold C. Mueller. *Money and Banking in Medieval and Renaissance Venice.* Vol. 1. Baltimore: Johns Hopkins University Press, 1985.

Langmuir, Gavin. *Toward a Definition of Antisemitism.* Berkeley: University of California Press, 1990.

Lansing, Carol. "Conflicts over Gender in Civil Courts." In *The Oxford Handbook of Women and Gender in Medieval Europe*, edited by Judith M. Bennett and Ruth Mazo Karras, 118–32. Oxford: Oxford University Press, 2013.

Lauer, Rena. "Cretan Jews and the First Sephardic Encounter in the Fifteenth Century." *Mediterranean Historical Review* 27 (2012): 129–40.

———. "In Defence of Bigamy: Colonial Policy, Jewish Law, and Gender in Venetian Crete." *Gender & History* 29 (2017): 570–88.

———. "Jewish Law and Litigation in the Secular Courts of the Late Medieval Mediterranean." *Critical Analysis of Law* 3 (2016): 114–32.

———. "Jewish Women in Venetian Candia: Negotiating Intercommunal Contact in a Premodern Colonial City, 1300–1500." In *Religious Cohabitation in European Towns (10th–15th Centuries)*, edited by John Tolan and Stéphane Boissellier, 293–309. Turnhout: Brepols, 2015.

Libson, Gideon. *Jewish and Islamic Law: A Comparative Study of Custom During the Geonic Period.* Cambridge, MA: Harvard University Press, 2003.

Linder, Amnon. "The Legal Status of Jews in the Byzantine Empire." In *Jews in Byzantium: Dialectics of Minority and Majority Cultures*, edited by Robert Bonfil, Oded Irshai, Guy S. Stroumsa, and Rina Talgam, 149–218. Leiden: Brill, 2012.

Lorberbaum, Menachem. *Politics and the Limits of Law: Secularizing the Political in Medieval Jewish Thought.* Stanford, CA: Stanford University Press, 2001.

Lourie, Elena. "Mafiosi and Malsines: Violence, Fear, and Faction in the Jewish Aljamas of Valencia in the Fourteenth Century." In *Crusade and Colonisation: Muslims, Christians, and Jews in Medieval Aragon*, 69–102. Hampshire: Variorum, 1990.

Luttrell, A. T. "Venice and the Knights Hospitallers of Rhodes in the Fourteenth Century." *Papers of the British School at Rome* 26 (1958): 195–212.

Madero, Marta. "The Servitude of the Flesh from the Twelfth to the Fourteenth Century." *Critical Analysis of Law* 3 (2016): 133–56.

Malkiel, David. "Renaissance in the Graveyard: The Hebrew Tombstones of Padua and Ashkenazic Acculturation in Sixteenth-Century Italy." *AJS Review* 37 (2013): 333–70.

Malkin, Irad. "Postcolonial Concepts and Ancient Greek Colonization." *Modern Language Quarterly* 65 (2004): 341–64.

Maltezou, Chryssa. "Byzantine 'Consuetudines' in Venetian Crete." *Dumbarton Oaks Papers* 49 (1995): 269–80.

———. "From Crete to Jerusalem: The Will of a Cretan Jew (1626)." *Mediterranean Historical Review* 10 (1995): 189–201.

———. "The Historical and Social Context." In *Literature and Society in Renaissance Crete*, edited by David Holton, 17–47. Cambridge: Cambridge University Press, 1991.

———. "Métiers e salaries en Crète vénitienne (XVe siècle)." *Byzantinische Forschungen* 12 (1987): 321–41.

Marchetto, Giuliano. *Il divorzio imperfetto: I giuristi medievali e la separazione dei coniugi.* Bologna: Il Mulino, 2008.

Marcus, Simon. "Herkev ha-yishuv ha-yehudi ba-'i Kritim biyemei ha-shilton ha-venetsiani" [The Composition of the Jewish Community on the Island of Crete in the Days of Venetian Rule]. *Sinai* 60 (1967/68): 63–76.

Margaritis, Stephen. *Crete and the Ionian Islands Under the Venetians.* Athens: Liontiadis, 1978.

Marx, Alexander. "A Jewish Cause Célèbre in Sixteenth-Century Italy." In *Studies in Jewish History and Booklore*, edited by Alexander Marx, 107–54. New York: JTS, 1944.

McCleery, Iona. "What Is 'Colonial' About Medieval Colonial Medicine? Iberian Health in Global Context." *Journal of Medieval Iberian Studies* 7 (2015): 151–75.

McDougall, Sara. *Bigamy and Christian Identity in Late Medieval Champagne.* Philadelphia: University of Pennsylvania Press, 2012.

McKee, Sally. "Domestic Slavery in Renaissance Italy." *Slavery & Abolition* 29 (2008): 305–26.

———. "Greek Women in Latin Households in Fourteenth-Century Crete." *Journal of Medieval History* 19 (1993): 229–49.

———. *Uncommon Dominion: Venetian Crete and the Myth of Ethnic Purity.* Philadelphia: University of Pennsylvania Press, 2000.

———. "Women Under Venetian Colonial Rule in the Early Renaissance." *Renaissance Quarterly* 51 (1998): 34–67.

Memmi, Albert. *The Colonizer and the Colonized.* Translated by Howard Greenfield. Boston: Beacon, 1965.

Menache, Sophia. "Faith, Myth, and Politics: The Stereotype of the Jews and Their Expulsion from England and France." *Jewish Quarterly Review*, n.s. 73 (1985): 351–74.

Menchi, Silvana Seidel, and Diego Quaglioni, eds. *Coniugi nemici: La separazione in Italia dal XII al XVIII secolo.* Bologna: Il Mulino, 2000.

Meyer, Hannah. "Gender, Jewish Creditors and Christians Debtors in Thirteenth-Century Exeter." In *Intersections of Gender, Religion and Ethnicity in the Middle Ages*, edited by Cordelia Beattie and Kirsten A. Fenton, 104–24. Houndmills: Palgrave Macmillan, 2011.

Migliardi O'Riordan, Giustiniana. "Elementi di diritto bizantino nella consuetudine veneziana dei secoli XI e XII." *Byzantinische Forschungen* 22 (1996): 111–17.

Miret y Sans, Joaquim, and Moïse Schwab. "Documents sur les juifs Catalans aux XIe, XIIe, et XIIIe siècles." *Révue des Études Juives* 68 (1914): 49–83, 174–97.

Molho, Anthony. *Marriage Alliance in Late Medieval Florence*. Cambridge, MA: Harvard University Press, 1994.

Morrison, Robert. "A Scholarly Intermediary Between the Ottoman Empire and Renaissance Europe." *Isis* 105 (2014): 32–57.

Möschter, Angela. *Juden in venezianischen Treviso (1389–1509)*. Hannover: Hahnsche Buchhandlung, 2008.

Mueller, Reinhold. *Immigrazione e cittadinanza nella Venezia medievale*. Rome: Viella, 2010.

———. "The Jewish Moneylenders of Late Trecento Venice: A Revisitation." *Mediterranean Historical Review* 10 (1995): 202–17.

———. "Les prêteurs juifs de Venise au moyen âge." *Annales ESC* 30 (1975): 1277–1302.

———. "The Status and Economic Activity of Jews in the Venetian Dominions During the Fifteenth Century." In *Wirtschaftsgeschichte der mittelalterlichen Juden: Fragen und Einschätzungen*, edited by Michael Toch and Elisabeth Müller-Luckner, 63–92. Munich: R. Oldenbourg, 2008.

Muir, Edward. "The Sources of Civil Society in Italy." *Journal of Interdisciplinary History* 29 (1999): 379–406.

———. "Was There Republicanism in the Renaissance Republics? Venice After Agnadello." In *Venice Reconsidered: The History and Civilization of an Italian City State*, edited by John J. Martin and Dennis Romano, 137–67. Baltimore: Johns Hopkins University Press, 2002.

Nicol, Donald M. *Byzantium and Venice: A Study in Diplomatic and Cultural Relations*. Cambridge: Cambridge University Press, 1998.

Nirenberg, David. *Anti-Judaism: The Western Tradition*. New York: W. W. Norton, 2013.

———. *Communities of Violence: Persecution of Minorities in the Middle Ages*. Princeton, NJ: Princeton University Press, 1996.

———. "Hope's Mistakes." *New Republic*, 13 February 2008.

O'Brien, Darren. *The Pinnacle of Hatred: The Blood Libel and the Jews*. Jerusalem: Magnes Press, 2011.

O'Connell, Monique. *Men of Empire: Power and Negotiation in Venice's Maritime State*. Baltimore: Johns Hopkins University Press, 2009.

Ogren, Brian. *Renaissance and Rebirth: Reincarnation in Early Modern Italian Kabbalah*. Leiden: Brill, 2009.

Ortalli, Edgardo. "La perizia medica a Bologna nei secoli XII e XIV: Normativa e practica di un istituto giudiziario." *Deputazione di storia patria per le provincie di Romagna: Atti e memorie* 17–19 (1969): 223–59.

Papadia-Lala, Anastasia. "The Jews in Early Modern Venetian Crete: Community and Identities." *Mediterranean Historical Review* 27 (2012): 141–50.

Parush, Adi. "The Courtroom as Theater and the Theater as Courtroom in Ancient Athens." *Israel Law Review* 35 (2001): 118–68.

Paudice, Aleida. *Between Several Worlds: The Life and Writings of Elia Capsali*. Munich: M-Press, 2010.

Phillips, Roderick. *Putting Asunder: A History of Divorce in Western Society*. Cambridge: Cambridge University Press, 1988.

Po-chia Hsia, Ronnie. *The Myth of Ritual Murder: Jews and Magic in Reformation Germany*. New Haven, CT: Yale University Press, 1988.

Porges, Nathan. "Elie Capsali et sa Chronique de Venise." *Revue des études juives* 77–79 (1923– 24): 77:20–40, 78:15–34, 79:28–60.

Powell, Eve Troutt. *A Different Shade of Colonialism: Egypt, Great Britain, and the Mastery of the Sudan*. Berkeley: University of California Press, 2003.

Prawer, Joshua. *The Crusaders' Kingdom: European Colonialism in the Middle Ages*. New York: Praeger, 1972.

Rabinowitz, Louis I. *The Herem Hayyishub: A Contribution to the Medieval Economic History of the Jews*. London: Goldston, 1945.

Ravid, Benjamin. "All Ghettos Were Jewish Quarters, but Not All Jewish Quarters Were Ghettos." *Critical Inquiry* 10 (2008): 5–24.

———. "How 'Other' Really Was the Jewish Other? The Evidence from Venice." In *Acculturation and Its Discontents: The Italian Jewish Experience Between Exclusion and Inclusion*, edited by David N. Myers, Massimo Ciavolella, Peter H. Reill, and Geoffrey Simcox, 19–55. Toronto: University of Toronto Press, 2008.

———. "The Legal State of the Jews in Venice to 1509." *Proceedings of the American Academy for Jewish Research* 54 (1987): 169–202.

———. "The Venetian Government and the Jews." In *The Jews of Early Modern Venice*, edited by Robert C. Davis and Benjamin Ravid, 3–30. Baltimore: Johns Hopkins University Press, 2001.

Ravitzky, Aviezer. "The God of the Philosophers Versus the God of the Kabbalists: A Controversy in Fifteenth-Century Crete (Heb MSS Vatican 105 and 254)." In *Studies in Jewish Manuscripts*, edited by Joseph Dan and Klaus Herrmann, 139–70. Tübingen: Mohr Siebeck, 1999.

Ray, Jonathan. *The Sephardic Frontier: The "Reconquista" and the Jewish Community of Medieval Iberia*. Ithaca, NY: Cornell University Press, 2008.

Roberti, Melchiorre. *La magistrature giudiziare veneziane*. Vol. 1. Padua: Tipografia del Seminario, 1907.

Roberts, Simon. "The Study of Dispute: Anthropological Perspectives." In *Disputes and Settlements: Law and Human Relations in the West*, edited by John Bossy, 1–24. Cambridge: Cambridge University Press, 1983.

Robinson, John Harvey. *New History: Essays Illustrating the Modern Historical Outlook*. New York: Macmillan, 1912.

Romano, Dennis. "Equality in Fifteenth-Century Venice." *Studies in Medieval and Renaissance History* 6 (2009): 125–45.

Rosanes, Shlomo. *Divrei yimei Yisrael be-Togarmah* [History of the Jews of the Ottoman Empire]. Tel Aviv: Dvir, 1930.

Rosen, Lawrence. *The Anthropology of Justice: Law as Culture in Islamic Society*. Cambridge: Cambridge University Press, 1989.

Rosensweig, Bernard. *Ashkenazi Jewry in Transition*. Waterloo, Ontario: Wilfrid Laurier University Press, 1975.

Roth, Cecil. "The Qualifications of Jewish Physicians in the Middle Ages." *Speculum* 28 (1953): 834–43.

Rozen, Mina. *The History of the Jewish Community of Istanbul: The Formative Years, 1453–1566*. Leiden: Brill, 2002.

Ruben, Miri. *Gentile Tales: The Narrative Assault on Late Medieval Jews*. Philadelphia: University of Pennsylvania Press, 2004.

Ruggiero, Guido. *The Boundaries of Eros: Sex Crime and Sexuality in Renaissance Venice*. Oxford: Oxford University Press, 1985.

———. "The Cooperation of Physicians and the State in the Control of Violence in Renaissance Venice." *Journal of the History of Medicine and Allied Sciences* 33 (1978): 156–66.

———. *Violence in Early Renaissance Venice*. New Brunswick, NJ: Rutgers University Press, 1980.

Rytina, Steve, and David L. Morgan. "The Arithmetic of Social Relations: The Interplay of Category and Network." *American Journal of Sociology* 88 (1982): 88–113.

Sabar, Shalom. "Childbirth and Magic: Jewish Folklore and Material Culture." In *Cultures of the Jews*. Vol. 2, *Diversities of Diaspora*, edited by David Biale, 369–420. New York: Schocken Books, 2006.

Santschi, Elisabeth. "Affaires pénales en Crète vénetienne (1407–1420)." *Thesaurismata* 13 (1976): 47–80.

———. "Contrats de travail et d'apprentissage en Crète vénitienne au XIVe siècle d'après quelques notaires." *Revue Suisse d'Histoire* 19 (1969): 34–74.

———. "Contribution à l'*étude de la communauté juive en Crète vénitienne au XIVe* siécle, d'après des sources administratives et judiciaires." *Studi Veneziani* 15 (1973): 177–212.

———. "Procès criminels en Crète vénetienne (1354–1389)." *Thesaurismata* 7 (1970): 82–96.

Sassoon, David Solomon, ed. *Ohel Dawid: Descriptive Catalogue of the Hebrew and Samaritan Manuscripts in the Sassoon Library, London*. 2 vols. London: Oxford University Press, 1932.

Schlössinger, Max. "Delmedigo." *Jewish Encyclopedia*, s.v. "Delmedigo." New York: Funk and Wagnalls, 1903.

Scott, James C. *Weapons of the Weak: Everyday Forms of Peasant Resistance*. New Haven, CT: Yale University Press, 1985.

Scott, Joan W. *Gender and the Politics of History*. New York: Columbia University Press, 1988.

Sennett, Richard. *Flesh and Stone: The Body and the City in Western Civilization*. New York: W. W. Norton, 1994.

Shatzmiller, Joseph. "Halikhatam shel yehudim l'arkhaot shel goyim be-Provanz be-yemei ha-beinayim" [Jews Going to Gentile Courts in Provence in the Middle Ages]. In

Divrei ha-kongress ha-olami ha-khamishi l'madaei ha-yahadut [Proceedings of the Fifth World Congress of Jewish Studies], edited by Pinchas Peli and Avigdor Shin'an, 2:375–81. Jerusalem: Ha-Igud ha-'olami le-mada'e ha-Yahadut, 1973.

———. *Jews, Medicine, and Medieval Society.* Berkeley: University of California Press, 1994.

———. *Médecine et justice en Provence Médiévale: Documents de Manosque, 1262–1348.* Aix-en-Provence: Publications de l'Université de Provence, 1989.

———. *Shylock Reconsidered: Jews, Moneylending, and Medieval Society.* Berkeley: University of California Press, 1990.

Shatzmiller, Maya. *Her Day in Court: Women's Property Rights in Fifteenth-Century Granada.* Cambridge, MA: Harvard University Press, 2007.

Shaw, James E. *The Justice of Venice: Authorities and Liberties in the Urban Economy, 1550–1700.* Oxford: Oxford University Press, 2006.

Shmuelevitz, Aryeh. "Capsali as a Source for Ottoman History, 1450–1523." *International Journal of Middle East Studies* 9 (1978): 339–44.

Siegmund, Stefanie B. "Division of the Dowry on the Death of the Daughter: An Instance in the Negotiation of Laws and Jewish Customs in Early Modern Tuscany." *Jewish History* 16 (2002): 73–106.

Simonsohn, Uriel. *A Common Justice: The Legal Allegiances of Christians and Jews Under Early Islam.* Philadelphia: University of Pennsylvania Press, 2011.

Smail, Daniel Lord. *The Consumption of Justice: Emotions, Publicity, and Legal Culture in Marseille, 1264–1423.* Ithaca, NY: Cornell University Press, 2003.

———. "Factions and Vengeance in Renaissance Italy: A Review Article." *Comparative Studies in Society and History* 38 (1996): 781–89.

Soloveitchik, Haym. "Can Halakhic Texts Talk History?" *AJS Review* 3 (1978): 153–96.

Spyridakis, Stylianos V. "Notes on the Jews of Gortyna and Crete." *Zeitschrift für Papyrologie und Epigraphik* 73 (1988): 171–75.

Stacey, Robert C. "The English Jews Under Henry III." In *The Jews in Medieval Britain: Historical, Literary, and Archeological Perspectives*, edited by Patricia Skinner, 41–54. Woodbridge, Suffolk: Boydell, 2003.

Starr, Joshua. "Jewish Life in Crete Under the Rule of Venice." *Proceedings of the American Academy for Jewish Research* 12 (1942): 59–114.

———. *The Jews in the Byzantine Empire, 641–1204.* Athens: Verlag der "Byzantinisch-Neugriechischen Jahrbücher," 1939.

———. *Romania: The Jewries of the Levant After the Fourth Crusade.* Paris: Éditions du Centre, 1949.

Steiman, Ilona. "Making Illuminated Haggadot in Venetian Crete." *Mediterranean Historical Review* 27 (2012): 161–73

Steinschneider, Moritz. "Candia: Cenni di storia letteraria." *Mosè: Antologie Israelitica* (1879– 83), 2:411–16, 456–62; 3:53–59, 281–85, 421–26; 4:303–8; 5:401–6; 6:15–18.

Stow, Kenneth. *Alienated Minority: The Jews of Medieval Latin Europe.* Cambridge, MA: Harvard University Press, 1992.

———. *Jewish Dogs: An Image and Its Interpreters: Continuity in the Catholic-Jewish Encounter.* Stanford, CA: Stanford University Press, 2006.

———. "Jews and Christians: Two Different Cultures?" In *"Interstizi": Culture ebraico-cristiane a Venezia e nei suoi domini dal Medioevo all'Età Moderna,* edited by Uwe Israel, Robert Jütte, and Reinhold C. Mueller, 31–46. Rome: Edizione di storia e letteratura, 2010.

———. "Papal and Royal Attitudes Toward Jewish Lending in the Thirteenth Century." *AJS Review* 6 (1981): 161–84.

Stuard, Susan Mosher. "Brideprice, Dowry, and Other Marital Assets." In *The Oxford Handbook of Women and Gender in the Middle Ages,* edited by Judith M. Bennett and Ruth Mazo Karras, 148–62. Oxford: Oxford University Press, 2013.

Süssmann, Arthur. *Die Judenschuldentilgung unter König Wenzel.* Berlin: Lamm, 1906.

Taitz, Emily. *The Jews of Medieval France: The Community of Champagne.* Westport, CT: Greenwood Press, 1994.

Thiriet, Freddy. *La Romanie vénitienne au Moyen Age: Le développement et l'exploitation du domaine colonial vénitien (XIIe–XVe siècles).* Paris: Editions E. de Boccard, 1975 [1959].

Thomas, Georg Martin, ed. *Commission des Dogen Andreas Dandolo für die Insel Creta vom Jahre 1350.* Munich: Verlag der K. Akademie, 1877.

Tiepolo, Maria Francesca. "Note sul riordino degli archivi del Duca e dei notai di Candia nell'Archivio di Stato di Veneizia." *Thesaurismata* 10 (1973): 88–100.

Tirosh-Samuelson, Hava. *Between Worlds: The Life and Thought of Rabbi David ben Judah Messer Leon.* Albany: SUNY Press, 1991.

Toaff, Ariel. "Gli insediamenti ashkenaziti nell'Italia settentrionale." In *Gli ebrei in Italia,* edited by Corrado Vivanti, 155–71. Turin: Einaudi, 1996.

———. *The Jews in Medieval Assisi, 1305–1487: A Social and Economic History of a Small Jewish Community in Italy.* Florence: L. S. Olschki, 1979.

———. *Love, Work, Death: Jewish Life in Medieval Umbria.* Translated by Judith Landry. Oxford: Littman Library, 1996.

———. *Pasque di sangue: Ebrei d'Europa e omicidi rituali.* 2nd ed. Bologna: Il Mulino, 2008.

Trivellato, Francesca. *The Familiarity of Strangers: The Sephardic Diaspora, Livorno, and Cross-Cultural Trade in the Early Modern Period.* New Haven, CT: Yale University Press, 2009.

Tsougarakis, Nickiphoros I. *The Latin Religious Orders in Medieval Greece, 1204–1500.* Turnhout: Brepols, 2012.

Varanini, Gian Maria, and Reinhold C. Mueller, eds. *Ebrei nella Terraferma veneta del Quattrocento.* Florence: Firenze University Press, 2005.

Vassilaki, Maria, ed. *The Hand of Angelos: An Icon Painter in Venetian Crete.* Farnham, Surrey: Lund Humphries, 2010.

Verlinden, Charles. "La Crète, debouché et plaque tournante de la traite des esclaves aux XIVe et XVe siècles." In *Studi in onore di Amintore Fanfani,* 3:591–669. Milan: Giuffrè, 1962.

Veronese, Alessandra. "Mobilità, migrazioni e presenza ebraica a Trieste nei secoli XIV e XV." In *Scritti in onore di Girolamo Arnaldi offerti dalla Scuola nazionale di studi medioevali*, edited by Andrea Degrandi and Ovidio Capitani, 545–82. Rome: Istituto storico italiano per il Medio Evo, 2001.

Vlassi, Despina. "La tariffa delle spese giudiziare pubblicata a Cefalonia nel 1511." *Studi Veneziani* 7 (1983): 233–52.

Vogel, Hans Ulrich. *Marco Polo Was in China: New Evidence from Currencies, Salts, and Revenues*. Leiden: Brill, 2013.

Walker, Sue Sheridan, ed. *Wife and Widow in Medieval England*. Ann Arbor: University of Michigan Press, 1993.

Walzer, Michael, Menachem Lorberbaum, and Noam Zohar, eds. *The Jewish Political Tradition*. Vol. 1, *Authority*. New Haven, CT: Yale University Press, 2000.

Weinberger, Leon. *Jewish Poets in Crete*. Cincinnati: Hebrew Union College Press, 1985.

Westreich, Elimelech. *Temurot be-ma'amad ha-ishah be-mishpat ha-'ivri: massa bein masorot* [Transitions in the Legal State of the Wife in Jewish Law: A Journey Among Traditions]. Jerusalem: Hebrew University Magnes Press, 2002.

Winer, Rebecca Lynn. *Women, Wealth, and Community in Perpignan, c. 1250–1300*. Aldershot: Ashgate, 2006.

Woolf, Greg. *Becoming Roman: The Origins of Provincial Civilization in Gaul*. Cambridge: Cambridge University Press, 1998.

Wray, Shona Kelly. "Instruments of Concord: Making Peace and Settling Disputes Through a Notary in the City and Contado of Late Medieval Bologna." *Journal of Social History* 43 (2009): 733–60.

Yerushalmi, Yosef Hayim. *"Diener von Königen und nicht Diener von Dienern": Einige Aspekte der politischen Geschichte der Juden*. Munich: Carl Friedrich von Siemens Stiftung, 1995.

Yuval, Israel. *Two Nations in Your Womb: Perceptions of Jews and Christians in Late Antiquity and the Middle Ages*. Translated by Barbara Harshav and Jonathan Chipman. Berkeley: University of California Press, 2006.

Zinger, Oded. "Women, Gender, and Law: Marital Disputes According to Documents from the Cairo Geniza." PhD diss., Princeton University, 2014.

Index

abandonment, 137–38, 147–49

Adamero, Joste (Joseph), 58

Adelman, Howard Tzvi, 121, 152–53

Adret, Solomon ibn, 48, 104, 111, 117–19, 125, 127, 162, 165–66, 179, 257n7

adultery, 188–89

agency, expressed through colonial justice system, 11, 14, 117, 197–98

Alchana de Negroponte, 169

Alfonso III, king of Aragon, 95

Allemanus, Elia, 41

Anastassu, wife of Lazaro, 148–49

anathema, 113–14

angaria (labor tax), 91, 170, 258n25

Angura, Abraham, 62

Angura, David, 58

Angura, Saphira (wife of Parnas Buchi), 156–60

appeals, judicial, 90–93, 117

Aragon, 134

Arbel, Benjamin, 52–53, 100

Artom, Elias, 8

Ascandrani, Bonadona, 179

Ascandrani, Samuel, 179

Ashkenazi, Malkiel Cohen (Melchiele Theotonicus), 43

Ashkenazi, Meir, 69

Ashkenazi, Moses Cohen, 42

Ashkenazi, Samuel Cohen, 36

Ashkenazi, Yitzhak (Isaac), 42

Ashkenazi Jews: bigamy banned by, 144; in Cretan leadership, 42; on Crete, 13, 41–43, 217n79; customs of, 47–48, 226n172; influence of, 47–49, 226n172; and litigation, 125

Ashtor, Eliyahu, 85

assimilation, 104

Astarita, Tommaso, 161

Astruc (Astrug) family, 40

Astrug, Elia, 110

Astrug, Meir, 108

Astrug, Solomon, 40–41, 62, 126, 139–41, 146, 155

Avogaria di Comun, 17

Avonale, Georgius and Philippus, 106

Baduario, Albanus, 132, 135

Balbo, Chaluda, 45

Balbo, Chana, 109

Balbo, Çigio (Tziona), 45, 109

Balbo, Isaiah, 109, 166–67

Balbo, Judah, 62, 106, 109

Balbo, Lazaro, 62, 174

Balbo, Michael, 42

Balbo, Shabbetai (Sambatheus), 109

Balbo, Solomon Cohen, 36

Barcelona, 177–78

Baron, Salo, 104, 176, 257n5

Bartzeloni, Judah, 178

beit din (Jewish court): authority of, 5, 103, 120–21, 153; in Candia, 29, 102; colonial justice system in relation to, 103–4, 112–18; and divorce, 127, 131; and fraudulent marriage, 136; and marriage cases, 142, 144–45

Belo, Tam, 182–85

Ben Judah, Gershom, 144

Benton, Lauren, 118

Berger, Michael, 130

Bernardino di Siena, 37

bigamy, 49, 142–46, 148–49, 155, 253n71, 253n72

Black Death, 4, 12, 14, 31, 37, 65, 87

blood libel, 94, 98–99. *See also* lamb crucifixion

Boccaccio, Giovanni, *Decameron*, 20–21, 23

Bonavita, Ottaviano, 91–92

Bonfil, Robert, 196, 197

Bonhomo, Leonardo de, 58

Boniface of Monferrat, 17

Acknowledgments

Though Crete may be one, no book or its author is an island. I have relied on a great number of people and institutions to support and nurture me over the course of the research and writing of this book. Research undertaken in Venice and Israel was supported by Harvard University, the Memorial Foundation for Jewish Culture, the Gladys Krieble Delmas Foundation, Targum Shlishi, and the Medieval Academy of America. At Oregon State University (OSU), I was able to take time away from teaching to focus on essential writing and revision through generous fellowships from the Center for the Humanities and the Hundere Endowment for Religion and Culture. OSU's Center for the Humanities also funded cartography for this book, with maps ably and speedily made by Gordon Thompson. The College of Liberal Arts and the Center for the Humanities jointly funded indexing through a generous faculty publication grant. Thank you also to the staff at the Archivio di Stato in Venice and the National Library of Israel in Jerusalem.

I have been lucky to have exceptional, generous, and exacting mentors, including William Chester Jordan, Michael McCormick, Rachel Greenblatt, and the late Angeliki Laiou. Above all, Daniel Lord Smail's guidance, humanity, and unique perspective have shaped me and my thinking in many positive ways. I am grateful to Dan, Kathleen, and the whole Smail family. In Venice, Reinhold Mueller opened his home and became a trusted friend and purveyor of books I didn't even know I needed. (I did.) In Israel, Benjamin Arbel and David Jacoby became and continue to be scholarly role models and prized interlocutors.

My colleagues at Oregon State University have been generous sounding boards and sympathetic critical readers of my work, including Thom Bahde, Courtney Campbell, Marisa Chappell, Sharyn Clough, Neil Davison, Anita Guerrini, Trina Hogg, Joy Jensen, Jonathan Katz, Christopher McKnight Nichols, Michael Osborne, and Kara Ritzheimer, among many others. I thank the OSU Center for the Humanities junior women's writing group, particularly

Mila Zuo, Ana Ribero, and Tekla Bude. I happily acknowledge the fruitful conversations I have had about this project with two of my exceptional former students (now friends): Jennifer Meissner and Elizabeth Nielsen. In its final stages, Elizabeth read the book cover to cover with her especially keen eye, spotting infelicities and suggesting innumerable ways to make it better.

Many colleagues have become friends through this process, and many colleagues and friends alike have willingly and patiently engaged with me on this project over a period of nearly a decade. I am grateful to Mika Ahuvia, Christine Axen, Courtney Bruntz, the late Drew Cayton, Christoph Cluse, Rowan Dorin, Federica Francesconi, Rachel Furst, Charlotte Newman Goldy, Jennifer Gordon, Liora Halperin, Ethan Katz, Jessica Marglin, Sara McDougall, Kara Olive, Moria Paz, Alan Stahl, John Tolan, Ryan Wilkinson, Oded Zinger, and Judith Zinsser, among many, many others. I also thank those at USC's Center for Law, History, and Culture for helpful feedback on Chapter 5. Thank you to Renée Levine Melammed for necessary encouragement in the final stages of this book.

At a pivotal moment, Robert Finlay appeared in Oregon, as if on cue, and helped me enormously improve the first half of the manuscript. Sally McKee's meticulous, frank, and thoughtful comments on the entire book have made it significantly better. Jerry Singerman, Erica Ginsburg, and Hannah Blake at Penn Press have made the process of publication both transparent and remarkably painless. It goes without saying, but I will do so anyhow: any and all infelicities and mistakes are solely my own.

It would be impossible to express the fullness of my gratitude to my family on these pages. So let me at least mention my wonderful parents, Phyllis and Chaim Lauer, who have always supported me as I took unexpected paths; my grandparents, Sara and Moshe Farkas and Rose and Aaron Lauer, of blessed memory, each of whom embodied the two most essential acts of support (feeding and educating); my sisters, Dvora, Aviva, and Adina, for modeling what it means to be strong, independent *neshei chayil* to me and to their children; and my in-laws, Barb and Ivo Osterloh, for their resilience and affection. And finally, to my best reader and critic, my teammate, my husband, Yiftach (Kevin) Osterloh. *Betzar herchavtah li.*